Landscape, Religion, and the Supernatural

RELIGION, CULTURE, AND HISTORY

SERIES EDITOR
Kristian Petersen, Old Dominion University

A Publication Series of
The American Academy of Religion
and
Oxford University Press

PARABLES FOR OUR TIME
Rereading New Testament Scholarship after the Holocaust
Tania Oldenhage

MOSES IN AMERICA
The Cultural Uses of Biblical Narrative
Melanie Jane Wright

INTERSECTING PATHWAYS
Modern Jewish Theologians in Conversation with Christianity
Marc A. Krell

ASCETICISM AND ITS CRITICS
Historical Accounts and Comparative Perspectives
Edited by Oliver Freiberger

VIRTUOUS BODIES
The Physical Dimensions of Morality in Buddhist Ethics
Susanne Mrozik

IMAGINING THE FETUS
The Unborn in Myth, Religion, and Culture
Edited by Vanessa R. Sasson and Jane Marie Law

VICTORIAN REFORMATION
The Fight over Idolatry in the Church of England, 1840–1860
Dominic Janes

SCHLEIERMACHER ON RELIGION AND THE NATURAL ORDER
Andrew C. Dole

MUSLIMS AND OTHERS IN SACRED SPACE
Edited by Margaret Cormack

REAL SADHUS SING TO GOD
Gender, Asceticism, and Vernacular Religion in Rajasthan
Antoinette Elizabeth DeNapoli

LITTLE BUDDHAS
Children and Childhoods in Buddhist Texts and Traditions
Edited by Vanessa R. Sasson

HINDU CHRISTIAN FAQIR
Modern Monks, Global Christianity, and Indian Sainthood
Timothy S. Dobe

MUSLIMS BEYOND THE ARAB WORLD
The Odyssey of 'Ajamī and the Murīdiyya
Fallou Ngom

MUSLIM CIVIL SOCIETY AND THE POLITICS OF RELIGIOUS FREEDOM IN TURKEY
Jeremy F. Walton

LATINO AND MUSLIM IN AMERICA
Race, Religion, and the Making of a New Minority
Harold D. Morales

THE MANY FACES OF A HIMALAYAN GODDESS
Haḍimbā, Her Devotees, and Religion in Rapid Change
Ehud Halperin

MISSIONARY CALCULUS
Americans in the Making of Sunday Schools in Victorian India
Anilkumar Belvadi

DEVOTIONAL SOVEREIGNTY
Kingship and Religion in India
Caleb Simmons

ECOLOGIES OF RESONANCE IN
CHRISTIAN MUSICKING
Mark Porter

GLOBAL TANTRA
Julian Strube

LAUGHTER, CREATIVITY, AND
PERSEVERANCE
Ute Hüsken

WORLD OF WORLDLY GODS
*The Persistence and Transformation of Shamanic
Bon in Buddhist Bhutan*
Kelzang T. Tashi

LANDSCAPE, RELIGION, AND THE
SUPERNATURAL
Nordic Perspectives on Landscape Theory
Matthias Egeler

Landscape, Religion, and the Supernatural

Nordic Perspectives on Landscape Theory

MATTHIAS EGELER

OXFORD
UNIVERSITY PRESS

Oxford University Press is a department of the University of Oxford. It furthers
the University's objective of excellence in research, scholarship, and education
by publishing worldwide. Oxford is a registered trade mark of Oxford University
Press in the UK and certain other countries.

Published in the United States of America by Oxford University Press
198 Madison Avenue, New York, NY 10016, United States of America.

© Oxford University Press 2024

Some rights reserved. No part of this publication may be reproduced, stored in
a retrieval system, or transmitted, in any form or by any means, for commercial purposes,
without the prior permission in writing of Oxford University Press, or as expressly
permitted by law, by licence or under terms agreed with the appropriate
reprographics rights organization.

This is an open access publication, available online and distributed under the terms of a Creative
Commons Attribution – Non Commercial – No Derivatives 4.0 International licence (CC BY-NC-ND 4.0),
a copy of which is available at http://creativecommons.org/licenses/by-nc-nd/4.0/.

Enquiries concerning use outside the scope of the licence terms should be sent to
the Rights Department, Oxford University Press, at the above address.

You must not circulate this work in any other form
and you must impose this same condition on any acquirer.

Library of Congress Cataloging-in-Publication Data
Names: Egeler, Matthias, 1980– author. | American Academy of Religion.
Title: Landscape, religion, and the supernatural : Nordic perspectives on
   landscape theory / Matthias Egeler.
Description: New York, NY : Oxford University Press, [2024] |
   Series: Religion, Culture, and History series |
   Includes bibliographical references and index.
Identifiers: LCCN 2023043011 (print) | LCCN 2023043012 (ebook) |
   ISBN 9780197747360 (hardback) | ISBN 9780197747384 (epub) |
   ISBN 9780197747391 | ISBN 9780197747377
Subjects: LCSH: Landscapes—Philosophy. | Landscapes—Religious aspects. |
   Supernatural. | Folk religion—Iceland.
Classification: LCC BH301.L3 E39 2024 (print) | LCC BH301.L3 (ebook) |
   DDC 712—dc23/eng/20231122
LC record available at https://lccn.loc.gov/2023043011
LC ebook record available at https://lccn.loc.gov/2023043012

DOI: 10.1093/oso/9780197747360.001.0001

Printed by Integrated Books International, United States of America

For Odele, og allt gott fólk á Ströndum

Contents

Acknowledgments	xi
Prelude	1
1. Introduction and Exposition	4
Landscape, Religion, and the Supernatural: Introduction to Theories and Concepts	4
Analyzing Landscape and the Supernatural	4
Religion, the Supernatural, and Folk Belief	8
Landscape	14
Looking at Landscapes: Ideology and Way of Seeing	15
Living in Landscapes: Dwelling, Place, and Home	19
Strandir: Exposition of an Icelandic Landscape	35
The Church in Strandir	40
Common Elements and Story Patterns of the Supernatural Landscape	45
Sources and the Local Cultural Context of the Project	67
2. Twelve Movements: Aspects of the Engagement with the Supernatural Landscape	73
Theses on the Supernatural Landscape	73
1: Time and Memory	75
2: Repeating Patterns	87
3: Identity	104
4: Morality	123
5: Labor	137
6: Playfulness and Adventure	150
7: Power and Subversion	163
8: Sound	177
9: Emotions	189
10: Coping with Contingency	205
11: Home and Unhomeliness	218
12: Nature and Environment	239
3. Coda	256
Theses on the Supernatural Landscape	256
Transformations between the Country and the City	256

X CONTENTS

4. Encore	278
Theses on the Supernatural Landscape	278
Being-in-a-Place? Retrospect and Prospects	279
Landscape: A Vignette	279
Landscape: A Panoramic View	283
Country and City: Being-in-a-Place and Looking-at-a-Place	293
Bibliography	303
Index	329

Acknowledgments

The research for this publication was funded by the Deutsche Forschungsgemeinschaft (DFG, German Research Foundation; project number 453026744) and supported by the Institut für Nordische Philologie of the Ludwig-Maximilians-University in Munich, the Wissenschaftskolleg zu Berlin, the University of Iceland Research Center in Strandir—The Folklore Institute (Rannsóknasetur Háskóla Íslands á Ströndum—Þjóðfræðistofa), and the community of Strandabyggð. I owe particular thanks to Jón Jónsson, the director of the Folklore Institute, for his untiring support with all manner of issues from the academic to the practical. Throughout my work on this book, Jón's advice, always generously given, has been crucial, and without him this book would be nothing like what it is now—I am not sure it would even have been written. A thank-you also to Jón's family, especially Ester Sigfúsdóttir and Dagrún Ósk Jónsdóttir: thank you very much both for your hospitality in Kirkjuból and for the discussions of Strandir folklore! To the community of Strandabyggð I would like to give a heartfelt thanks for their hospitality, help with accommodation, and support in all manner of practical issues. To Hafdís Sturlaugsdóttir, María Hildur Maack, and the Environmental Institute of the Westfjords (Náttúrustofa Vestfjarða) at Hólmavík, I owe thanks for liberally sharing their expertise and research results, and especially for granting me access to the maps and field notes that resulted from the research that Hilmar Egill Sveinbjörnsson undertook for Náttúrustofa in 1999. Náttúrustofa Vestfjarða also supported me with the loan of technical equipment. During the publication process, I have received much valuable help for which I would like to thank the series editor Robert Yelle; the two reviewers of this volume, Daniel Sävborg and a second, anonymous reviewer, who have given me very valuable feedback; and Clive Tolley for his fantastic copyediting. In Germany, I owe particular thanks to Wilhelm Heizmann, Nora Kauffeldt, Claudia Pichlmayr, Johanna Schreiber, and Katharina Schubert. In Strandir and elsewhere in Iceland: Ásdís Jónsdóttir and the whole *Steinadalsætt*; Anna Björg Þórarinsdóttir; Ágúst Þormar Jónsson; Birkir Þór Stefánsson; Brynja Rós Guðlaugsdóttir; Eiríkur Valdimarsson; Gaia Alba and Guido Antonio Di Carlo; Guðbrandur

Sverrisson; Guðlaugur Bjarnason; Gunnhildur Halldórsdóttir and Sigurkarl Ásmundsson; Halldór Þorsteinsson; Jóna Ingibjörg Bjarnadóttir; Lárus Jóhannsson; Magnús Ásbjörnsson; Marta Sigvaldadóttir; Matthías Sævar Lýðsson and Hafdís Sturlaugsdóttir; Óla Friðmey Kjartansdóttir and Ingþór Ólafsson; Peter Weiss and the University Center of the Westfjords in Ísafjörður; Rakel Ýr Stefánsdóttir; Salbjörg Engilbertsdóttir and Sverrir Guðbrandsson; Sigmundur Sigurðsson; Sigurður Marinó Þorvaldsson; Skúli Gautason; Úlfar Eyjólfsson; Úlfar Örn Hjartarson and Hjörtur Þór Þórsson; Unnar Ragnarsson; Valdís Einarsdóttir and the Museum Byggðasafn Dalamanna in Laugar; Vignir Rúnar Vignisson; and several people whose names I never managed to find out—thank you!

Prelude

It is New Year's Eve of the year 1948. We are in one of the wards of the National Hospital in Reykjavík, the best hospital in Iceland, where they bring all the worst cases. A journalist is sitting by the bedside of Jóhann Kristmundsson. Jóhann has just come out of the operating theater and is in a bad way. For more than half a month, he has had a high fever; a few weeks later, he will have one of his legs amputated; a few years later, he will commit suicide. He is the only survivor of a snow avalanche that had hit his farmhouse and buried everybody in it for several days. Of the seven members of the household who were present at the time of the disaster, most were killed instantly when the snow smashed into the building, broke its outer walls, and filled every room. Jóhann remained conscious, but he was helplessly trapped. Immediately after the impact, one other person was still capable of speech, the teenager Jónas, a son of a relative living on the farm. He kept asking Jóhann to help his daughter Ásdís, a two-year-old toddler, saying "she was so cold." But Jóhann could not move, and at some point the boy fell silent. It was only four days later that the postman came to deliver the mail to the remote farmhouse, discovered what had happened, and fetched help. By the time the neighbors had come and dug the victims out, Jónas and one of Jóhann's daughters still showed signs of life, but they were already beyond saving. Both died within a few hours of their discovery. Only Jóhann lived on.

The journalist makes some token gestures of sympathy and asks Jóhann whether he is up to talking about the event. Jóhann says that it was all the same to him, as he was in any case seeing the happenings unfold before his inner eye, and he could then just as well tell others about them. So, with the journalist's occasional prompting, Jóhann gives an account of the weather conditions of those fateful days, the unprecedented avalanche that had hit

---

Landscape, Religion, and the Supernatural. Matthias Egeler, Oxford University Press. © Oxford University Press 2024.
DOI: 10.1093/oso/9780197747360.003.0001

2 LANDSCAPE, RELIGION, AND THE SUPERNATURAL

an area where in living memory no avalanche had ever come down before, of how the family was drinking coffee when the snow hit, of his time trapped in the cold white mass, of the death of every family member in the house, and of the difficulties that his rescuers had with transporting him south from his remote farm in the valley Goðdalur far up in the Westfjords. Then, right at the end of the interview, the journalist changes tack. While before he had presented himself as sympathetic, he now suddenly points the finger at who he sees as the culprit for the accident. He asks:

> Is it true that the dwelling house in Goðdalur was built on a place of enchantment (*álagablettur*), which it was not allowed to disturb or tamper with?

The question, of course, implies the answer. The journalist is aware that Jóhann Kristmundsson, being a modern man and an energetic modernizer with a foible for progress and a certain contempt for old superstitions, had ten years previously erected a new farmhouse at what he thought would be the best spot, on top of a geothermal field which would provide an easy way of heating the building. Neighbors and relatives had warned him against building there, as this spot traditionally was regarded as an *álagablettur*: a "place of enchantment" which was untouchable and the violation of which would lead to immediate punishment. By asking his question, the journalist thus lays the blame for the disaster squarely at Jóhann's own feet—and Jóhann in his answer accepts this blame:

> Yes, that is true. In Goðdalur there is more than one place of enchantment (*álagablettur*). There is, for instance, a place of enchantment in a wetland within the home-field which you may not mow. When it was mown, cows would die from the hay, horses fall down dead and so on. Another place of enchantment was on what they call Bólbarð; you couldn't move anything there, as the old story goes. I picked a fight with this tradition and built a house there, which is now in ruins.

Having gotten this admission of guilt, the journalist takes his leave. On the way out, he asks Jóhann whether he would return to his farm. Jóhann answers that he would not, as "the tragedy stood too clearly before his eyes for him to go on struggling at that place—a place which forever would remind him of doom and destruction."

A few days later, the newspaper *Vísir* published this interview, which took up two broadsheet pages, under a heading which instantly made clear who the newspapermen thought was to blame for the deaths at Goðdalur:

TRAGEDY IN GOÐDALUR:
Picked a fight with enchantment—and now the farm is in ruins.
Interview with Jóhann Kristmundsson, farmer from Goðdalur.

In printing this interview, the newspaper not only indulged in the kind of victim-blaming that has given some branches of the journalistic profession such a bad name, but it also created a strikingly public monument to the continued power of beliefs in the rule of supernatural presences over the landscape. While the Cold War was getting into its stride, here a newspaper published in a western European capital could still deal with the power and terrors of the supernatural landscape as a matter of fact.[1]

---

[1] The account given here closely follows this newspaper publication: Anonymous 1949. Another interview published in a supplement of the newspaper *Morgunblaðið* (Valtýr Stefánsson 1949) throws some doubt on the objectivity of the reporting in *Vísir*; this will be discussed in greater detail in the section "Home and Unhomeliness" in the second chapter of this volume.

1
Introduction and Exposition

Landscape, Religion, and the Supernatural: Introduction to Theories and Concepts

Analyzing Landscape and the Supernatural

This book presents a study of the interlocking of landscape, religion, and the supernatural. The exact meaning of each of these concepts is highly contested—something the following chapters will treat as an opportunity rather than as a hindrance. The contested nature of these concepts will be made to bear fruit by bringing together a broad range of theorizing from the fields of landscape theory, folkloristics, and the study of religions to show the analytical usefulness that various theoretical perspectives can have in different circumstances. In order to do this, the focus will be on a geographical area whose characteristics mirror key elements that have been prominent in different schools of landscape theory. This area is the district of Strandir in the Icelandic Westfjords, where the Goðdalur tragedy took place in 1948 and where the local engagement with the landscape has been documented in great detail since the early nineteenth century. Given the firm empirical base that has resulted from two centuries of systematic documentation, Strandir provides a perfect laboratory case to explore the potential of a broad range of current and classic theorizing on landscape, religion, and the supernatural.

The aim of this exploration resembles what Diana L. Eck called the "grammar of sanctification" of a sacred geography:[1] it aims to provide a synthesis of some of the most central questions that govern the relationship between landscape, religion, and the supernatural. While all my main data are drawn from a single region—as Max Weber has previously noted, any research that hopes to be of lasting value today has to be specialized research[2]—the analysis of these data draws on theories that have been developed across

[1] Eck 2012, 17.
[2] Weber 1946, 135.

Landscape, Religion, and the Supernatural. Matthias Egeler, Oxford University Press. © Oxford University Press 2024.
DOI: 10.1093/oso/9780197747360.003.0002

a broad range of different cultural backgrounds. Even though I will explore the potential of these theories through a single regional data set, the wide-ranging materials on which these theories have originally been developed will ensure that the final results will not only be applicable to Iceland but also will open up heuristic questions that can be applied in at least some other cultural contexts, too.

"Landscape," "religion," and the "supernatural" are all highly contested terms that have been understood (or defined) in many different ways. For the purpose of this study, "landscape" will be used as a heuristic term designating the physical, topographical environment of a geographically restricted area both as it is culturally interpreted through both narratives and behaviors, and as it is transformed into abstract representations. The reason for this choice, and what it means, will be explained in what follows. It is even less possible to define "religion" than "landscape" in a reasoned manner that goes beyond the strictly heuristic. As the historian of religions Jörg Rüpke has pointed out, ultimately all academic understandings of "religion" in one way or another have their roots in the common everyday usage of this word,[3] even though scholarly analysis can reach very different conclusions from this (more or less) common starting point.[4] The same may be said of "supernatural." My approach starts from the basic assumption that definitions are not descriptions of ontological realities, but ways of highlighting perspectives. For me, a definition is a lens that helps to see certain things better, while at the same time it obscures others. In what follows, I will therefore use a range of "lenses" to bring different objects into sharper focus.

To answer the question this book poses—*What are the main ways in which landscape, religion, and the supernatural interrelate?*—the following discussion will oscillate between theory and empirical material. The present chapter, "Introduction and Exposition," has two parts, one theoretical and one empirical. The first section, "Landscape, Religion, and the Supernatural: Introduction to Theories and Concepts," gives a concise introduction to some of the main lines of classic theorizing in the study of religions and in the interdisciplinary field of landscape theory. It thus presents a cross-section of current and classic thinking on concepts like

---

[3] Rüpke 2007, 27.
[4] On the challenges of defining "religion" cf., for instance, Sävborg and Valk 2018b, 15; Meyer and Houtman 2012, 9–13; Zinser 2010, 35–80; Rüpke 2007, 26–27; Auffarth and Mohr 2006; Kehrer 1998; Ahn 1997.

"religion," the "supernatural," or the various ways in which "landscape" has been conceptualized. This chapter does not present anything "new," but it sets the scene concerning the state of the discussion in landscape theory and the study of religions. The next section, "Strandir: Exposition of an Icelandic Landscape," provides an introduction to the empirical material that stands at the center of this study: this chapter outlines basic aspects of social and economic organization and of traditional ways of engaging with the landscape in Strandir. This is intended as a backdrop for the following, more specific analyses, giving the reader a general idea of the context in which the phenomena are embedded that stand in the center of the following chapters.

After this theoretical and empirical introduction, the main chapter of the book presents "Twelve Movements: Aspects of Engagement with the Supernatural Landscape." This chapter consists of twelve sections that use very specific theorizing and empirical phenomena from Strandir to discuss how landscape, religion, and the supernatural relate to the themes of "Time and Memory," "Repeating Patterns," "Identity," "Morality," "Labor," "Playfulness and Adventure," "Power and Subversion," "Sound," "Emotions," "Coping with Contingency," "Home and Unhomeliness," and "Nature and Environment." The main thrust of this chapter is to highlight a range of aspects that are of particular importance for the relationship between landscape, religion, and the supernatural. Each of the sections of this chapter takes its starting point from a set of current and classic theorizing on the theme of the section. It then contrasts this theorizing with pertinent empirical material from Strandir in order to highlight the importance of the respective theme and to show the strengths and, where necessary, limitations of the state of current theory, and to highlight what the Icelandic material suggests as the most fruitful ways of approaching these themes. The "twelve movements" of this part of the book show how landscape works as a network of places intensely connected with associations and interpretations, and with forms of practice that are interdependent with these associations and interpretations. In this landscape, its "sacralization" happens cumulatively through the sacralization of a broad range of specific individual places; to effect such "sacralization," a wide spectrum of strategies is brought to bear on these places. This landscape is very emphatically both material and cultural, and its materiality and its religious and supernatural elements are interdependent and reflect complex dialectics. I propose that the main factor determining this dialectic is land use. Many other studies of landscape and place have put their emphasis on power relations as a determining factor of

INTRODUCTION AND EXPOSITION 7

the human relationship to the landscape;[5] yet this is not confirmed by the material from Strandir.[6] While power plays an important role, it is only one factor among many, and it seems to affect the relationship to the landscape primarily when it influences land use; that is, land use is the primary effective factor, and power is a secondary one. Whether this is a broader phenomenon or a specific quirk of the Strandir data set—which does not focus on the perspective of the "powerful," but on the perspectives of farmers and shepherds—further studies will have to decide, but the material presented in what follows will demonstrate the need for such further studies. So, in short, this core part of the book will serve not only to highlight the analytical usefulness of existing theorizing on landscape but also to critique some of the emphases that have dominated this theorizing.

The section "Coda" then turns toward "Transformations between the Country and the City." While the central section of the book focuses on the rural landscape as a place of habitation and agricultural work, this coda focuses on landscape as something looked at by the urban visitor, who is essentially an outsider and perceives the landscape in a manner that is fundamentally different from how it is perceived by the people who live and work in it on an everyday basis. The coda turns from an inside to an outside perspective by shifting its focus from the agricultural countryside to the way the supernatural landscape is represented in the town of Hólmavík. While Hólmavík, which in 2020 had 329 inhabitants, elsewhere would hardly register as a focus of settlement, within Strandir it stands out as a population center and in structural terms fulfills urban functions:[7] it is the location of the regional administration, both in terms of the secular state and of the Lutheran Protestant national Church of Iceland; it is the regional commercial hub; it has a museum and even a research institute of the University of Iceland. In Hólmavík, we will meet the supernatural landscape primarily as something that is enjoyed aesthetically in its transformation into other

---

[5] E.g., Cresswell 2015, 19 ("Place, at a basic level, is space invested with meaning in the context of power"); Soja 1996; Cosgrove 1998; and W. J. T. Mitchell's classic volume *Landscape and Power* (2002a). Within toponomastics, the comparatively recent development of "critical place-name studies" is programmatically focused on questions of power: Rose-Redwood and Alderman 2011; Rose-Redwood et al. 2010; Berg and Vuolteenaho 2009.

[6] Cf. Bigon 2016, 4–5, who criticizes the exaggerated preoccupation of "critical place-name studies" with political power (see the note above). This preoccupation has been noted as problematic even within the field of "critical place-name studies" (Rose-Redwood et al. 2010, 466).

[7] As Bätzing 2020, 16–17, has highlighted, in the thinly settled environments of Iceland and northern Scandinavia, the minimum population for a city in the sense of a central settlement with important functions for its surroundings lies at only two hundred inhabitants.

8 LANDSCAPE, RELIGION, AND THE SUPERNATURAL

media, especially art, and is an object of the superficial attentions of international consumer society.

The book closes with an "Encore," which both looks back at the theories and materials discussed in the preceding chapters and on toward how to frame the main lines of my analysis terminologically. This chapter presents a summary of important conclusions; this highlights points in current theorizing that are particularly enlightening for the analysis of landscape, as well as ones that call for revision. A synthesis of these points leads me to propose "being-in-a-place" and "looking-at-a-place" as concepts to formulate the contrasting central traits of two typical and idealized views of landscape: the rural and the urban. "Being-in-a-place" and "looking-at-a-place" reflect the differences between the inside perspective of the rural agricultural population versus the outside perspective of the urban visitor (or absentee landowner). This complementary pair of ideal types is offered as a tool to analyze how the land is engaged with that includes both the urban, middle- and upper-class perspective, which to date has dominated landscape theory to the virtual exclusion of other perspectives, and the rural, agricultural and working-class perspective that has hitherto largely formed a blind spot in the theorization, and whose richness and complexity has rarely been appreciated. While the exact degree of its transferability to other cultural contexts will have to be determined by further comparative research, I hope that this pair of ideal types can at least serve as a heuristic matrix for how one can approach a multiplicity of perspectives on and ways of engaging with the landscape that so far has been rendered largely invisible by an undue focus on a limited range of social contexts.

Religion, the Supernatural, and Folk Belief

In a survey of definitions of "religion," Christoph Auffarth and Hubert Mohr have identified six components or dimensions which form the basis of most attempts to define "religion." Religion, they note, is normally defined (1) as "faith," "world view," or "belief"; (2) as a social organization or "church"; (3) as "ritual action"; (4) as "ethics," a store of rules governing moral behavior; (5) as "symbolic system"; (6) as a "feeling," as something based on emotions.[8] In the following discussion, every one of these aspects—as well

---

[8] Auffarth and Mohr 2006, 1612.

as some aspects not highlighted by Auffarth and Mohr—will at one point or another come to the fore, and the theories and methods that I will use to approach them will be selected according to what opens up the most interesting perspectives on the matters at hand. I will thus apply different approaches to different aspects of the material with no intention of maintaining theoretical purity or consistency. Rather, my approach will resemble what Claude Lévi-Strauss called "bricolage"[9] in that I will use theories of religion in an eclectic and pragmatic manner: I will draw on different theories in a consciously heuristic way that makes the use of any given theory dependent exclusively upon its explanatory power. According to context, I will thus touch upon a broad range of both historical and contemporary approaches, including Friedrich Schleiermacher's conceptualization of religion as a feeling of absolute dependency,[10] Edward B. Tylor's "minimum definition of Religion, the belief in Spiritual Beings,"[11] Birgit Meyer's conceptualization of "religion as a practice of mediation through which a distance between the immanent and what lies 'beyond' it is posited and held to be bridged, albeit temporarily,"[12] or Thomas A. Tweed's spatial definition, according to which religions "are confluences of organic-cultural flows that intensify joy and confront suffering by drawing on human and suprahuman forces to make homes and cross boundaries."[13] If the reader will forebear with this heretical take on theorizing, I think they will ultimately find it congenial to understanding the many things that happen in the landscape.

A particular terminological challenge is how best to refer to the landscape in which the colorful spectrum of phenomena analyzed here takes place. A common way of referring to landscapes that point to symbolic meanings beyond their mere materiality is as "symbolic landscape";[14] "mythological landscape"[15] (or "storied landscape"),[16] "religious landscape,"[17] and "sacred landscape"[18] are also established terms. But "symbolic," "mythological," and "storied" only grasp associations of the landscape with narratives and abstract symbolisms, while failing to highlight the practices that are connected

---

[9] Cf. Lévi-Strauss 1966, 16–17.
[10] Cf. Corrigan 2016, 512.
[11] Tylor 1871, 383.
[12] Meyer 2012, 24.
[13] Tweed 2006, 54 (original in italics); cf. Yelle 2019, 15–16.
[14] Cf. Backhaus and Murungi 2009; Cosgrove 1998.
[15] E.g., Faulstich 1998.
[16] Hawes 2017.
[17] Hahn 2002.
[18] E.g., Käppel and Pothou 2015; Adler et al. 2013; Jordan 2003; Cancik 1985–1986.

10 LANDSCAPE, RELIGION, AND THE SUPERNATURAL

to parts of the landscape: the landscape is not just a place to tell stories about but also and especially a place to *do* things in. The terms "religious" and "sacred" are better suited to grasp the latter aspect of the landscape—the landscape as a place of praxis—but are too formal and emphatic to be ideal descriptions of some common motifs connected with the landscapes analyzed in the following chapters: at the very least, it is counterintuitive to use the terms "religious" or "sacred" about a landscape that is connected with a burlesque story about a troll, even if this story constitutes the founding legend of a church (which some, but not all, burlesque troll stories do). The term "sacred" in particular suggests a marked state of exception;[19] but in the landscapes of the everyday, the exception is often very small, even if it is there *in nuce*. Also the material discussed in the following suggests that the "sacred" strictly speaking is too exceptional to form the basis of a general approach: in the Icelandic documentation on landscape, the vernacular term for "sacrality," *helgi*, is used only very rarely and then most commonly in connection with the most extreme occurrences.[20] Since in this book I do not focus on the exception, but on the everyday, I have therefore settled on employing the phrase "supernatural landscape," which seems like a suitably intuitive umbrella term for the landscapes of the everyday analyzed in the following chapters. In other cultural situations, the term "supernatural" may be unsuited,[21] and it is not used here with far-reaching theoretical aspirations. Yet for the landscapes at hand it largely avoids misleading associations and thus seems heuristically useful.

Both the concept of the supernatural and the empirical material that I draw on in this study have long stood at the center of a lively and fruitful debate in the field of folkloristics or folklore studies. Daniel Sävborg in particular has presented enlightening discussions of the concept of the supernatural with recourse to Nordic material both of the Middle Ages and the

---

[19] Cf. Yelle 2019, 20.

[20] Most examples in the corpus discussed here refer to the valley of Goðdalur, where an avalanche wiped out most of a family who allegedly had violated a "sacred" place; see section "Home and Unhomeliness." The two other examples of the use of *helgi* that I have become aware of are connected with prohibited places at the farm of Svanshóll; see the section "Coping with Contingency." There as well, however, there is a connection to the Goðdalur tragedy, if an indirect one: the term is used in a description of "places of enchantment" on the farm by Ingimundur Ingimundarson, whose sister Svanborg Ingimundardóttir was the wife of Jóhann Kristmundsson and died in the Goðdalur avalanche. Ingimundur's emphatic choice of words therefore may be colored by the loss his family had suffered through the alleged agency of such a supernatural site.

[21] Cf. Frog 2020, 455; Sävborg and Bek-Pedersen 2018b, 6; Sävborg and Valk 2018b, 16; Tolkien 2014, 28. A promising alternative in intercultural contexts could be the category of transcendence as recently foregrounded by Robert A. Yelle (2019, esp. p. 14), but in the specific context at hand, it would lead to a counterintuitive use of language.

more recent folklore record.[22] One of the basic problems of the term is the question whether a definition of the supernatural should be based on a mainstream modern-day perspective of what is "supernatural," or on the emic perspective of Nordic cultures.[23] A modern mainstream definition could be as simple as "something that does not exist in reality," but as Sävborg rightly highlights, such a definition would be too anachronistic and too dependent on individual religious belief or worldview to be very useful as an analytical tool. More relevant, therefore, is the emic view. Etymologically, the English term "supernatural" and its various counterparts in a range of European languages go back to the Medieval Latin *supernaturalis*, which denoted something that exists beyond the laws of nature through the intervention of either God or the devil: medieval learned views assumed that the supernatural has been put beyond natural laws by either miracles (*miracula*, i.e., acts of God) or magic (*magica*, i.e., acts of the devil).[24] The resulting semantic spectrum of the term is close to the evocations of the word "supernatural" in everyday speech to this day, which illustrates that the use of the term "supernatural" for approaching phenomena found in Western cultural contexts is largely unproblematic and pragmatically useful.[25] In the context of the present analysis, it is also exculpated by the linguistic fact that Icelandic has known the word *yfirnáttúrlegt*—which is a calque of *supernaturalis* or one of its many variants that are found across European languages, such as German "übernatürlich" and Danish "overnaturlig"—at least since the first half of the twentieth century, which is the period that forms the focus of the empirical part of this study.

The common root that Sävborg has shown for both the "divine" and the "magical" aspects of the traditional (Latinate) European supernatural is also important for another aspect of this study: the way it combines analyses of a set of materials that may seem disparate, but that are held together by the same logic that underlies the range of the Medieval Latin term *supernaturalis* as encompassing both the "divine" and the "magical." Viewed through the lens of the semantics of *supernaturalis*, the present study of the supernatural landscape considers elements that encompass both the "divine" as represented by the Lutheran Protestant national Church of Iceland, and the "magical" as represented by the many aspects of so-called folk belief that in

---

[22] Sävborg and Valk 2018b, 15–17; Sävborg and Bek-Pedersen 2018b, 6–7; Sävborg 2016.
[23] Sävborg 2016, 119–120.
[24] Sävborg and Bek-Pedersen 2018b, 6; Sävborg 2016, 120.
[25] Sävborg and Valk 2018b, 16–17; Sävborg 2016, 121.

12 LANDSCAPE, RELIGION, AND THE SUPERNATURAL

practice form an equally prominent part of this supernatural landscape but would find little favor in the eyes of the Church authorities.[26] A perspective focused on the normative views of religious specialists would separate these two aspects and maybe investigate the one as "religion" and the other as "folk belief." Yet while approaches that implicitly adapted a normative, often specifically Protestant position throughout much of the twentieth century time and again underlay the study of religions, already by the 1980s the adoption of such implicitly theological views by researchers in the study of religions was harshly criticized.[27] Beyond its institutional frame, there is no fundamental difference between folk religion and institutionalized religion; as the folklorist Linda Dégh put it: "Western folk religion as a belief system is the informal doppelgänger of mainstream Christian philosophy based on the Bible and its testimonial interpretations."[28] With a similar thrust, Ülo Valk has emphasized that popular storytelling about encounters with the supernatural constitutes a counterdiscourse to the official, hegemonic, institutional discourse as it is represented by societal authorities such as the Church. Valk contrasts "authoritarian culture" with "the more democratic heteroglossia of folkloric voices," highlighting the necessity to view both as alternatives on equal footing rather than as "higher" versus "lower" (representing "the elite" versus "the folk"). In his view as in that of other folklorists, the "vernacular beliefs" of folk religion are not separate from and opposed to institutionally organized religion, but rather both can be thought of as having a symbiotic relationship that can be described as a complex ongoing dialogue between different voices in society.[29]

A closing of the analytical gap between folk religion (as the religion of the "common people" and the object of folkloristics) and institutionalized religion (as the religion of the "elite" and the historically dominant object of the study of religions) was performed not only by folklorists like Dégh and Valk, but in a very similar manner also from the perspective of the study of religions. To pick just one recent example, several contributors to the discourse on material religion have highlighted how the study of religions needs to overcome its former biases toward perspectives deeply

---

[26] Cf. the in-depth discussion in Sävborg 2016, 121–127, which pursues the question how "magic" can be viewed as a key to understand the peculiarities of entities like trolls or the dangerous being Selkolla in both Old Norse literature and later Scandinavian folklore, all of whom an intuitive use of language today would classify as supernatural.

[27] For instance, Gladigow 1988; Ruel 1997.

[28] Dégh 2001, 262.

[29] Valk 2012, esp. p. 26 (with a survey of further literature).

INTRODUCTION AND EXPOSITION 13

colored by normative Christian, especially Protestant, views. Thus, Matthew Engelke emphasized what he called the "crypto-Protestantism" that underlay conceptualizations of religion such as that of Edward Burnett Tylor; instead of continuing such Protestant biases, Engelke called for an alternative approach focusing on lived experience[30]—which is arguably exactly what stands at the center of folkloristic approaches like those of Dégh or Valk. Birgit Meyer and Dick Houtman similarly emphasized that the study of religions needs to take a fresh look at the different varieties of Protestantism: such new investigations would have to shed the Protestant view of Protestantism as a religion of the intellect and interiority and investigate the realities of lived Protestantisms, which may result in a picture rather different from that painted by its normative theological self-perception.[31] Importantly, such studies would bring exactly the kinds of counterdiscourses to the fore that were highlighted by Valk.

Such overlapping research discourses in folkloristics and the study of religions show that, as Sävborg and Valk have noted, folkloristics and religious studies are indeed related disciplines.[32] The data set that forms the core of this book is the supernatural landscape of the Strandir district of Iceland, and Icelandic material of this kind has so far been studied primarily from the perspective of folkloristics.[33] In this volume, I aim to show that this material has much to tell us as well for questions and theories that belong to the field of the study of religions. Incidentally, this means that this book will constitute one of the studies of different varieties of Protestantism called for by Meyer and Houtman; yet its main interest will lie in approaches to the relationship between religion, the supernatural, and the landscape. I hope that my attempt to make folkloristic materials—and sometimes also folkloristic methods—fruitful for the study of religions will make a contribution not only to our understanding of the mechanisms that govern the supernatural landscape but also to intensifying the dialogue between the two disciplines of folkloristics and the study of religions, which indeed have much to tell each other.

---

[30] Engelke 2011, 12.

[31] Meyer and Houtman 2012, 12–13; Meyer 2012, 12.

[32] Sävborg and Valk 2018b, 8. Cf. Asplund Ingemark 2006, 4.

[33] For instance, see the volumes on landscape and supernatural folk storytelling: Gunnell 2008; Sävborg and Valk 2018a.

Landscape

The term "landscape" (in a way quite similar to some of its equivalents in other European languages, such as German "Landschaft") has two roots: an early medieval English and an early modern Dutch one. Already in Old English, there was a noun *landscipe*, a very old Germanic word corresponding to Old Saxon *landscepi* and Old High German *lantscaf*. This Old English *landscipe* denoted "a tract of land, region," just as the Old High German *lantscaf* translated as "regio, provincia, patria," "region, province, fatherland."[34] The modern English word "landscape," however, is not derived from this Old English predecessor; rather, it is a loanword from the Dutch. In the first instance, Dutch *landschap* referred to an area of land inhabited and cultivated by human beings; and from there, the term was transferred to paintings that depicted such areas of land.[35] In early modern England, Dutch landscape paintings became hugely fashionable among the wealthier sections of society and were imported in large numbers. The importation of these paintings also left its mark on contemporary language, as it was accompanied by the importation of the Dutch term *landschap* as a technical term of painting. As such it became established as a word of the English language from the late sixteenth century onward.[36] Historically speaking, therefore, an English "landscape" in the first instance is a painting of an inland scene. Thus, one can to this day speak of "a landscape by William Turner" or "a landscape by John Constable." In this sense, as a landscape painting or a painted landscape, a landscape is something purely to be looked at.

The relationship between the viewed (painted) landscape and its viewer implies a sense of separation: one does not interact with a painted landscape, one looks at it, and the use of perspective in European art since the Renaissance even suggests that one looks at it from an (if imaginary) distant vantage point. This separation, as well as the restriction of the relationship between the landscape and its viewer to the visual, also reverberates in a broader meaning of the term that had developed by the 1640s at the latest, when it appears in the poetry of John Milton: that of a prospect of a natural inland scenery that could be taken in at a glance from one point of view.[37] In

---

[34] Bosworth and Toller 1898, 619 (s.v. "land-scipe"); Schenk 2001, §1.

[35] Schama 1996, 10.

[36] *OED*, s.v. "landscape, n."; cf. Schama 1996, 10. On the German term *Landschaft*, whose historical development followed largely parallel lines, cf. Schenk 2001, §1.

[37] *OED*, s.v. "landscape, n.," meaning 2a.

this usage, "landscape" has been transferred back from the canvas onto the land. Yet while now it again refers to a piece of ground, this ground is still *looked at* from *a distance*.

The sense of landscape as a lived-in rather than a looked-at space—the former being what the Dutch landscape painters of the sixteenth century had represented—seems to have been regained only rather late. From the late nineteenth century onward, landscape starts to emancipate itself again from paintings and views, and the word is attested as being used to refer to an area of land with its specific characteristics.[38] A "landscape" is now an area of a specific character and with specific land forms that can be distinguished from its neighboring landscapes, which have a different character; one may think of a desert landscape or an Alpine landscape. Such landscapes—just as the landscapes of painting had necessarily been—are generally of a limited (though not small) size: whether one views landscape as a prospect seen from a particular perspective or as an area defined by specific characteristics, both ways of conceptualizing landscape imply that its extent cannot be infinite. One way or another, the term "landscape" carries connotations of a certain coherence, which by implication limits the size it can have. Sometimes, this restriction has even been seen as a central defining criterion. Thus, Jaromír Beneš defines landscape as "a geographical space that can be comprehended by an individual or a group of inter-related individuals, the functional and structural links of which can be understood and described within a space so defined."[39]

This excursus on the history of landscape as a word of the English language was necessary because, quite as Rüpke noted for the term "religion," the usage of a word in everyday speech is the starting point for its use in academic discourse. This very much is also the case for "landscape" as a critical term, whose focuses have oscillated between the gaze of the distant viewer and the area characterized by specific features.

Looking at Landscapes: Ideology and Way of Seeing

The long history of landscape as a prospect that can be painted or looked at from one single spot has repercussions in some important theoretical

---

[38] *OED*, s.v. "landscape, n.," meaning 2b.
[39] Beneš and Zvelebil 1999, 74.

16 LANDSCAPE, RELIGION, AND THE SUPERNATURAL

discourses on the term.[40] An early example is the stance taken by Raymond Williams in his classic work on *The Country and the City* (1973), where he argues: "A working country is hardly ever a landscape. The very idea of landscape implies separation and observation."[41] For him, a landscape is something that is viewed by an observer who is separated from it. Much more recently, Tim Cresswell follows this usage by describing landscape as a purely visual idea, likewise treating it as scenery that is seen by a viewer who remains outside it. On this basis, Cresswell constructs a fundamental difference between the concept of "place" (more on this later) and the concept of "landscape": for him, a place is something that one is within, while a landscape is something that one always remains outside of, because it is defined by being looked at from the outside. In Cresswell's words: "We do not live in landscapes—we look at them."[42]

The most prominent—and indeed ground-breaking—representative of an approach that focuses on landscape as something that is looked at was Denis Cosgrove (1948–2008).[43] At a time when geographers studying landscape were primarily interested in landscape as physical topography,[44] Cosgrove established a way of looking at landscape that saw it as a "way of seeing."[45] This way of seeing, he proposed, was anything but objective, but deeply bound up in issues of ideology and power. Cosgrove, who professed

---

[40] There is a vast literature on space/place and landscape; the following survey of some main lines of thought focuses on classic approaches that had a particular impact on research in the field. For book-length general overviews, cf. Tally 2013; Hubbard and Kitchin 2011. Among classic texts on landscape, milestones of particular importance were W. J. T. Mitchell's *Landscape and Power* (2002); Tim Ingold's *The Perception of the Environment* (2000); Keith H. Basso's *Wisdom Sits in Places* (1996); Simon Schama's *Landscape and Memory* (1996); and Christopher Tilley's foundational *A Phenomenology of Landscape* (1994, with the follow-up volumes Tilley and Bennett 2004; Tilley 2008; Tilley 2010). For a (nonexhaustive) cross-section of research on landscape particularly (but not only) in its relationship to religion, see also Young 2022, 79–108; Sävborg and Valk 2018a; Hawes 2017; Beinhauer-Köhler et al. 2017; Käppel and Pothou 2015; Hermann and Mohn 2015; Chadwick and Gibson 2013; Feldt 2012; Janowski and Ingold 2012; Walsham 2011; Olshausen and Sauer 2009; Corrigan 2009; Knott 2005; Smith 2004; Jordan 2003; Lane 2002; Hahn 2002; Rinschede 1999; Faulstich 1998; Hirsch and O'Hanlon 1996; Chidester and Linenthal 1995; Alcock and Osborne 1994; Smith 1987; Meining 1979; Smith 1978; Paffen 1973. For very useful overviews over developments in the geography of religions through the twentieth century, see Kong 1990; Kong 2001. For an attempt at an encyclopaedic summa of the relationship between religion and nature, cf. Taylor 2005a; more recently, for example von Stuckrad 2019. Important contributions go back at least as far as Bronislaw Malinowski's *Argonauts of the Western Pacific* (1922) and his *Coral Gardens and Their Magic* (1935).

[41] Williams 1973, 120.

[42] Cresswell 2015, 17. Cf. DeLue and Elkins 2008, 93–94; Bender 2002, S105.

[43] See Lilley 2011 for an overview of his work. Key publications on landscape are Cosgrove 2008; Cosgrove 1998 (orig. ed. 1984); Cosgrove and Daniels 1988; Cosgrove 1985.

[44] One exception is "humanistic geography," which will be discussed later and which Cosgrove (1985, 45, 56–59) explicitly rejected.

[45] Cosgrove 1985, 45, 46, 47, 55; Cosgrove 2008, 20; Cosgrove 1998, xiv, xx, xxv, 1, 13; Kühne et al. 2018, 11–12; Lilley 2011, 122.

a broadly Marxian understanding of society and culture,[46] developed much of his thinking on the art and culture of the Italian and English Renaissance and the representations of landscapes that arose in this context, and whose underlying principles were expounded in great detail by contemporary treatises often written by the artists themselves. Landscape, as Cosgrove understood it on this basis, was a way of representing and shaping the physical environment that was based on the development of linear perspective, which in turn was bound up with measuring, accounting, surveying, and mapping. The application of this perspective to the country marked its subjugation under the control of the city: it reflected a visual power that mirrored the power inherent in property rights. Even in endeavors as seemingly innocent as painting and garden design, the concept of landscape as it was originally framed in the fifteenth and early sixteenth centuries ultimately achieved the "transformation [of space] into the property of individual or state."[47] Cosgrove's concept of landscape as a "way of seeing" thus saw landscape as "bourgeois, individualist and related to the exercise of power over space":[48] "Landscape is thus a way of seeing, a composition and structuring of the world so that it may be appropriated by a detached, individual spectator to whom an illusion of order and control is offered through the composition of space according to the certainties of geometry."[49] This illusion often went hand in hand with very real power wielded by the patrons of artists and the owners of landscape paintings. At the same time, the landscape way of seeing also implied a distance from the world, which by people of a certain class would be approached only through its refraction in a painting, a poem, or a Claude Glass.[50]

To approach landscape in a controlled way, Cosgrove and Daniels offered a methodological sketch drawing on classics of both art history and anthropology.[51] Arguing that landscape should be seen as an image or symbol, they proposed that it can be analyzed through the concept of *iconography*, understood as the study of symbolic imagery. Basing their iconographic method on classic work in art history by Aby Warburg, Erwin Panofsky, and Ernst Cassirer, Cosgrove and Daniels presented a two-step approach to the

[46] Cosgrove 2008, 20, 22; Cosgrove 1998, xiii, xv–xvi.
[47] Cosgrove 1985, 46.
[48] Cosgrove 1985, 45.
[49] Cosgrove 1985, 55.
[50] Cosgrove 1985, 55. On the Claude Glass, cf. later.
[51] Cosgrove and Daniels 1988, 1–4; Cosgrove 2008, 33. Cf. Warburg 2018; Geertz 1973. For a more recent discussion of landscape iconography, see Hoelscher 2009.

18 LANDSCAPE, RELIGION, AND THE SUPERNATURAL

meaning of images. In its first step, their method identifies conventional, consciously used symbols, but it does not stop there; rather, it goes on to enquire into the "intrinsic meaning" of a representation that can be grasped in the unconscious underlying principles and basic attitudes that have gone into its making. These can be termed "symbolic forms," whose achievement it is to structure the world in a way specific to each culture. Cosgrove and Daniels also highlighted the close relatedness of iconographic and ethnological research by pointing out the parallelism between Aby Warburg's conceptualization of images as encoded texts and Clifford Geertz's conceptualization of culture as a text. In particular, Cosgrove and Daniels found that the working methods of Warburg and his colleagues closely paralleled Geertz's two steps of "thick description" and "diagnosis":[52]

> setting down the meaning particular social actions have for the actors whose actions they are, and stating, as explicitly as we can manage, what the knowledge thus attained demonstrates about the society in which it is found and, beyond that, about social life as such.

While Cosgrove's and Daniels's methodological sketch of landscape iconography has been criticized for being too general to provide much guidance for concrete landscape studies,[53] it illustrates that even the study of landscape as a primarily pictorial "way of seeing" is not just an art-historical, but a deeply anthropological endeavor.

While Cosgrove reduced "landscape" to a particular historical manifestation of a way of seeing the world—which seems of limited analytical usefulness and therefore will not be emulated here[54]—his approach marks a fundamental insight: landscape is not an objective "given," but an ideological construct.[55] As he put it in a nutshell: "the landscape idea is a visual ideology."[56] Cosgrove was thus a pioneer of what is now sometimes called a "constructivist" approach to landscape, which analyzes landscape as a social construct that is not simply a given physical object, but created through individual as well as social processes. A constructivist view of landscape differs fundamentally from essentialist and positivist approaches, which

---

[52] Geertz 1973, 27.
[53] Lilley 2011, 122.
[54] Cf. also the criticism voiced by Ingold 1993, 154.
[55] Cf. Lilley 2011, 121.
[56] Cosgrove 1985, 47.

respectively view landscape as a totality with an objectively existing intrinsic nature or essence (essentialism) or as an object that is best approached by counting and measuring its constituent parts (positivism).[57] The following analysis will take such a constructivist approach, though with the slight qualification that its constructivism is moderate rather than radical: as already recognized by Cosgrove himself, it is not just that culture shapes landscape; landscape also shapes culture.[58] The physical topography may only be the raw material for the construction of a cultural landscape, but its properties also impose restrictions on which cultural constructs are possible and which needs these constructs have to meet.[59]

Living in Landscapes: Dwelling, Place, and Home

However much scholars such as Williams, Cosgrove, and Cresswell wanted to reduce landscape to a visual phenomenon—something to be looked at or a "way of seeing"—such approaches did not stand unchallenged. While the use of the term "landscape" in the context of the history of art has had a tremendous impact on its semantic range, the connection between this word and the language of painting is not an exclusive one. As already mentioned, as a word, "landscape" already existed before it became associated with art. In this early form, "landscape" did not refer to a view, but to a territory: Old English *landscipe* denoted "a tract of land, region"; Old High German *lantscaf* meant "regio, provincia, patria" ("region, province, fatherland"), and thus a territory whose definition was primarily a political one; even Dutch *landschap* originally referred to an area of land inhabited and cultivated by human beings, and only later on became the term par excellence for a landscape painting that depicted exactly such an area.[60] While the tremendous success of Dutch landscape painting for a while shifted the emphasis of the word from the depicted area to the artwork depicting an area, the word "landscape" never entirely shook off its connection to the actual land that was represented in art.

A second strain of scholarship on landscape does not focus on landscape as something primarily to be looked at, but in continuation of the word's original meaning focuses on landscape in the sense of an inhabited

---

[57] For a survey see Kühne et al. 2018.
[58] Lilley 2011, 121.
[59] Cf. Bender 2002, S104.
[60] Bosworth and Toller 1898, 619 (s.v. "land-scipe"); Schenk 2001, §1; Schama 1996, 10.

20 LANDSCAPE, RELIGION, AND THE SUPERNATURAL

area. Thus, Tim Ingold defined landscape in a way markedly different from Cosgrove's purely visual "way of seeing": "the landscape is the world as it is known to those who dwell therein, who inhabit its places and journey along the paths connecting them."[61] Instead of a way of seeing, landscape here is a place of dwelling and of movement, defined by places and paths. It is something that one cannot only look *at*, but that one can look *around in*;[62] or as Rachael Ziady DeLue put it: "a thing that we live *within*."[63] Similarly, criticizing the concept of landscape as something to be looked at from an indigenous Pueblo perspective, Leslie Marmon Silko rejected the assumption that the viewer "is somehow *outside* or *separate from* the territory he or she surveys" and emphasized that viewers "are as much a part of the landscape as the boulders they stand on."[64]

Space and Place

In theorizing on the human relationship to space, dwelling and being *inside* places has been an important theme since at least the 1950s. One scholar who played a particularly prominent role was the French philosopher Gaston Bachelard (1884–1962). In his classic *La poétique de l'espace* (1958),[65] Bachelard attempted to develop a theory of the human relationship to and a poetics of space. His topic was not so much geographical space as the space of the imagination, which he approached through the example of the house, focusing on the most intimate space of human habitation and thus putting the place of dwelling into the center of his approach to space. He particularly investigated where the human attempt to dwell somewhere turned out well, focusing on "quite simple images of *felicitous space*" in an approach for which he coined the term "topophilia."[66] Looking at the house, he focused on personal spaces which are loved and suggest safety and comfort. Importantly, Bachelard noted that such personal, lived-in spaces become qualitatively different from the space that is accessible to the measurements of a surveyor:[67]

> Space that has been seized upon by the imagination cannot remain indifferent space subject to the measures and estimates of the surveyor.

---

[61] Ingold 1993, 156.
[62] Ingold 1993, 166, 171.
[63] DeLue and Elkins 2008, 104.
[64] Silko 1996, 265–266.
[65] Bachelard 1994 (1958); cf. Cresswell 2015, 29–30, 39–40; Tally 2013, 114–116.
[66] Bachelard 1994 (1958), xxxv–xxxvi (quotation: p. xxxv; emphasis original).
[67] Bachelard 1994 (1958), xxxvi.

INTRODUCTION AND EXPOSITION 21

It has been lived in, not in its positivity, but with all the partiality of the imagination.

Lived-in space is filled with meaning and thereby is qualitatively changed, and has become something different from the "indifferent space" of the surveyor. The measuring rod of the land surveyor can only capture certain aspects of space; others are a work of the imagination, which is just as important for human life but much more difficult to quantify.

Even more influential—in spite of his political aberrations[68]—has been the German philosopher Martin Heidegger (1889–1976).[69] In his thinking, the concept of dwelling became the fundamental analytic category through which he approached the human relationship to space. Heidegger formulated his ideas in greatest detail in his lecture "Bauen Wohnen Denken" ("Building Dwelling Thinking"), originally delivered in 1951.[70] The way he presented his argument now seems alien. His pervasive references to "divinities" and "the godhead" today seem like esoteric obfuscation, and his idea that we can approach existential truth through the etymologies of words is an anachronism at least as striking as the 1949 news report of the Icelandic tabloid *Vísir* on the Goðdalur tragedy: Heidegger's etymological method was a direct regression to the late antique methodology that Isidore of Seville in the sixth century formulated in his *Etymologies*,[71] and as such it was based on a fundamental disregard for the pragmatic nature of language, that is, the fact that the meaning of words is determined by their use, not by some absolute "essence."[72] But for all its failings, Heidegger's contribution presented an early formulation of what, if clad in a different terminology, would become widely established tenets of spatial theory that are still fundamental today.

Heidegger argued that dwelling is essentially how humans exist—*are*—in the world: in their strict sense, *being* and *dwelling* for him were identical, and so was *building* in its putative original meaning:[73]

[68] Cf. Garrard 2012, 120–122.
[69] On Heidegger's influence in spatial theory cf. Cresswell 2015, 19, 27–29, 37, 48–50, 94–95; Tally 2013, 47, 64–66; Vergunst et al. 2012, 3; Basso 1996, 106; Rose 1993, 51.
[70] Heidegger 1993.
[71] Ed. Lindsay 1911.
[72] See Heidegger 1993, esp. pp. 348–351, with the programmatic statement: "It is language that tells us about the essence of a thing" (p. 348).
[73] Heidegger 1993, 349.

> *Bauen* originally means to dwell. Where the word *bauen* still speaks in its original sense, it also says *how far* the essence of dwelling reaches. That is, *bauen, buan, bhu, beo* are our word *bin* in the versions: *ich bin,* I am, *du bist,* you are [. . .]. What then does *ich bin* mean? The old word *bauen,* to which the *bin* belongs, answers: *ich bin, du bist* mean I dwell, you dwell. The way in which you are and I am, the manner in which we humans *are* on the earth, is *buan,* dwelling. To be a human being means [. . .] to dwell.

This essentialized concept of building = being = dwelling Heidegger then took to be the basis of the creation of what he termed "locales." A locale is not just something that is given, but it is created by an act of building (= being = dwelling), and only after its existence has thus been established does it "gather" spaces around it. Heidegger used the example of a bridge over a river: by being built, a bridge turns a certain spot on the river into a locale; and this then *"gathers* the earth as landscape around the stream."[74] The act of building in the form of building a bridge creates a "locale" from a mere exchangeable spot, and this locale then in turn acts as a catalyst that orders the spots surrounding it into a landscape of meaningful spaces. Heidegger, somewhat esoterically, conceptualized this ordering as a "gathering" of "earth and sky, divinities and mortals."[75] But behind this romantic mystification stood an idea which is still fundamental in theorizing today: a geographical spot is not meaningful for human beings just because it is a geographical spot, but requires a human act of doing something with it—be it physically or mentally—to turn it into a meaningful "locale." These locales, which have been established by humans, then transform the other spots around them into a meaningful landscape. That the land is meaningful is not just a given; its meaning is created by the acts of human beings.

In contemporary spatial theory, what Heidegger had termed a "locale" would be termed a "place." In the decades since Heidegger was writing, the concept of "place" has become established as one of the most fundamental concepts in the "spatial turn" of the arts and humanities. In their most common conceptualization, the two basic analytic units in approaches inspired by the "spatial turn" are "place" and "space."[76] Of these, "space" is the

---

[74] Quotation: Heidegger 1993, 354.

[75] E.g., Heidegger 1993, 355.

[76] For surveys cf. Cresswell 2015; Hubbard and Kitchin 2011. Foundational was Tuan 1977. A notable exception to the standard usage described in the following is Michel de Certeau (1984), who exactly inverts the otherwise predominant definitions of space vs. place: cf. Cresswell 2015, 70.

geometrical space of the natural sciences, the sort of space that can be measured with a tape measure. The concept of "place" is based on "space" with a twist: "place" is a section of "space" that has been connected with human "meaning" and "significance."[77] In Heidegger's example, a place is where the bridge has been built, and the construction of the bridge is what creates a place out of mere space.

The two concepts of space and place are thus directly dependent on each other: "space" is the raw material from which "place" is created by adding an element of meaning. In difference to Heidegger's example of the bridge, this meaning does not presuppose a physical change, but can be a purely mental construct. Yi-Fu Tuan, the central proponent of "humanistic geography" and one of the classic theorists of the space/place distinction,[78] illustrated both the effect and the elusiveness of this process of the creation of place by quoting an anecdote about the two famous physicists Niels Bohr and Werner Heisenberg. In his memoirs, Heisenberg reminisced about a visit to the Danish castle of Kronberg that he made together with Bohr, and during which Bohr remarked to Heisenberg:[79]

Isn't it strange how this castle changes as soon as one imagines that Hamlet lived here? As scientists we believe that a castle consists only of stones, and admire the way the architect put them together. The stones [...] constitute the whole castle. None of this should be changed by the fact that Hamlet lived here, and yet it is changed completely. Suddenly the walls and the ramparts speak a quite different language. The courtyard becomes an entire world, [...], we hear Hamlet's "To be or not to be." Yet all we really know about Hamlet is that his name appears in a thirteenth-century chronicle. No one can prove that he really lived, let alone that he lived here. But everyone knows the questions Shakespeare had him ask, the human depth he was made to reveal, and so he, too, had to be found a place on earth, here in Kronberg. And once we know that, Kronberg becomes quite a different castle for us.

Well before the space/place distinction was formulated, Bohr here got to the heart of the difference between what later theorizing would call "space" and

---

[77] The word "meaning" seems to be the word most often, and certainly most prominently, used to define "place"; cf. Cresswell 2015, 19.

[78] Cf. Rodaway 2011; Cresswell 2015, 19, 35.

[79] Heisenberg 1972, 51; quoted by Tuan 1977, 4.

24 LANDSCAPE, RELIGION, AND THE SUPERNATURAL

"place." As "space," "a castle consists only of stones"; but being the castle where Shakespeare set his *Hamlet*, it was filled with so many associations of deeply important actions and thoughts that it became something different: what Tuan would call a "place." Remarkably—and remarked on as such by Bohr—this process was independent of any actual "belief" in the narrative that gave the place meaning: Bohr was well aware of the tenuous claim that Hamlet, and especially Shakespeare's Hamlet, has to historical veracity; yet still he felt the effect that the story had on the castle, and felt it deeply. A story does not need to be believed to work; it just needs to have been told.[80]

Bohr and Heisenberg were not the only people outside the academic discourse on "space" to observe the foundational role of the space/place distinction. The case through which the following discussion will approach the relationships between landscape, religion, and the supernatural will be the district of Strandir in the Icelandic Westfjords. One of the medieval texts that is referred to most frequently in the landscape mythology of Strandir is *Finnboga saga ramma*, the "Saga of Finnbogi the Strong," a prose narrative about the exploits of the farmer-hero Finnbogi the Strong that was probably written in the early fourteenth century.[81] The action of this saga is not restricted to Strandir, and it found an intense reception in other parts of Iceland, too. We get a glimpse of how this reception worked through a text by Finnur Kristjánsson from 1978, in which Finnur told of some of his memories of growing up in early twentieth-century Iceland.[82] In Finnur's case, his childhood experiences were located in northern Iceland in the area of Flateyjardalur valley, where crucial early parts of the Saga of Finnbogi the Strong are set. He told how his first encounter with the saga took place through the medium of writing, but how this then deeply affected his perception of his local landscape. When he was still a little boy, he was spending an evening helping an old woman to card wool. Then an uncle of his came and said: "That is a shame that you should not read the Sagas of Icelanders, my good boy, read this one," handing him a copy of the Saga of Finnbogi. At first, Finnur read the text only because he did not like carding wool, but then he was gripped by the saga, especially by the way it changed his relationship to the landscape around his home farm. The first few chapters of the saga tell

---

[80] Cf. the parallel results of recent research on "non-religion": Stacey 2020.

[81] *Finnboga saga*, ed. Jóhannes Halldórsson 1959, 251–340; trans. Kennedy 1997. In general on the close connections between medieval literature and recent folk storytelling in Iceland cf., for instance, Frog and Ahola 2021; Sävborg and Valk 2018a; Sävborg and Bek-Pedersen 2018a; Sävborg and Bek-Pedersen 2014a, 2014b; Sävborg 2014; Mitchell 2014. In a wider Nordic perspective, cf. Frog 2014.

[82] Finnur Kristjánsson 1978, esp. pp. 8–9.

INTRODUCTION AND EXPOSITION   25

how its hero, Finnbogi the Strong, was abandoned as an infant (quite like Moses) and got his name. For the first years of his life, he grew up under the preliminary name Urðarköttur, "Scree-Cat," because as a baby he had been found abandoned in a field of scree (*Finnboga saga*, chs. 2–4). As a young man, however, he saved the life of a rich Norwegian by the name of Finnbogi. This marked the beginning of a lasting friendship. One day, the two were riding together, when Finnbogi started feeling queasy; and when they reached a large rock on the mountain slope, they stopped there. By this rock, Finnbogi died, and as part of his legacy, he bequeathed not only his weapons but also his name to Urðarköttur—who thus became the Finnbogi who would later be known as Finnbogi the Strong (*Finnboga saga*, chs. 8–9). The stone where this happened henceforth was called Finnbogasteinn: "Finnbogi's Stone."

Already the medieval saga text emphasized the importance of the stone where this occurrence took place: as the Norwegian chose the place for his final rest, the saga made him say: "We'll stop here, and it may be that at this spot something worth reporting about our journey will happen."[83] After summarizing the episode of the saga that is set at Finnbogasteinn, Finnur described the effect that this reading had on him in the following words:[84]

There is now no need to recapitulate more from this saga, but my interest had been awakened for Eyri in Flateyjardalur valley [one of the places where the saga is set] and the scree there where the lad [. . .] cried between grey stones. And from the farmyard at home in Halldórsstaðir I saw Finnbogasteinn ["Finnbogi's Stone"] standing out against the sky, black, rounded. It had grown with reading the saga and loomed as if it was higher than before.

Thus came spring, lambing, sheep-shearing, and I was the shepherd.

After this it was much more fun to be a shepherd. [The farm of] Kinnarfell had come to life a little, and now I always had some errand to attend to at Finnbogasteinn ["Finnbogi's Stone"], jumped on top of it, stood there for a good while—from there one had a better view of the livestock. The stone was like a solid foundation of a living story, and thus if one shouted a lot and loud and rose up a little and was lucky, some people on the farms could see the lad outlined against the sky on the stone.

[83] *Finnboga saga*, ed. Jóhannes Halldórsson 1959, 251–340, at pp. 268–269; trans. Kennedy 1997, 230.
[84] Finnur Kristjánsson 1978, 9.

26 LANDSCAPE, RELIGION, AND THE SUPERNATURAL

Reading the saga had utterly changed Finnur's relationship to his home environment. He now took an interest in the landscape of the valley, and especially in the key locations of the early life of the eponymous hero of *Finnboga saga*: the scree field where Finnbogi had been left to die as an infant; and the isolated boulder where he received his name. One of the aspects that make Finnur's testimony particularly remarkable is how he describes how, after reading the saga, he started actively interacting with the boulder Finnbogasteinn. Having read the saga, he made his work as a shepherd provide him with opportunities to spend time at his new favorite place. He also embraced the stone with all his senses: Finnur did not just look at it from a distance (though he did that, too), but climbed on top of it, jumped around on it, and shouted from it to attract attention to himself. Finnur did not quite say so, but the way he not only enjoyed being at the stone but also wanted to be seen there might suggest that on some level he was identifying himself with the saga hero, who in a classic fairy-tale pattern started from humble beginnings to rise to glory and wealth, thus providing the perfect fantasy for a young shepherd boy. But being at the stone not only prompted Finnur to dream: Finnbogasteinn also turned out to be a remarkably good place from which to herd his flock, as it gave him a good view of the pastures. In this way dreams and the everyday, storytelling and work interlaced, and "after this it was much more fun to be a shepherd." The saga site had acquired a deep, invigorating meaning for Finnur: by connecting it with a key moment in a heroic biography, reading the saga had turned the stone from "space" to "place," and Finnur's clear reminiscences of how this came about constitute a remarkably self-conscious account of the underlying process. The transformation of his perspective that Finnur described is exactly the transformation from space to place that also underlies Bohr's remark to Heisenberg, but while the great physicists only stated the result, the shepherd actually gave voice to the process that led there.

In Finnur's account another property of a "place" is made very explicit, one that Tuan highlighted as a central definitional feature: it provokes a pause in movement. For Finnur, Finnbogasteinn not only became connected with the saga narrative and thus with associations that turned it into much more than its mere materiality, but it also became one of his favorite locations to interrupt his rambles through the landscape. This is closely mirrored by Tuan's definition:[85]

---

[85] Tuan 1977, 6.

"Space" is more abstract than "place." What begins as undifferentiated space becomes place as we get to know it better and endow it with value. [...] The ideas "space" and "place" require each other for definition. From the security and stability of place we are aware of the openness, freedom, and threat of space, and vice versa. Furthermore, if we think of space as that which allows movement, then place is pause; each pause in movement makes it possible for location to be transformed into place.

Finnbogasteinn fits these criteria with striking accuracy: Finnur's reading had—at least for him, and it is important to note that perceptions of what is a "place" vary not only over time but also between individuals—endowed Finnbogasteinn with value and turned it into a place where he loved to stop, and did so as much as his other obligations allowed.

The anecdotes told by Heisenberg and Finnur Kristjánsson both speak of an emotional reaction and attachment to places: they experienced their places on a deeply emotional level. This emotional component of human experiences of and relationships to places has long been an important part of the discourse on space and place. In has played a prominent role already for Tuan's "humanistic geography," which had its heyday in the 1970s, when Tuan approached both positive and negative relationships to places: two of his major monographs are dedicated to the affectionate relationship of *Topophilia* (1974), which he defined as the "the affective bond between people and place or setting,"[86] and the horror of *Landscapes of Fear* (1979).[87] From the perspective of the study of religions, a particularly important concept that Tuan developed to approach this aspect of place is "geopiety."[88] He coined this term to designate a religious concept referring to a relationship of mutual, reciprocal reverence and care between human beings, deities, and nature and the land. Tuan found variants and manifestations of geopiety just as much in the environmentalist movement as in patriotism,[89] which he thus viewed through a place-focused religious analytical lens. At the same time, he also applied the concept to more classically religious phenomena such as the density of shrines and other cultic and sacred sites in the rural landscape of ancient Greece.[90] As a critical term, "geopiety" thus seems custom-made

---

[86] Tuan 1990 (1974), 4.
[87] Tuan 1990 (1974); Tuan 2013 (1979).
[88] Tuan 1976.
[89] Tuan 1976, 13, 23–29.
[90] Tuan 1976, 17–18, 21.

28 LANDSCAPE, RELIGION, AND THE SUPERNATURAL

for describing situations that involve a dense inscription of supernatural concepts into the landscape.

Tuan, as one of the most important founding fathers of a "humanistic geography" that put a central focus on the study of emotions as part of the experience of places, was an early pioneer, but by no means the last scholar to approach places and landscapes through the feelings they are connected to. In the context of the "emotive turn" of the arts and humanities that has been proclaimed in recent years,[91] research on emotions is also thriving in landscape studies. This is amply illustrated by Debbie Felton's *Landscapes of Dread in Classical Antiquity*,[92] and even more recently by Camilla Asplund Ingemark's and Dominic Ingemark's proposal of the theoretical concept of "emotional topography."[93] They argued that one of the common themes running through the existing research on the spatiality of emotions is that certain locations provoke particular emotions.[94] This they combined with a social and a temporal aspect, particularly emphasizing the temporal one: the emotions evoked by a place can change depending on the time of the day, the time of the month, or even the time of the year: a place that feels perfectly safe during daytime can become scary after nightfall. This often has a social dimension: a park can feel safe during the day, when one does not meet anybody more threatening than a dog walker, but can turn scary at night by becoming associated with marginalized social groups such as prostitutes and criminals.[95] Or as the same phenomenon was described by Sävborg and Valk: a visit to a cemetery during daytime may evoke sweet memories and a sense of tranquility, but at night the same place may evoke fear.[96]

It should be emphasized that the emotions elicited by particular places are extremely changeable over time and between different social groups. A classic example is the Alps, which only during the eighteenth and nineteenth centuries turned from a place viewed with horror to a desirable place to take a holiday.[97] So there is no intrinsic link between certain types of places and certain emotions; the exact workings of the entanglement of place, emotions, time, and social framework have to be analyzed for every place in every period of every society anew. What is important, however, is

---

[91] For overviews cf. Corrigan 2016; Corrigan 2008a; Stubbe 1999.
[92] Felton 2018.
[93] Asplund Ingemark and Ingemark 2020, esp. pp. 167–171, 248–250.
[94] Asplund Ingemark and Ingemark 2020, 167.
[95] Asplund Ingemark and Ingemark 2020, 169–170. Cf. Frog 2020, 464.
[96] Sävborg and Valk 2018b, 11.
[97] Macfarlane 2008 (2003).

that—irrespective of its changeability—this quadruple entanglement exists, and we will meet it also in Strandir. At the same time, the following case studies will illustrate how difficult it can be to decide from archival material how a place was perceived on an emotional level. Who knows whether a ghost story is really about fear as terror, rather than about fear as a titillation that eases the boredom of long hours of monotonous work?

Tuan's distinction between "space" and "place" has become the most common basic premise in current research on space in the arts and humanities. It is not, however, the only distinction that is used in scholarship. Terminologically developed along different lines, but in some ways functionally equivalent to the space/place distinction is the concept of social space or socially produced space that was foregrounded by Henri Lefebvre (1901–1991). For Lefebvre it was fundamental to emphasize the created character of space: "(Social) space is a (social) product."[98] Lefebvre developed his most central contributions to the discourse on space through his work as a Neo-Marxist theorist of the modern city, which he analyzed with a strong focus on social hierarchies and power relations. He thus understood social space as an expression of modes of production and focused on how this space was created and contested; a strong emphasis of his work was on how space, as a central object of struggles over its meaning, is not fixed, but constantly changing. While he did not explain his terminologies with complete consistency, generally speaking Lefebvre distinguished the "perceived space" of everyday social life, which is the place of *spatial practice*; the "conceived space" of planning, surveying, and cartography, which is captured and codified in *representations of space*; and the *representational spaces* that are "lived" through the symbols and images they are connected to, and which are spaces of the literary and artistic avant gardes that are able to subvert the boundaries between the other types of space. (Lefebvre refers, among others, to the surrealist painter René Magritte.) As a lifelong political activist and intellectual pioneer of the political Left, the practical potential of representational spaces to subvert the spatial practices of the capitalist system was one of his central concerns. Terminology to Lefebvre was not as important as the concrete work of analyzing power relations.[99] This focus on power relations will also inform important parts of the following analyses of material from Strandir.

[98] Lefebvre 1991, 26 (emphasis original).
[99] Lefebvre 1991 (orig. ed. 1974), esp. pp. 27, 33, 38–40; cf. Cresswell 2015, 17–19, 64–66, 69; Shields 2011.

30 LANDSCAPE, RELIGION, AND THE SUPERNATURAL

Lefebvre's work was one of the starting points from which Edward W. Soja (1940–2015) set out when he developed his category of "Thirdspace."[100] Writing within the paradigm of what he called a radical postmodernist perspective, Soja proposed a critique of binary conceptualizations of spatiality, arguing for a "trialectics of spatiality." According to Soja, one should distinguish three categories of space. In his terminological system, *Firstspace* is the "real" material space that can be measured empirically, or what Bachelard described as the space of the surveyor; *Secondspace* refers to ideas about space and to cognitive or mental representations of space; while *Thirdspace* is space that is lived and practiced. Soja's Thirdspace transcends the distinction between material (First-)space and mental (Second-)space: it is fundamentally characterized by being both/and: it is both material and also mental, both objective and also subjective, both real and also imagined. Soja put a particular emphasis on the characteristic of Thirdspace to combine the real and the imagined, and to reflect the importance of this trait of Thirdspace he coined the term of the "real-and-imagined"; in Soja's own words: "Simultaneously real and imagined and more (both and also . . .), the exploration of Thirdspace can be described and inscribed in journeys to 'real-and-imagined' (or perhaps 'realandimagined'?) places."[101] A justified criticism of the concept of Thirdspace, however, is that Soja programmatically uses the term in such a broad and abstract way that its concrete, specific meaning becomes elusive.[102] Furthermore, as a combination of the material "reality" of the geographical world with its mental imaginings and ascriptions of meaning, there is little—if indeed anything—that marks Thirdspace as fundamentally different from the common conceptualization of "place" as the synthesis of the "space of the surveyor" with the meanings ascribed to it by the imagination and cultural practices of human beings.

Another counterpoint to "place" has been proposed by Michel Foucault (1926–1984): in a radio lecture delivered in 1966, he coined the concept of the heterotopia, which since the 1980s has gained immense popularity in spatial research.[103] A heterotopia is a place that in some fundamental way is

---

[100] Soja 1996 (his capitalization); cf. Cresswell 2015, 69–70; Kugele 2016, 40–42; Latham 2011; Shields 2011, 282.

[101] Soja 1996, 11.

[102] See Latham 2011, 384, and cf. programmatically Soja 1996, 2 ("I use the concept of Thirdspace most broadly to highlight what I consider to be the most interesting new ways of thinking about space and social spatiality"), 22 ("the radical openness and limitless scope of what is presented here as a Thirdspace perspective").

[103] Foucault 2017; cf. Dünne et al. 2006, 292–295, 317–329 (with a revised version of the lecture delivered in 1967). Specifically on the usefulness of the concept in the study of religions: Mohn 2007.

"other": Foucault defined it as a space which is entirely different. He assumed that there is probably no society which does not create heterotopias. In different societies, such heterotopias can be places that are sacred or forbidden, or sanatoria, institutions for the mentally ill, or prisons. Such heterotopias can always be dissolved, changed, or created anew: a society's heterotopias depend on their respective historical contexts; they are not unchangeable or permanent. Heterotopias furthermore often combine several incompatible spaces in one and the same place, and they are recurrently connected with breaks in time, which makes them related to their temporal equivalent, "heterochronias"; as examples, Foucault referred to gardens, cemeteries, or museums. While some heterotopias can aim at stability (like museums), other heterotopias can be highly temporal, such as fairs or nudist holiday villages, where a completely different set of rules applies for a limited period of time. Foucault also saw a fundamental characteristic of heterotopias in the existence of a mechanism which closes them off and isolates them from their surroundings. And finally, heterotopias call all other spaces into question: they either create an illusion that exposes the illusory character of all other reality, or they create a real space of perfect order, whose total order stands in contrast to the chaos of normal space—Foucault's examples are brothels and the tight, totalitarian ordering of a colonial settlement.[104] In a way, a heterotopia could be described as the general category of place (which is usually defined as space made meaningful by some kind of marking) with an extra marker that sets it apart with particular emphasis.

Home and Dwelling

This overview of perspectives on space and place could be expanded further; other concepts that one could mention, for instance, are the concept of the "non-place" that was coined by Marc Augé (b. 1935),[105] or the distinction between "smooth" and "striated" space that has been proposed by Gilles Deleuze (1925–1995) and Félix Guattari (1930–1992).[106] Some such further perspectives will be introduced in the course of the discussion. For the present purpose, however, the most important point to highlight is that one of the core functions of most of the different ways of structuring space has long been seen in the creation of "home."

---

[104] Foucault 2017, 11, 12, 14, 15, 16–17, 18; Foucault 2006, 320, 321, 322, 324, 325.
[105] Augé 2014; cf. Merriman 2011; Cresswell 2015, 78, 81–82, 108, 146; Günzel 2013, 94–98.
[106] Deleuze and Guattari 1988, 551–581; Dünne et al. 2006, 381–384, 434–446; Holland 2013, esp. pp. 41–44, 123–126; Tally 2013, 135–139.

32 LANDSCAPE, RELIGION, AND THE SUPERNATURAL

Implicitly or explicitly, the concept of "home" has stood in the center of attention of even the early theorists of space. By developing his poetics of space on the example of the intimate spaces of the house—*the* home par excellence—Bachelard placed "home" at the heart of his thinking. Analyzing the house and its rooms, Bachelard focused on beloved spaces, "simple images of *felicitous space*."[107] He highlighted that the root of the human attachment to such places is that they "concentrate [. . .] being within limits that protect":[108] in this conceptualization, "home" is an archetypical safe space. Similarly, Heidegger has his meditation on dwelling culminate in the image of a house:[109]

> Let us think for a while of a farmhouse in the Black Forest, which was built some two hundred years ago by the dwelling of peasants. Here the self-sufficiency of the power to let earth and sky, divinities and mortals enter *in simple oneness* into things ordered the house. It placed the farm on the wind-sheltered mountain slope, looking south, among the meadows close to the spring. It gave it the wide overhanging shingle roof whose proper slope bears up under the burden of snow, and that, reaching deep down, shields the chambers against the storms of the long winter nights. It did not forget the altar corner behind the community table; it made room in its chamber for the hallowed places of childbed and the "tree of the dead"— for that is what they call a coffin there: the *Totenbaum*—and in this way it designed for the different generations under one roof the character of their journey through time.

Like Bachelard, also Heidegger's concept of the ideal-typical place of dwelling put great emphasis on its protective aspects: half of his evocation of traditional dwelling talks of its protective, sheltering aspects, while the other half outlines the close relationship that it establishes to the "divinities" and the dead. In Heidegger's thinking, dwelling, which he claimed to be "*the basic character* of Being,"[110] consists half of shelter and half of spirituality.

This approach has had a deep impact not least in humanistic geography. Tuan defined geography as "the study of the earth as the home of people"[111]

---

[107] Bachelard 1994 (1958), xxxv.
[108] Bachelard 1994 (1958), xxxvi.
[109] Heidegger 1993, 361–362. Cf. Cresswell 2015, 27–29.
[110] Heidegger 1993, 362.
[111] Tuan 1991, 99.

and thus put the concept of "home" right at the heart of the discipline. Aspects of his definition of "home" mirror the double thrust of Heidegger's conceptualization of dwelling as both sheltered and spiritual: "home is a unit of space organized mentally and materially to satisfy a people's real and perceived basic biosocial needs and, beyond that, their higher aesthetic-political aspirations."[112] In this definition, "a people's [...] basic biosocial needs" correspond to Heidegger's emphasis on the sheltering aspect, the meadows, and the spring of his Black Forest farmhouse, while "their higher aesthetic-political aspirations" mirror Heidegger's "hallowed places," "altar corner," and the "simple oneness" of "divinities and mortals."

Approaches such as Tuan's and Heidegger's have, however, also drawn considerable criticism. Thus, Cresswell pointed out how "romantic and nostalgic" Heidegger's vision was;[113] this romantic nostalgia was also not just a feature of the example of the Black Forest farmhouse, but permeated Heidegger's thoughts on dwelling, which elsewhere talk of horse carriages, statues of saints, castles, and cathedrals:[114] over large stretches, Heidegger's writing reads like a medievalizing romance. Given that he framed his thoughts on dwelling in postwar Germany in the face of far-reaching devastation, it certainly contains a strong element of escapism.

Other criticism has been voiced by feminist and postmodern writers.[115] Thus, Gillian Rose has charged the paradigm of humanistic geography with being masculinist: in her assessment, it uses men as its implicit norm and falsely presupposes that the experiences of men can represent all experiences. She especially attacked the concept of "home" that is common in humanistic geography:[116]

> The claim that home is the exemplar of place is persistent in humanistic work. Although it was often noted that home need not necessarily be a family house, images of the domestic recur in [the work of humanistic geographers] as universal, even biological experiences. [...] This enthusiasm for home and for what is associated with the domestic, in the context of the erasure of women from humanistic studies, suggests to me that humanistic geographers are working with a masculinist notion of home/place.

---

[112] Tuan 1991, 102.
[113] Cresswell 2015, 37.
[114] Heidegger 1993, 354–355.
[115] Cf. Rodaway 2011, 429–430.
[116] Rose 1993, 53; cf. Cresswell 2015, 40.

34 LANDSCAPE, RELIGION, AND THE SUPERNATURAL

In marked contrast to this masculinist view of home, some—but not all—feminist researchers have seen the family as a major site of the oppression of women.[117] Any analysis of "home" thus has to recognize the broad spectrum of different experiences made by different people, where for some, "home" is perceived as protective, while for others it is stifling and abusive. These experiences differ not only along lines of gender. Thus, Black feminist writing can propose very different arguments on the basis of very different experiences: the Black feminist author bell hooks has described home as a comparatively sheltered place of subversion and resistance in an otherwise oppressive, racist, hate-filled environment.[118] The value, or lack thereof, of "home" for different people, what role "home" plays for them, and how it can be utilized politically and even subversively, thus has to be assessed strictly on a case-by-case basis.

The main set of data discussed in the following chapters to a large extent represents a "male" perspective.[119] Farm life in Strandir in the early twentieth century—the period which forms the center of gravity of the present study for the very pragmatic reason that it has left us with a record of its supernatural landscape almost unequalled both before and after—was characterized by a strongly gendered division of labor. In general, work out of doors was men's work, and work indoors was women's work. This was more a rule of thumb than strictly adhered to,[120] yet in some cases this division was maintained with staggering thoroughness. A striking example is the diary that Þorsteinn Guðbrandsson (1858–1923), farmer at Kaldrananes and a keen diarist, kept during the year 1918.[121] His diary strictly kept to things that happened out of doors, and from the diary alone it would be impossible to say how old Þorsteinn was or what his family relationships were. He never even mentioned his wife by name; she only got a single mention as "mother" when she gave money to their daughter for a journey.[122] Þorsteinn's (men's) world was not the world inside the house, which pointedly was none of his business, but that of outdoor agricultural work. Correspondingly, there is a strong tendency in our sources to view the wider landscape where this

---

[117] Rose 1993, 54–56.
[118] Cresswell 2015, 40–41; McKittrick 2011, 244–246; Rose 1993, 53; hooks 1990.
[119] It shares this limitation, though in a less pronounced fashion, with Cosgrove's studies of landscape: Cosgrove 1998, xvii–xviii; Cosgrove 2008, 24–25.
[120] See Dagrún Ósk Jónsdóttir 2021; Willson 2019.
[121] Ed. Jón Jónsson 2018a.
[122] Jón Jónsson 2018b, 6.

outdoor work took place through the lens of a male perspective: the perspective of the predominantly male laborer who worked this land.

Even so, the perspective of Strandir storytelling is never exclusively a male and/or hegemonic one: again and again, women, servants, and the poor also get a voice, and the "rich" as well as the "authorities"—both ecclesiastical and secular—are quite often taken down a peg.[123] Even though it is predominantly "male" in outlook, subversion and the questioning of power structures thus still form a prominent trait of this storytelling culture. This comparative sensibility to power and abuse may have its roots in the pervasive poverty that characterized much of life in Strandir in the early twentieth century, and that united Strandir society in a shared experience of scarcity. The perspective of the poor male laborer is often quite decidedly male, but just as often and just as much it is the perspective of the poor and subaltern. In this, the Strandir view of landscape is markedly different from Cosgrove's conceptualization of landscape as the bourgeois "way of seeing" of the urban landowner or W. J. T. Mitchell's description of "landscape" as "something like the 'dreamwork' of imperialism."[124]

Strandir: Exposition of an Icelandic Landscape

The approach taken in this book builds on the historical ambivalence of the term "landscape," whose meaning oscillates between a way of seeing and a place of dwelling. Drawing on a wide range of theoretical and empirical landscape studies, it shows the analytical usefulness that both perspectives have in different circumstances.[125] With this in mind, the book focuses on an area whose characteristics mirror key elements that the different schools of thought in landscape theory have highlighted. This area is the district of Strandir in the Icelandic Westfjords (Map 1.1). This chapter presents an introduction to Strandir as a region. It gives an overview of its social and economic structure, of the history of the Church there, and of the available sources on the area's supernatural landscape. Furthermore, a central concern is to present an exposition of the typical characteristics of the individual,

---

[123] A study of women in Icelandic folk storytelling is currently in preparation by Dagrún Ósk Jónsdóttir under the working title "Virtuous, Rebellious and Monstrous Women in Icelandic Folk Legends."

[124] Mitchell 2002d, 10 (criticized as an exaggeration already by Cosgrove 1998, xix; Cosgrove 2008, 27).

[125] Cf. Schenk 2001, §1.

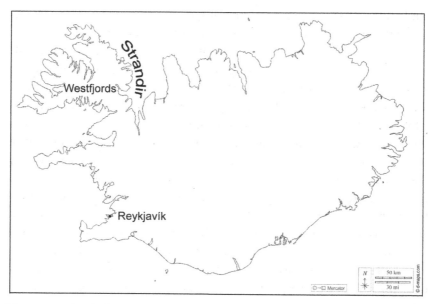

Map 1.1 Iceland, showing the geographical setting of the Westfjords and Strandir.

largely independent working farm that is the basic element in the makeup of the landscape of Strandir, one of isolated farmsteads whose supernatural places constitute the lion's share of the supernatural landscape of the region. These farms are typically characterized by specific and recurrent patterns of storytelling and spatial organization. This introduction will outline these patterns in order to provide a context for the discussions of specific themes in the relationship between landscape and religion that form the focal point of the following chapters.

Strandir exhibits the central features of the different definitions of "landscape" in the academic discourse to date. It has the potential to represent both a place of dwelling and a "way of seeing": Strandir is a place of dwelling that gives its inhabitants a common sense of identity as *Strandamenn*, "people of Strandir"; and it is a place that at times is impossibly picturesque and is thus not only inhabited but also draws the gaze of the viewer, whose gazing has recurrently been transformed into art. Strandir is of limited size (reflecting another defining feature of "landscape" as an area of restricted extent), but it is large and varied enough to offer a broad range of phenomena for analysis. Furthermore, making Strandir the site for an analysis of the relationship of landscape, religion, and the supernatural fits its self-image. Icelandic folk tradition has long viewed Strandir as the home of Icelandic magic and all manner of things uncanny. The district is for Iceland what the Harz Mountains around the Brocken are for Germany: the traditional center of (imaginings of) witchcraft, and thus a place saturated with the supernatural. This does not mean that the makeup of its supernatural landscape is markedly different from that of any other region of Iceland—it probably isn't, though this statement comes with the caveat that no other studies of Icelandic supernatural landscapes on a regional scale have been undertaken to date—but it means that local people are very open to the questions asked in the following chapters. In Strandir, no farmer is particularly surprised if a foreign researcher takes an interest in the story places, sacred spots, and supernatural sites on their land.

According to medieval Icelandic historiography, the history of Strandir begins in the ninth and tenth centuries, soon after the first discovery of Iceland by Norwegian seafarers around the year 860. Its first settlement, primarily by settlers from Scandinavia, in the decades after the discovery of Iceland is described in considerable detail but with questionable reliability by the medieval Icelandic *Landnámabók* or *Book of Settlements*.[126] The period of first settlement, c. 870–930, when the bulk of the land was settled, is known as the Settlement Period and has since its literary treatment in the medieval Sagas of Icelanders played a central role in Icelandic identity. It is the formative period of Iceland, in which its major landscape features were first named. Some of the first-generation settlers that play the most central roles in the accounts of the Settlement Period in medieval Icelandic literature were still prominent in the folklore of the nineteenth and twentieth centuries, which identifies their graves with hills and rock outcrops. For Strandir, the single most important (but by no means only) such figure is Steingrímur *trölli*:[127] Steingrímur the Troll was the first settler and name giver of Steingrímsfjörður ("Steingrímur's Fjord"), the largest fjord in Strandir, and also the fjord's central parsonage at Staður claimed him as its founding hero and located his grave in the mountains above the church. From there, he was said to protect shipping as far as he could see from his grave mound.[128]

---

[126] Ed. Jakob Benediktsson 1968; Sturlubók-recension translated by Hermann Pálsson and Edwards 1972. On its problems as a historical source: Egeler 2015c; Jakob Benediktsson 1966–1969.

[127] His nickname *trölli* is a weak form of the common word for "troll," which is a standard way of forming nicknames in Icelandic.

[128] See Egeler forthcoming a.

38 LANDSCAPE, RELIGION, AND THE SUPERNATURAL

During the Settlement Period, the population of Iceland primarily adhered to the vernacular "pagan" religion of pre-Christian Scandinavia, though there were Christians among the new settlers right from the beginning.[129] In the year 999/1000, Iceland collectively converted to Christianity by decision of its General Assembly, since in this early phase of its history Iceland was still a republic. In 1262–1264, Iceland became part of Norway, which in turn through the Kalmar Union in 1397 merged with Denmark. When King Christian III of Denmark in the mid-sixteenth century decided that his realm would embrace the Reformation in the form of Lutheran Protestantism, Iceland, as a subject to the Danish crown, was forced to follow suit. Icelandic resistance to the Reformation was crushed with the beheading of the last Catholic bishop of Hólar, Jón Arason, in 1550, and Lutheranism has been the dominant confession in Iceland ever since. Iceland remained part of Denmark until 1944, when it declared its independence on the basis of state treaties that in the preceding decades had allowed it increasing degrees of home rule and sovereignty.

The district of Strandir historically encompassed the east coast of the West Fjords and its hinterland, from the southern tip of Hrútafjörður fjord to the northern end of the bay of Skjaldabjarnarvík. Traditionally, this area was subdivided into the communities of (from north to south) Árneshreppur, Kaldrananeshreppur, Hrófbergshreppur, Hólmavíkurhreppur, Kirkjubólshreppur, Fellshreppur, Óspakseyrarhreppur, and Bæjarhreppur. One of the main purposes of these administrative units was to organize the annual collection of the sheep from the mountain pastures. Today, this is no longer the basis for the political structure of the district. Hrófbergshreppur, Hólmavíkurhreppur, Kirkjubólshreppur, Fellshreppur, and Óspakseyrarhreppur now all form Strandabyggð. Bæjarhreppur, which covers the western coast of Hrútafjörður and its hinterland, was reassigned from Strandir to the Norðurland district in 2012.

Strandir covers an area of about 3,500 km² and is inhabited very thinly: in 2020, it had a mere 609 permanent residents, two-thirds of whom were living in the region's two villages, Hólmavík (329) and Drangsnes (70). To some extent, this extremely low number of inhabitants is a recent development. In the early twentieth century, the region was important for its good fishing grounds, but the collapse of the herring fisheries in the 1950s has made large-scale fishing unprofitable and thus destroyed much of the district's

---

[129] On the pre-Christian religious history of northern Europe, see Schjødt et al. 2020.

economic basis. From the second half of the twentieth century onward, this has led to a massive population drain, and the demographic situation has still not stabilized. Since 1998 alone, when there were still 853 people living in Strandir, the total population of the region has decreased by a staggering 29 percent.[130]

Hólmavík and Drangsnes, the two villages of the district, provide central infrastructural services, including schools, a medical center, a police station, the regional bases of the state utility companies, the district's only commercial automobile workshop, and trade. Hólmavík was founded as a trading post in the 1890s; the trading association Kaupfélagið, which together with a shop of the merchant house Riis formed the core around which Hólmavík grew, went out of business only in 2019. Both Hólmavík and Drangsnes still to some extent live off shrimp processing (Hólmavík) and fishing (Drangsnes). Hólmavík is also now the seat of the only remaining priest of the Icelandic Lutheran Protestant national Church in Strandir.

Apart from the two villages, the settlement pattern is based on scattered farmsteads. Almost all farms are located by the shore; structurally, they tend to own a strip of land that runs from the shore into the mountains, allowing access to both land and marine resources. While the upper parts of some valleys historically were able to sustain farms, conditions were only ever favorable in locations that are more or less directly coastal. The actual highlands are uninhabitable. Many of the old farms are now abandoned; those that still exist are often located several kilometers from the next neighbor. Few young people remain; today, at most social occasions everybody under the age of forty stands out as young. Until a couple of decades ago, local community centers would host dances every Saturday; but these dances, which were notoriously riotous and the thought of which can still make the eyes of old people light up, have now ceased. Hand in hand with the drop in population numbers, social isolation is becoming a greater problem every year. Virtually every year, also, more farms are either entirely abandoned or turned into mere summer houses.

The economy of the remaining working farms is typically based on sheep husbandry. Sheep are kept outdoors for about half of the year; for the other half they are stabled and fed from the hay that the farmers make during the summer months. Most of the hay production necessary for seeing the flock through the winter takes place on specially tended hay fields in the

---

[130] Statistics Iceland, https://hagstofa.is, last accessed 23 November 2020.

40 LANDSCAPE, RELIGION, AND THE SUPERNATURAL

immediate surroundings of the farmhouse: this is the *tún* or "home-field," which is often fenced in to protect its grass against the free-running sheep and has connotations of being the private part of a farm. While the mountain areas are open and universally accessible, there is an expectation that you stay outside people's *tún* unless you have permission to enter.

Around the turn of the nineteenth to twentieth centuries, part of the sheep flock was still kept for dairy. The dairy sheep were gathered together every evening, penned in special night pens, and milked in the morning, after which they were released for the day to be collected again in the evening. Today, sheep are bred mostly for meat, with fur and wool generating some additional income. Soon after lambing (in late April and May), the ewes and their lambs are now left to roam and to find their way into the upper parts of the valleys and up into the mountain pastures. There, they fend for themselves and do as they please for the whole summer. In September, the sheep are gathered from the uplands in a major communal effort and are sorted, and their owners decide which sheep are kept for breeding and which are sent to the slaughterhouse.

The Church in Strandir

Iceland has been Christian since the early Middle Ages. According to medieval Icelandic historiography, the island instituted Christianity as its state religion on the General Assembly of the year 999/1000.[131] By the sixteenth century, Iceland had become part of Denmark, and so during the Reformation it had to follow the lead of the Danish king Christian III and become Protestant—which was not a popular move. Jón Arason, the last Catholic bishop of Hólar, whose refusal to adopt Lutheranism led to his execution in 1550, is still a kind of popular hero who on one of the stained-glass windows of the (Lutheran Protestant!) church of Akureyri is depicted much like a saint or martyr. While by and large Protestantism was enforced, Icelandic churches long maintained an almost Catholic visual appearance, as the lavishness of their decoration was limited only by the available resources rather than by Protestant austerity. Also some devotional practices were carried over almost seamlessly, especially the cult of Guðmundur the Good.

---

[131] For a critical overview of the conversion history of Iceland, see Jón Viðar Sigurðsson 2020.

Guðmundur Arason (1161–1237), or Guðmundur the Good, was a son of one of the most prominent northern Icelandic families of his day and is a well-attested historical figure.[132] He was ordained a priest in 1185 and made himself a name through his charity and religious fervor, and he early on acquired a reputation as a miracle worker who was equally adept at exorcizing supernatural monsters and in healing the sick. In 1201, Guðmundur became bishop-elect of Hólar and was consecrated bishop (a ceremony which had to be performed in Norway) in 1203. As bishop of Hólar, Guðmundur soon entered into a dispute with a number of northern Icelandic chieftains. The bone of contention was which courts had the right to judge clerics: Guðmundur, contrary to established custom, claimed that only the bishop (i.e., he himself) had a right to judge clerics, whereas until then there had been no distinction between clerics and the laity before the law. The conflict escalated, and after a skirmish in 1208, in which a prominent representative of the "laicist" faction was killed, Guðmundur was driven out of Hólar.

The following years were rather turbulent. Guðmundur repeatedly lost and regained his grip of the see at Hólar. He twice had to leave Iceland for Norway, where he was forced to spend almost a decade in all. He made enemies both of the chieftains and the common farmers, and he was involved in skirmishes several times when conflicts boiled over into open violence. In 1232, the archbishop of Trondheim (his ecclesiastical superior) officially removed Guðmundur from his office. He died five years later, in March 1237.

Guðmundur's lifelong struggle to expand the power of the Church against the traditional rights of the secular chieftains had devastating effects on his diocese, the political situation within Iceland, and Icelandic independence, as it kept necessitating Norwegian mediation in what should have been internal Icelandic affairs. Only a generation later Iceland submitted to Norwegian rule, as internal conflicts had spun out of control to such a degree that external rule had become preferable to what in effect was a state of almost civil war. Nevertheless, after Guðmundur's death his memory took on an increasingly rosy tinge. In 1315, his remains were disinterred and placed in a shrine, where they became an object of intense devotion and pilgrimage. There are indications that his cult even spread to Norway.[133] Guðmundur was never formally canonized. In the face of the Reformation, Jón Arason

---

[132] On Guðmundur the Good cf., for instance, Kuldkepp 2018; Ciklamini 2008; Ciklamini 2006; Ciklamini 2004; Cormack 1994, 99–100. A translation of his medieval Life is Turville-Petre and Olszewska 1942 (with a concise overview of his biography: pp. xxi–xxiv).

[133] Egeler 2015a, 110–111.

42 LANDSCAPE, RELIGION, AND THE SUPERNATURAL

made an attempt to effect Guðmundur's formal canonization, but failed, being inconvenienced by being beheaded. Nevertheless, in cultic reality—if not in theological theory—Guðmundur is the most popular saint of Iceland.

Since the category of a "saint" does not exist in Lutheran Protestant Iceland, Guðmundur is not called a saint, though for all practical aims and purposes he is described and treated as one.[134] In Strandir, as indeed in many parts of Iceland, from the nineteenth to the twenty-first century, Guðmundur played an equally prominent role in storytelling, place-names, and cultic practice.[135] The general pattern is that Guðmundur—or as he is generally called with his pet name: Gvendur the Good—does all manner of good for the population in a very hands-on way. Guðmundur the Good is not concerned with doctrine, mystical introspection, or the saving of people's souls, but he looks after their survival and physical well-being. He blesses springs that supply the drinking water for farms, ensuring that their water promotes health and never fails in its supply; he blesses dangerous road sections to prevent deaths by drowning or rock fall; he subdues murderous ghosts; or he stops an avalanche from sweeping away a farm. Guðmundur the Good is thus very much a saint of the everyday. His most prominent presence in the landscape is through the springs that he is said to have blessed. Most of these springs are named either directly after him as Gvendarbrunnur ("Guðmundur's Well"),[136] or they are named from the healing powers they have received through his blessing and are called Heilsubót ("Restitution of Health").[137] The waters of at least one Gvendarbrunnur are still taken more or less regularly by visitors and are said to have healing powers.[138]

Strandir used to have three parishes.[139] The former parish of Árneshreppur has two churches, both of which are located at Árnes on the bay of Trékyllisvík, where they stand within 120 m of each other. The older church was consecrated in 1850, which makes it the oldest surviving building in the whole district; the more recent church was consecrated in 1991 and is thus

---

[134] On the afterlife of Catholic saints in Lutheran Iceland, cf. Cormack 2008.

[135] See the discussion of places connected with him in the following chapters. For a general discussion of holy wells in Iceland, including wells blessed by Guðmundur the Good, cf. Cormack 2007.

[136] In Strandir, I know of examples at Staður, Skjaldabjarnarvík, Drangar, Kálfanes, Tröllatunga, Kolbeinsá í Hrútafirði, and on the island of Grímsey. Cf. the later discussion.

[137] Examples in Kambur, Kaldbakur, and Hrófberg.

[138] The claim of Einar Ólafur Sveinsson (2003 [orig. ed. 1940], 153) that the belief in the healing powers of wells blessed by Guðmundur belonged to pre-Reformation times is contradicted by both the archival evidence and to some extent even by contemporary practice.

[139] The following is based on the database of Icelandic churches, http://www.kirkjukort.net/, last accessed 3 December 2020.

Fig. 1.1 The two churches at Árnes and the mountain Reykjaneshyrna (in the left half of the picture), which has provided the inspiration for the design of the new (1991) church. The farm below the cliffs toward the right margin of the picture is Finnbogastaðir. There, Finnbogi the Strong killed the troll woman Kleppa, who plays a central role in the founding legend of the church at Staður. © M. Egeler, 2019.

the newest church in Strandir. The "New Church" in Árnes is also architecturally the most daring church building of the district. Its avant-garde design is inspired by the natural environment of the area and especially by the mountain Reykjaneshyrna, whose striking shape is alluded to by the design of the church's roof. Also the building material used for key elements was sourced locally, with the altar resting on rock pillars taken from the local shoreline.[140] The place of worship of Strandir's most remote inhabited area is thus the one that most explicitly sites itself in the local landscape and local nature (Fig. 1.1).

The parish of Hólmavík covers the churches in Kaldrananes (1851), Staður (1855), Kollafjarðarnes (1909), and Hólmavík (1968), as well as the chapel in Drangsnes (1944). Hólmavík became the seat of the local priest only in 1948; before then, the main church of the parish was the one at Staður. The former preeminence of Staður is reflected in the rich story landscape in which it is set, and which contrasts markedly with the rather less storied modern church in Hólmavík. According to its traditional founding legend, the church at

---

[140] Magnús H. Magnússon 1991.

44 LANDSCAPE, RELIGION, AND THE SUPERNATURAL

Staður was originally located beyond a deep ravine in the mountains above its present-day location. This place was so cut off from its surroundings that it could only be reached across an arch of rock that formed a natural bridge across the ravine. At the time when this first church was in use, the valley of Staðardalur was still inhabited by the pagan troll woman Kleppa. Kleppa had a huge part in shaping and naming the land in this valley: she built an important mountain road across Flókatunga at the head of the valley, and three farms were named after herself (Kleppustaðir, "Kleppa's-Steads"), her husband Skerpingur (Skerpingsstaðir, "Skerpingur's-Steads"), and her temple (Hofstaðir, "Temple-Steads"). Since Kleppa was a pagan, however, she hated and was greatly troubled by the sound of the church bells. In the end she tried to solve the problem posed by their ringing by using violence: she took her ax and smashed the rock arch that alone gave access to the church. This strategy backfired, however. Without the rock arch giving access to its former location, the church had to be relocated to where it still stands today, down in the valley, and Kleppa had to move away. To escape the ringing of the Christian bells, the pagan troll went to the northernmost part of Strandir in Árneshreppur and took refuge with Finnbogi the Strong in Finnbogastaðir—who, ironically, was later to build the first church in Árneshreppur, which in a roundabout way led to Kleppa's death. Thus, the founding legend of Staður does not revolve around a saint, but around a pagan troll, and through this troll it binds places in a large part of Strandir together into a single landscape of storytelling and ecclesiastical structure.[141]

The third Strandir parish used to be the parish of Prestbakki, which served the churches at Prestbakki (1957), Óspakseyri (1939), and Staður on the Hrútafjörður fjord (1884). Today, most of this third parish no longer belongs to Strandir. The parishes of Árneshreppur and Hólmavík are now served by a single priest, whose seat is in Hólmavík, and who also covers Óspakseyri, but not Prestbakki or Staður on the Hrútafjörður fjord.[142]

The church in Hólmavík, which is now the main parish church of Strandir, is located in a prominent position above the harbor, and by accident or design it is oriented to directly face the harbor entrance. It is one of the largest and most dominant buildings in the village and the largest church in the district. This church is used quite often for concerts, as well as for ecclesiastical

---

[141] For a mid-nineteenth-century record of this story, which is still alive today, see Jón Árnason 1954–1961, 1: 144–145.

[142] Storytelling from the old parish of Prestbakki will form the focus especially of the section "Power and Subversion."

purposes. Services are held somewhat irregularly, but nobody's church attendance has ever been particularly regular. Given the scattered settlement pattern that is characteristic of Strandir, and which could make the way to church a very long one, in inclement weather (and sometimes in not so inclement weather) motivation to undertake the trip to the nearest church has long been shaky. From 1918, we possess the diary of Þorsteinn Guðbrandsson at Kaldrananes, who owned and was in charge of the maintenance of the church there. A phrase that with only very minor variation recurs more than half a dozen times in his entries for 1918 is this: "Ekki var messað, enginn kom til kirkju," "No service was held; nobody came to church."[143]

Common Elements and Story Patterns of the Supernatural Landscape

To explore the relationship between landscape, religion, and the supernatural, this study draws on a "thick description"[144] and analysis of examples from the supernatural landscape of Strandir. In Strandir, we meet a Western European society whose richness of supernatural traditions runs counter to the narrative of secularization and where the "disenchantment" of the world postulated by Max Weber never seems to have happened,[145] or has only recently been starting to gain ground. The resulting wealth of supernatural heritage makes the landscape of Strandir an outstanding case study to pursue the mechanisms at work in how a stretch of land is turned into a supernatural landscape.

The landscape of Strandir is characterized by scattered farmsteads that are sometimes located kilometers from their next neighbor, with often vast stretches of open, extensively used agricultural land in between. The

---

[143] Ed. Jón Jónsson 2018a, 16, 21, 27, 29, 36, 41 (28 March, 19 May, 20 May, 14 July, 28 July, 14 October, 26 December).

[144] Cf. Geertz 1973, 3–30.

[145] Weber 1946, 139, 148–149, 155. Cf. Yelle and Trein 2020; Yelle 2013. Authors such as Josephson-Storm 2017 or Asprem 2014 have harshly criticized the idea of disenchantment. Since the empirical material underlying the present study is a clear case of a landscape of the supernatural that has not been disenchanted, it can be taken as a concrete case study of an absence of disenchantment in a recent and contemporary European context. Whether this has more general implications for the discussion of Weber's concept of disenchantment, however, is outside the remit of this book, which focuses on the internal mechanisms by which the supernatural landscape works rather than on the implications of its continued existence for our ideas of the "disenchantment" of Europe at large (which, for instance, might well have taken place in other European landscapes, even if it has done so only to a limited extent in the landscape of Strandir).

experience of most international visitors to the region is very much colored by this openness: when asked about their experience, most visitors stress how they are awed by the vast emptiness of the landscape. This feeling of emptiness is further enhanced by the fact that there is hardly any higher vegetation to block the view in any direction, so even in mountainous areas the landscape constantly seems laid out to a larger scale, and with fewer things in it, than would be the case in the densely settled, tree-grown areas of temperate Europe.

Such first impressions, however, are deceptive. As physically empty as the landscape may seem, it is densely endowed with cultural semantics, many of which reflect an intense play with ideas of supernatural presences and occurrences. In order to ease the reader's way into this cosmos, in this section I give an overview of the most common elements and story patterns from which the supernatural landscape of Strandir is constructed. To this end, I focus on the basic constituent unit of this landscape: the individual farmstead. Thus, I outline an ideal type of an early twentieth-century Strandir farm, in the sense in which the term was defined by Max Weber: a heuristic synthesis of features that recur but are not present in all concrete cases, and which combine into a coherent, utopian mental image that in this particular way is not found anywhere in reality, but which rather forms a heuristic reference point for scholarly analysis.[146]

For a Strandir farm, the construction of such an ideal type makes sense not least because the traditional elements of the landscape are strongly standardized and repetitive. In the far-reaching standardization of its main elements, the supernatural landscape of Strandir recalls the emphasis that classic theorists like Emile Durkheim or Clifford Geertz have put on the character of "religion" as a "system" or even a "unified system."[147] On one farm

---

[146] Weber 1985 (1904), 189–190, esp. p. 190: An *Idealtypus* "wird gewonnen durch einseitige Steigerung eines oder einiger Gesichtspunkte und durch Zusammenschluß einer Fülle von diffus und diskret, hier mehr, dort weniger, stellenweise gar nicht, vorhandenen Einzelerscheinungen, die sich jenen einseitig herausgehobenen Gesichtspunkten fügen, zu einem in sich einheitlichen Gedankenbilde. In seiner begrifflichen Reinheit ist dieses Gedankenbild nirgends in der Wirklichkeit empirisch vorfindbar, es ist eine Utopie, und für die historische Arbeit erwächst die Aufgabe, in jedem einzelnen Falle festzustellen, wie nahe oder wie fern die Wirklichkeit jenem Idealbilde steht."
[147] Durkheim 1915, 47 ("A religion is a unified system of beliefs and practices relative to sacred things, that is to say, things set apart and forbidden—beliefs and practices which unite into one single moral community called a Church, all those who adhere to them."); Geertz 1973, 90 ("a *religion* is: *(1) a system of symbols which acts to (2) establish powerful, pervasive, and long-lasting moods and motivations in men by (3) formulating conceptions of a general order of existence and (4) clothing these conceptions with such an aura of factuality that (5) the moods and motivations seem uniquely realistic*," italics in original).

after another, the same belief traditions and stories recur, and sometimes established story patterns recur even where they do not really fit the local topography. Frog has coined the term "otherworlding" for the process by which places are turned into locations of an (in this case supernatural) "other," and he has highlighted that this process often works through common narrative patterns: as he notes, only "[t]he recognizability of this pattern makes it a meaningful paradigm."[148] In other words, if a process of otherworlding of a place is to be socially successful, it must be recognizable and repeated, as only wide repetition allows it to become naturalized.

Such use of strongly standardized narrative patterns and wide repetition is exactly what we see on Strandir farms. However, this does not mean that every farm has the same stories; this is not the case, and there is no farm that I know of that has the full set of stories and belief traditions outlined herein. Rather, there is something like an established corpus of stories and belief traditions from which individual farms make individual selections: what distinguishes the story landscape of one farm from that of another is not so much absolute originality as the individual way stories and beliefs derived from a common tradition are localized on its land. The ideal type of a Strandir farm outlined below reflects this common tradition rather than any specific individual farm.

A traditional Strandir farm—that is, a farm established before the far-reaching mechanization of Icelandic agriculture in the second half of the twentieth century—has roughly between 150 and 300 named sites. This extremely dense microtoponymy was connected at least partly with the organization of the agricultural workflow; historical documents associate the practical value of the microtoponymy of Strandir farms particularly with shepherding. Not all the names are purely practical, however. While documentation is very unequal, every farm for which reasonably detailed twentieth-century descriptions are extant is ascribed at least one, but mostly several places connected with supernatural belief traditions and stories. While documentation is too patchy to make meaningful quantifications, I estimate a lower single-digit percentage of a farm's named sites to typically be in the supernatural category. This may not look like much, yet for well-documented farms several supernatural places are almost invariably attested.

The engagement with these places takes two forms, mirroring the juxtaposition of "beliefs and practices" that since Durkheim has been part of many

---

[148] Frog 2020, quotation: p. 461.

48 LANDSCAPE, RELIGION, AND THE SUPERNATURAL

definitions of religion:[149] ideas about the nature of these places ("beliefs") are formulated in stories,[150] which are connected with behaviors ("practices"). The behaviors associated with supernatural places overwhelmingly consist in what has been termed "rituals of avoidance":[151] people tend to ensure that supernatural places are not violated in order to protect themselves against negative repercussions, or just because they want to preserve the place because they like its story. The degree of care taken varies hugely between individuals, and as far as the extant documentation allows us to say, it has always done so.

The narrative traditions connected with the supernatural places of Strandir are much more varied than such "rituals of avoidance," but at the same time they are very strongly patterned: stories connected with specific types of places tend to have specific narrative structures and to contain specific motifs. Such patterning of the storytelling tradition is a common trait of (at least European) folk storytelling. The consistency of this patterning has facilitated classic studies like Vladimir Propp's influential study of Russian fairy tales, *Morphology of the Folktale*,[152] or the common practice of structuring folk storytelling through tale type catalogues and motif catalogues.[153] Yet while a wealth of research exists on the classification and structure of folk storytelling, it can only be applied to a very limited extent to the Strandir storytelling that forms the focus of this book. The work on structure and typology that has been undertaken to date mostly concerns the more elaborate genres of folk storytelling, such as fairy tales in the specific sense of German *Märchen*. However, most of the storytelling about supernatural places in Strandir belongs to the legend genre. This material has hitherto not been the focus of research and, for instance, is not at all covered in the classic *The Types of the Folktale* by Antti Aarne and Stith Thompson.[154] An exhaustive study of the legends of Strandir as a genre has yet to be undertaken and lies beyond the scope of this book. Nonetheless, it is clear that specific types of supernatural places tend to be connected with specific types of stories that contain specific motifs and follow specific recurrent narrative structures. I will now highlight typical characteristics of these stories

---

[149] Durkheim 1915, 47 (see the preceding note).

[150] On the importance of storytelling for the cultural construction of places in a folkloristic perspective, see Sävborg and Valk 2018b, 8. On the importance of stories for the creation of a feeling of the reality of religious beliefs, cf. Luhrmann 2020, xiii, 25–57.

[151] On the term "ritual of avoidance," see Chadbourne 2012, 76.

[152] Propp 1968.

[153] E.g., Christiansen 1958; for Iceland: Jón Árnason 1954–1961, 6: 315–330; Einar Ól. Sveinsson 1929 with a focus on the genre of fairy tales (*Märchen*).

[154] Thompson 1961; new, expanded edition: Uther 2004.

as they are connected with the places of the supernatural that are typical of a Strandir farm.

"Places of Enchantment": *álagablettir*

One of the most common types of belief traditions on Strandir farms is the *álagablettur* (plural: *álagablettir*), or "place of enchantments."[155] The term *álagablettur* is not an academic term, but a word that is in common use in vernacular discourse. Typically, a Strandir *álagablettur* is a place where it is forbidden to cut the grass or to make other changes to the landscape; in a rarer variant, the forbidden place consists in a stretch of water where it is forbidden to fish.[156] A violation of this injunction would lead to punishment in the form of mishaps whose nature is normally unspecified. Typically, such mishaps consist in the death of livestock or agricultural work accidents, sometimes involving severe injuries, among the members of the household. The Goðdalur tragedy, which was ascribed to the violation of an *álagablettur*, is unusual for being the most vicious disaster connected with an *álagablettur* in Strandir, and also for the time span of several years that passed between the construction of the new farmhouse on the alleged *álagablettur* and the avalanche that destroyed it. More typically, violation of an *álagablettur* is thought to lead to accidents or death of livestock that are either immediate or at least occur within the year in which the site was violated.

Stories about such violations of *álagablettir* and the ensuing punishment are common and tend to follow a standard narrative pattern of PROHIBITION—VIOLATION—PUNISHMENT—REFORM: an *álagablettur* is known; a young farmer takes over farming and does not believe in the power of the *álagablettur*; he (the culprit is always male) violates the place against better advice (which is generally given by a woman, who is often of an older generation); accidents happen that teach him the error of his ways; and henceforth he respects the *álagablettur*. In a variant of this pattern that likewise is attested repeatedly, an *álagablettur* is violated out of ignorance; then a dream appearance warns the culprit off; and reform ensues. In either version of the standard story, an *álagablettur* thus functions, to use Foucault's term, as the ultimate heterotopia: a place that is set apart by the presence of

---

[155] For a discussion of *álagablettir* in general, see Gunnell 2018a; specifically on the *álagablettir* of Strandir, see Dagrún Ósk Jónsdóttir and Jón Jónsson 2019; Dagrún Ósk Jónsdóttir and Jón Jónsson 2021.

[156] The emphasis that an *álagablettur* puts on prohibitions makes it the closest thing on a typical farm to the "*sacred things, that is to say, things set apart and forbidden*" that Emile Durkheim had seen as the heart of "religion": Durkheim 1915, 47 (italics original); see the earlier note.

50 LANDSCAPE, RELIGION, AND THE SUPERNATURAL

supernatural powers, and therefore is untouchable. It should be noted, however, that in spite of its (theoretically) untouchable nature, storytelling about *álagablettir* is generally about their violation: even with respect to one and the same *álagablettur*, storytelling can repeat the pattern of PROHIBITION— VIOLATION—PUNISHMENT—REFORM again and again. Even while claiming the truth of an *álagablettur*, the stories thus emphasize that this truth was never accepted by all members of society and was an object of ongoing discussion.

A typical *álagablettur* in Strandir is an area of good grass that is both small and clearly demarcated, for example by being located in a sharply delineated hollow or on top of a hill with sharply delineated banks. So while *álagablettir* are considered dangerous, they constitute a controlled danger, as their clear demarcation normally means that there is no risk of violating them accidentally.[157] Often, the forbidden grass is also located in an area that makes one wonder why anybody would want to cut it in the first place. So in practice, not touching an *álagablettur* is frequently not much of an economic loss. A typical *álagablettur* seems to constitute a trade-off where the yield of a small amount of difficult land is exchanged for the feeling that by not touching this land, one can control the danger of accidents and animal diseases. Thus, such *álagablettir* seem to contribute a way of dealing with contingency and a basic feeling of the precariousness of life.

This function of addressing the precariousness of the human condition makes *álagablettir* something rather more specific than the common phenomenon of attributing mishaps, ill luck, and disasters to supernatural or divine agents, which in the history of religions is attested again and again. When Lisbon was destroyed by a catastrophic earthquake in 1755, many contemporaries interpreted this as punishment caused by the wrath of God.[158] Similarly, though in a more systematic fashion, E. E. Evans-Pritchard in his classic study of witchcraft among the Azande saw the central and pervasive function of the Azande concept of witchcraft as explaining the underlying reasons for any coincidence that led to injury: witchcraft explained

---

[157] *Álagablettir* certainly are among and may even be *the* most clearly demarcated supernatural places in Strandir. This emphasis on their boundaries recalls the importance that Heidegger in his *Building Dwelling Thinking* ascribed to boundaries, where he argued that "the boundary is that from which something *begins its essential unfolding*" (Heidegger 1993, 356, emphasis original). In the case of an *álagablettur*, however, the point of the boundary is not so much the beginning as the marking of an end: its sharp boundary marks the end of safe working space more than the beginning of the presence of the supernatural, for what is important to the farmer is the safety outside rather than the danger inside it.
[158] Bühler 2016, 172.

INTRODUCTION AND EXPOSITION 51

why people were killed when a granary collapsed just as they were sitting in its shade.[159] In cases like the earthquake of Lisbon or Azande witchcraft, the divine/supernatural is offered as a reason for why something bad has happened. The "natural philosophy" (to use Evans-Pritchard's term)[160] of the *álagablettur* subtly differs from this common pattern by focusing not so much on the explanation of ill luck that has already occurred as on the prevention of ill luck that might occur in the future: in the first instance, an *álagablettur* offers a conceptual way of preventing ill luck, and only secondarily serves for its retrospective explanation. This positive, preventative function may be the reason why *álagablettir* were so extremely widespread: whenever detailed historical accounts of Strandir farms exist, *álagablettir* feature so regularly that we can assume that in the early twentieth century almost every working farm had at least one.

Humanoid Supernatural Beings: The Hidden People and Trolls

Most accounts of *álagablettir* do not explain why cutting the grass there leads to retribution. A significant minority of descriptions, however, specify that the grass growing on the *álagablettur* belongs to the *álfar* or "elves," and that the accidents resulting from the violation of the *álagablettur* are their punishment for the theft of their property.[161] Today, the *álfar* or *huldufólk* ("hidden people") are by far the most advertised part of the supernatural cosmos of traditional and not-so-traditional Iceland, featuring widely in newsprint, coffee-table books, television documentaries, and other popular media and publications. No travel book about Iceland today can do without at least one chapter about "the Icelandic elf belief." This was not always so: in travelogues and other publications about contemporary Iceland from the nineteenth and the early twentieth centuries, there is little or no interest in "elves," and

---

[159] Evans-Pritchard 1937, 63–83.
[160] Evans-Pritchard 1937, 63.
[161] In general on Icelandic *álfar,* see Gunnell 2020b; Gunnell 2018b; Ármann Jakobsson 2015; Gunnell 2007; Einar Ólafur Sveinsson 2003, esp. pp. 170–183. The largest single collection of stories about *álfar* probably is still Jón Árnason 1954–1961, 2: 3–124. On their international reception, see Egeler 2020b. With the exception of the origin story of the *álfar*, the following outline is based specifically on traditions about *álfar* in Strandir. Whether there is regional variation between *álfar* in different parts of rural Iceland is still a lacuna in the existing research to date. While historically *álfar* are not the only earth-dwelling beings of Iceland, they have since the Middle Ages gained considerable prominence; "dwarfs" (*dvergar*), for instance, have largely disappeared from Icelandic folk belief, and where they or places named from them occur, they seem to be merging with *álfar*. In Strandir, all dwarf places connected with any amount of narrative lore are also connected with elves, suggesting that the two categories of beings have largely collapsed into one. On dwarfs and their far-reaching disappearance from Icelandic folklore, see Gunnell 2020a; Einar Ólafur Sveinsson 2003, 72, 93, 159–160, 286, 298–299, 302, 309.

52   LANDSCAPE, RELIGION, AND THE SUPERNATURAL

where "elves" are mentioned they tend to be described as an obsolete belief of the past. It was only after the Second World War that Icelandic tourism marketing and travel writing about Iceland began promoting the now well-established cliché that Iceland is "the land where people believe in elves." The underlying causes of this change still remain virtually uncharted territory.[162]

The "elves" (singular *álfur*, plural *álfar*) of traditional Icelandic folk belief and folk storytelling share complex historical connections with the Tinker Bell-style fairies of present-day international pop culture, as both have their roots in part in early medieval Ireland and Scotland.[163] Yet since the early Middle Ages, their characters have taken such deeply divergent lines of development that by the twentieth century they had virtually nothing in common. While the fairies of international pop culture, with their diminutive size and dragonfly wings, are creations of Shakespeare and the Victorians,[164] traditional Icelandic "elves" are beings of countryside life through and through. Today, this is no longer true of all Icelandic elf lore: the ideas about elves that Icelandic urban media and spiritualists such as Erla Stefánsdóttir have widely propagated are deeply influenced by the international New Age and by Victorian fairy iconography, making "the Reykjavík fairy" of the twenty-first century a very different being indeed from the traditional "rural elf." The following outline focuses on the latter, as this is the kind of "elves" widely attested in traditional storytelling from Strandir, whereas the influence of the New Age fairy, which in Iceland is very much an invasive species, is strongest in urban habitats.[165]

In traditional Icelandic folk storytelling, the "elves" form a parallel rural society of otherworldly farmers that live in much the same way as their human neighbors. Just like human farmers, elves keep livestock, and just like in human farming, their livestock consists mostly in sheep. They have to work just as hard as human beings, and can be met driving their flock or just sitting somewhere, mud-soaked and resting after a hard day's labor in the hay fields. By and large, however, their efforts pay greater dividends. Recurrently, descriptions of elf encounters emphasize the colorful—which means: expensive—clothing they are wearing, showing their society as not simply parallel to the human one, but as more affluent. In a society scarred by

---

[162] Cf. Egeler 2020b.
[163] Cf. Einar Ólafur Sveinsson 2003, 174–175.
[164] Cf. Purkiss 2007; Martineau 1997.
[165] Cf. Ármann Jakobsson 2015, 217, 219–220. A detailed study of the changes wrought by urbanization and the influence of New Age concepts and international Anglophone pop culture still remains to be written, and I hope to return to the topic of these contemporary developments elsewhere.

pervasive scarcity—in Iceland, even periods of hunger recurred throughout much of the nineteenth century—this additional wealth, however little it may seem now, marked the parallel world of the elves as a fantasy of a better life. Wish-fulfillment fantasies also appear in connection with elves in other ways: a shepherd may ask an elf to help him find his lost sheep, and receive this help; or somebody may have a love affair with one of the hidden people. At the same time, however, their world is not without its shadows. A common theme of elf stories is problems in childbirth: elf women can die in childbed, and their orphaned babies can be heard crying in the rocks. Also their economy is not safe from threats: if humans cut the grass that feeds their flocks, their livestock starves.

Thus, the hidden people are not all-out different; they are different enough to be markedly Other, but they can be related to in both good and bad aspects.[166] A nineteenth-century origin story of the hidden people paints them as siblings of humankind.[167] This story relates that on one occasion God announced that he would come to visit Adam and Eve, and so Eve started washing and dressing up their children to give this elevated guest an appropriate welcome. She did not, however, have enough time to wash all of them before God's arrival, and since she was embarrassed that some of her children were dirty, she hid them when God arrived. But nothing can be hidden from God, and so he knew full well that some of the children were being withheld from meeting him. This vexed him, and he declared that what was hidden from him should remain hidden forever. So the hidden people came into being.

It is hard to say to what extent this origin story of the hidden people was representative of Icelandic views before it was popularized by its publication in Jón Árnason's *Icelandic Folk and Fairy Tales*.[168] Its underlying sentiment of a close relatedness between humans and the hidden people certainly resonates with many aspects of Strandir storytelling. Jón Árnason's story integrates the elves into a Christian worldview, and in narratives from Strandir it is common for them to be described as Christian: in many locations, prominent rocks are identified as their churches, and it is repeatedly recounted that one can hear the sound of bells and religious hymns

---

[166] Cf. Frog 2020, 458 on the incremental nature of "otherworlding": "Commensurability is [. . .] salient: the familiar or recognizable forms a frame of reference against which fractions of difference become emphasized."

[167] Jón Árnason 1954–1961, 2: 7.

[168] The clergy often preferred to demonize them, cf. Einar Ólafur Sveinsson 2003, 84–85, 132, 173–174.

54   LANDSCAPE, RELIGION, AND THE SUPERNATURAL

from there. Also in their physical appearance, Strandir storytelling depicts the hidden people as close to human beings to the point of being virtually indistinguishable. A recurrent narrative pattern of stories about encounters with elves goes as follows: 1. people on the road meet strangers, and think that the strangers are person X or from farm Z; 2. the people reach a human habitation and tell of the encounter; 3. they are informed that person X / the persons from farm Z were somewhere else entirely; 4. it is concluded that the strangers encountered on the road must have belonged to the hidden people.

Not only storytelling but also the typical location of "elf settlements" (*álfabyggð*) in the landscape reflects their closeness to human society. While there are individual exceptions, the location and appearance of such "elf settlements" follow a recurring pattern. Typically, an "elf settlement" is located close to the farm buildings, not more than a few minutes on foot and often directly abutting land that is in intense use, such as sheep pens: these otherworldly siblings of humankind live in direct proximity to human society. Consequently, the "elf settlement" is often visible from the farm buildings. It normally takes the form of an isolated hill, rock, or large boulder. Its size generally remains within a human scale: a normal elf hill may have the size of a small garage or of a two-story building, but it stays within a human scope. While Strandir has cliff faces that can reach a height of several hundred meters, connecting such landmarks with the elves is extremely unusual. Traditional elves are the same size as human beings, and their abodes move within the same scale. Most "elf settlements" have a cliff face or an area of exposed smooth rock on at least one side, which may mirror the wood-paneled facade of a nineteenth-century turf-built farmhouse. Traditional *álfar* are very much, as "fairies" in nineteenth-century rural Ireland used to be called, the (mostly) "good neighbors." In 1940, the Icelandic medievalist and folklorist Einar Ólafur Sveinsson formulated a hypothesis about one of the functions of the Icelandic elf belief that, while old, still seems valid: "In very many stories of the hidden folk it is as if loneliness and longing for the society of men cried out to nature until hillocks and rocks and hillsides opened and were filled with hidden folk."[169] The elves may be part of the landscape because this barren northern landscape is so empty that, to the human mind, it needs filling, and fill it they do. Elf hills and elf rocks are among the most common places of the supernatural on Icelandic farms.

---

[169] Einar Ólafur Sveinsson 2003 (orig. ed. 1940), 290.

Another common element of the supernatural landscape, and one that stands in a multilayered contrast to belief and storytelling about elves, is trolls (Icelandic *tröll*, plural *tröll*).[170] Trolls appear widely in Strandir storytelling. In these stories, they are described as beings of the past, sometimes even the primordial past, who inhabited the land already before the arrival of human settlers and Christianity. As beings of the pre-Christian period, they are fierce adherents of paganism and abhor the Christian faith; church bells terrify them and drive them away.

Trolls do not live in the habitable lowlands where humans build their farms. Rather, their world is the mountains, from which in the past they descended to wreak havoc—or tried to do so, for often they were thwarted. They are huge, and their size has allowed them to alter the shape of the land: they can dig a fjord, create multitudes of skerries, and single-handedly build important roads. Even Grímsey, the largest island of Strandir, was created by a troll woman. Thus, they have an almost cosmogonic aspect, in that the traces of their strength are visible throughout the physical landscape.

In a number of cases, this cosmogonic aspect has led to an association between them and the mythical founding heroes of farms; some farms even outright claim troll women as their founders. At the same time, most stories about trolls are humorous. For all their power, trolls are not very bright, and they often become the topic of raucous high tales of the triumph of human wit over their elementary strength and their unbridled sexual desires. It is thus a common pattern of troll stories that the troll first performs feats of great strength, but is then either outwitted by a human opponent or outmaneuvers itself through its very own stupidity. Many of these tales end with the demise of the troll: when a troll is hit by the first rays of the morning sun, it turns to stone. In four cases, bizarrely, a troll woman commits suicide by drowning herself in a waterfall.

Petrified trolls are a common part of the landscape and have a typical troll geology as a free-standing stone pillar consisting of horizontal layers of material reminiscent of layers of basalt columns. Geological structures of this

---

[170] In general on trolls, cf. Simek 2018; Ármann Jakobsson 2017; Einar Ólafur Sveinsson 2003, 163–170. In medieval Icelandic literature, trolls overlap with or are part of various categories of giants, on which see Egeler 2021b; Clunies Ross 2020; Ármann Jakobsson 2009; Ármann Jakobsson 2008; Ármann Jakobsson 2006; Ármann Jakobsson 2005; Schulz 2004 (which is the most detailed analysis of Old Norse giants to date). The following outline is based on troll stories from Strandir. As it is the case with the *álfar*, also for trolls regional variation has not yet been studied. At least some of the traits of Strandir trolls, especially their role in founding narratives, could be specific to the region (Jón Jónsson, pers. comm.).

56 LANDSCAPE, RELIGION, AND THE SUPERNATURAL

type form as the outer walls of lava tubes and, being harder than the surrounding rock, tend to weather out of slopes and cliff faces. The physicality of the land here directly governs the storytelling about trolls. Stories about trolls in most cases are directly tied to such stone pillars, and the relationship between the stories and the geological formations is governed by a largely fixed pattern: where there is one stone pillar, it is almost invariably a petrified troll woman;[171] if there is more than one pillar, the others are the troll woman's husband, livestock, and (in one case) children. Thus, troll stories show a strong preference for the female sex: when a troll acts, it is normally female, and male trolls are introduced only to make up numbers to allow the troll story to tally with the observable number of petrified trolls in the landscape.

Overall, trolls form a multilayered foil of the local traditions about *álfar* or "elves": while elves are believed in (at least by some people) and looked upon with considerable seriousness, trolls only appear in stories that are not believed in and that are predominantly farcical in character; elves live close to the farm buildings, while trolls haunt the mountains; elves simply inhabit the landscape, while trolls shape and create it; elves are beings of the contemporary present, while trolls belong to the deep, often primordial past; elves are still thought to be alive, while trolls have all turned to stone; elves are Christian and ring church bells of their own, while trolls were pagan, owned heathen temples, and could not stand the sound of ringing bells and were driven away by them; elves can equally be male and female, while trolls that play active roles in narratives are almost invariably female only; elves are human-sized, while trolls are gigantic; elves can appear as the lovers of humans of either sex, while trolls are almost always rapists who abduct human men and try to force them to become their paramours—or even eat them (Table 1.1). In a way, elves and trolls are the supernatural inside and outside the ordered life of the farm. But such a generalization only indicates a general tendency. The elf woman in the story of "The Elf Woman at Ullarvötn" (*Álfkonan hjá Ullarvötnum*)[172] in many ways lives and behaves like a typical troll, while some trolls are fondly looked upon as the founders of farms. Distinctions between the typical categories of beings and their

---

[171] The only exception that I am aware of is the rock pillar Hvítserkur, which narratively is explained as a petrified male troll. Hvítserkur is not actually located in Strandir, however, though he is said to have originated from there. See chapter 2, section "Sound."

[172] Jón Árnason 1954–1961, 1: 97–99.

Table 1.1 *Álfar* ("Elves") and *tröll* ("Trolls") as a Contrasting Pair

Álfar ("Elves")	*Tröll* ("Trolls")
Part of belief (serious)	Part of storytelling (comic)
Close to the farms	Highlands and borders
Inhabiting the landscape	Creating the landscape
Present	Primordial past
Alive	Petrified
Christian	Pagan
Owning churches and church bells of their own	Owning pagan temples and driven away by church bells
Both sexes active	Only female sex active
Lovers	Abductors and consumers of men
Human size	Huge size

characteristic behaviors are upheld only to a certain degree, and while there are clear trends, they may not be valid for every case.

Founders' Burial Mounds

Another type of place that, like petrified trolls, inscribes the deep past into the land of a farm is founders' burial mounds.[173] Like *álagablettir*, elf settlements, or petrified trolls, such mounds also form an emic category, that of "mounds of people of olden times" (singular *fornmannahaugur*, plural *fornmannahaugar*). Founders' burial mounds are typically natural hills that tradition identifies as the last resting place of the man, woman, or troll who first founded the farm, or who was the first settler in a larger geographical unit, such as a valley or fjord. The incumbents of such mounds, whether they be human or troll, are typically eponymous heroes, who are said to have given their name to the locality they have founded: Steingrímur in Steigrímshaugur ("Steingrímur's Mound") is the mythical first settler of Steingrímsfjörður ("Steingrímur's Fjord"); Hvít in Hvítarleiði ("Hvít's Grave") is the troll foundress of the farm of Hvítarhlíð ("Hvít's Slope").

---

[173] Cf. Einar Ólafur Sveinsson 2003, 153; Egeler forthcoming a; Egeler 2022. Burial mounds are hugely important through all periods of Nordic storytelling and literature; see, for instance, Sävborg 2011; Gunnell 2014; Gunnell 2019.

58 LANDSCAPE, RELIGION, AND THE SUPERNATURAL

The physical appearance of such mounds is not standardized very strongly. Their size varies hugely, ranging from a couple to a couple of dozen meters. Their shape and composition likewise are not predefined. The mound Gestur in Miðdalur is an oval, rounded hillock, while Steingrímshaugur on Staðarfjall is a flat-topped rock outcrop, and Mókollshaugur has an almost uncanny resemblance to the Bent Pyramid of Dahshur. Their location shows a certain preponderance of sites that overlook the farm, fjord, or valley founded or first settled by the mound's incumbent. Exceptions are plentiful, however; instead of overlooking their land, the mounds of founders may well be located in the middle of the farmland or be tucked away in a remote corner of the mountains above it. Sometimes, the location of the mound is related to the range of the local church bells or the rays of the sun; in such cases, the story goes that before death the founder stipulated a burial where they could hear (or inversely: would never be bothered by) the ringing of church bells, or where the sun always (or: never) shines on their grave. Occasionally, the view from the mound is important, as the founder buried in the mound can be said to extend a certain protection to the area that the mound overlooks or in which it is located.

Such founders' burial mounds are often so obviously natural in origin as to have aroused comments to that effect as early as the eighteenth century. Yet such an awareness did not stop people telling stories about the mounds, or rather, telling the same story about them. With few exceptions, founders' burial mounds are connected with stories that closely adhere to a standardized narrative pattern, which runs as follows:

> The founding hero/heroine NN, who was the first to settle here and from whom the farm/fjord is named, is buried in NN's Mound (NN's-*haugur*) together with his/her chest of treasure. Before his/her death, he/she pronounced a warning against trying to break into the mound, but in the comparatively recent past such an attempt was made nevertheless. When the would-be mound-breakers took their spades and crowbars to the mound, however, they suddenly saw that the local church/their farm was on fire. They rushed home to help put out the blaze. Yet when they arrived at the burning church/farm, they did not find it engulfed in flames; everything there was in order. This experience so spooked the mound-breakers that they gave up their attempt to rob the founder's treasure. The hole that they dug before they stopped was never backfilled, and it can still be seen today and is testimony to the truth of the story.

INTRODUCTION AND EXPOSITION 59

This story pattern is one of only very few cases—indeed, maybe the only one—where a traditional story overrides topography. Generally, in Strandir there is a complete match between the actions that unfold in a folk narrative and the place where it is set, so that every occurrence described in a tale makes perfect sense in the place where it is said to have played itself out. Often one can trace the movements of the protagonists step by step. The narrative of the founder's mound breaks this rule. It is recurrently told about mounds from which there is no line of sight to the church or farm that is reputedly seen burning, making the action as described by the tale impossible. Sometimes, this is taken into consideration through auxiliary additions to the standard plot; for example, the mound-breakers have forgotten an important tool, so one of the men (they are always men) has to go back to the farm/church and then sees it burning and fetches the others. In other cases the story is just left unchanged, and it is told in a matter-of-fact manner, even though it is impossible in its local setting.

Types of Ghosts: The Sad, the Murderous, and the Harmless
Another traditional type of place that refers to the deep past is *útburður* sites.[174] An *útburður* is a "borne-out one," the ghost of an infant that shortly after its birth was borne out into the wilderness and left there to die. Both folklore and medieval Icelandic literature associate the practice of infanticide with the pagan past of Iceland before its conversion to Christianity in 999/1000. In Strandir folklore, the one who "bears out" a child is always a villain, and typically a pagan one. (The inverse does not hold true, though: not every pagan is said to have committed infanticide, only the evil ones.) In the landscape, this abominable act has left traces forever after: the ghosts of such exposed children can be heard crying at the places of their deaths, sometimes specifically in bad weather, when their suffering appears to be greatest. An *útburður* site is marked as the place of an unforgivable ancient crime, and of never-ending pain. Such places can be located quite far from the farm buildings—at a pass high in the mountains, for instance—but do not have to be in remote locations: at least occasionally an *útburður* site could be located even in the immediate vicinity of the farmhouse. *Útburður* sites do not seem to have a typical physical appearance: the crying of the infant ghost can be

---

[174] See chapter 2, section "Morality." For a general discussion of the various types of Icelandic "ghosts" and revenants, including those introduced in the following, cf. Einar Ólafur Sveinsson 2003, 183–188.

60 LANDSCAPE, RELIGION, AND THE SUPERNATURAL

located at a rock, on a mountain pass, or by a stretch of road, with no rules for what such a place looks like. If anything, the criterion for identifying an *útburður* site is an auditory one: recurrently, they are exposed places where the howling of the wind forms a central part of the local soundscape.

Also other types of ghosts form a common supernatural phenomenon on Strandir farms. The most important type of ghost, or at least the type most prominent in storytelling in Strandir, is the *draugur* (plural *draugar*). A Strandir *draugur* can come into being in a range of ways. Most ghosts of this type are dead people who by the use of magic powers have been conjured up from their grave by somebody with a grudge against a family or an individual, and henceforth haunt their victims to order, as it were. Even when their original target dies, their hauntings continue, as they are inherited by the next generation of the victim's family. Other *draugar* came into being as restless dead persons who are driven by a desire to avenge a (real or imagined) wrong done to them by a member of the family that they haunt forever after. Ghosts of this kind can appear equally as discorporate entities and in very much a physical form as effectively living corpses, the embodied walking dead.

Unlike all supernatural presences described so far, *draugar* are located on rather than within farms: while they tend to haunt specific farms, they are not restricted to specific locations on the land of these farms, but can wreak their havoc wherever on the farm it pleases them. Thus, they can attack people traveling on the access roads to a farm; they can kill sheep in the sheep house; they can manifest themselves inside the farm's kitchen or parlor; or they can ride the roof of the farmhouse, making its timbers creak so violently that everybody inside fears that the roof framework will give way. The reason for *draugar*'s mobility is that most of them are primarily tied to persons and families rather than places: with rare exceptions such as the *draugur* of Feykishólar, a farm's ghost exists as such because it haunts the family living there, not because it is attached to the place itself. When a family member goes traveling, the ghost can even accompany this person and pursue its malicious business wherever the traveler stops off. According to a recurrent storyline, some inexplicable mayhem arises at a farm, and shortly afterward a person arrives who is known to be haunted by a *draugur*: the mischief of the *draugur* has announced the impending arrival of its main victim.

A somewhat different category of what in English would be called "ghosts," but in Icelandic are not typically referred to as *draugar* but rather as *skotta*, *fylgja*, or *slæðingur*, are the souls of people who have died at specific dangerous places and have then remained attached to the place of their untimely demise. Such ghosts have a limited geographical range, though they do not have to be attached exclusively to the landscape features where they died. A recurring story pattern is exemplified by the ghosts who are resident on certain skerries off the farm of Broddanes: these ghosts commute between these skerries and the mainland, being normally resident on the skerries but repairing to the farmhouse at Broddadalsá to avoid particularly unpleasant weather. In contrast to the notoriously vengeful *draugar*, such ghosts may be dangerous, but they do not have to be.

Christianity: Paradise, Patron Saints, and Churches

Christianity is also present in the landscape of Strandir, though its presence is often largely depleted of actual religious or spiritual significance, especially—but not only—where the former official state religion of Iceland is concerned, Lutheran Protestantism. Thus, probably the most common Christian-mythological place-name on farms in Strandir is Paradís, "Paradise." The name Paradís obviously harks back to the Garden of Eden, but a Paradís has no spiritual significance, being simply a small sheltered place, typically a hollow or a spot embraced by cliffs, that offers protection from the wind while letting the sun in, and is hence a good spot to eat one's packed lunch while working out of doors. A Paradís also often cannot be looked into from the farmhouse and thus offers some rare privacy in a landscape which, lacking higher vegetation, is extremely open and exposed over huge stretches.

Another category of Christian places has already been introduced in the survey of the Church in Strandir: the wells blessed by Guðmundur the Good. These are not "holy wells" in the sense known from Ireland—that is, saints' cult sites as objects of pilgrimage on special occasions where devotees can ask specific wishes to be fulfilled. A Gvendarbrunnur ("Guðmundur's Well") can become such a pilgrimage site—in recent decades, this seems to have happened to the one at Kálfanes near Hólmavík—but more typically it is not a pilgrimage site that is distant, exceptional, and visited on extraordinary

62 LANDSCAPE, RELIGION, AND THE SUPERNATURAL

occasions, but rather an everyday part of the basic makeup of farm life: a typical Gvendarbrunnur is located on the land of the farm (so one does not have to undertake a pilgrimage there, as it is an essential part of home), and it is exceptional first and foremost because of the reliability of its water supply, which never dries up and never freezes. In 2019, at least one farm in Strandir still drew its drinking-water supply from the water blessed by Guðmundur the Good, which through hoses and pipes was directly funneled to the tap over the kitchen sink. The sacrality of a Gvendarbrunnur is a very homely and utterly pragmatic one: it is holy by reliably ensuring your daily coffee, being in the first place the source of your drinking water and only secondarily a place of the manifestation of the saint's power.

Before the Reformation the Icelandic clergy attempted Guðmundur's formal canonization; though this was never realized, in practice he was a well-established local Catholic saint with a cult that is attested as far afield as the Norwegian province of Telemark.[175] In post-Reformation Strandir, he is never called a "saint": in a nod toward Lutheran orthodoxy, he is merely called "Bishop Guðmundur" or simply Guðmundur the Good. Yet for all that Catholic terminology is avoided, in storytelling he remains exactly the sort of miracle-working saint that the Reformation had set out to abolish. Also in other respects, the purging of the Catholic landscape by the Reformation was only half-successful. Place-names such as Krossholt ("Cross Hill") still remind us of the free-standing crosses that dotted the coast and the countryside before they were removed after the Reformation.

Lutheran orthodoxy has done little to replace the former presence of Catholicism in the landscape. Typically, the presence of the Lutheran Church is reflected only in the churches themselves and in place-names that refer to these churches, priests, and the way to church, such as Kirkjuholt ("Church Hill"), Kirkjuvöllur ("Church Field"), Prestsengi ("Priest's Meadow"), Prestbakki ("Priest Ridge"), Prestavað ("Ford of the Priests"), or Prestaskarð ("Pass of the Priests"). Recurrently, however, even such names have a sting, and at least oral tradition of the twentieth century tended to deflate any sacred connotations of such names to the brink of parody. Prestaskarð ("Pass of the Priests") on the land of Víðidalsá farm was said to be so called not

---

[175] Egeler 2015a, 110–111.

INTRODUCTION AND EXPOSITION   63

because it was on the way to church, but because the priests of Tröllatunga used this pass when they went shopping in Skeljavík.[176] On the land of Svanshóll in Kaldrananes, Prestavað ("Ford of the Priests") and nearby Prestatjörn ("Pond of the Priests") allegedly got their names when a priest fell into the cold water there.[177] The hill Oddshóll ("Oddur's Hill") allegedly took its name from an occasion when a certain Pastor Oddur was seen delousing himself there.[178] The presence that the actual official religion of Strandir shows in its landscape is thus remarkably meager. Protestant churches and parsons are far outnumbered by elf dwellings, quasi-Catholic holy wells, and places of enchantments.

Nonsupernatural Narratives

The story landscape of Icelandic farms is not restricted to religious and supernatural narratives. These in fact only make up a small part of the overall storytelling tradition, albeit one which Icelanders themselves also felt to be privileged. The Icelandic folklorist Einar Ólafur Sveinsson noted already in 1940 that stories containing supernatural elements evoke a particular interest and are preserved in oral tradition better than others,[179] something borne out by the material produced by local people from Strandir: in the contributions of Sigurður Gunnlaugsson, Sigurður Rósmundsson, or Magnús Steingrímsson to the local journal *Viljinn* from the 1920s,[180] for example, traditions about places with supernatural connotations tend to be narrated in more detail than those concerning other places; the lists of places and place-names compiled by Símon Jóhannes Ágústsson (1904–1976) in the 1960s take particular note of and give more details about places of the supernatural than they do with any other kind of place;[181] and when Ingimundur Ingimundarson (1911–2000), who farmed at

---

[176] *SÁM* Guðrún S. Magnúsdóttir 1978b, 4.
[177] *SÁM* Ingimundur Ingimundarson s.a. (b), 1.
[178] See chapter 2, section "Power and Subversion."
[179] Einar Ólafur Sveinsson 2003 (orig. ed. 1940), 63.
[180] *SÁM* Sigurður Gunnlaugsson 1929b; *SÁM* Sigurður Rósmundsson s.a.; *SÁM* Magnús Steingrímsson 1929.
[181] *SÁM* Símon Jóh. Ágústsson s.a. (b); *SÁM* Símon Jóh. Ágústsson 1964; *SÁM* Símon Jóh. Ágústsson s.a. (a); *SÁM* Símon Jóh. Ágústsson s.a. (c).

64 LANDSCAPE, RELIGION, AND THE SUPERNATURAL

Svanshóll in Kaldrananeshreppur, composed a detailed description of his farm, he singled out its supernatural traditions for special treatment.[182] Hence there is an emic justification for analyzing the landscape of Strandir with particular focus on the supernatural: also within Strandir, the supernatural in the landscape has long been felt to be somehow different from, say, haymaking in the landscape, and deserving of special attention.[183] As we shall see, the distinction between the supernatural landscape and the haymaking landscape is not as clear-cut as one might think; but the point still deserves highlighting that an analysis of the supernatural landscape not only reflects the etic perspective of academic research but also an emic fascination.[184]

Yet however that may be, the landscape of Strandir does not exhaust itself in its supernatural occurrences. In addition to supernatural stories and beliefs, it is also home to a plethora of nonsupernatural storytelling traditions. Some of these are just as strongly patterned as any of the stories about elves, founders' graves, trolls, or Guðmundur the Good that have been introduced earlier.

Maybe the most widespread nonsupernatural traditional story type in Strandir is the tale of the two dead shepherds.[185] This story is connected with at least twelve locations throughout Strandir. It is generally tied to a smallish pile of stones or large tussock, which it interprets as a burial site. Specifically, this burial is not a formal one, but a *dys*, which means a quickly dug, makeshift grave that may consist in nothing more than a few stones thrown over a body; a *dys* is often associated with execution sites and places of violent conflict. This alleged burial site tends to be located toward the edge of the intensely used part of a farm's land, and it is connected with a story that follows a very simple and very consistent pattern:

---

[182] *SÁM* Ingimundur Ingimundarson s.a. (a).

[183] This recalls Tanya M. Luhrmann's programmatic argument that "all human groups distinguish what counts as natural from what is beyond the natural," and that it would even be "somewhat insulting to assume that non-Western people don't think of objects like rocks and gods as being real in different ways, as if they had a less subtle ontology than we moderns" (Luhrmann 2020, 5).

[184] In Europe, this fascination has a history of almost two millennia at least: already Pausanias's *Description of Greece* from the second century AD puts a striking focus on the mythological and religious places of the Greek landscape. Cf. Hawes 2017.

[185] See chapter 2, section "Coping with Contingency."

Two shepherds from this and the neighboring farm got into an argument. The argument got out of hand, the two shepherds started to fight, and they killed each other. They were buried side by side in the same grave.

Almost invariably, the victims of the fight remain anonymous; in the one case that I am aware of where a name is given, they both have the same name. Also the cause of their fight tends to be unknown, and the story sometimes even explicitly emphasizes that it is unknown. Where such alleged burial places have a name, it tends to be extremely generic, such as Strákadys ("Burial of the Lads"), Strákaskarð ("Pass of the Lads"), or Smalaþúfa ("Tussock of the Shepherds"). Detail is thus consistently lacking, making the grave of the two shepherds a common landscape monument to the "unknown quarrelsome young man."

Summary: The Farm as a Unit of Subsistence and Storytelling

To summarize, the ideal type of an early twentieth-century Strandir farm takes up a strip of land that reaches from the coast up into the mountains. This land contains just short of a dozen types of places with religious or supernatural associations; most of these associations are formulated in short stories that tend to follow clearly established patterns (Map 1.2). The farmhouse is located relatively close to the coast and the coastal road. Close to the farm buildings, there is an *álagablettur* or "spot of enchantments" that it is forbidden to tamper with, and whose violation leads to accidents and mishaps of all kinds. Often, but not necessarily, this is associated with a dwelling or church of the hidden people, whose property the *álagablettur* is and who dwell in a clearly distinct hill or rock. The main water supply of the farm is provided by a Gvendarbrunnur that has been blessed by Guðmundur the Good; this blessing is the reason why it never fails. The *álagablettur*, elf dwelling, and blessed spring are typically located in close vicinity to the farmhouse, on or adjacent to its intensely farmed home-field or *tún*. Somewhat further out from the farmhouse, place-names may mark the way to a church, or a location where some past parson did something undignified and entertaining; a little hollow by the name of Paradís provides shelter from the cold wind and privacy from prying eyes; a place where somebody died in an accident is haunted by more or less harmless ghosts. In the wasteland on the margins of the farm the ghost of a dead

66 LANDSCAPE, RELIGION, AND THE SUPERNATURAL

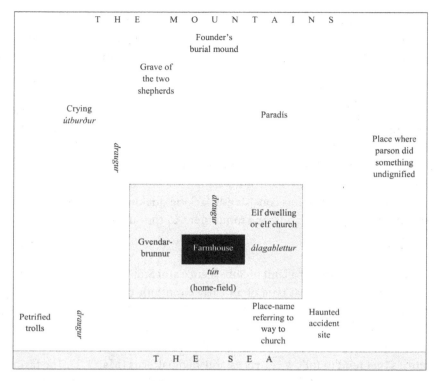

Map 1.2 Schematic map of the ideal type of a Strandir farm. No single farm that I am aware of has all the places marked here, but each of these places is a typical and recurring feature of the landscape of belief and storytelling of which most old farms seem to represent a repetition and variation.

infant can be heard crying, two dead shepherds are buried under a small pile of stones, and a troll has been caught by the rays of the sun and turned into a stone pillar. In the mountains high above the farm, the burial mound of its founding hero watches over it. Anywhere on its land, the unlucky may encounter a *draugur*, who has been harassing the farming family for generations.

This ideal type is an abstraction that in this form is not found anywhere in real-life Strandir; in practice, a well-documented large farm will have some four or five of the sites that are brought together in this ideal type, and a small one will have fewer. But even though this ideal type is, by its very nature, not "real," it can serve as an introduction to what the reader may expect when encountering concrete farms. Most importantly, it provides an introduction to what is "normal"

Sources and the Local Cultural Context of the Project

This study is based on a range of published as well as archival materials, which it combines with fieldwork undertaken in 2019 and 2021. (All references made to "now" or "today" should be understood to refer to 2019.) While fieldwork constituted only one aspect of the study, its contribution was fundamental, as only field research allowed the establishment of the exact relationship between the existing published and archival collections and the actual landscape, and to take not only narratives but also practice into consideration as a vital part of the analysis.

The classic printed sources for landscape, religion, and the supernatural in Strandir are editions of "traditional" folk narratives, many of which focus on aspects of "folk belief." The systematic collection of such folktales began in the mid-nineteenth century. Probably the single most important collection of Icelandic folklore is Jón Árnason's *Íslenzkar þjóðsögur og æfintýri* ("Icelandic Folk and Fairy Tales"). Around the middle of the nineteenth century, Jón Árnason collected around 2,600 legends from all over Iceland, of which he was able to publish a two-volume selection in 1862–1864;[186] his complete corpus was published only a century later,[187] and to this day it constitutes the largest single collection of Icelandic folk narrative. Other collections used in the current study include those by Ólafur Davíðsson, Árngrímur Fr. Bjarnason and Helgi Guðmundsson, Þorsteinn M. Jónsson, or Jón Thorarensen.[188] These printed collections are generally organized according to thematic rather than geographical criteria: a typical category would be "legends about churches," but not "legends from Kollafjörður," which can make it difficult to find stories that are relevant for specific places rather than specific themes. In recent years, however, the accessibility of this

---

[186] *Sagnagrunnur. A Geographically Mapped Database of Icelandic Folk Legends,* by Terry Gunnell and Trausti Dagsson, https://sagnagrunnur.com at https://sagnagrunnur.com/instructions/, last accessed 4 December 2020; Jón Árnason 1862–1864.

[187] Jón Árnason 1954–1961.

[188] I have used the following editions of these sometimes much-reprinted works: Ólafur Davíðsson 1978–1980; Árngrímur Fr. Bjarnason and Helgi Guðmundsson 1933–1949; Þorsteinn M. Jónsson 1964–1965; Jón Thorarensen 1971. It should be noted that this is not an exhaustive list of the printed sources used in this study.

type of source for geographically focused studies has been greatly increased by the *Sagnagrunnur* database of Icelandic folk legends, which presents a distribution map of some 10,000 Icelandic legends as found in the major folklore collections. The collections that underlie this digital mapping project were mostly compiled between the mid-nineteenth and the early twentieth century,[189] and this date range is also representative of the legends from printed sources used in this study.

The following study is, however, not restricted to the material brought together in such folktale collections. Rather, I have also drawn on a broad range of local and national Icelandic publications that do not have a specific focus on local storytelling, but contain considerable amounts of it in passing, such as journals, newspapers, or (auto-)biographies. The journal *Strandapósturinn*, "The Strandir Post," has been of particular importance. *Strandapósturinn* is a yearbook which has been published since 1967 and contains a florilegium of texts about Strandir and by inhabitants or former inhabitants of Strandir; the spectrum of the contributions covers official announcements, poetry, memoirs, academic studies, folktales, discussions of local place-names, and much more. It has a particular value as a venue created by local people for local people that engages with local concerns and viewpoints, and thus makes the emic perspective of Strandir directly accessible to the etic observer.

These published sources have been crucially supplemented with archival material. One major category of such archival material is recordings of interviews that the folklore department of Stofnun Árna Magnússonar, the "Árni Magnússon Institute" of Icelandic studies in Reykjavík, conducted in Strandir especially in the 1970s. In the course of these interviews, local residents were questioned about local stories, place-names, and traditional types of supernatural phenomena. Many of these interview recordings have been digitized, creating a huge searchable corpus that documents local traditions in the third quarter of the twentieth century.[190] Other important archival materials were files held in Hólmavík by Rannsóknasetur Háskóla Íslands á Ströndum—Þjóðfræðistofa ("The University of Iceland Research Center in Strandir—The Folklore Institute") and Náttúrustofa Vestfjarða á

---

[189] *Sagnagrunnur. A Geographically Mapped Database of Icelandic Folk Legends*, by Terry Gunnell and Trausti Dagsson, https://sagnagrunnur.com, last accessed 4 December 2020.
[190] *Ísmús—íslenskur músík- og menningararfur*, https://www.ismus.is/, last accessed 4 December 2020.

Hólmavík ("The Nature Research Center of the Westfjords in Hólmavík"), which pertain to local research and local folklore collecting undertaken over recent decades. Central, furthermore, were files of Örnefnastofnun Þjóðminjasafns ("The Place-Name Institute of the National Museum"), which operated from 1969 to 1998.[191] Especially during the 1970s, the Place-Name Institute conducted a large-scale campaign of interviewing people from Strandir about the place-names of their farms and the stories connected with them. Typically, interviewees were elderly people who had lived and worked on the respective farms for several decades, and were thus intimately familiar with them, even though in some cases they had moved away long before the actual interview was conducted. In many cases, their statements thus reflect their experiences during their formative years in the early decades of the twentieth century, when most of the informants had grown up on the farms they were describing. The originals of these files are now held by the Árni Magnússon Institute in Reykjavík and have recently been made accessible through an online database.[192]

This rich assemblage of printed and archival material has provided an important starting point for the present study. In spite of its richness, however, it has its limitations. Generally, all the sources described herein are focused on stories and place-names: they give descriptions of vast assemblies of microtoponyms, many of which they furthermore connect with longer or shorter narratives. However, hardly any of the archival material, and none of the published sources, is accompanied by detailed maps with a sufficient resolution to identify accurately the exact landscape features that specific names and stories are connected to. Even the digital mapping project of the *Sagnagrunnur* database only locates stories on the level of farms, but it does not attempt to define their exact locations on the lands of these farms. However, to fully understand the relationship between landscape, storytelling, and belief traditions, the *exact* locations of stories and beliefs need to be determined: to analyze, say, the role of a "place of enchantment" (*álagablettur*) or of an abode of supernatural entities on a farm, it is insufficient to just know that one existed on this farm. Rather, it is necessary to know *where exactly* it was located, as only this allows conclusions to be drawn—or at least sound working hypotheses to be developed—about the

---

[191] See https://www.arnastofnun.is/is/ornefnastofnun-islands, last accessed 4 December 2020.
[192] *Nafnið.is*, by Emily Lethbridge, https://nafnid.is/, last accessed 27 January 2022.

role it played in daily life on the farm: it makes a world of difference whether a story place or supernatural site is located next to the farmhouse or on the margins of the farmland up in the mountains.

This challenge is linked with another systematic lacuna in the existing material: this material gives names of places and stories connected to them, but it hardly ever contextualizes these names and stories within the concerns of daily life. When, how often, and by whom was a particular place visited? What resources did it provide for the farm? What role did it play in its agricultural workflow? Such questions can be crucial for understanding the place of story sites and sites of supernatural belief traditions in everyday life; yet it is very rare that they are addressed explicitly by the existing material. To establish these kinds of contexts, it was necessary to identify the exact locations of places of storytelling and belief in the landscape, which then provided a key to their use and thus the lived context of belief and narrative.

Research for the necessary in-depth localization of landscape-related belief and storytelling was undertaken during a total, so far, of eight months of fieldwork as a guest researcher at the University of Iceland Research Center in Strandir—The Folklore Institute in Hólmavík. The challenges posed by this process varied hugely. In some cases, some or all historical locations were well known to one member or another of the farming family that now works the land. Yet many farms that were still inhabited in the 1970s are now abandoned, and even where continuity of habitation exists, the locations of places attested in archival material is now often unknown even to the current landowners. Occasionally, such cases could be resolved by elderly citizens who in their youth worked on such now-abandoned farms, but often such knowledge was not available. In such cases, the only way of locating places was to collect all available material about the farm in question and to try to collate maps, the different extant descriptions of the farms, the local topography, and the meaning of topographically descriptive place-names. Often this would allow for the reconstruction of enough of the local network of place-names to be able to triangulate the exact landscape feature that the site being searched for was to be identified with. For every such place, this necessitated a "close walking" of the old farmland that used historical accounts and the meaning of semantically clear place-names as guides through the landscape. This was a time-consuming process, but confronting discursive (if patchy) descriptions of farms and the statements made by their toponyms with the concrete landscape features of the locality in many cases allowed the identification of sites with virtual certainty. In other cases, especially where similar features in the local landscape repeated or where toponyms were too generic, even a "close walking" of the landscape failed to yield identifications.

The local community was invariably extremely sympathetic to locating and mapping the local places of storytelling and folk belief. During my stay as a guest researcher at the Folklore Institute in Hólmavík, the project was communicated widely through public lectures held in the museum Galdrasýning á Ströndum (The Museum of Sorcery and Witchcraft) in Hólmavík and in other venues in the Westfjords, through an exhibition in the context of a local art festival, via the Folklore Institute's Facebook account (which has considerable reach within the community), and not least through word of mouth, both through the Folklore Institute and whenever I was able to meet the current owners of farmland that I was interested in. In principle, Icelandic legislation allows free access to all land that is not specifically fenced in; yet even so, permission was sought (and invariably granted) whenever possible.

One reason why the project received such an open welcome in the local community is that its line of enquiry built upon interests that have a long tradition of being addressed by local people in local venues. Farmers in Strandir started writing accounts of the place-names and place-stories of their farms already well before the middle of the twentieth century. Striking early examples are found in issues of the journal *Viljinn* ("The Will") from the 1920s. *Viljinn* was edited by the local young men's association Geislinn and was produced during the winter months, when there was less agricultural work to do and people had more time for other occupations. Since printing was not available, issues were written by hand and then circulated from farm to farm in a kind of reader-circle system. A number of issues from the 1920s consisted in descriptions of local farms written by their owners, in which the farmers gave detailed accounts of the microtoponymy of their land and summarized a plethora of stories connected with these place-names. In later decades, discussions of place-names and place-name stories formed, and continue to form, an important part of the range of topics commonly discussed in the regional yearbook *Strandapósturinn*, "The Strandir Post." Thus, talking of places, place-names, and their stories has a long and deeply rooted tradition in Strandir, which meant that making enquiries about the whereabouts of place-names never raised an eyebrow. Rather, the topic by default was considered as intrinsically interesting, and a researcher's interest was always warmly welcomed.

For reasons of space, both published and archival sources are quoted in translation, with only key words given in the Icelandic original. All translations are mine unless stated otherwise. Icelandic persons are referred to by their given names; this does not express familiarity, but follows Icelandic usage and naming conventions, as most Icelanders do not have family names, but given names and patronymics.

2

Twelve Movements

Aspects of the Engagement with the Supernatural Landscape

Theses on the Supernatural Landscape

A landscape consists of places.

The mythology and praxis of the landscape establishes cross-connections between these places.

The constituent places of landscapes are intensely endowed with associations and interpretations, and with forms of practice that are interdependent with these associations and interpretations.

Landscapes are experienced in the specificity and materiality of their constituent places, and in the paths, sight lines, and panoramas that connect them. The engagement with individual places takes precedence over the engagement with their wider contexts.

The "sacralization" of landscapes happens cumulatively through the sacralization of their specific individual places, on which a broad spectrum of strategies is brought to bear.

Landscape mythology is experienced not so much through the narrative arch of its plotlines as through the places to which its constituent parts are connected, and their distribution in space.

The landscape is both material and cultural. Its materiality and its supernatural elements are interdependent and reflect a complex dialectic, in which the physicality of the landscape plays a major role for its interpretations. The main factor that determines this dialectic is everyday land use.

Certain types of place traditions tend to latch on to elements of the topography which stand out and draw attention. This attention seems to function as a catalyst on which the tradition crystallizes.

Landscape, Religion, and the Supernatural. Matthias Egeler, Oxford University Press. © Oxford University Press 2024.
DOI: 10.1093/oso/9780197747360.003.0003

Mythological constructions of landscapes take place on different levels, from the strictly local to the regional.

The praxis and mythology of the landscape can be intensely private, entirely public, and everything in between.

Place-names both remember and are the source of the creation of new narratives.

Place-names, sight lines, everyday use, weather phenomena, and the physical topography of the land are the main factors that inspire and help to locate supernatural traditions. These traditions are based on a preexisting store of established motifs that is predetermined by the local culture of storytelling and belief.

The supernatural landscape emplaces and handles fear.

The supernatural landscape is funny.

Roads attract and are focal points of stories.

Beware of the troll.

In the landscape, what is important is repeated. Repetition both results from and constitutes importance, and importance can be measured by the intensity of this repetition.

Identities are both expressed in and constituted through cultural and religious constructions of landscapes, especially landscapes of home.

Landscape naturalizes cultural and religious knowledge through constant, repeated actualization in encounters with both the physical landscape and its mediations.

Landscape creates the possibility to experience traditional narratives and thus contributes to naturalizing the belief in their truth. Seeing is believing, even though belief is unimportant.

Landscape is normative. It tells its inhabitants what to do and what not to do.

The experience and meaning of landscape are based on its character as a taskscape. This is not true where landscape is transformed into a way of seeing.

The landscape as taskscape is filled with supernatural associations by taking places important for everyday labor and connecting them with motifs taken from the established stock of motifs of local traditional storytelling.

Landscape as a way of seeing expresses power as seen through the eyes of outside authority.

Landscape as a place of habitation and work expresses power as seen through the eyes of the subaltern laborer.

There is no absolute division between landscape as a place of habitation and landscape as a view.

The landscape is a soundscape where real sounds can take on a supernatural meaning just as supernatural sounds can be perceived as if they were real. Different parts of the supernatural landscape are differentiated by different soundscapes.

Landscape is a focal point and magnifier of a broad range of both shallow and intense emotional reactions.

Landscape as a place of habitation provides modes for creating illusions of safety and harnessing the powers of the supernatural to offset contingency. This is a central aspect of the contribution that the supernatural landscape makes to the construction of "home."

It is all about the sheep. If it is not about the sheep, then it is about fishing.

The supernatural landscape is a self-protecting environmentalist system. It is just not very good at it.

The way a landscape is perceived by outsiders can have little to do with how it is perceived by the people actually living there.

The human perception of the landscape, irrespective of whether it is that of outsiders or of local people, and its real properties are two different things. Sometimes they are two very different things.

1: Time and Memory

In modern-day theorizing, space and time have a difficult relationship. When Michel Foucault formulated the spatial turn of the arts and humanities in a lecture held in 1967, he put the study of time and the study of space into a seemingly direct opposition: while the nineteenth century had been characterized by an obsession with history and historical development, he argued, his present was an "epoch of space."[1] Yet at the same time, Foucault noted the entanglement of spatial and temporal categories. Formulating his concept of the heterotopia, the space that is fundamentally "other," he also

---

[1] Foucault 2006, 317.

76   LANDSCAPE, RELIGION, AND THE SUPERNATURAL

observed that such heterotopias are often connected with "heterochronias," times that are fundamentally "other":[2] the fair, for instance, is not only determined by the spatial boundaries of the fairground but also by the time of the market days.[3]

Time is also entangled with space through memory. What is remembered is the past, and places can play a central role for the process of remembering and thus for the preservation of "history." This is why Jóhann Kristmundsson never resumed farming at Goðdalur: the memories of the days under the avalanche and everything he lost in it were just too vivid there, as places bring memory into focus. A pioneer of the study of places of memory was Maurice Halbwachs (1877–1945), who introduced the concept of "collective memory" and applied it to an analysis of *La topographie légendaire des Evangiles en Terre Sainte* (1941).[4] In this study he showed how the "Legendary Topography of the Gospels in the Holy Land" illustrates how the "collective memory" is a reconstruction of the past that adapts its image of the past to the needs of the present.[5] "Memory" is not an "absolute" recollection of the past, but a (re-)construction that is performed by and for each present anew, and in the face of which the question of the "truth" of the past becomes immaterial.

Later generations of researchers developed the question of place and memory in different directions.[6] In the 1980s, Pierre Nora put his focus on the places of memory and coined the term *lieu de mémoire* to denote places—both physical and metaphorical—in which memory crystalizes with particular intensity, especially places and objects of national remembrance.[7] In the 1990s, Aleida Assmann likewise focused on *Erinnerungsräume* ("spaces of memory"),[8] while Jan Assmann took his starting point from the concept of "collective memory" to develop the concept of "cultural memory."[9] Assmann explicitly relates his concept of "cultural memory" to space and the landscape, describing landscape as one of the "storage media" (*Speicherungsmedien*) of cultural memory: for him, landscape is a mnemonic aid that helps maintain the contents of cultural memory, which come to mind when certain places are encountered.[10]

---

[2] Foucault 2017, 12, 16; Foucault 2006, 324.

[3] Further on the importance of the temporal aspect (including "magical time") of legends about supernatural places cf. Sävborg and Valk 2018b, 13; Benozzo 2004, 55–84.

[4] Halbwachs 2003.

[5] Halbwachs 2003, 20–21.

[6] For a broad discussion of the concept of memory in Nordic contexts, albeit restricted to the premodern period, see Glauser et al. 2018.

[7] Nora 1984–1992.

[8] Assmann 1999.

[9] Assmann 2007 (orig. ed. 1992).

[10] E.g., Assmann 2017, 131–132. Cf. Assmann 2007 (1992), 60.

TWELVE MOVEMENTS 77

Other approaches not only see the preservation of "memory" as one of the functions of landscape but put "memory" at the very heart of landscape. Simon Schama in his classic *Landscape and Memory* highlights "memory" as its most fundamental constituent element:[11]

> [A]lthough we are accustomed to separate nature and human perception into two realms, they are, in fact, indivisible. Before it can ever be a repose for the senses, landscape is the work of the mind. Its scenery is built up as much from strata of memory as from layers of rock.

Another prominent representative of a memory-focused approach to landscape is Robert Macfarlane. He not only highlighted how "memory and landscape layer and interleave,"[12] but his approach also converged with that of Assmann in that both of them developed the connection between landscape and memory into a distinctly textual metaphor. Assmann, attempting to conceptualize the makeup of the "sacred landscapes" of Australian Aboriginal mythology and ancient Near Eastern as well as ancient Roman cult, described landscapes as "topographical 'texts' of cultural memory."[13] In a similar vein, Macfarlane proposed that "[w]e *read* landscapes, in other words, we interpret their forms in the light of our own experience and memory, and that of our shared cultural memory."[14] For Assmann and Macfarlane, landscape thus becomes a text written in the ink of cultural memory.

This use of the metaphor of "landscape as text" is a common feature of approaches based on the concept of "(cultural) memory": as Assmann has stated programmatically, the theory of cultural memory investigates "the textuality of the past."[15] In this discourse, the past is treated as a "text," and landscape is one of the "media" in which this text is stored and can be "read." At the same time, the converse is not necessarily true: not all approaches to landscape that use the metaphor of text are based on memory theory. James and Nancy Duncan took their starting point from literary theory when

---

[11] Schama 1996, 6–7. For examples of scholars directly quoting and building on this passage, which has become one of the most-quoted passages in landscape theory, see Paturel 2019, 18; Wattchow 2013, 89; Tolia-Kelly 2013, 331; Ingold 2012, 2; Eck 2012, 11–12. Other recent books foregrounding the importance of "memory" for understanding landscape are Chadwick and Gibson 2013; Stewart and Strathern 2003.

[12] Macfarlane 2018, 101.

[13] Assmann 2007 (1992), 60 ("topographische 'Texte' des kulturellen Gedächtnisses").

[14] Macfarlane 2008 (2003), 18.

[15] Assmann 2017, 9: "Im Rahmen der Sprachlichkeit unseres Weltverhältnisses, wie es die Hermeneutik erschlossen hat, untersucht die Theorie des kulturellen Gedächtnisses die Textualität der Vergangenheit."

78 LANDSCAPE, RELIGION, AND THE SUPERNATURAL

they proposed that landscapes can be read "in much the same way as literary texts," and that they "can be seen as texts which are transformations of ideologies into a concrete form."[16]

I will here introduce two places of the supernatural from Strandir, each of which in a different way throws a spotlight on the potential and limitations of the memory perspective and the metaphor of landscape as a "text." These examples—located at the farms of Krossnes in Árneshreppur and Kleifar in Selströnd in Strandabyggð—then lead to the question of the role of the past in the landscape, and more specifically how places compress time and make the past present in the here and now.

*

The farm of Krossnes in Árneshreppur is today one of the northernmost inhabited farms of Strandir, and it was a working farm until a couple of years ago. Krossnes has comparatively little fertile land, but it owns about 4.5 km of shoreline. This shoreline traditionally provided the farm with a solid income from driftwood, which is the only local source of large timber, and which was processed in the farm's own sawmill. The economic importance of the seashore resources is reflected in a large number of microtoponyms that refer to coastal features: about eighty place-names on the land of the farm are located at or close to the coast. This translates into an average of one place-name per every 60 m, which helped to locate new driftwood with great accuracy.[17] What makes Krossnes interesting in the present context, however, is not the clear relationship between its economy and its landscape of place-names and stories,[18] but the way the stories connected with its toponymy inscribe time depth and memory into its land.

One of the small-scale place-names on the shoreline of Krossnes is the name Hempusteinn, "Cassock Stone" (Fig. 2.1). The story connected with this place was published in the 1940s. According to the local farmer Skarphéðinn Njálsson (1899–1995) and an anonymous group of "several others," it ran as follows:[19]

Hempusteinn ("Cassock Stone")

On the land of the farm of Krossnes ("Cross Peninsula") in Árneshreppur in the district of Strandir there is a belt of cliffs beyond the so-called Skötuvík

---

[16] Duncan and Duncan 1988, 117. Cf. Cosgrove 2008, 33–34; Mitchell 2002c, 1; Cosgrove 1998, xxv–xxvi. See also the use of the reading metaphor by Ladino 2019, 18.

[17] *SÁM* Haukur Jóhannesson s.a. (a), 2.

[18] See the section "Labor."

[19] Árngrímur Fr. Bjarnason and Helgi Guðmundsson 1933–1949, 3: 111.

Fig. 2.1 Hempusteinn ("Cassock Stone"), which forms the end of a belt of cliffs on the coastline of Krossnes. © S. Klose, 2023, reproduced with permission.

Bay, which runs out into the sea. That is steepest at the front by the sea, but becomes less steep where it comes up against the slope [of the coast]. Right at the front it is called *Hempusteinn* ("Cassock Stone"). A long time ago, a priest's cassock was found there on the rock, and it has its name from that. It was said that there was a dwelling place of the elves (*álfabyggð*) in these rocks, and Hempusteinn was the church of these elves. Others say that these elves' priest had his abode in Hempusteinn, and their church was in a different place.

In the olden time (*fornöld*) Krossnes was called a great land of spirits (*vættaland*). Some of them will not yet have died out. Therefore the land there was sanctified with crosses, and the farm has its name from that.

On a superficial level, this short account interprets the microtoponym "Cassock Stone" and the name of the farm itself as memorializing aspects of the history of the farm: the names are related to a tradition about the existence of an elf church or an elf parsonage in "Cassock Stone" and to a prehistory of the farm as a place that was densely inhabited by supernatural entities that were largely (though not entirely) exorcized with the help of crosses that gave the farm its name Krossnes, "Cross Peninsula." Taking the story at face value, the place-names encapsulate history and the memory of this history.

80 LANDSCAPE, RELIGION, AND THE SUPERNATURAL

Such a reading of this testimony would be entirely in line with much of the theoretical discourse. Marc Augé, for instance, emphasized the commemorative function of toponyms on the example of French street names. Augé highlighted that these street names have a minimalist but pervasive historical dimension: an exhaustive exegesis of the street names of Paris would have to muster the whole history of France since its conquest by Julius Caesar. The streets of France are thus saturated with history, and every journey through a French town involves an everyday, mechanical kind of immersion in history that is prompted by the historical names that one cannot avoid passing.[20] In this way, place-names can contribute to the creation of Pierre Nora's *lieux de mémoire* or Aleida Assmann's *Erinnerungsräume*, or to the storing of cultural memory in the landscape, following Jan Assmann's conceptualization of landscape as one of the storage media of cultural memory.

Yet in a subtle way the story told earlier makes clear that the causality between story and name is not quite as straightforward as it is in the official French toponymy that Augé had in mind. Approaches that emphasize the commemorative function of toponyms imply a causal relationship between place-name and story where the story came first and the place-name was created afterward in order to commemorate the story. In such cases, the place-name gives presence in the landscape to a preexistent story. The account from Krossness does not seem to follow this pattern. The storytelling tradition recorded in the 1940s lets a partial instability shimmer through, where the place-name is a stable element, but the stories connected with it are not. According to this account, there seems to have been general agreement about the place-name "Cassock Stone" as such, which indeed recurs in other sources. But this testimony does not present the established place-name as the consequence of an established story. Rather, it presents three different stories about the place and conflates these stories without fully integrating them into a seamless whole. First, there is a story that a priest's cassock was found at the "Cassock Stone" (which is actually not entirely impossible, as the former parsonage of Árnes is located directly across the bay of Trékyllisvík; so one of the priest's cassocks could conceivably have been blown off a washing line and across to the opposite shore). Second, there is a story that identified the rock formation as the church of the local elves, where their priest would have worn his cassock while celebrating divine service. Third, there is a story according to which the rock was the parsonage of the local elf community, where their priest lived and could easily have lost one of

[20] Augé 2014, 73–74.

his garments. These stories have in common that each of them offers an implicit or explicit explanation for the place-name "Cassock Stone"; what they do not share is the actual storyline.

If one compares this situation with the French street names that Augé used as his example for the classic commemorative function of place-names, it is as if somebody had taken the Rue Jules-César in the twelfth arrondissement of Paris and made up three different stories about who or what Julius Caesar was, and what this Caesar had to do with Paris. In comparison to the classic way of looking at place-names, Icelandic storytelling time and again turns the underlying mechanism on its head: repeatedly, one can observe that place-names are not invented to commemorate (hi)stories, but stories are invented to explain place-names. In Iceland, such invention has a history that goes back as far as documentary evidence exists; Þórhallur Vilmundarson showed it, indeed, to be a central narrative mechanism in medieval Icelandic literature.[21]

As a pervasive habit of storytelling, this narrative mechanism even seems to occur yet again in the statement about Krossnes cited earlier. This statement not only offers three implicitly competing explanations of the place-name "Cassock Stone" but also an explanation of the farm name Krossnes, "Cross Peninsula." This farm, so the story goes, was named from the crosses used to exorcize the spirit beings (*vættir*) that inhabited its land. The explanatory story is striking for its indecisiveness: it states that the farm is named from the crosses that were used to rid the place of its supernatural entities, but immediately backpedals to state that some of them are still there anyway. One explanation would be that a story has been invented here to explain the place-name, but that because of its focus on the meaning of this place-name the story struggles to remain in tune with other local traditions such as those about the elf church in Hempusteinn, where the spirit beings of the land were still said to abide and therefore could not have been driven out.

These examples show that there is more to Icelandic place-names than simply commemorating the past. These place-names not only remember but also form cues for the invention of new stories about the past. They are catalysts in an ongoing process of the invention and reinvention of local history. In this culture of commemoration and storytelling, the toponyms are fixed in space—none of the three variants of the story of the "Cassock Stone" had any doubt about where it was located—but the history that underlies

---

[21] Þórhallur Vilmundarson 1991, esp. pp. xxx–xli; cf. McTurk 1994–1997, 166–170; Egeler 2018b.

82 LANDSCAPE, RELIGION, AND THE SUPERNATURAL

them can be intrinsically fluid. The "strata of memory" that Simon Schama compared with "layers of rock" seem more akin to the uncertain underground offered by shifting river sands, which may be layered but are intrinsically unstable rather than solid as bedrock.

*

Another kind of fluidity is displayed by traditions about an elf hill on the farm of Kleifar on the north coast of Steingrímsfjörður. In the mid-1970s, Guðmundur Jóhannsson drew up an account of the place-names and stories of this farm. This account represents memories of the state of things in the early twentieth century; Guðmundur himself was born in 1903 and had lived at Kleifar from 1921 to 1943, and one of the sources of his knowledge was Guðbjörg Torfadóttir, the daughter of a famous farmer at Kleifar; she died in 1923, at the age of seventy-eight. About a prominent rocky hill in the center of the home-field of Kleifar, only a couple of minutes' walk from the farmhouse, the two remembered the following:[22]

> In the middle of the home-field below the farmhouse is a grass-grown hill, which during my [Guðmundur Jóhannsson's] time was called Álfhóll ("Elf Hill"). Guðbjörg said that it had been called Nónhóll ("3 O'Clock Hill"), because from the farmhouse it was 3 o'clock there [i.e., the sun stood over it at 3 o'clock]. It was a belief of some people that elves (*álfar*) dwell in the hill; some people said that on holy days they heard singing from there. Guðjón Guðlaugsson, Member of Parliament, who was farmer at Kleifar and founder of the Steingrímsfjörður Trading Association and its first managing director, erected a flagpole on the hill and had a flag hoisted when he received ships in Hólmavík. The flagpole will still have been standing when Guðjón moved away, for the next farmer, Þórður, thought such things unnecessary and in jest called the hill Gálgahóll ("Gallows' Hill").

Looking at this hill through the lens of current theorizing is again revealing. As a place that differs from its surroundings by belonging to the elves, it exemplifies not merely Foucault's concept of the heterotopia, but the interlinking of spatial heterotopia and temporal heterochronia. The remark that "some people said that on holy days they heard singing from there" implies that the elves were celebrating mass on the high holy days. Thus, on

---

[22] *SÁM* Guðmundur Jóhannsson and Guðrún Magnúsdóttir 1975, 2.

the feast days of the Church, the heterotopia of the elf hill merged with the heterochronia of the Christian liturgical calendar.

The way Guðmundur Jóhannsson described the history of this hill furthermore brings us back to the concept of memory. The elf hill is a place where memories of the history of the farm crystallize. In a more straightforward way than with the "Cassock Stone" Hempusteinn, the elf hill of Kleifar emerges as both a local *lieu de mémoire* in Pierre Nora's terminology and an example of Jan Assmann's proposal to see the landscape as one of the storage media of cultural memory. The hill inscribes cultural memories of both supernatural entities and political symbols into the land of the farm and thus allows the farming landscape to be "read" as a text that tells of supernatural as well as of human history.

Even more interestingly, the hill therefore also illustrates a different type of the stratification of memory from that seen at the "Cassock Stone." In Guðmundur's account, the hill went by three names over the years: it was Álfhóll, "Elf Hill," because elves dwelled there; it was Nónhóll, "3 O'Clock Hill," because the sun stood over it at 3 o'clock; and it was Gálgahóll, "Gallows' Hill," because one farmer mocked the flagpole that his self-important predecessor had erected there. Thus, at least parts of the tradition show a clear change over time, rather than just a general fluctuation such as we met at the "Cassock Stone." In the course of this change, the toponymy and the associated (hi)stories of this hill show exactly the kind of firm stratification that Simon Schama implied when noting that landscape is "built up as much from strata of memory as from layers of rock."[23]

The hill also shows potential limitations in common metaphors in landscape theory. In particular, it problematizes the metaphor of "reading" the landscape as a text inscribed with memory. The account given by Guðmundur Jóhannsson is unusually detailed, and it is particularly valuable for how it spells out the varying perspectives that people had on the hill at different times: for some (but not others) it was a place inhabited by elves, where some (but not others) claimed to hear the music of the elves' divine service; for some it was a place of political display; but later on others saw this display merely as a flaunting of the pretentiousness of the political class. The elf hill of Kleifar thus emerges as a place of contention and of an ongoing and developing construction of meaning, mirroring exactly the emphasis

---

[23] Schama 1996, 6–7.

84 LANDSCAPE, RELIGION, AND THE SUPERNATURAL

that Halbwachs put on the constructed nature of "collective memory" in the Holy Land.

For this contention to become visible, however, an unusually dense documentation is necessary, which is often not available. We are only able to see the contending interpretations of Kleifar because Guðmundur chose and was able to highlight them. If he had preferred not to give as encyclopedic an account of this place, we would have received a much less multifaceted "reading" of this landscape. This in turn raises the nagging suspicion: if a source paints a coherent picture of a landscape, may this indicate not so much the internal coherence of this landscape as a certain one-sidedness of the source material? Should we perhaps be less willing to give credence to a reading of a landscape the more coherent it is?

*

Place-names have repeatedly been called "mnemonic pegs" that fix myths and stories (including historical narratives) to particular spots in the landscape and thus help to remember them.[24] This has direct implications for the relationship between landscape and time; as Christopher Tilley puts it: "named locations [...] act so as to fuse time and space," as names connect places with narratives, which have the effect of introducing an element of temporality.[25] Such a perspective can also be applied to the microtoponymy of Icelandic farms: not only farm names like Krossnes ("Cross Peninsula") but also the names of sometimes very small landscape features on the land of these farms evoke a history both legendary and mundane that equally encompasses elf priests and the scorn felt by normal farmers for the political self-representation of those in power. The names in the landscape encapsulate its history, and through these names this history can be "read" like a book printed on topography instead of paper.

Yet at the same time, the examples from Krossnes and Kleifar highlight another aspect even more than a simple inscription of memory. The passing of time almost invariably means change, and the "meanings" of landscapes also change constantly: these are not fixed, but subject to a permanent process of creation, recreation, adaptation, and even obliteration.[26] As Barbara Bender phrased it: "*Landscape is time materialized. Or, better, Landscape is time materializing*: landscapes, like time, never stand still."[27] Sometimes,

---

[24] Brink 2013, 35; Tilley 1994, 33. Cf. earlier on the concept of the *lieu de mémoire*.
[25] Tilley 1994, 33.
[26] Cosgrove and Daniels 1988, 8; Bender 2002.
[27] Bender 2002, S103.

this constancy of change has even been made a topic within the landscape itself: Renaissance landscape painting incorporated the idea of change and the passage of time through devices such as the memento mori or ruined buildings.[28]

Both the "Cassock Stone" of Krossnes and the elf hill of Kleifar share this inherent fluidity of the landscape and illustrate it in different ways: the "Cassock Stone" is connected with different stories that all explain the same name in different ways and thus show the inconstancy of this storytelling, and the elf hill of Kleifar has a whole stratigraphy of different names that were applied to it over time. The names of the land are not just "mnemonic pegs" but are also part and parcel of the processes through which memory is changed and reinvented.

This constant change is fundamentally characterized by an insight that Halbwachs formulated about collective memory: it does not simply represent the past, but it is made by and for the present.[29] The stories that we—and place-names—tell about the past are first and foremost just that: stories. Such stories can and do change for many reasons, and their changes can go hand in hand with the changes undergone by the status of the places they are connected to.[30] Some simply change by mistake and through forgetting, others because people have different views of the past and ways of engaging with the land. As Bender emphasized: landscapes are a recording of the past, but they are not just *a* recording, as landscapes are subjective, polyvalent, and multivocal.[31] One person's story is another person's lie—or, less confrontationally, just another person's joke, as we saw in the renaming of the elf hill at Kleifar as Gallows' Hill. Understandings of the past depend on social relations. As such, they do not have to be political—it would be difficult to find a political message in the stories of the "Cassock Stone" Hempusteinn—but they *can* be deeply political.[32] This is an aspect of the landscape that we will come back to in more detail later.[33]

The shifting names across the land and the various ways of telling stories about them make a constancy of change visible that is a fundamental characteristic of the landscape. At the same time, however, local traditional stories also help bridge the gap between the present and the alleged happenings of

---

[28] Cosgrove 1985, 57–58.
[29] Halbwachs 2003, 20–21. Cf. Egeler 2019a.
[30] Cf. Sävborg and Valk 2018b, 10.
[31] Bender 2002, S103.
[32] Bender 2002, S104.
[33] See the section "Power and Subversion."

the past: there seems to be an overall tendency in the landscape for temporal differences to be leveled and the past to become part of the present.[34] Already Halbwachs in his classic study of the legendary topography of the Holy Land noted that, if seen from the perspective of pilgrims, the legendary sites of the Gospels have an effect of conveying a kind of sensual certainty of the truth of the legendary stories, and the way they achieve this effect is that the places "where it happened," where Jesus walked, turn the past into a part of the present where it is possible to touch it and where one thinks one can directly experience it.[35] In this experience, the past stops being the past and, mediated by the "place where it happened," becomes part of the present, largely or entirely erasing the chronological time lag between the "happening" and the visitor of the place. Bachelard has ingeniously described this mechanism in the two images of a frozen theater set and of compression. Imagining the past as a theater constituted by memories tied to places, Bachelard points out that "the stage setting"—that is, the places that our memories are connected to—"maintains the characters in their dominant rôles":[36] memories are fixed to places, and while we like to think of these memories as organized in time, actually they are organized in space, wherein time is compressed: "In its countless alveoli space contains compressed time. That is what space is for."[37]

Something similar also seems to be happening in the examples of Krossnes and Kleifar. The elf hill of Kleifar gave the stories about elves on this farm so much presence that "some people said that on holy days they heard singing from there": being inscribed into the land close by the farmhouse, memories of stories about elves were imbued with enough power to turn these elves into entities that some inhabitants of the farm perceived as real living neighbors. Similarly, sites like the "Cassock Stone" with its elf parsonage or elf church established an imaginary continuity between the deep supernatural prehistory of the farm and its present that allowed the supernatural to be asserted right into the here and now, or as the testimony from the 1940s puts it: "In the olden time Krossnes was called a great land of spirits. Some of them will not yet have died out." Supernatural story places are not only a function of memory that is directed at the past; they also give this past a place in the space of the present.

---

[34] Cf. the observation by Bender 2002, S108–S109, that in the perception of the nonacademic local population the various chronological strata of a Cornish landscape would sometimes merge into an undifferentiated "history."

[35] Halbwachs 2003, 13–14.

[36] Bachelard 1994 (1958), 8. Cf. Cresswell 2015, 29–30.

[37] Bachelard 1994 (1958), 8.

2: Repeating Patterns

Repetition and the extensive use of recurring patterns are a central element of how human beings approach the world they inhabit. As Diana L. Eck put it in her study of the sacred geography of India: "Those things that are deeply important are to be widely repeated."[38] Consequently, when she described the "grammar of sanctification" that rules the construction of the religious landscape in India, she put repetition, duplication, and homologies right at the center of her approach.[39] Throughout India, local hills and mountains can be interpreted as parts of the Himalayas, and local rivers can be imagined as being fed by the River Ganges, thus duplicating the pan-Indian holy mountains and India's most holy river in the local and regional landscape.[40] Basing her analysis of the "grammar of sanctification" of the Indian landscape centrally on this element of reduplication, Eck presents a landscape-focused formulation of a broader mechanism that the folklorist Albert Eskeröd, working in a different field and on very different material, had proposed already in the 1940s. Eskeröd noted that in the different Scandinavian storytelling traditions he was studying, there were elements which tended to dominate individual local traditions. One of his examples is that folk storytelling along the Halland coast of Sweden is dominated by stories about mermaids, whereas in Östergötland and its surrounding areas the supernatural entity of choice was the *myling*, the ghost of a murdered newborn child. To describe this phenomenon, Eskeröd coined the term *traditionsdominanter*, for which he himself proposed the English rendering "dominant traditions," while later folklorists generally preferred "tradition dominants":[41] Eskeröd defined these as "elements that in the general popular tradition dominate different groups within this tradition."[42] Such "tradition dominants" have a prominence which leads to their domination, and this essentially means repetition, throughout the tradition.

The repetition that Eck and Eskeröd identified in their areas of study is also of central importance for the religious and supernatural landscape of Strandir: when engaging with beliefs and storytelling here, one again and

---

[38] Eck 2012, 5.
[39] Eck 2012, 17–41, esp. pp. 17, 39.
[40] Eck 2012, 18, 36–39, 131–188.
[41] Eskeröd 1947, 79–81, 357; Honko 1981, 23–24; Tangherlini 1990, 378; Sävborg and Valk 2018b, 20.
[42] Eskeröd 1947, 81.

88 LANDSCAPE, RELIGION, AND THE SUPERNATURAL

again meets the same stories and ideas repeated on the land of one farm after another. It almost seems as if no area of Strandir could bear the thought of being without its own local manifestation of a certain set of legends and beliefs. Conversely, many places are not just the object of one simple story, but the focal point of complex traditions; yet on closer scrutiny, it turns out that the constituent parts of these traditions are again mirror images of recurring narratives that are widely distributed throughout the region.

I present two examples that illustrate the importance of repeating patterns from two different angles. The first example introduces a narrative that, with only minor variation, recurs in a number of different places throughout Strandir; the second example is of a single place with a complex story, whose elements mirror a range of different storytelling motifs that are likewise found throughout the region and, in one case, throughout the wider Christian world. Thus, this chapter highlights not only the importance of repeating patterns in the supernatural landscape but also some of the complexity that is generated by their use.

*

On the southeastern coast of the fjord of Kollafjörður, a small gravelly spit of land juts out into the sea: Hnyðjueyri, "Gravel Bank of the Rootstock (*hnyðja*)." Where it faces the open sea with a broad beach of black sand, the shoreline of Hnyðjueyri is strewn with driftwood, and just above the beach, a selection of the best logs has been stacked up into neat piles (Fig. 2.2). This part of the coastline belongs to the land of the farm of Broddanes. In 1976, Guðbrandur Benediktsson, who had been born in 1887 and had farmed Broddanes from 1927 to 1968, told the following story about the name and occurrences connected with Hnyðjueyri:[43]

> It is said that an old woman lived at Hnyðjueyri ("Hnyðja's Gravel Bank" /"Rootstock Gravel Bank"), called Hnyðja ("Rootstock"). She had two sons, who went to sea and caught fish on Kollafjörður. But one time, when they were at sea, it got stormy and the brothers' boat capsized. They both perished there. She then ordained that henceforth fish should not be caught nor a boat perish on Kollafjörður. So it has been since then. The gravel bank is well placed for flotsam and jetsam, and rootstocks (*hnyðjur*) have often been washed ashore there.

---

[43] *SÁM* Guðrún S. Magnúsdóttir 1976c, 7.

Fig. 2.2 Hnyðjueyri ("Hnyðja's Gravel Bank"/"Rootstock Gravel Bank"), where the driftwood and the rootstocks that stand at the core of its place-name are plentifully washed ashore. © M. Egeler, 2019.

Guðbrandur then goes on to describe the location of Erlendsboði ("Erlendur's Skerry") and Erlendsbás ("Erlendur's Rock Basin"), where the two brothers—one of whom was called Erlendur—drowned and one of the bodies was washed ashore.[44]

Guðbrandur's story is interesting in a number of ways, one being how he manages to tell a story that derives the place-name Hnyðjueyri from an old woman called Hnyðja while at the same time clearly showing that he is perfectly aware of the real origin of the name in the driftwood that is washed ashore there, containing many a rootstock (*hnyðja*). As with the "Cassock Stone" Hempusteinn discussed in the preceding section, here, too, the place-name is both the basis of and much more stable than the stories that are told about it: the place-name "Rootstock Gravel Bank" is derived from its natural characteristics, but then imaginatively developed into a story about a Ms. Rootstock. In the present context, however, the main importance of this story is that, with only minor variations, it is repeated all over Strandir.

[44] *SÁM* Guðrún S. Magnúsdóttir 1976c, 7–8.

90 LANDSCAPE, RELIGION, AND THE SUPERNATURAL

Geographically and thematically one of the closest repetitions of the story is found at the farm of Þambárvellir in Bitrufjörður, one fjord to the south from Hnyðjueyri. This farm takes its name from the river Þambá, whose name in turn is derived—at least by local tradition—from the troll woman Þömb.[45] This Þömb had two sons, both of whom drowned in the rapids of Strákafoss ("Waterfall of the Lads") when they were fishing for trout.[46] The reaction of the bereaved mother exactly mirrors that of the old woman at Hnyðjueyri: "Then the old woman [i.e., Þömb] ordained for the Þambá river that no trout (*silungur*) should go into it, and that nobody should perish in it. As far as is known, these have both come to pass."[47] Þömb then took her chest of gold and withdrew into the waterfall of Kerlingarfoss ("Waterfall of the Crone"/"Waterfall of the Troll Woman"), where she has remained ever since.[48] A variant of the story tells simply that she committed suicide by throwing herself into the waterfall.[49]

Þömb's tribulations in turn are mirrored by the fate of Kráka in the fjord of Veiðileysa. Kráka is said to have been an old woman who, together with her two sons, lived at Krákutún. Both of Kráka's sons drowned while trying to land their boat, upon which the bereaved Kráka decreed that it would no longer be possible to fish in the fjord, but at the same time nobody would perish ever again in trying to land. Kráka later drowned herself in a waterfall a short distance above Krákutún, which since then has been called Krákufoss, "Kráka's Waterfall."[50]

The story about Kráka was told by two brothers, Guðbrandur Sveinn Þorláksson and Annes Þorláksson, who were both born at Veiðileysa and lived there respectively from 1921 to 1959 and from 1917 to 1949.[51] Guðbrandur and Annes told the story about the curse of the absence of fish, but just as Guðbrandur Benediktsson had made clear his doubts about how his own story explained the name Hnyðjueyri, so, too, Guðbrandur and Annes emphasized that all was not as it was told: for they pointed out that

---

[45] "Af skessum, bófum og draugum" at the local news webpage *strandir.is* (https://strandir.is/af-skessum-bofum-og-draugum/, accessed 10 July 2020; later moved to http://strandir.saudfjarsetur.is/af-skessum-bofum-og-draugum/, 5 January 2021).

[46] Or Arctic char; the term *silungur* covers both.

[47] *SÁM* Magnús Kristjánsson 1977, 5.

[48] *SÁM* Magnús Kristjánsson 1977, 6.

[49] "Af skessum, bófum og draugum" at the local news webpage *strandir.is* (https://strandir.is/af-skessum-bofum-og-draugum/, accessed 10 July 2020; later moved to http://strandir.saudfjarsetur.is/af-skessum-bofum-og-draugum/, 5 January 2021).

[50] *SÁM* Guðrún S. Magnúsdóttir 1975a, 7–8.

[51] *SÁM* Guðrún S. Magnúsdóttir 1975a, 1.

TWELVE MOVEMENTS   91

there actually were fish in the fjord of Veiðileysa, in spite of the story of the curse.[52]

Such doubts about the literal truth of the story also characterize another variant of the tale. This variant is set at Reykjarfjörður, which is the next fjord immediately to the north of Veiðileysa. At the farm of Reykjarfjörður, which shares the name of the fjord, the pertinent story is recorded through the testimony of both Jóhann Hjaltason and Guðmundur Ágústsson;[53] the latter was born in 1912 and farmed at Reykjarfjörður from 1924 to 1930.[54] It goes as follows. Close by the home-field of the farm runs the river Óveiðisá, "Catchless River," which has its source in the lake Búrfellsvatn. Once, two sons of a widow, who was living at Reykjarfjörður, drowned while fishing in the river (or the lake);[55] after this the widow decreed that henceforth there would be no fish in either the lake or the river. And indeed there is no fishing in either Óveiðisá or Búrfellsvatn. Yet while Guðmundur Ágústsson knew and told the story, he found himself unable to let it stand without comment: the river, he pointed out, is so shallow that one could not really imagine anybody drowning in it, and for the same reason it was also unsurprising that there was no good fishing to be had in it.[56] So he made it clear that he viewed at least part of the curse as superfluous: the river being what it is, it was so bad for fish that there wasn't anything to curse there to start with.

The last variant of the story is set at the lake of Þiðriksvallavatn. This version is connected with former building remains that, after the construction of a water power plant and a dam, are now submerged under the waters of the lake; before they disappeared, they were located on the gravel banks of Byrgiseyrar on the northern shore of the lake. A story recorded in the 1950s and again in the late 1970s related that these buildings had once been inhabited by a widow and her two sons. When both boys drowned while fishing on the lake, the widow decreed that henceforth there should be no walkable ice on Þiðriksvallavatn before Advent and that it should not be possible anymore to practice fishing on the lake;[57] and as the transcript of the

---

[52] *SÁM* Guðrún S. Magnúsdóttir 1975a, 7–8. The presence of fish also stands in a certain tension to the name of the fjord, as Veiðileysa means "Catchless Sea," "Sea where no Fish is caught" (cf. *brimleysa*, "calm (smooth) sea": Geir T. Zoega 1910, s.v. "brim-lauss"; Cleasby and Gudbrand Vigfusson 1874, s.v. "brim-lauss"). This name may have been a factor for why the story of the curse was located at Veiðileysa.

[53] *SÁM* Jóhann Hjaltason s.a. (c), 5; *SÁM* Guðrún Magnúsdóttir 1974a, 3.

[54] *SÁM* Guðrún Magnúsdóttir 1974a, 1.

[55] Jóhann Hjaltason locates the drowning in the river, Guðmundur Ágústsson in the lake (*SÁM* Jóhann Hjaltason s.a. (c), 5; *SÁM* Guðrún Magnúsdóttir 1974a, 3).

[56] *SÁM* Guðrún Magnúsdóttir 1974a, 3.

[57] *SÁM* Magnús Steingrímsson 1953b, 1; *SÁM* Guðrún S. Magnúsdóttir 1978d, 5.

92 LANDSCAPE, RELIGION, AND THE SUPERNATURAL

tale from the 1950s concludes: "For the most part both appear to have come to pass."[58]

So in sum, in five locations in Strandir essentially the same story is told: after the only two sons of a poor widow or old woman drown in a fishing accident, the woman curses the body of water that killed them to be without fish forever after; in most cases, this curse is counterbalanced by the promise that nobody would ever drown in this body of water again. In two of the five cases, the bereaved mother then commits suicide by drowning herself in a waterfall, or—taking on a more strongly supernatural aspect—she moves into a waterfall to continue living her (undead?)[59] life there. Strikingly often, the truth of the story is doubted by the informants who are telling it; but they tell it nevertheless. The literal, historical truth of the tale does not seem to be what matters. What matters, what both marks the tale as important and constitutes its importance, is its repetition: in a tale like that of the bereaved widow, we see the supernatural landscape of Strandir being constructed out of repeating patterns.

*

Right from its beginnings in the 1960s, the annual journal *Strandapósturinn*, "The Strandir Post," has been dedicated to the conservation and celebration of the cultural life of Strandir. It is edited by a regional association, the Átthagafélag Strandamanna, which is an association for people from Strandir who have left the district but want to maintain contact; its name could be translated roughly as "Heritage Association of People from Strandir." The journal thus reflects something very close to a local view of Strandir by and for people from Strandir. While most early covers of The Strandir Post feature distinctive, easily recognizable buildings and landscape features, that of the third issue, published in 1969, spotlights a curiously rough and small-scale structure. It reproduces a watercolor of a hummock crowned by a small cairn of angular stones; a weathered piece of driftwood sticks out of the top of this cairn, which may once have been a piece of a rootstock. The perspective chosen for the picture looks up at the cairn from a viewpoint close to the ground, so both the cairn and the piece of wood are silhouetted against the

---

[58] *SÁM* Magnús Steingrímsson 1953b, 1.

[59] Cf. the story of the sorceress Gullbrá, who at the end of her life takes her gold, moves into a waterfall, and appears to live a life there that is more monstrous than human: Jón Árnason 1954–1961, 1: 140–144.

Fig. 2.3 The cover of the third issue of *Strandapósturinn*, published in 1969, showing a painting of the cairn atop Kross by Halldór Þorsteinsson. Reproduced with permission.

sky. This creates an effect that makes them seem to be towering above the viewer, even though the size of the stones provides a rough scale and makes clear that the structure is not very big (Fig. 2.3). Neither on the cover itself nor anywhere inside the journal is the image explained: it is presented as if known to the reader as a matter of course. As it happens, there are at least two historic photographs from the mid-twentieth century extant that show that

Fig. 2.4 Historic photograph (c. 1945–1950) of Kross ("Cross"), looking from the cairn with the rootstock toward the church of Kaldrananes. Reproduced with permission of Halldór Þorsteinsson.

the cairn and its rootstock during this period drew enough attention to be photographed repeatedly (Fig. 2.4).[60]

A year earlier, the cover of the preceding issue of *Strandapósturinn* had shown a watercolor of the rock towers of the Broddar, which are traditionally identified as the burial place of the founding hero of an important farm, and over the next seven years followed a series of covers that sported photographs of regional churches.[61] At first glance, it may seem puzzling why a small drystone cairn was chosen for a purpose which otherwise was served by towering rock pinnacles and prominent religious buildings. On closer scrutiny, however, this choice makes a lot of sense, as the rootstock-crowned cairn of 1969 forms a perfect transition from ancient heroes to ecclesiastical structures.

What is shown on the cover image is the cairn that crowns a rocky hill near the church of Kaldrananes on Bjarnarfjörður. This hill bears the name Kross, "Cross." Kaldrananes is one of the central places of Strandir, being one of the few farms with a church. The church at Kaldrananes was served by the priest of Staður, not having one of its own; it nonetheless formed an important

---

[60] In addition to the historic photograph reproduced here (Fig. 2.4), cf. also a photograph roughly dated to 1940–1965 in the collection of the National Museum of Iceland, inventory no. ÞJ_Str-65, digitized at https://sarpur.is/, 2 February 2022.

[61] Broddar: issue 2 (1968). Churches: issues 4 (1970) to 10 (1976).

regular social focus of the fjord. The first church there was probably built in 1317;[62] the current church is a small wooden building erected in 1851, which makes it the second-oldest surviving building in Strandir, after the old church of Árnes (1850). Together with three residential houses and a large stable building, it is located in the middle of a broad tongue of land that juts into the fjord from its south coast. It is a walk of about 800 m along the farm track that leads past the church to the end of this tongue of land, where Kross towers over its surroundings.

The crown of the hill is demarcated by a rocky step that encircles it and on two of its sides forms perpendicular rock walls several meters in height. Its top is formed by a rough, slightly sloping plateau some 30 m in diameter. In the center of this plateau, on a rocky outcrop next to a deep hollow, the cairn has been erected from which to this day (2019) the piece of rootstock sticks up into the sky, overlooking the fjord. The rootstock that is embedded in the cairn today is still the same one that was depicted on the journal cover of 1969: even after half a century of weathering, its distinctive shape remains clearly recognizable. This is the more remarkable as the cairn has been rebuilt in the recent past. The interrupted patterns of growth of lichen on the stones make clear that the current drystone cairn was piled up comparatively recently; but it still had the same piece of driftwood reinserted that some fifty years earlier was deemed iconic enough for the cover image of *Strandapósturinn*.

Why this place and this specific piece of driftwood is so important is explained by an undated, but probably mid-twentieth-century account written by Matthías Helgason:[63]

Up on Höfði ("Headland") and right at the front of it there are very high rocks. The place there is called Kross ("Cross"), where it adds most to the height. An old-fashioned wooden cross stands there, set into a ruined pile of rubble that is there. It was not considered feasible to mess with that. Many years ago, it is said that a certain farmer of [Kaldrana-]Nes called it a superstition (*hindurvitni*) not to use this piece of rootstock just like any other that should turn up. Therefore he takes it home with him and intends to burn it. For some reason it came about that he did not have to stick it under his cooking pot at that very hour, for the next morning people noticed a

---

[62] Cormack 2018, 77, note 9.
[63] *SÁM* Matthías Helgason s.a. (c), 6–7.

96 LANDSCAPE, RELIGION, AND THE SUPERNATURAL

man sauntering with this rootstock down to Höfði, and he replaced it carefully at the same place; as for himself, he certainly spread the word that the dreams he had during the night were heavy. After this, it has never been messed with.

Down below, Höfði is all grown with grass. It [the soil] is the thinner on the gravel the higher one gets, however[.] About that [there is] an old tradition that there is treasure hidden there. Around the middle of the last [i.e., the nineteenth] century, it is told that some young men thought that they would investigate that treasure chest and dug into the gravel ridge. They had not been digging long, when one of them happened to look homewards to the farm and saw that it is all engulfed in bright flames. They then stopped as quickly as possible. There are no stories about any damage arising from this, but the effort left its mark, since there is a very big hollow there, clearly made by human hands.

This account testifies to a local tradition that identified the piece of the rootstock in the cairn as a "cross" and saw it as standing under supernatural protection; furthermore, it claimed the existence of hidden treasure, which was likewise supernaturally protected. A man who disbelieved the inviolability of the "cross" was disabused of his skepticism by a dream vision, and a group of young lads that tried to dig up the treasure was scared off by a vision in which they saw the nearby farm burning. In neither case was any actual harm done: the powers that protect this place were satisfied when its would-be desecrators stood down. No revenge was enacted on them.

The physical appearance of the piece of rootstock in the cairn makes its identification as a "cross" at first seem somewhat puzzling: irrespective of the angle from which one looks at this log of driftwood, it is not cruciform, but only consists of a main trunk from which the base of one root goes off at a shallow angle. If anything, it is more reminiscent of a hockey stick than a cross. In all likelihood, the key to why it came to be described as a "cross" is found in the toponymy of the place. Matthías Helgason's description makes it quite clear that the name Kross ("Cross") in the first instance is attached to the rocky hill that overlooks the fjord; and only after stating this does Matthías call the piece of rootstock an "old-fashioned wooden cross" ("fornfálegur trékross").[64] Following the usual Icelandic pattern of how place-names trigger stories, this suggests that Matthías's identification of the

---

[64] *SÁM* Matthías Helgason s.a. (c), 6.

rootstock as a cross follows the guidance provided by the name of the place. The implicit logic seems to be this: since the place is named from a cross, the one upstanding piece of wood to be seen there must be that cross.

The interpretation of the rootstock as a cross ultimately appears to be an echo of the Catholic practice of erecting standing crosses. Up to the Reformation, this was common also in Strandir. A fourteenth-century story about one of the miracles worked by Guðmundur the Good mentions "harbor crosses" ("hafnarkrossar"),[65] which the story suggests were rather tall; this seems to indicate that erecting standing crosses at harbors was not only a fairly common but indeed a landscape-defining practice. Kross at Kaldrananes overlooks a tiny present-day harbor as well as the former landing installations of a now-defunct fish-processing plant: hence the place-name Kross may indeed be rooted in such a "harbor cross"—it overlooks a location that has been the preferred harbor site at least throughout much of the twentieth century, and which could have served this purpose for a very long time. Since the hill Kross is the highest hill overlooking the landing site, it would have been a perfect location for a harbor cross: on this hill, such a harbor cross would not only have overlooked the harbor but also would have gone a long way to making the location of the harbor more visible from the sea, serving as a beacon both spiritual and maritime.

Place-names formed with *Kross-* are among the more common toponyms, and even the specific arrangement at Kaldrananes has a close structural parallel elsewhere in Strandir. If the aforementioned suspicion is correct and Kross is named from a former harbor cross, then it would have formed a landmark for those who were coming to the church at Kaldrananes by boat. Similarly, at least according to local tradition, a standing cross functioned as a landmark on the way to the church at Tröllatunga on the south side of Steingrímsfjörður: there, most approaches to the former church led past the hill Krossholt, "Cross Hill," where it was said a cross used to stand.[66] The same pattern is repeated here: a hill named from a pre-Reformation cross marks the way to church. The only difference is that at Kaldrananes, the name derived from the original medieval cross seems to have reflected back on a piece of driftwood erected on top of the cross hill. It appears that the present-day rootstock on Kross has acquired its supernatural characteristics as a contact relic of a place-name.

---

[65] Jón Sigurðsson and Guðbrandur Vigfússon 1858–1878, 1: 607; Cormack 2018, 78.
[66] *NV* Hilmar Egill Sveinbjörnsson 1999, n. p. (Tröllatunga, no. 94).

98 LANDSCAPE, RELIGION, AND THE SUPERNATURAL

Other major elements of the Kross tradition also repeat patterns that recur elsewhere in Strandir. Matthías Helgason's account of how a disbeliever removed the rootstock from Kross in order to burn it, but was then seen returning it after a dream, closely mirrors a story told at Þorpar on Steingrímsfjörður. The object of this story is the hill Gullhóll. On one occasion, when a new stable building was being erected at the farm, the workers started fetching stone from Gullhóll to use for the construction work. However, an elf woman came (it can be assumed, in a dream) and proclaimed that if people didn't stop taking stone from the hill, the ones who did so would get "something worse" from it.[67] Just like the Kross rootstock, the hill is still there and looks untouched.[68] Another parallel is provided by a story set at Brúará, a farm north of Kaldrananes but still located within the district of Kaldrananeshreppur. This story focuses on the restitution of material that had been removed from a supernatural place, but which in this example is brought about in a somewhat more robust manner. A farmer at Brúará was once building a new sheep house in the immediate vicinity of the farm's *álagablettur*. Since he did not believe in the *álagablettur*, he had the sods of grass for the roof of the sheep house cut inside the enchanted area. By evening, the roof was covered and the sheep house finished, and everybody went to bed. But when the inhabitants of the farm got up the next morning, they found that the sheep house had collapsed overnight—so everybody rushed to return all the sods of grass to the place of enchantment.[69] Many a transgression against a supernaturally protected place, it seems, does not last longer than an unquiet night.

Another repeating pattern is the motif of the fire illusion. The story about Kross relates that when some lads decide to put the tradition of the buried treasure to the test and start digging for it, it suddenly seems to them as if the farm at Kaldrananes was on fire. They break off their work and run to put out the flames; yet at the farm they find that all is well. After this, they never resume the digging work, but neither do they fill back the hole that they have already dug, so this hole remains to this day as a testimony to the occurrence.

---

[67] *NV* Hilmar Egill Sveinbjörnsson 1999, n. p. (Þorpar).

[68] It generally is a common motif to receive instructions in dreams; for some other instances from Strandir, cf. Jón Árnason 1954–1961, 1: 97–99; *SÁM* Haukur Jóhannesson 1988, 30; *SÁM* Pétur Guðmundsson and Guðmundur Guðmundsson s.a., 13; or the story about the origin of the monster Selkolla, where it is a repeated motif of the narrative that dire consequences ensue whenever a dream request from a supernatural/dead being is refused (Árngrímur Fr. Bjarnason and Helgi Guðmundsson 1933–1949, 2: 88–91; Cormack 2018, 90–91). Even more common are straightforward prophetic dreams; for an example set at Kaldrananes, see Jón Árnason 1954–1961, 3: 441.

[69] Lárus Jóhannsson, pers. comm.

What is interesting about this story is that the whole narrative, including all its details, is a set piece. One of the classic types of story sites in Strandir is the founder's burial mound: in a number of places, local tradition identifies the location where the first settler at a farm or fjord was buried, and many of these founders' graves are connected with exactly the same story as is told about the treasure hunters at Kross: the rumor of buried treasure at some point led to an attempt to dig up this treasure, but when people were doing so, the nearest farm or church was suddenly seen burning; when everybody then rushed off to help put out the flames, it was found that all was well with the buildings; but afterward, the digging work was never resumed, and the hollow that had already been dug was never backfilled. In Strandir, this story and variants of it are connected with at least half a dozen places:[70] Steingrímshaugur ("Steingrímur's Burial Mound") on the mountain of Staðarfjall, reputed to be the burial mound of Steingrímur the Troll, the eponymous founding hero of Steingrímsfjörður;[71] Ljúfuholt ("Ljúfa's Hill"), the reputed burial mound of Ljúfa, the founding heroine of the farm of Ljúfustaðir ("Ljúfa's Steads") in Fellshreppur;[72] Skiphóll ("Ship Hill") in Brunngil, where Gull-Bárður, the legendary first settler at the top of Bitrufjörður, is said to be buried in his ship;[73] Mókollshaugur ("Mókollur's Burial Mound"), the reputed grave of (Mó-)Kollur, the eponymous founding hero of the fjord of Kollafjörður;[74] the twin mounds of the Önundarhaugar ("Önundur's Burial Mounds"), where Önundur Wooden-Foot, the founding hero of Kaldbaksdalur, is buried in the one and his ship in the other mound;[75] and the hill Ljótunn, which is the burial site of the identically named founding heroine Ljótunn, who founded Ljótunnarstaðir ("Ljótunn's Steads") in Bæjarhreppur.[76] The complex of the founder's burial mound and the fire illusion protecting it forms a firmly established pattern of storytelling that is, in different places, repeated again and again with only very minor variation.

While Kross is connected with exactly the same wonder narrative as these founders' graves, it still somewhat stands apart from them: no tradition explicitly identifies Kross as a burial site. It may, however, be a factor here that

---

[70] The following list is likely to be incomplete.

[71] *SÁM* Magnús Steingrímsson 1929, 10; Helgi Guðmundsson 1933–1937, 1: 352–353; *SÁM* Magnús Steingrímsson 1953a, 33–34; *SÁM* Magnús Steingrímsson 1953c, 5.

[72] *SÁM* Þórður Bjarnason s.a., 6; *SÁM* Guðrún S. Magnúsdóttir 1976e, 6.

[73] Óla Friðmey Kjartansdóttir and Ingþór Ólafsson, pers. comm.

[74] Interview with Þorvaldur Jónsson recorded on 13 December 1973 (SÁM 91/2573 EF—24, https://www.ismus.is/i/audio/id-1014865, 5 July 2020).

[75] *SÁM* Guðrún S. Magnúsdóttir 1975b, 2. Cf. Egeler 2022.

[76] *SÁM* Skúli Guðjónsson 1978, 7.

100 LANDSCAPE, RELIGION, AND THE SUPERNATURAL

in Christian iconography every hill crowned by a cross evokes Golgotha, and Golgotha not only is the place of the crucifixion of Christ but also the burial site of Adam: since Origen of Alexandria (c. AD185–253) at the latest, it is a common (though not universally endorsed) idea that the Cross of the crucifixion was erected directly above the grave of Adam, the first human being.[77] Golgotha is thus not only the place of the crucifixion but also the founder's burial mound of the founder of humanity as a whole—an interpretation which is highlighted not only in Origen's *Commentaries on Matthew* and subsequent theological works but also by a rich tradition of Catholic iconography that frequently places a representation of Adam's skull at the foot of the Cross.[78]

At the same time, trying to contextualize Kross in this wider tradition of Christian literature and iconography may be overthinking things; for at least occasionally, the motif of the fire illusion that protects a treasure is also connected with places that are not normally viewed as founders' grave mounds. This is the case at Tröllatunga, which I had already mentioned earlier as providing another example of a hill that was formerly crowned by a standing cross. About 350 m south of the former church of Tröllatunga, the hill Gullhóll, "Gold Hill," rises above the home-field. Gullhóll is a substantial, well-rounded, reasonably symmetrical hill some 30 m in diameter with a deep, sharply delineated hollow at its top; between the top of the hill and the farm there is an open line of sight (Fig. 2.5). A number of sources relate that gold is hidden in this hill, but it is protected by a fire enchantment; thus, for instance, a description of Tröllatunga from the 1970s recounts: "Gullhóll. There is a little hollow down into it and the story goes that gold is hidden there, but as soon as one digs into it, the church appears to be burning."[79]

At least one witness has considered it possible that Gullhóll could have been the actual burial mound of Steingrímur the Troll, which normally, and by the vast majority of witnesses, is identified with the rocky hill of Steingrímshaugur on Staðarfjall.[80] For the most part, however, Gullhóll is

---

[77] Ristow and Jászai 1970, col. 164.

[78] *Origenis Commentariorum series in Matthæum* 126 (*Patrologia Graeca* (Migne) t. xiii, col. 1777): "Venit enim ad me traditio quædam talis, quod corpus Adæ primi hominis ibi sepultum est ubi crucifixus est Christus, ut sicut in Adam omnes moriuntur, sic in Christo omnes vivificentur: ut in loco illo qui dicitur Calvariæ locus, id est *locus capitis*, caput humani generis resurrectionem inveniat cum populo universo per resurrectionem Domini Salvatoris, qui ibi passus est, et resurrexit." For a collection of prominent iconographic examples of the skull of Adam at the foot of the cross, see Ristow and Jászai 1970, cols. 164–165.

[79] *SÁM* Guðrún Magnúsdóttir 1975c, 10. Cf. Þorsteinn Erlingsson 1954, 348.

[80] Þorsteinn Erlingsson 1954, 348; cf. Egeler forthcoming a.

Fig. 2.5 The view from the top of Gullhóll ("Gold Hill") toward the farm buildings of Tröllatunga. The small area of trees by the houses marks the old cemetery, which would have been located directly by the church (dismantled in 1909). The hollow in the foreground is the hole, located directly below the highest point of Gullhóll, which reputedly resulted from an attempt to dig up the gold of the Gold Hill, until the vision of the burning church put an end to the digging. © M. Egeler, 2019.

not considered a grave mound, even though it looks much more like a real grave mound than many hills that are actually interpreted as such. So even if Kross is not a repetition of Adam's grave in Golgotha, connecting it with the fire illusion motif may bend, but it does not break, the storytelling pattern so common in Strandir.

Within Strandir, Kross is the only example of its kind. While there are many place-names referring to crosses, nowhere else has such a cross been re-erected, and be it in the form of the rootstock of a piece of driftwood. Yet even though Kross is unique, it is not in the least idiosyncratic. Rather, it is composed of a combination and repetition of patterns that can be seen repeating throughout Strandir, and even of repeating patterns that are a common heritage of much of Christianity. Kross is a version of an Icelandic harbor cross; it is Golgotha described through the imagery of a founder's burial mound; it is an abode of the supernatural that scares off its violators in ways elsewhere

102 LANDSCAPE, RELIGION, AND THE SUPERNATURAL

observed at dwelling places of the hidden people. Golgotha, the location of the original Cross, is described as the center of the world already in the early Christian theology of Antiquity; as Cyril of Jerusalem put it in the fourth century: τῆς γὰρ γῆς τὸ μεσώτατον ὁ Γολγοθᾶς οὗτός ἐστιν, "this Golgotha is the center of the world."[81] The hill of Kross in a way serves as a center which mirrors much of the storytelling world of Strandir in a manner that makes it blatantly clear just how much this world is constituted of new combinations, adaptations, and sometimes virtually unchanged multiplications of repeating patterns.

*

In a famous essay on landscape and place-lore in the Irish region of Connemara, Tim Robinson offered a meditation on the Connemara coastline as a kind of fractal: a geometrical form that is composed of the repetition of "self-similar" shapes that replicate each other at different scales.[82] While I do not want to push the analogy too far, the cultural construction of a supernatural landscape also seems to have something of a fractal about it, if only in the loose sense that it contains a strong element of repetition and replication on different scales.

These different scales of repetition are one of the most important implications of the examples presented in the preceding pages. The story about the curse of the bereaved widow has illustrated the wholesale repetition of a story which, with minor or no changes, recurs in a broad range of places across the whole region; and Kross has shown how a single, complex place may, as a whole, be one of a kind, but is still a combination of widely recurring motifs. The scales of the immediate locality and the wider region are inseparably interconnected. Every famous story is repeated and localized at one site after another. Every farm uses a selection of much the same storytelling motifs to inscribe supernatural presences into its land, even if some degree of individuality is achieved by combining the same narrative patterns in different, new ways.

The fundamental importance of recurring patterns perceptible in such examples mirrors observations already made in the wider scholarly

---

[81] *Catechesis XIII: De Christo crucifixo et sepulto* XXVIII (*Patrologia Graeca* (Migne) t. xxxiii, col. 805). Cf. Ristow and Jászai 1970, col. 164 with further attestations.
[82] Robinson 1996b, 78–102.

discourse, such as Eck's emphasis on reduplication in her "grammar of sanctification" of the Indian landscape, or Eskeröd's concept of the "tradition dominant." This central importance of repetition is a characteristic not only of the cultural construction of supernatural landscapes, but of popular culture more broadly. The stories that people tell each other tend to follow clearly established narrative patterns that recur widely within their respective cultures of storytelling: this is the reason why Vladimir Propp in his *Morphology of the Folktale* was able to find a common narrative pattern underlying Russian fairy tales,[83] and why Antti Aarne and Stith Thompson were able to propose an international typology of folk storytelling whose usefulness has stood the test of time.[84] This, in a completely different medium and cultural context, is also the reason why the administration of the Yosemite National Park built a parking lot at Tunnel View to allow visitors to the park to take photos of the same landscape prospect that Ansel Adams had made famous through *Clearing Winter Storm, Yosemite*, a black and white photograph taken in 1935 that was to become one of North America's most celebrated—and most repeated—nature photographs.[85] Human cultural production does not aim for innovation, but for replication, if maybe sometimes replication with a twist.

Such patterning also applies to the supernatural landscape, a landscape constructed out of individual places that, however, are not individualistic: the basic element of the sacred landscape is the repetition of established patterns and motifs that recur widely. Important stories are repeated in many different places; and places that are important are connected with stories that recur elsewhere. This also means that repetition can be taken as an indicator of importance. We know that *Clearing Winter Storm, Yosemite* is a famous photograph because nearly every visitor to Yosemite takes their own snapshot of the same view; and we know that the story of the bereaved widow must have been important because it was repeated so widely. In a sense, repetition both results from and constitutes importance, and the importance of an individual tradition or story pattern within the regional cultural context can be measured by the intensity of its repetition.

[83] Propp 1968.
[84] Thompson 1961; new, expanded edition: Uther 2004.
[85] Stoll 2015, fig. 4.1 and pp. 113–114.

104 LANDSCAPE, RELIGION, AND THE SUPERNATURAL

3: Identity

Denis Cosgrove has highlighted the importance of landscape for the construction of identities, pointing to the frequent role that landscape images (such as the oak tree as a symbol) have played for the imaginative creation of new identities.[86] More recently, Diana L. Eck in her study of the sacred geography of India puts particular emphasis on the importance of sacred places and the mythology of the landscape for the construction of regional and national identities: in her approach, it is especially the interlock of landscape and religion that becomes central to identity formation. A central focus of her book lies on how pilgrimage routes and the interconnectedness of pilgrimage sites create "a sense of location and belonging"[87]—which is a core part of a sense of identity. Eck highlights how in India this is achieved through the "footsteps of pilgrims [which] are the point of departure in creating the lived landscape,"[88] and how regional focuses on particular pilgrimage places can contribute to the formation of a regional sense of identity.[89] Such creations of identity out of pilgrimage can be of fundamental importance. Thus, for the Indian anthropologist Iravati Karve the experience of the great pilgrimage to Pandharpur in Maharashtra gave her "a new definition of Maharashtra: the land whose people go to Pandharpur for pilgrimage."[90] Even the Indian sense of "nationhood" has been related to the intricate network of pilgrimage sites that connects locations throughout the subcontinent.[91]

While Eck presents a strictly empirical study focused on the specifics of Indian cases, Thomas A. Tween has made a much more general attempt to outline a spatial theory of religion. His endeavor returns time and again to the construction of identities through religious ideas and spatial practices; he proposes that religions play an important role in the construction of a home, a homeland, and a collective identity.[92] In Tweed's own words: "Religions [. . .] involve homemaking. They construct a home—and a homeland. They delineate domestic and public space and construct collective identity."[93]

---

[86] Cosgrove 1998, xxi.
[87] Eck 2012, 6.
[88] Eck 2012, 12.
[89] Eck 2012, 12.
[90] Eck 2012, 12–13; Karve 1962, 22.
[91] Eck 2012, 15–16, cf pp. 42–105.
[92] Tweed 2006, 75, 97, cf. pp. 111, 166; on his concept of a homeland, see Tweed 2006, 109–113.
[93] Tweed 2006, 75.

Questions of the formation of identities thus form a recurrent theme in research on landscape, space, geography, and religion.[94] In Strandir, too, there appears to be a link between beliefs and stories of the supernatural and the construction of local and regional identities. The present section pursues this theme through three examples, one of them with a strictly local focus—a single farm—while the second and third have broader regional focuses involving a number of major fjords of Strandir and even the Westfjords as a whole. These examples are the farm of Hvítarhlíð in Bitrufjörður, where the name of the farm and the myth of its foundation by a troll became the object of a local controversy; the story of the troll Kleppa, which starts in Staðardalur in central Strandir but concludes in the northern part of Strandir in Árneshreppur; and the folktale of how a group of trolls tried to separate the Westfjords from the Icelandic mainland, only to end up being turned to stone in prominent public places in Kollafjörður and Steingrímsfjörður.

*

On the north coast of Bitrufjörður, the farm of Hvítarhlíð now languishes in a state of semi-abandonment. It perches on the slope above the coastal road no. 68, from which it is reached via a gravel track leading past a junk yard filled with everything from discarded furniture to an old clinker-built fishing boat. At the end of this gravel track, there are several buildings in different states of use or decay. Some stables and storage barns are visibly the oldest buildings still standing; they are boarded up, and from inside a window splattered with bird droppings an oversized plastic Santa Claus is waving a cheerful greeting. We have come to Hvítarhlíð for a structure located directly behind this cluster of buildings.

Hvítarhlíð is an old farm that has accumulated its share of stories. A now-drained bog below the farmhouses was said to be the hiding place of a copper cauldron full of gold;[95] two cliffs were thought to be inhabited by the hidden people.[96] Most of the storytelling about Hvítarhlíð is connected with its name, however—and what this name means is not as straightforward as one might think. An early written attestation of the farm and its name is found in a land register entry dated 24 June 1890, in which the then-owner of Hvítarhlíð and six witnesses from neighboring farms define and testify to the location of the

---

[94] Other in-depth case studies from recent years that focus on themes of religion, identitiy, and landscape are Walsham 2011; Torri 2020. Cf. also Brace et al. 2006.

[95] *SÁM* Einar Magnússon 1999, 3.

[96] *SÁM* Einar Magnússon 1999, 6.

106 LANDSCAPE, RELIGION, AND THE SUPERNATURAL

property's boundaries.[97] The importance of this entry lies in the spelling it uses for the name of the farm: Hvítahlíð, not Hvítarhlíð. The former is what one would expect: Hvítahlíð has a straightforward meaning "White Slope," which would be a very typically Icelandic place-name, whereas Hvítarhlíð does not lend itself to an equally obvious analysis. Yet a little over a century after this land register entry was signed, Einar Magnússon, who then owned and farmed Hvíta(r)hlíð, wrote a description of the place-names of his farm which opted for the unlikely form Hvítarhlíð as the correct name of the farm. In his account from 1999, Einar connected the name with legends about the farm's founding heroine and her grave, which he described as located in the immediate vicinity of the farm buildings and which lies just behind the building with the Santa in its window:[98]

> Right at the bottom of Miðvöllur, above the cattle-house, is Hvítarleiði ("Hvít's Grave"), a big and long hummock; a tradition relates that the female first settler (*landnámskona*) of the estate is buried there, together with her money chest at her feet, and the estate takes its name from her. These enchantments (*álög*) rest on Hvítarleiði that one may not mow there; the farmer who does that will lose his best cow or the hay will burn. Hvítarleiði has now for a long time been the only hummock in the home-field (*tún*), and I hope that it stays there in the future. One may suppose that Hvítarleiði is one of the oldest place-names of the estate.

Thus, as Einar saw things in the 1990s, the correct name of the farm was Hvítarhlíð, which meant "Hvít's Slope," "Slope of Ms. White" (*hvítar* being the feminine genitive form of the adjective *hvítur*, "white"); and the Hvít from which the farm was named was the settler who had first established the farm, and who was buried in an enchanted grave located a little upslope from the byre. The "enchantments" that lie on the grave are of exactly the kinds that are typical for any *álagablettur* in Strandir; in fact, Einar himself uses the word *álög* to describe the magic which protects it, which is the very word from which the term *álagablettur* is derived. Since *álagablettur* is not an academic term but a commonplace word of everyday speech for such "places of enchantment," this use of language is unlikely to be accidental. Hvít's grave is a classic *álagablettur* in everything but the curious detail that it is *also* the grave

---

[97] S. E. Sverrisson 1890, 75.
[98] *SÁM* Einar Magnússon 1999, 7.

of a founding heroine—which is a common category of sites, except that normally such founders' graves are distinct from "places of enchantment."

If the spelling used in 1890 truthfully reflects the attitudes current at the time, then in the late nineteenth century Hvíta(r)hlíð was a "White Slope" (*Hvítahlíð*), whereas by the late twentieth century it had become "Hvít's/ Ms. White's Slope" (*Hvítarhlíð*), the farm founded by the heroine Hvít ("Ms. White") that came with the full mythical accoutrements of enchantments and hidden treasure. Rather than Max Weber's disenchantment,[99] an extensive enchantment of the farm seems to have taken place.[100] This enchantment was enacted by providing the farm with a story of an eponymous founder figure, which means an origin story that is directly tied to the identity of the farm. Thus, this enchantment addresses exactly the question that Camilla Asplund Ingemark has proposed as the central question raised by narratives of enchantment. According to her, such narratives ask: "What does it mean to be human and how is human identity constructed in relation to the extra-human forces of existence [. . .]?"[101] At Hvíta(r)hlíð farm, this question is answered by invoking a founder figure Hvít, identifying her grave, and ascribing supernatural properties to it, thereby giving the farm both a deep history and a close link to the supernatural that transcends the ordinary material aspects of everyday human life.

How this happened probably had a lot to do with pronunciation. In everyday speech, inside a compound the final -*r* of a genitive like *Hvítar* ("of Hvít/ of Ms. White") is not very distinct; people are generally aware of it and pronounce it when they focus on speaking clearly, but in normal speech such a final -*r* of a genitive ending inside a compound becomes virtually silent.[102] In practice this means that the pronunciation of Hvítahlíð and that of

---

[99] Weber 1946, 139, 148–149, 155. Cf. Yelle and Trein 2020; Yelle 2013.

[100] Cf. Sävborg and Valk 2018b, 12 on "the role that belief narratives play in the supernaturalisation of the everyday world."

[101] Asplund Ingemark 2006, 1. In research on Weber's disenchantment thesis, Asprem has highlighted that conversely also disenchantment has been used to shape identities, showing that in the right circumstances, both the absence and the presense of (dis)enchantment can be an important component of identity formation: Asprem 2014, 539–540.

[102] Interestingly, people claim that they pronounce such final -*r* in interior position of compounds, even though they don't, or rarely do; the claim that this -*r* is pronounced reflects an awareness of what they would say if they overenunciated, rather than reflecting the reality of everyday speech. In the files of the Icelandic Place-Name Institute (nafnid.is), pertinent mistakes or corrections of spellings recur regularly if rarely; in most cases, the clear etymology of the place-names ensures a correct spelling, and most variation occurs where a name makes linguistic sense both with and without the internal -*r*. For instance, some considerable confusion about the internal -*r* has been noted for Reykja(r)nes in Árneshreppur, whose name means much the same thing with or without the -*r* ("Peninsula of Steam(clouds)"): *SÁM* Haukur Jóhannesson and Helgi Jónsson 2007, 3–4.

108 LANDSCAPE, RELIGION, AND THE SUPERNATURAL

Hvítarhlíð are almost identical, and Hvíta(r)hlíð can be understood equally well as "White Slope" and as "Slope of Ms. White." "White Slope" is the "obvious" reading in the sense that place-names formed according to the pattern "[color] + [topographical feature]" are commonplace: Hvítá ("White River"), Svartiflói ("Black Bog"), Grænihjalli ("Green Rock Terrace"), or Rauðagil ("Red Gully") are some examples of this pattern from Strandir. Yet being commonplace, such an explanation is also slightly boring, and since the Middle Ages Icelandic storytelling has indulged in extrapolating persons from toponyms that are actually just topographically descriptive. Thus, the *Book of Settlements* could interpret Gufuskálar, whose name "Houses of Steam" refers to local geothermal activity, as the foundation of a certain Ketill *gufa*, "Cauldron Steam."[103] In this medieval example, a farm name that refers to a characteristic topographical feature was reinterpreted as containing the name of the farm's founder ("Mr. Steam"), and exactly the same seems to have happened also at Hvíta(r)hlíð. Facilitated by a linguistic ambiguity, the pedestrian name "White Slope" was read against the grain to provide a founding heroine Hvít ("Ms. White"), setting the farm apart from other places named in a more ordinary manner.

Now this Hvít, or "Ms. White," acquired a large, very visible grave above the byre, which was left untouched when all the rest of the meadow was leveled off. To this grave accrued an air of unfathomable age as well as stories of enchantments and treasure and other marvels. Stefán Gíslason, who through his parents and grandparents had long-standing connections to Hvítarhlíð and grew up on the neighboring farm of Gröf, remembers that when he was little he was told that Hvít, whose grave is rather larger than a human one would be, was a female troll (*tröllkona*); and yet the children at the farm loved to play at her grave and were allowed to do so as long as they did not make too much noise, as undue noise would bring the wrath of the *álagablettur* down upon them. In their play, the children closely engaged with the grave. A depression in the hummock that forms the visible part of the grave was said to mark the boundary between Hvít's head and her torso, but became the focus of the children's discussion when one of them suggested it might not be located between her head and torso but between Hvít's body and her chest of money.[104]

---

[103] *Landnámabók*, ed. Jakob Benediktsson 1968, ch. H97; Egeler 2018a, 65–71.
[104] Stefán Gíslason 2008, 8.

TWELVE MOVEMENTS   109

In short, the founding heroine had become a colorful supernatural person that was deeply established at the farm. Then, however, bureaucracy intervened. In early 2006, the local council decided that it was high time to renew the road signs in the district, and so a newly designed set was produced that replaced the old signs. When Stefán Gíslason saw the new sign, he suddenly found Hvítarhlíð renamed: the new sign had done away with "Ms. White" and gave the name of the farm as Hvítahlíð, "White Slope." The old sign, meanwhile, had been unceremoniously dumped on the ground.[105]

One reaction to this was a public complaint by Stefán Gíslason about this official treatment of his ancestral homestead, where his parents and grandparents had farmed until 1956. First, Stefán wrote an account of the incident that he published on his personal blog.[106] His text struck a chord. A few days later it was republished on the local online news platform *strandir.is*,[107] and a fortnight after its first online publication it was taken up by the local print media and was printed in the newspaper *Bændablaðið*, "The Farmers' Paper."[108] While this did not help in any practical sense—the road sign was never changed back—the text is an important document that not only testifies to the view of those directly affected, but through its double republication also shows that this view, rather than being a personal idiosyncrasy, resonated with people. As the editorial preface to the republication of Stefán's text in *Bændablaðið* put it: "The topic seemed urgent to *Bændablaðið* and [. . .] the article [. . .] should greatly concern farmers in the whole country."[109]

In his article, Stefán not only retold the traditions about "Ms. White's Grave" Hvítarleiði and the childhood experiences that he and his brother had there but also highlighted the value and importance of place-names in connection with stories more generally. He noted: "The farm names carry stories in themselves that make life a tiny bit richer than it would otherwise be, even if the stories begin to fade. For this reason there is a cultural value in the farm names." Commenting on his photographs of the old road sign lying discarded on the ground, he emphasizes that this occurrence shows a

---

[105] Stefán Gíslason 2008, 8 (with photographic documentation).

[106] "Að breyta bæjarnöfnum," at https://stefangisla.blog.is/blog/stefangisla/entry/537569/, first published 12 May 2008, last accessed 8 July 2020.

[107] "Að breyta bæjarnöfnum," at http://strandir.is/ad-breyta-baejarnofnum/, first published 18 May 2008, last accessed 8 July 2020; later moved to http://strandir.saudfjarsetur.is/ad-breyta-baeja rnofnum/, 5 January 2021.

[108] Stefán Gíslason 2008.

[109] Stefán Gíslason 2008, 8.

110 LANDSCAPE, RELIGION, AND THE SUPERNATURAL

disappearance of an old cultural heritage that he sees as the obligation of the present generation to preserve for those that come after it. Particularly significant is a remark in which Stefán weighs the new official form of the farm name against the old one:

> Naturally that [i.e., Hvítahlíð, "White Slope"] had seemed the better and more logical name to somebody, but at the same time it has made its contribution, with ignorance and short-sightedness, to the eradication of the story which follows the farm name. Certainly the slope (*hlíð*) is often white (*hvít*) in winter, but which slope in this part of the country is not?

This remark highlights Stefán's feeling that the form Hvítahlíð, "White Slope," is banal and makes no contribution to the farm that goes beyond a platitude which could be applied to every place in the region: "White Slope" lacks both character and individuality and strips the farm of its specificity. In other words, he sees the official (officious?) "correction" of the farm name as a threat to the farm's identity. This fear, of course, is not unfounded: the figure of the farm's founding heroine Hvít is intrinsically tied up with the farm's name, and founding figures tend to be central constituents of a place's identity, not just at Hvíta(r)hlíð. Hvít in certain ways plays much the same role as a classical Greek hero, providing a more-than-human name-giver and reference point for a small geographical and social unit. One may think of local Greek heroes such as Hippothoon, a son of Poseidon and the eponymous hero of the Attic phyle Hippothoontis, who was a name-giving ancestral figure for a subsection of the Athenian population and, as such, the recipient of a cult.[110] While of course Hvít was not the recipient of anything that could be called worship, her grave was still the reference point of "rituals of avoidance"[111] (prohibition of noise and mowing); it had a mythology of its own; and—being an *álagablettur*—it exerted a certain supernatural power, or at least the threat of such power. Hvít was a "heroine" in a sense that, while not identical with the Greek, comes remarkably close to it.

None of the more otherworldly aspects of Hvít and her grave is foregrounded in Stefán's article. Stefán is concerned with something much more of this world: the loss of the farm's inherited identity. On the official plane, his writing did not make much of a difference: the new road sign

---

[110] *Pausanias* I.v.1–2; I.xxxviii.4; I.xxxix.3; Stoll 1884–1937 (*Hippothoon*), col. 2692.
[111] On the term "ritual of avoidance," see Chadbourne 2012, 76.

stayed, and to this day it reads "Hvítahlíð." On the farm itself, however, at least something could be done. After the work gang who had replaced the signs had left the old one simply dumped by the roadside, somebody took the discarded sign and put it up next to Hvítarleiði: the road sign has become the headstone for the grave of the founding troll (Fig. 2.6). Thus, Hvít lives on as a fixed part of the farm's landscape. It is one of the melancholy ironies of Strandir that, with the farmhouse now standing empty for most of the year, the dead troll actually seems to have outlived her farm.

*

In a puzzling inversion of their more usual role as burlesque antiheroes, trolls in Strandir appear to be a recurrent feature of local and even regional identity formation. In Bitrufjörður, there are three farms whose name is believed to be derived from a troll or troll-like being. There is Hvítarhlíð, named from the troll woman Hvít; some 4 km west of Hvítarhlíð lies Einfætingsgil farm, "Glen of the One-Legged One," whose name is said to refer to a one-legged "troll witch" (*skessa*); and across the fjord directly to the south of Hvítarhlíð

Fig. 2.6 Some of the abandoned buildings of Hvíta(r)hlíð, with Hvítarleiði, "Hvít's Grave," in the foreground in the right-hand corner of the picture. At the head of the grave, the old road sign with the spelling "Hvítarhlíð" now functions as a headstone. © M. Egeler, 2019.

112 LANDSCAPE, RELIGION, AND THE SUPERNATURAL

lies Þambárvellir, named from the troll woman Þömb.[112] The importance of these farms' trolls is strictly local: each plays a role only for a single farm. In addition to such highly local troll stories, there are also troll founding narratives that have a regional range.

In the overview of the ecclesiastical organization of Strandir in the Introduction, I summarized the origin legend of the church at Staður, which is one such tradition of regional importance.[113] In the storytelling tradition about Staður and the valley of Staðardalur, the troll woman Kleppa is connected with the building of the highland road up to Steingrímsfjarðarheiði at Flókatunga; the naming of the farmsteads of Kleppustaðir ("Kleppa's-Steads," her own farm), Skerpingsstaðir ("Skerpingur's-Steads," where her husband Skerpingur lived), and Hofstaðir ("Temple-Steads," where her temple was located); and the reshaping of some landscape features that led to the relocalization of the church to its present site at Staður. Thus, the narratives about Kleppa already cover the whole valley of Staðardalur; but this is not yet all. There are also traditions about Kleppa that are located in the northern part of Strandir in Árneshreppur. The story goes that Kleppa did her best—or her worst—to rid Staðardalur of Christianity; but at some point she had to accept her defeat, and rather than living in a Christian valley, she decided to move north. Crossing the mountains of Trékyllisheiði, she traveled to Árneshreppur, where she finally arrived at Finnbogastaðir. Finnbogastaðir is a farm of considerable historical importance that traces itself back to the first settlement of Iceland during the Viking Age; its legendary founder Finnbogi the Strong is the hero of a medieval saga.[114] Kleppa does not appear in the medieval saga, but in modern folk tradition her narrative latches on to that of the famous settler. Stories recorded in the nineteenth and twentieth centuries claim that, after leaving Staðardalur, she approached Finnbogi, who at the time was still a pagan, and asked him for leave to live on his farm.[115] Finnbogi granted her request, and for a while things went well; but it did not last. In due course, Finnbogi converted to Christianity and built a church. Kleppa was not happy and behaved accordingly. On one occasion, she took her scissors, cut all the grass in a good grass field very close to the

---

[112] On both farms and their trolls, see the post "Af skessum, bófum og draugum" on the local news webpage *strandir.is* (https://strandir.is/af-skessum-bofum-og-draugum/, posted 22 February 2005, accessed 10 July 2020; later moved to http://strandir.saudfjarsetur.is/af-skessum-bofum-og-draugum/, 5 January 2021).

[113] See chapter 1, section "The Church in Strandir."

[114] See chapter 1, section "Living in Landscapes: Dwelling, Place, and Home."

[115] Jón Árnason 1954–1961, 1: 144–145; *SÁM* Pálína Þórólfsdóttir 1980, 4.

TWELVE MOVEMENTS   113

ground, and proclaimed that it would never grow back properly again, which indeed came to pass (this sounds like blaming the troll for the consequences of overgrazing).[116] Somewhere else she pissed on a field with such enthusiasm that it turned into a bog and remained so until the arrival of modern drainage in the twentieth century.[117] In the end, Finnbogi climbed up the mountain that towers above Finnbogastaðir, broke a huge rock out of its cliffs, and hurled it down on Kleppa; according to one version of the tale, he did this while Kleppa was squatting down to piss on a field she wanted to turn into bog land.[118] Finnbogi's aim was true, and to this day Kleppa remains buried under the rock. It now forms a small rocky hill which is located in a boggy grass field between the farm and the mountain, and bears the troll's name: Kleppa (Fig. 2.7).[119]

Taken together, the stories about Kleppa thus not only pervade the valley of Staðardalur and are entangled with the important parsonage there, but they also throw a bridge to the northernmost outpost of the Church in Strandir: the old church of Árnes, which was built in 1850 and is the oldest extant ecclesiastical building in the district, lies barely 1 km to the northwest of the hill Kleppa, and the story gives the building of the first local church as the reason for why the troll is buried under this hill and why two large areas of Finnbogastaðir are boggy and half-barren. The actions that the antiheroine Kleppa takes upon the arrival of the Church create both landscapes, the one around the church at Staður and the one around the church at Árnes (Map 2.1). Conversely, this means that Kleppa as a focus of storytelling constitutes a connecting link between them and thus forms part of the creation not just of local, but regional identity.

*

Another troll story about the creation of regional landmarks and indeed a whole regional landscape is the tale of the three trolls who wanted to separate the Westfjords from the rest of Iceland (Map 2.2). This story was collected by

---

[116] Jón Árnason 1954–1961, 1: 145; *SÁM* Guðmundur P. Valgeirsson 1979, 4; *SÁM* Pálína Þórólfsdóttir 1980, 4. In Pálína Þórólfsdóttir's telling the troll turns into an old woman with magical abilities who wants to buy land that Finnbogi does not want to sell. (In modern Icelandic, *kerling* can simply be an old woman, but often it is used for a female troll; thus, the word creates a certain fluidity between the two categories.) On environmental aspects of the supernatural landscape, see section "Nature and Environment."

[117] *SÁM* Pálína Þórólfsdóttir 1980, 4.

[118] *SÁM* Guðmundur P. Valgeirsson 1979, 7–8.

[119] *SÁM* Guðmundur P. Valgeirsson 1979, 7–8; *SÁM* Pálína Þórólfsdóttir 1980, 4; *SÁM* Jóhann Hjaltason s.a. (a), 4.

Fig. 2.7 The farm of Finnbogastaðir with Kleppa, which is the small, distinct hill in the middle of an otherwise level grass field to the left of the farm, under which the troll Kleppa is buried. In the background, the mountain from which Finnbogi the Strong threw the rock which forms Kleppa. © M. Egeler, 2019.

Jón Árnason in the middle of the nineteenth century, and to this day it has a pervasive presence in the area. As Jón Árnason recorded it,[120] once upon a time ("í fyrndinni," "a long time ago") there were three trolls who wanted to dig a canal across the narrowest point of the Westfjords between Kollafjörður and Gilsfjörður, and while they were at it they also wanted to create islands. Two trolls worked on this task on the western side, a male and a female, and because the water was very shallow there and islands therefore easy to create, they made good headway; the material they dug out of the mainland formed all the many islands in Breiðafjörður. But in the west it did not go at all so well, because the work was down to a single troll woman and the water was much deeper, so her islands all sank and she merely created submerged skerries. Now the trolls on both sides worked through the night and lost track of time. When they saw dawn coming, the trolls who were at work in the west quickly ran back across the mountain pass of Steinadalsheiði to try

---

[120] Jón Árnason 1954–1961, 3: 279–280. Jón Árnason transcribed the tale himself in 1861: Jón Árnason 1954–1961, 3: 638.

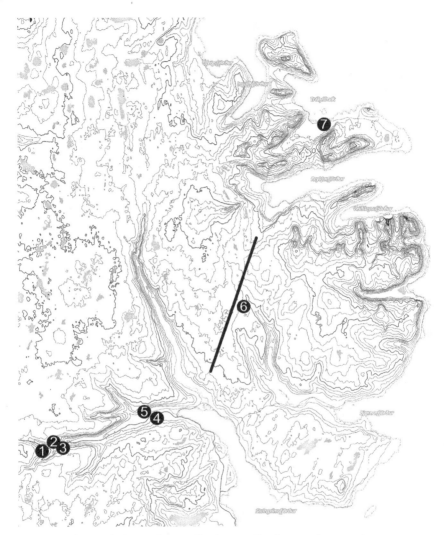

Map 2.1 The mythology of the troll Kleppa, which extends over a large part of Strandir. 1: Flókatunga, where Kleppa created a major mountain route. 2: Her farm Kleppustaðir. 3: Skerpingsstaðir, "Skerpingur's-Steads," the farm of her husband, Skerpingur. 4: Hofstaðir, "Temple-Steads," the location of her temple. 5: Staður, where the parish church came to be located because of Kleppa's interference. 6: Rough location of one of the historic routes across the highlands of Trékyllisheiði, which Kleppa crossed to escape the spread of Christianity. 7: Finnbogastaðir, where Kleppa found shelter but after the coming of Christianity wrought mayhem, and where consequently she was killed and remains buried to this day. Árnes is a couple of minutes' walk to the west of Finnbogastaðir. Base map created on Inkatlas.com; © OpenStreetMap contributors (openstreetmap.org), Inkatlas.

116 LANDSCAPE, RELIGION, AND THE SUPERNATURAL

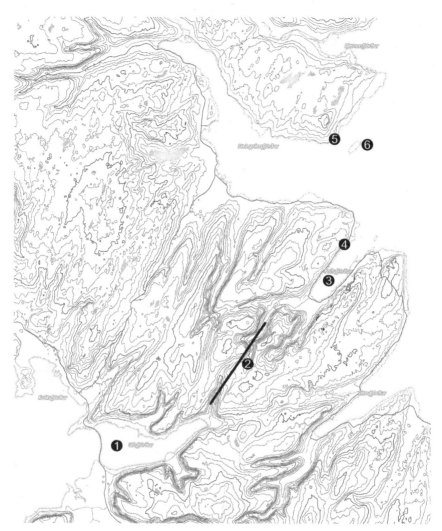

Map 2.2 The story of the trolls that tried to separate Strandir from the Icelandic mainland, which, like the story of Kleppa, extends over a large part of Strandir (and beyond). 1: Gilsfjörður, the southwestern end of the troll canal-building project. 2: Steinadalsheiði, which the southern troll work gang crossed when they noticed that they were being overtaken by the light of day. 3: Kollafjörður, the northeastern end of the troll canal. 4: The Drangar, the petrified trolls of the southern work gang. 5: Kerling, the petrified troll who had been digging from the north. 6: Grímsey, the island that this troll cut from the mainland, with her petrified ox Uxi, an offshore rock. Base map created on Inkatlas.com; © OpenStreetMap contributors (openstreetmap.org), Inkatlas.

to find shelter in Kollafjörður; but when they reached the shore there, the sun came up and they turned to stone. As Jón Árnason records the resulting place-names, these stones were then called the Drangar ("Rock Towers") and stand near Kollafjarðarnes. In Danish maps from the early twentieth century, the Drangar are still named as such;[121] today, the two trolls are known as Karl and Kerling, "Man" and "Crone."

Meanwhile, the troll woman who had been working on the eastern end of the canal project also lost track of time and did not look up from her work until it started to get light. Then she jumped northward over Steingrímsfjörður and stopped at the cliffs of Malarhorn, where the sun shone on her. She was extremely angry that she hadn't managed to make more in terms of islands than a few skerries and some tiny islands only suitable as breeding grounds for birds. In her anger, she drove her spade into Malarhorn cliff with such force that it broke a large piece out of the rock; this is the island of Grímsey, the only big island that the troll woman managed to create, and, as Jón Árnason writes, "people say that the layering of stone on the island is exactly the same as in Malarhorn, and from this it is easy to see that it is broken from this rock." At the eastern end of the island is a rock shaped like an ox, which is called Uxi, "ox." This ox belonged to the troll woman. The animal happened to stand on the island when the troll broke it off from the mainland, and the sun rose on it just as on its owner, turning it to stone.

Jón Árnason's version of the story does not give a reason for why the trolls tried to dig a channel across the narrow neck of land that connects the Westfjords to the rest of the Icelandic mainland. The idea of digging such a canal may express a certain feeling on the part of the storyteller that the Westfjords are a place of their own and really distinct from the southern parts of Iceland. Today, however, local opinion in Steingrímsfjörður has it that the trolls wanted to separate the Westfjords in order to check the spread of humankind across the island, which was accompanied by Christianity and therefore deeply disagreeable to the troll population.[122] In this view, the trolls become the prehuman native inhabitants of Iceland that try to secure a space for themselves and in the attempt create the region's landscape as it has been from the earliest times of human habitation; and the Westfjords become,

---

[121] *Generalstabens Topografiske Kort*, sheet *Tröllatunga—33 Óspakseyri N.V.* (drawn 1912, published 1914).

[122] Jón Jónsson, pers. comm.; this view is also mentioned in Regína Hrönn Ragnarsdóttir's travel blog article "The 3 Trolls who wanted to separate the Westfjords from the Mainland of Iceland," https://guidetoiceland.is/connect-with-locals/regina/the-westfjord-trolls-who-wanted-to-separate-the-westfjords-from-the-mainland-of-iceland-folklore, last accessed 11 July 2020.

118   LANDSCAPE, RELIGION, AND THE SUPERNATURAL

deep down, the land of the trolls. The tale is comparable to those in which trolls like Hvít appear as the founders of farms; it is just that the foundation element is formulated not on a local but on a regional scale.

The story has a very strong presence in and beyond the region. The narrative is widely known and easily accessible: Jón Árnason's text of the story has been printed repeatedly;[123] it is found online in several open-access databases;[124] it is the object of Icelandic travel writing;[125] it was quoted in foreign travel writing about Iceland already in the nineteenth century;[126] it is summarized on local signposting; it has been turned into teaching material for Icelandic children;[127] in 2019, it was made the topic of an episode of an Icelandic children's TV series;[128] it has, in a number of variants, time and again been recorded from oral tradition;[129] and the regional journal *Strandapósturinn* has repeatedly used the trolls, the ox, and their island as cover images.[130] Recently, *Strandapósturinn* has also reprinted the story.[131]

---

[123] Jón Þorkelsson 1899, 80–81; Jón Árnason 1954–1961, 3: 279–280 (printed in several editions); *Strandapósturinn* 52 (2020), 139–140.

[124] For instance, https://www.snerpa.is/net/thjod/troll-ve.htm, https://baekur.is/bok/000428529/0/90/THjodsogur_og, and others; all last accessed 11 July 2020.

[125] See Regína Hrönn Ragnarsdóttir's travel blog article "The 3 Trolls who wanted to separate the Westfjords from the Mainland of Iceland," https://guidetoiceland.is/connect-with-locals/regina/the-westfjord-trolls-who-wanted-to-separate-the-westfjords-from-the-mainland-of-iceland-folklore, last accessed 11 July 2020.

[126] E.g., Howell 1893, 148.

[127] Material on the webpage of the Icelandic teaching association *netskoli.is*: https://netskoli.is/kennsla/verkefni_skoda.aspx?ContentID=9263969588, last accessed 11 July 2020.

[128] *Leiðangurinn—Leitin að tröllunum* ["The Expedition—The Search for the Trolls"], https://www.ruv.is/sjonvarp/spila/leidangurinn/27893, accessed 10 July 2020, broadcasted online 26 June 2019–27 April 2021.

[129] *SÁM* Matthías Helgason s.a. (a), 2–3; *SÁM* Guðrún S. Magnúsdóttir 1975e, 3–4; *SÁM* Haukur Jóhannesson 2008, 3; *SÁM* Guðrún S. Magnúsdóttir and Guðjón Guðmundsson 1976, 1. For the most part, these variants follow the same main lines as the version published by Jón Árnason. A notable exception is a version that Guðrún S. Magnúsdóttir collected from Magndís Aradóttir, who had lived in Drangsnes from 1919 to 1955 (*SÁM* Guðrún S. Magnúsdóttir 1975e, 3–4). In her version, the troll woman of Drangsnes had a husband. The two got into an argument about who should lead the ox on its leash. The woman in the end got so angry that she stomped her foot with such force that the piece of land on which her husband and the ox were standing broke off the mainland. The piece of land formed Grímsey, the ox fell into the water immediately in front of it and there turned to stone, and the husband drowned and disappeared. In another version, told by Guðjón Guðmundsson, the troll woman used the ox to pull Grímsey out into the sea; this is why the ox is now located on the place at the tip of the island where it is (*SÁM* Guðrún S. Magnúsdóttir and Guðjón Guðmundsson 1976, 1). In a version told by Guðmundur Ragnar Guðmundsson in 1970, the husband of the troll woman actually became the ox Uxi (interview recorded on 8 July 1970; *SÁM* 91/2359 EF—13, https://www.ismus.is/i/audio/id-1013089, 12 July 2020). What remains constant in all versions is the direct connection of the tales to the same real-world landscape features and their association with trolls.

[130] Issues 16 (1982), 34 (2001), 39 (2007), 43 (2011).

[131] *Strandapósturinn* 52 (2020), 139–140.

Fig. 2.8 Uxi, the "Ox," just off the northeastern tip of Grímsey. © M. Egeler, 2019.

Most monumentally and most permanently, however, the story is given presence through the landscape features whose origin it purports to explain. Grímsey, the island created by the spade of the troll woman, is the largest island in Strandir. It is visible from large parts of the Strandir coast, including much of Steingrímsfjörður; as a central landmark for orientation at sea, it has been the location of a lighthouse since 1915. Uxi, the "ox," likewise is visible from many kilometers of the coastline—and from many viewpoints it does indeed look strikingly like an ox (Fig. 2.8). The petrified troll woman who created Grímsey is known as Kerling, the "Crone": she is a well-signposted rock pillar in a central location in the village of Drangsnes (whose name means "Peninsula of the Rock Pillar" and refers to the troll): she stands right between a café and the public swimming pool (Fig. 2.9).

Even the two trolls who were caught out by the sun in Kollafjörður used to be located in an extremely public place. Today, their location is fairly hidden. The current road runs on an escarpment some 20 m above the waterline from which, driving by, one only catches a short glimpse of the two pinnacles that represent the two petrified trolls. Before the construction of the current road, however, the route used to run directly on the edge of the water. Where it passed the two trolls, it was framed by the trolls on the seaward side and by cliffs and steep rocky slopes on the landward side (Fig. 2.10). Already the maps of the Danish General Staff from the 1910s clearly mark both the trolls

Fig. 2.9 The troll landscape of the village of Drangsnes: the rock pillar is Kerling, the "Crone," the petrified troll who created the island of Grímsey and who owned the "Ox" Uxi, both of which are visible in the distance. © M. Egeler, 2019.

Fig. 2.10 The two trolls Karl ("Man") and Kerling ("Crone") on the shore of Kollafjörður. These are the two trolls that worked on the western end of the canal project, digging from Gilsfjörður toward Kollafjörður. Note the track that runs just inland from the petrified trolls: this track represents a now-disused utilization phase of the coastal road, which runs toward the pass road over Steinadalsheiði that the trolls had also used. © M. Egeler, 2019.

TWELVE MOVEMENTS 121

and the cliffs behind them, and show the road as running between the trolls and the cliffs.[132]

The association between the location of the trolls and the old coastal road mirrors the importance that has been ascribed to roads and paths in some classic theorizing on landscape: the movement that takes place along roads and paths is a central part of what holds landscapes together. Tim Ingold in particular has emphasized the fundamental importance of movement, of roads and paths, for understanding space, landscape, and place. He even goes so far to argue that "place" is dependent on the existence of paths: if one wants to reach a place, one has to follow a path of one kind or another. "Thus there can be no places without paths, along which people arrive and depart; and no paths without places, that constitute their destinations and points of departure."[133] The Kollafjörður trolls are a case in point that this central importance of roads and paths is valid also for the supernatural landscape: roads, paths, and tracks are among the landscape features along which the supernatural landscape is organized. The same also holds true to a certain extent for the story of Kleppa discussed earlier, as Staður and Finnbogastaðir/Árnes are connected by a highland route that the troll also used to travel between the main places of the story. Both troll stories are organized along major travel routes.

In Kollafjörður, the location of the trolls directly next to the old coastal road made them impossible to miss. The story of the three trolls is a tale of regional importance, but it is also a "roadside tale" whose setting people would have passed by very frequently. In the case of the trolls, the regional importance of their story used to correlate with the importance of their location, since the road led to the pass over the Steinadalsheiði highlands to Gilsfjörður, from where the trolls had come. Steinadalsheiði is the shortest route to the southern side of the Westfjords, and until about the middle of the twentieth century, it was one of the most important passes leading

---

[132] *Generalstabens Topografiske Kort*, sheet *Tröllatunga—33 Óspakseyri N.V.* (drawn 1912, published 1914). The Danish surveyors have marked the trolls as "Drangar" ("Rock Towers"), using the topographically descriptive name that is also found in Jón Árnason's transcript of the narrative.
[133] Ingold 1993, 167. Cf. Moor 2016; Ingold 2010.

122 LANDSCAPE, RELIGION, AND THE SUPERNATURAL

south.[134] Like two stone sentinels, the petrified trolls would greet anybody coming from there to Steingrímsfjörður and remind them that people in the Westfjords always thought they were special, even before there were people.

*

This section first introduced the farm of Hvítarhlíð in Bitrufjörður. The controversy about its correct name provides an unusually explicit example of the role that the myth of a founding heroine can play in a farm's sense of identity. Since this founding heroine turns out to be a female troll, this example also affirms the importance that trolls in Strandir can gain as founding figures. A second set of case studies then pursued this theme of founding trolls further. It introduced the folktale of how the troll woman Kleppa moved from Staðardalur to Finnbogastaðir in Árneshreppur as well as the story of the three trolls that, through a failed attempt to separate the Westfjords from the Icelandic mainland, created important landscape features in central Strandir, some of which can be seen as landmarks that seem to memorialize a Strandir "sense of being special." These landmarks had and have a remarkable presence in the public space of Strandir, being two rock pillars located by the side of a formerly important road, another rock pillar next to the public swimming pool of a village, and the largest island of the region. Thus, the examples discussed here approached the theme of identity both on a local and on a regional stage.

Eck, in her investigation of the sacred geography of India, has emphasized the importance of the footsteps of pilgrims for the construction of regional and even supraregional identities on the subcontinent.[135] In Lutheran-Protestant Strandir, pilgrimage does not play a prominent role in religious life.[136] Yet the location of the petrified trolls in Kollafjörður directly by the side of a formerly important road highlights that footsteps are important even so: while local identity—in the sense of the relation to the immediate home on the farm as the smallest unit of reference—is based on the name, stories, and practices of the place one lives at, all relations one has to the wider region beyond the home farmstead are based on places one goes to or looks at from afar. The trolls at Kollafjörður, or the maritime rock of Uxi, can

---

[134] Jón Jónsson, pers. comm.; cf. Kålund 1877–1882, 1: 631, who mentions this pass as a "meget benyttede vej" ("much-used route").

[135] Eck 2012, 12.

[136] It is not entirely unknown either, however, as people do occasionally visit holy wells blessed by Guðmundur the Good.

stand for the importance of such places one goes to or regularly sees in the distance. In the encounter with their physical presence, they evoke narratives that are widely shared within the community; and thus they add an important facet to the region's identity.

The construction of identities is a complex process that is not all about landscape. Yet landscape does play a part in it: it actualizes the particular, shared meaning that narratives or practices endow places with, and through constant, repeated actualization this meaning is made part of a widely shared and deeply naturalized cultural knowledge. Landscape thus plays a prominent role in the process of "formulating conceptions of a general order of existence and [. . .] clothing these conceptions with [. . .] an aura of factuality" that Geertz suggested as a core function of religion.[137] The story of the three trolls was able to gain regional importance because it is connected with public places that are constantly seen and encountered. Changes in the way the landscape is used can undermine such a mechanism on the basis of direct encounters; but since the trolls—because their locations were so very public—had already gained their regional importance before the Kollafjörður road was moved away from them, the physical encounter seems to have been replaced by a transferral of the trolls into other media: now, they appear on TV and in print, as when the Kollafjörður trolls provide cover images for *Strandapósturinn*. The photograph of the trolls can stand in for the real place, just as the place stands in for the story connected with it; and it appears to be secondary whether this connection between place and story is actualized directly at the place or at one remove. But because the story is connected to the place, which in turn is inextricably connected to the region, the story still acts through the place to make its contribution to the region's identity.

4: Morality

From the 1960s onward—and thus at roughly the same time when much of the toponymy and place-lore of Strandir was collected by Icelandic folklorists and local enthusiasts—Keith Hamilton Basso undertook a long-term ethnographic study among the Western Apache. In 1996, this resulted in his

---

[137] Geertz 1973, 90 (italics in original): "a *religion* is: *(1) a system of symbols which acts to (2) establish powerful, pervasive, and long-lasting moods and motivations in men by (3) formulating conceptions of a general order of existence and (4) clothing these conceptions with such an aura of factuality that (5) the moods and motivations seem uniquely realistic.*"

124 LANDSCAPE, RELIGION, AND THE SUPERNATURAL

landmark monograph *Wisdom Sits in Places*, which soon became established as the central case study for, among others, the relationship between landscape and morality. In this book, Basso presented a foundational analysis of broader patterns, general mechanisms, and specific individual cases of how members of a Western Apache community viewed the landscape as a depository of wisdom and moral guidance.

In this society, the landscape both helped individuals to lead good lives and could be used to voice criticism of specific misdemeanors. The basic mechanism through which landscape could fulfill these functions was the link between the land, its toponyms, and the stories that were connected with these toponyms. Western Apache storytelling contains a rich repertoire of narratives that convey moral messages by—sometimes very drastically—illustrating the consequences of bad behavior. Telling such stories could be used as a means of addressing perceived misbehavior without explicitly confronting the culprit about what he or she had done: there would be no need for an explicit personal rebuke, as the person who had violated a rule would understand the analogy between his or her behavior and that described in the story. When such a story was told in their presence, they would understand that their behavior had been noted, judged, and fallen short of expectations, while the analogy of the story would tell them how they should have behaved. Such narratives, furthermore, were closely connected with specific named locations in the landscape. This link between place and story added another layer to the possible moral applications of place storytelling: the criticism that was expressed by telling a traditional story would act on the person at which it was directed not only in the moment when it was spoken but also later on when the culprit would be reminded of the moral issue every time they encountered the place where the story was set.

Basso, as one of his examples, tells the story of a young woman who during a ritual had violated the proper code of conduct. A few days after her indiscretion, her grandmother, without explicitly raising the issue of the specific offence, told a traditional tale that presented an analogy to the girl's misbehavior. The girl stood up, left without a word, and afterward made sure not to repeat her mistake. Two years after the incident Basso gave her a lift in his car, and the two fell to talking about what had happened on that occasion. When they passed a place which featured in the story the grandmother had told, Basso pointed it out. At this, the woman said that she was well aware of it, stating: "I know that place. It stalks me every day."[138]

---

[138] Basso 1996, 57.

The moral system was not only memorialized in the landscape; through it, the system constantly acted on the members of this society, providing continuous guidance for acceptable behavior. A place connected with a story that commented on certain types of undesirable behavior would in this way "stalk" a person who had violated the established code of conduct: at every encounter, such a place had the potential to evoke the story and thus remind them of the moral rule which they had violated.[139]

While in Strandir I have never encountered an active use of place-lore as a means of moral rebuke, there is certainly a considerable amount of storytelling that explains place-names through stories which seem to have a clear and marked moral thrust. So even if an explicit active use of the moral implications of the landscape does not play a major (if any) role, the local tradition of storytelling does invest considerable effort into formulating stories that reflect moral messages, connecting these messages to place-names, and locating them in often very public places. The landscape thus acts as a medium to propagate moral messages in the way recognized by W. J. T. Mitchell:[140]

landscape is [. . .] a physical and multisensory medium (earth, stone, vegetation, water, sky, sound and silence, light and darkness, etc.) in which cultural meanings and values are encoded, whether they are *put* there by the physical transformation of a place in landscape gardening and architecture, or *found* in a place formed, as we say, "by nature."

I will pursue this theme of the landscape as a mirror and medium of moral expectations through two groups of examples. First, I use the ghost Þorpa-Gudda and the skerry Sesselja to present material pertaining to social responsibility for the old and the poor, and then a local storytelling tradition about infanticide and the ghosts of crying children. All of these storytelling traditions as used in Strandir seem to have a common denominator in formulating a deeply felt obligation of care for the weakest members of society, and—through stories and place-names—they give this obligation a presence in the space of everyday life.

*

---

[139] Basso 1996, esp. pp. 48–59. Cf. Tilley 1994, 33.
[140] Mitchell 2002d, 14.

126   LANDSCAPE, RELIGION, AND THE SUPERNATURAL

A recurring topic of storytelling in Strandir is the suffering that people of wealth and power can bring upon the poorer and weaker members of society, either by abusing their power or by shunning their responsibilities. One common topic here is the consequences of sexual coercion;[141] another is the negligence—sometimes criminal—of the rich for the needs of the poor. The latter type is particularly interesting for how it embraces the moral ambiguities of its protagonists: rather than appearing as outright evil, the wrongdoers of such stories often seem merely flawed or even just normal, but the consequences of their actions are nothing less than disastrous. For these stories, moral behavior amounts not merely to avoiding evil, but to actively doing good.

Among the most famous stories of this kind in Strandir is the folktale of Þorpa-Gudda, which tells of how a farm quite literally comes to be haunted by its negligence of the poor. Þorpa-Gudda, "Gudda of Þorpar," is one of the best-known ghosts of Strandir, attached to the family that owns the farm of Þorpar on the south coast of Steingrímsfjörður. What is of interest here is the ghost's origin. As the story goes, during the early nineteenth century Þorpar was owned by a certain Gísli. He was a good farmer and the mayor (hreppstjóri) of the local community. An old woman was staying in his household called Guðbjörg (shortened to Gudda), who had never stayed at the same place for a long time. The latter detail is important because it created room for dispute. The Icelandic welfare system of the nineteenth century worked on the basis of origin: if a person became unable to look after themselves, the community where they had been born became liable to provide for them. The only exception to this was if a person had stayed in another community for a certain length of time, in which case the community that had become their de facto home was liable.[142]

Now Gísli found himself in the situation that people started saying that probably his community (and in practice this meant: he personally) was liable to provide for old Gudda. At this point he decided that it was high time to get rid of her. Making enquiries, he found out that the legal obligation to care for Gudda lay with the community of Selströnd on the opposite side of the fjord, where Gudda had been born; she had never stayed anywhere long enough for the legal obligation to be shifted elsewhere. So Gísli wrote to the mayor at Selströnd, informing him of his obligation to take over the

---

[141] See the section "Subversion."

[142] Jón Jónsson, pers. comm. The required length of time varied; before 1848, it was five years, and after 1848 it was extended to ten years: Gísli Gunnarsson 1990, 80.

care for Gudda. The Selströnd mayor denied that he was obliged to do so and refused to take on the old woman. Thus time went by with one mayor trying to get rid of her and the other refusing to take her on. Finally, Gísli had had enough: one morning he got up early and told his wife that he would now bring Gudda to Selströnd, whether the Selströnd mayor wanted it or not. Gudda was deeply upset and beseeched him to let her stay on his farm. Even Gísli's wife took sides with the old woman, arguing that they could afford to feed her and that she probably didn't have that long left to her anyway.

Gísli, however, would not be swayed. He had his men get a boat ready and they rowed the old woman over to Selströnd, where he put her ashore and told her to go to the mayor of Selströnd at Kleifar and to give him his regards. Gudda was furious. Swollen with anger, she told Gísli that he could not order her around any more, that she wasn't going to obey him any longer, and that she had left Þorpar unwillingly and would return there, "and it is uncertain who of us goes ashore there first."

Gísli ignored her and told his men to put to sea again and row home. When they arrived at Þorpar, they saw something floating at the beach; and on closer inspection, this turned out to be the body of old Gudda. When they found it, the corpse was still warm, and they were mystified how it could have reached Þorpar before them. Gísli now had a very bad feeling and regretted his coldness; but it was too late. Gudda was buried, but soon she started haunting Gísli and his farm. Whenever she was seen, she was creeping along on one elbow and one knee. "People said that this was because her thigh bone had been broken when she was found at the foreshore at Þorpar." The ghost, in the shape of the sea-battered corpse, has been following the members of the farming family of Þorpar ever since. "Folk belief made these stories bigger and bigger and blamed Gudda for all those mishaps that befell this extended family."[143]

The image of the ghost that, with broken bones, pursues its victims on all fours seems eerily modern and cinematographic. More to the point, it conveys a straightforward moral message in a remarkably blunt manner: those who can afford to support the poor have the obligation to do so, whatever legal technicalities may say. Playing itself out between Þorpar on the south coast and Kleifar on the north coast of Steingrímsfjörður, the story relates to a considerable geographical space, but it is grounded so specifically at the farm of Þorpar that the name of the ghost is formed as a compound of the personal

---

[143] Jón Thorarensen 1971, 1: 171–174.

128 LANDSCAPE, RELIGION, AND THE SUPERNATURAL

name of the dead woman and the place-name of the farm. This inseparably ties the ghost to the place, but it also makes the place evoke the ghost—and its moral message.

Even clearer is the connection between place and moral message in the case of Sesselja, whose story is located on the land of Kirkjuból, another farm on the south coast of Steingrímsfjörður. The story of Sesselja is short enough to give it in full. Grímur Benediktsson, who was born at Kirkjuból in 1927, told it in the following manner:[144]

> 600 m to 700 m from the shore at Hundatangi [on the land of Kirkjuból] is a skerry that is called Sesselja. The following story is told about how this name came about.
>
> A long time ago, the authorities of the district at Selströnd—which is now called Kaldrananeshreppur—sent men in a boat across Steingrímsfjörður to Kirkjuból with a pauper that the district was obliged to support (*sveitarómagi*), a girl by the name of Sesselja, about whom the authorities of the district at Selströnd said that she should be supported by the Tungusveit district. The authorities of the district in Tungusveit refused to accept the girl and they ordered the men to return with her and drove them out into the boat again and ordered them to row back.
>
> When they have come a certain distance from the land, they start discussing the quandary that they had gotten into, that they had not been able to pursue that affair that they had been instructed to take care of, and they are scared to come back again with the girl. Then they notice a skerry directly by the boat and decide to put the girl onto the skerry, and they leave her behind there. When the tide rose, the skerry was submerged and the girl drowned there.
>
> The skerry has been called Sesselja ever since.

The storyline of this folktale is very similar to that of the story of Þorpa-Gudda. There is no supernatural element and the direction of the action is inverted—here, the poor woman is brought south rather than north—but otherwise very much the same happens: the authorities in two communities on the northern and southern side of Steingrímsfjörður cannot agree on who has the duty to support a pauper, and as a result this pauper dies, even

---

[144] *SÁM* Grímur Benediktsson s.a., 3. Cf. also the version published by Gísli Jónatansson 1989, 123–124.

Fig. 2.11 The skerry Sesselja (in the center of the left half of the photograph) seen from the shore at Kirkjuból. © M. Egeler, 2019.

though both communities could easily have supported her. In the case of Þorpa-Gudda, this results in the creation of a ghost named from a place; in the case of Sesselja, it results in the creation of a place-name. Both at low tide and during storms, when the sea breaks on it in soaring plumes of spray, the skerry Sesselja is quite visible from the shore at Kirkjuból, and it has always been seen by many people, as the coastal road runs along this shore and has done so for as long as records exist (Fig. 2.11).[145] The name of the skerry is directly derived from the victim and thus memorializes the crime; thus, both the place and the name inscribe a moral code of behavior into the landscape by remembering the consequences that come to pass if this code of conduct is violated—and being located in public space, they make these consequences visible for all.

*

Just as much as adult paupers, and maybe even more so, due care for infants is a recurring theme of Strandir storytelling. One folktale of this kind is located at the farm of Víðivellir. In 1930, Jón Jóhannsson wrote an account of an event that happened to him in 1902, when he was working on a mountain meadow above the farm: while he and his father were making hay, they suddenly heard a child crying. Jón relates how the two men went to great lengths to determine the source of this crying and to ensure that every child they

---

[145] Cf. *Generalstabens Topografiske Kort*, sheet *Tröllatunga—33 Óspakseyri N.V.* (drawn 1912, published 1914).

130 LANDSCAPE, RELIGION, AND THE SUPERNATURAL

could think of was safe; but the only thing they found was that indeed everybody was safe, while the crying ultimately just disappeared and remained a mystery.[146] Another story is located at the boulder Selkollusteinn on the pass connecting Bjarnarfjörður with Steingrímsfjörður. Already in fourteenth-century hagiography, this glacial erratic is described as the place where the ghost Selkolla came into being, and this story is essentially one of child neglect. A man and a woman are tasked to bring a newly born baby girl to the church in Staður to be baptized, but at Selkollusteinn the two decide to put the baby on the ground and to take a break and have sex. While they are having sex, the infant dies and its body is taken over by an unclean spirit. Thus originates Selkolla, an unholy monstrosity that henceforth is to haunt the region to great destructive effect.[147]

Icelandic folklore, and indeed large parts of the wider Nordic cultural world, has an established type of ghostly supernatural being that results from infanticide. The historical background of this type probably lies in regional details of the conversion to Christianity. Medieval Icelandic historiography identifies the central episode of this long and complex process with a political decision made by the General Assembly in Þingvellir in the year 999/1000, when it was decided that Iceland should collectively become Christian, though certain pagan practices should, for the time being, remain legal. According to texts such as the twelfth-century *Íslendingabók* (*The Book of Icelanders*), this included the exposure of children (*barnaútburðr*).[148] This suggests that under the right circumstances the abandonment of newly born children was once an accepted practice, so firmly established before the conversion that it could be abolished only after a transition period.[149]

In the following centuries, the issue of child exposure became a lasting focus of storytelling. The word that *The Book of Icelanders* uses for the exposure of children is *barnaútburðr*, "bearing out of children." In its modern form *útburður*, "bearing out," this term is still in use, though now it primarily refers to a ghost that has come into being through such an act of infanticide by exposure. Margaret Cormack has recently proposed that the medieval Selkolla narrative "serves as a warning against infanticide,"[150] which coincides

---

[146] *SÁM* Jón Jóhannsson 1930, 5.

[147] Cormack 2018.

[148] *Íslendingabók* (ed. Jakob Benediktsson 1968, 3–28), ch. 7 (p. 17).

[149] On the exposure of children as a pre-Christian practice, cf. Lawing 2013; Mundal 1987; on the *útburður* as a supernatural being of folklore, see Cormack 2018, 84–86; Pentikäinen 1968, esp. pp. 190–224; Diljá Rut Guðmundudóttir 2016. On more recent social history, cf. Dagrún Ósk Jónsdóttir, forthcoming.

[150] Cormack 2018, 84.

TWELVE MOVEMENTS   131

with the conclusions drawn by Juha Pentikäinen in his monumental study of Nordic dead-child beings, who correlated the spread of *útburður*-stories with the condemnation of the exposure of infants by Christianity.[151] This approach offers an explanation of the historical roots of the storytelling tradition about dead-child beings; however, as the Selkolla story stands, it is not about intentional infanticide but about the consequences of gross neglect. This focus of the Selkolla story also resonates with the behavior of the protagonists in the Víðivellir memorate: the men who hear the crying do not assume that a crime has been committed, but that a child in distress needs help—upon which they in the most matter-of-course manner abandon their work to try to find the child and look after it.

This deeply felt concern for the welfare of children—any children— also recurs in other *útburður* tales in Strandir. However, not all *útburður* traditions are connected with enough narrative material to provide a basis for a detailed interpretation. At Finnbogastaðir in Árneshreppur, there was a place called Útburðarbás, "Rock Basin of the Exposed Child"; but already in the 1970s, any stories that might once have existed about Útburðarbás had been forgotten.[152] Finnbogi the Strong, the founding hero of Finnbogastaðir ("Finnbogi's-Steads"), was exposed as a child—the saga uses the words *bera út*, "bear out" (ch. 2)—but a poor man heard the crying of the baby (*barnsgrátr*), so Finnbogi was found, survived, and became a great hero (recalling and maybe alluding to the biography of Moses).[153] One wonders whether the Útburðarbás at Finnbogastaðir on some level alludes to the *bera út* that was a key moment of the biography of the farm's founding hero: *útburður* and *bera út* certainly mirror each other etymologically. Such a connection between the place on the farm and the farm's founding hero, however, is conjecture.

At Veiðileysa, likewise in Árneshreppur, there is an Útburðarhraun, "Rocky Area of the Exposed Child"; Guðbrandur Sveinn Þorláksson and Annes Þorláksson, who were both born at Veiðileysa (in 1921 and 1917, respectively), described Útburðarhraun as "a rock field of scree. It was said that a child had been exposed there (*borið út*). The track lies along it."[154] The next *útburður* site (moving south from Veiðileysa) used to be at Asparvík

---

[151] Pentikäinen 1968, 191.

[152] *SÁM* Guðrún S. Magnúsdóttir 1979a, 4; cf. *SÁM* Jóhann Hjaltason s.a. (a), 2.

[153] *Finnboga saga* (ed. Jóhannes Halldórsson 1959, 251–340), chs. 2–3. Cf. chapter 1, section "Living in Landscapes: Dwelling, Place, and Home."

[154] *SÁM* Guðrún S. Magnúsdóttir 1975a, 1, 6.

132 LANDSCAPE, RELIGION, AND THE SUPERNATURAL

in Kaldrananeshreppur, somewhere not far from the old farmhouses (though its exact location can no longer be determined). There was "a little rocky headland Einbúi, it was said that from there the wailing of an exposed child (*útburðarvæl*) could be heard, during bad weather."[155] At Svartiflói ("Black Bog") on the upland belonging to the farm of Víðidalsá in Hólmavíkurhreppur, a tradition recorded in the 1930s said "that during the pagan time a child was exposed (*borið út*) there"; this bog was notoriously bad as grassland, but there is no actual story about a haunting.[156] From the perspective of their narratives (or lack thereof), nothing much can be said about any of these places beyond that they were connected with the exposed child motif.

Much more complex are the interlinked traditions connected with the pass Ýluskarð and the valley Tungudalur, both of which are located on the south side of Steingrímsfjörður. Ýluskarð is a cleft in the mountain ridge between the valleys of Arnkötludalur and Tóftardalur that serves as a pass; it is still in regular use when sheep are herded. The sheep themselves likewise cross the mountain at this point, and do so with such frequency that their hoofsteps have created a clearly visible track that serves as a fine substitute for a human-made footpath. The name Ýluskarð means "Pass (or cleft) of Howling." Probably it was coined with reference to the wind which does indeed howl through Ýluskarð, as this cleft forms a natural wind channel whose winds, even on an otherwise quiet day, can be quite remarkable. Of all the *útburður* sites of Strandir, Ýluskarð is the one associated with the most detailed narrative traditions. Thus, around the middle of the twentieth century, Jóhann Hjaltason wrote:[157]

> [I]t is said that it receives its name from this, that in the past a child was exposed there (*borið út*). This exposed child (*útburður*) cannot be heard wailing there any longer, but knowledgeable and truthful people these days rather say that they have seen a light there which did not look natural.

The apparitions of lights that Jóhann mentions recur in at least one other testimony. Þorgeir Þorsteinsson had farmed the nearby farm of Hrófá from 1922 to 1954; in an interview conducted in the 1970s, he stated that he had seen the unnatural lights on the pass with his own eyes:[158]

---

[155] *SÁM* Jóhannes Jónsson s.a., 2.
[156] *SÁM* Stefán Pálsson 1934, 3.
[157] *SÁM* Jóhann Hjaltason s.a. (b), 3.
[158] *SÁM* Guðrún S. Magnúsdóttir 1978e, 4.

Ýluskarð, it was said there is an exposed child (*útburður*) there. Þorgeir saw a light there close around midnight, and that could not have been from natural causes.

The child (or children) thought to have haunted Ýluskarð are the only *útburður* beings in Strandir whose parentage is identified in the local storytelling tradition: "There the children of that Keralín were exposed (*borin út*), who lived at Kerasteinn by Tungudalur."[159] This Keralín was a famously unpopular person thought to have lived at one of the long-abandoned farms in Tungudalur. It seems rather puzzling from their location on the map why the storytelling tradition associates Ýluskarð and Tungudalur, as they are not contiguous but separated by the valley of Arnkötludalur. At the place itself, however, a connection is established by the local lines of sight: when one walks down from Ýluskarð on the eastern side of the mountain, one naturally faces exactly toward the entrance of Tungudalur, which one keeps in the center of one's view during almost the whole descent. The association between Ýluskarð and the inhabitants of Tungudalur was thus probably suggested by the experience of walking the track over the pass.

Tungudalur is connected with a number of traditions, of which the former residency of Keralín is the most prominent. Gísli Jónatansson (1904–1992), who lived at the nearby farm of Naustavík and was an important figure in the collection of Steingrímsfjörður folklore, in the mid-1980s wrote the following about this Keralín:[160]

Kerasteinn was the name of a farmstead pretty far towards the front of Tungudalur valley. It is told in stories about it that a man by the name of Eiríkur Keralín lived there. He is said to have been somewhat strange and was not popular. One thing was that he was said to have exposed (*borið út*) his children.

Once a guest is said to have come there, and then he hears the crying of a child, and he hears Eiríkur saying: "Somebody has to look after the child now that it has been allowed to live." Such is the folktale about this man, who was not popular. I think that the story may perfectly well have been the other way round, that they did not have fully developed children, and because people did not like this person, that it was then believed that

---

[159] Jón Kr. Guðmundsson 1989, 15.
[160] Gísli Jónatansson 1985, 128.

134 LANDSCAPE, RELIGION, AND THE SUPERNATURAL

he exposed (*borið út*) his children. And so as soon as this child was born healthier than the others, it lived with them, then he wanted to have it looked after well, now that destiny had let it live.

The way Gísli told and discussed the story again mirrors the ethos that was so fundamental for the memorate about the child's crying at Víðivellir. There, the men who had heard the crying had immediately dropped their work to find and help the child; here, the exposure of children is a misdeed associated with a cliché villain whose habit of infanticide correlates with his universal unpopularity. Intriguingly, furthermore, Gísli did not stop after reporting the common view that Keralín was a strange and unpopular man and a child murderer. Rather, he proposed a rereading of a traditional anecdote in which a seeming confession to infanticide is reinterpreted as an expression of the grief of a couple plagued by premature deliveries and stillbirths. When, in an anecdote told about him, Keralín says, "Somebody has to look after the child now that it has been allowed to live," this was commonly taken to mean that he had killed all others; yet Gísli suggested that it rather reflected his care for his only surviving child after all the others had been born before they were able to live. This take on the figure of Keralín is interesting not least because it shows how unimaginable the idea of the exposure of children seemed to Gísli: it is something that cannot even be ascribed to a traditional bogeyman. The default attitude is to look after children; and this is so ingrained that a contrasting foil becomes implausible even as part of a creepy story.

Thus, in sum, it seems that the *útburður* traditions of Strandir are dominated by an outlook that privileges care for children to the virtual exclusion of any other possibilities. Earlier, I mentioned Cormack's and Pentikäinen's approach to the moral interpretation of *útburður* tales, who classically read them as moral-spiritual warnings against infanticide and the exposure of children, and as a way to teach a half-pagan population the values of Christianity.[161] Within the modern storytelling tradition of Strandir, this function plays hardly any role any more: as Gísli Jónatansson's treatment of the Keralín story shows, the idea of infanticide is anathema to such a degree that it even loses its plausibility as a charge brought forward against a villain. Yet even so, these stories still seem to carry an echo of the original moral message of the *útburður* motif. The *útburður* traditions of Strandir inscribe the infant's suffering into the landscape and thus provide a constant

---

[161] See earlier; Cormack 2018, 84; Pentikäinen 1968, 191.

reminder of the duty of care that adults have for children. The example of the protagonists of the stories shows how adults are expected to behave: hearing an *útburður* crying first and foremost inspires an urgent desire to find and help the crying child.

Social responsibility here is lifted onto a supernatural plane, and correct behavior is exemplified by place-lore and made part of everyday space. For the locations of the ghostly crying children of Strandir are closely intertwined with everyday life: the Einbúi at Asparvík was located in the immediate vicinity of the old farm buildings; Svartiflói was partially mown and thus visited in the context of agricultural work; Selkollusteinn marks an important pass, just as Ýluskarð is an important bottleneck for shepherding; Útburðarhraun in Veiðileysa was located by the side of a path. Overwhelmingly, the *útburður* places of Strandir are located either in the immediate vicinity of dwellings—and thus were seen literally on a daily basis—or on roads, paths, and tracks, which would equally have ensured regular encounters. This made their "message" part of daily experience and the places themselves part of how this message was naturalized—which they did so successfully that the act they were originally meant to warn against stopped being plausible even as a crime.

*

In his study of landscape, place-names, and storytelling among the Western Apache, Basso on one occasion uses the metaphor of an abandoned theater stage to describe the effect that Apache place-lore has on the landscape it is connected with: the rich corpus of stories that are told about the land fill it with lively associations of a colorful cast of characters that once acted out these stories, and the land itself becomes "something resembling a theater, a natural stage upon the land (vacant now but with props still fully intact) where significant moral dramas unfolded in the past."[162] Almost exactly the same could be said about the landscape of Strandir—with the main difference perhaps that this northern stage in some cases not only consists of the props, but still contains the actors as well. When Jón Jóhannsson heard the spectral crying at Víðivellir in 1902 and Þorgeir Þorsteinsson in the 1970s spoke about how he saw the otherworldly lights at the "Pass of Howling," or when the ghost Þorpa-Gudda was blamed for all manner of accidents and mishaps at least until very recently, then the landscape of Strandir appears as a place where moral lessons were enacted not just in the deep past in order

---

[162] Basso 1996, 120–121 (quotation: p. 121).

136   LANDSCAPE, RELIGION, AND THE SUPERNATURAL

to be quoted in the present, but where this enactment, shifted onto the plane of the supernatural, continued well into the lived experience of the twentieth century. Some of this experience may even still be alive: the ghost of Feykishólar, who came into being through rape and murder and whose story will be pursued in another section, only recently drew attention back to himself by sabotaging the engines of two brand-new quad bikes.[163] The misdeeds of the past seem to echo through the rocks of mountains and shore alike, to be audible and visible even in the present if one has ears to hear and eyes to see. The wind still howls through the "Howling Pass" where the ghost of the dead infant used to cry, and even if one cannot identify the note of a cry in the noise of the wind, when exposed to it, not only visiting researchers but also locals are prompted to think of the story.

The preceding pages have reviewed traditional tales about the suffering inflicted on the poor by the unwillingness of the rich to fulfill their social duties, and of ghosts created when adults neglected their duty of care toward infants. In the Strandir landscape, these stories are made deeply present by their close connection with often very public places, including the network of roads and bridle paths whose importance for the supernatural landscape I highlighted in the preceding section. It appears that this presencing of such narratives is so strong that it can create convictions that the ghosts of past crimes have indeed been encountered. Whatever it was that Jón Jóhannsson "really" heard and Þorgeir Þorsteinsson "really" saw, they had experiences that they interpreted through the lens of traditional narratives; and this in turn means that, from their perspective, they had experienced the story. In this sense (which is all that matters for a scholarly investigation) these narratives remained "real" and present at least well into the twentieth century, and this very reality must have been a central element that gave them the power to naturalize their moral perspective. Maybe this subjectively experienced reality was the reason why this naturalization of their moral perspective was so effective that Keralín's infanticide in the end could be declared not only an abomination, but actually unimaginable and untrue. This self-dissolution of the narrative may well be the ultimate victory of the establishment of a moral system through landscape storytelling.

[163] Ingþór Ólafsson, pers. comm. Cf. section "Subversion."

5: Labor

The English word "landscape," as already highlighted in the introduction, is a loanword that has its origin in the Dutch term *landschap*; originally it was borrowed into English as a technical term of painting.[164] This origin in the world of (expensive, imported) art has accommodated the word in a context of "high culture" that it has never quite managed to shake off. Its roots in art and the culture of the middle and upper classes still reverberate when Simon Schama in his classic *Landscape and Memory* approaches landscape as a "work of the mind" that he investigates with recourse to hundreds of drawings, paintings, and prints,[165] or when Rachael Ziady DeLue and James Elkins present their attempt at a synthesis of landscape theory in, of all places, *The Art Seminar*.[166] Another consequence of this origin is that certain aspects of the human engagement with the landscape have been sorely neglected. Rather counterintuitively, since there are few things more solid and material than the landscape, this is particularly true for the physical engagement with the land. Tim Ingold defined *"landscape* [. . .] *as the taskscape in its embodied form,"*[167] that is, as an embodiment of the work and tasks that make up everyday working life, or in other words: as a physical place of physical labor. Yet this physical, labor-focused approach did not catch on. More than a decade after Ingold's definition Christopher Tilley and Wayne Bennett still had to note:[168]

> In virtually all the academic literature it is quite striking how disembodied written landscapes become. This is because virtually everything written about landscape is not only written on paper; it is principally derived from paper. Landscape is not bodily experienced; it becomes a variable historical or social discourse principally derived from maps, paintings, archives, and texts. Being "out there," bodily sensing place and relationships between places has hardly been that much on the agenda.

---

[164] *OED* s.v. "landscape, n."; see chapter 1, section "Landscape, Religion, and the Supernatural: Introduction to Theories and Concepts."

[165] Schama 1996, quotation: p. 7. Incidentally, his phrase of the landscape as a work of the mind was already anticipated by Georg Simmel (1913, n. p.: "ein geistiges Gebilde"), who in his writings on landscape (1885; 1913) likewise strongly focuses on its representations in and perception in the manner of art.

[166] DeLue and Elkins 2008.

[167] Ingold 1993, 162 (emphasis original).

[168] Tilley and Bennett 2004, 27.

138 LANDSCAPE, RELIGION, AND THE SUPERNATURAL

More than fifteen years after its first publication, this observation still stands: landscape is still approached primarily through highly encephalized metaphors like "meaning," "text," "orientation," or even "power," all of which have their value and justification but are largely blind to the physicality of the landscape. Even Robert Macfarlane, who approaches "landscape" through a combination of physical engagement and literature, still strongly focuses on intellectual metaphors like "memory."[169] Arguably, this perspective, which is pervasive throughout Macfarlane's writings, correlates with the specific shape that his physical encounter with the landscape assumes: Macfarlane consistently approaches the landscape through activities like hiking, walking, and camping, which are ultimately recreational in character. Thus, his approach has remained caught up in a middle-class world of leisure that, when all is said and done, is more about reading and daydreaming than about physical necessity.

The present section aims to fill this lacuna by highlighting an element that in Strandir is as pervasive as it is neglected in current theorizing: the close link between the supernatural and the experience of physical labor in the landscape. Ingold is one of the few scholars to have intuited the importance of this experience: "A place owes its character to the experiences it affords to those who spend time there. [...] And these, in turn, depend on the kinds of activities in which its inhabitants engage. [...] Thus whereas with space, meanings are *attached to* the world, with the landscape they are *gathered from* it."[170] In Strandir, the most important experience afforded by the land is the experience of labor, and this in turn fundamentally colors the experience of the supernatural. Encounters with the supernatural generally do not happen in contexts of leisure or during intellectual pursuits, but almost invariably in contexts of labor; and even where the encounter itself does not happen in a work context, it is at least told as if it does. The trolls that inhabit the mountains are encountered not during leisurely hikes, but when shepherds stumble over their lairs because they are searching for lost animals. An *álagablettur* brings its curse down onto a farm not when one has a picnic there, but when it is disturbed by agricultural work. The ghost of a child abandoned in the wilderness is heard crying when one is out in this wilderness to cut some grass.

---

[169] Macfarlane 2018, 101; Macfarlane 2008 (2003), 18.
[170] Ingold 1993, 155.

TWELVE MOVEMENTS   139

This section takes a story set in the uplands on the south coast of Steingrímsfjörður to pursue the link between labor and the supernatural through a group of interconnected examples relating to hay making, sheep husbandry, and the procuration of food. This investigation, during which we will encounter some exceptionally bad agricultural land as well as a range of mostly satanic supernatural beings, will show that the devil is in the details, and that those details tend to be work-related.

*

The story that stands in the center of this section is a tale by Guðmundur Jónsson from Selbekk (1904–1977). Guðmundur was an expansive story-teller devoted to detail, which makes a close reading of his story particularly revealing: Guðmundur's delight in storytelling and his concomitant attention to the minutiae of the progress of the plot means that many aspects of the storyline are made unusually explicit.

The story in question is called "Going for Iceland Moss (Who Called upon My Mother?)." This narrative presents itself as a kind of second-hand memorate: it tells of an event that happened to Guðmundur's mother when he was a young boy, so the incident told in the story would have taken place around 1910. At the time, Guðmundur and his family were living on the south coast of Steingrímsfjörður at Tungugröf farm, which is now abandoned. Remembering life there, Guðmundur tells his tale:[171]

> I want to talk about a little event that took place on a trip to collect Iceland moss that they went on, my mother, who was called Kristín, and Sigríður, a woman who was living with her, one spring evening to be productive and for fun. The weather was such that it was calm but hill fog shrouded the mountains all the way to the foothills, but in the lowland it was free of fog; grey weather but with the warmth of spring. The birdsong echoed with such wondrous gentleness in the good weather.
>
> The women could not resist the temptation and met up in order to go to the mountains and to get moss for themselves to make the food last longer for the homestead, as Iceland moss was and is considered wholesome and nourishing food. [. . .] The route which the women took to the moss lay di-agonally from Tungugröf westwards over Hrófá river, which separates the lands of Tungugröf and of Hrófá, and on the land of Hrófá was the place

---

[171] Jón Kr. Guðmundsson 1989, 14–16.

140   LANDSCAPE, RELIGION, AND THE SUPERNATURAL

that they wanted to get to, in the so-called Tóttardalur* valley. There they had gotten permission to gather moss from the farmer at Hrófá. So they went where the path lay across Hrófá and up along the brook which is called Ásendalækur. It comes from a shieling which is called Hrófársel. As soon as it reaches the shieling, there is a short stretch of way from there up a tilted, forested slope. There Álftaskarð ("Pass/Cleft of Swans") takes over, which cuts apart the belt of cliffs that lies all the way south on Bæjardalsheiði and is called Hrófáreggjar. The milk ewes were always driven over this pass and shepherded further up in Tóttardalur, and in this manner one also went with the train of horses that transported the hay through this pass, Álftaskarð ("Pass/Cleft of Swans"), which I think was correctly called Álfaskarð ("Pass/ Cleft of Elves"), named after old dwelling-places of elves. Not far from it is another pass in an extremely steep rocky slope of scree. That is called Ýluskarð ("Pass/Cleft of Howling"). There the children of that Keralín were abandoned, who lived at Kerasteinn at Tungudalur valley.

When the women came into Álfaskarð (that is Álftaskarð), they continued westwards along the belt of cliffs for around 15 minutes. Then they had come to the grassland directly below Ýluskarð. Once they had got there, they started to gather the moss; there was enough of it. They were quick to each fill their bag. And when they were done with that, they sat down and got themselves a bite of the provisions that they had with them.

As told earlier, there was a soot-black fog all the way down to the feet of the mountains. While the women were eating their bite, they heard my mother called two times. *Kristín* was said clearly with such a dark and unspeakable voice that they were given a fright. They both said there could be no question of it being a human voice. No human being could have such a voice. There is also not much likelihood that an ordinary person would be there on their way up on the edge of the mountain during that time in spring. If anybody had gone along the lower valley, then they would have seen him and met him, and from above nobody would have seen them because of the fog. Neither of them answered the call, they hurried away homewards on the same route they had come and did not become aware of anything on their way. With that this short story ends. It tells about one such phenomenon that we do not have an explanation for.

* Tóttardalur is an alternative spelling of Tóftardalur. (ME)

What lends this story its importance in the present context is the explicit connections that it establishes between supernatural places or experiences

TWELVE MOVEMENTS 141

and everyday work. The two women who go and have a spectral encounter are out, but not just for fun: "to be productive and for fun" ("sér til gagns og gamans") they venture into the mountains to gather Iceland moss, which was valued as a food item that, for instance, could be ground into a substitute for flour.[172] As the story puts it, the women wanted "to make the food last longer for the homestead." This allows a glimpse of the poverty and an everyday experience of scarcity that underlies their actions. Importantly, this poverty not only accompanies but drives the action. The supernatural is encountered during work (food gathering) that facilitates the fulfillment of basic needs.

In the story, the connection between this work and the encounter with the supernatural is reflected not only in the overarching plot of the narrative but also in Guðmundur's musings on Álftaskarð. He describes the real-world use of Álftaskarð ("Pass/Cleft of Swans") in great detail: it is used for sheep husbandry in order to access a valley suitable for shepherding ewes that were being milked—at the time, sheep were kept also as dairy animals—which happens to be the same valley where the two women gather Iceland moss and encounter the supernatural voice; and the pass was also used for transporting hay made in the uplands down to the farms. So the pass is important for farming and food production; and for this pass, Guðmundur proposes a reinterpretation which "corrects" its established name Álftaskarð ("Pass/Cleft of Swans") to Álfaskarð ("Pass/Cleft of Elves"), interpreting the rocky landscape in the vicinity of the pass as filled with elf rocks. So here again, a place of work is made a place of the supernatural, and in Guðmundur's expansive narration both aspects of the place are explicitly expounded.

Guðmundur's reinterpretation of Álftaskarð as Álfaskarð witnesses to a desire to maximize the presence of supernatural entities in the landscape: his story is the only testimony that I am aware of to name this a "Pass of Elves," whereas otherwise it is universally known as "Pass of Swans." In a way which is entirely idiosyncratic but the more interesting for that, Guðmundur takes a "normal" place of everyday working life and turns it into a place inhabited by supernatural beings. Since his interpretation of Álftaskarð as Álfaskarð is clearly (and in fact explicitly) nontraditional, this throws some doubt on how traditional his idea of a "dark and unspeakable voice" below Ýluskarð is. As we saw in the discussion of útburður narratives, Ýluskarð is traditionally haunted, but by the spectral crying of infants or by preternatural lights.[173]

---

[172] Jón Jónsson, pers. comm.
[173] For the attestations see the section "Morality."

142 LANDSCAPE, RELIGION, AND THE SUPERNATURAL

In Guðmundur's story, what is heard there is a terrifying dark voice—which seems a very unbabylike phenomenon and is certainly something that no *útburður* in Strandir is ever said to produce. Hence Guðmundur's story may be just that: his own—or his mother's—personal invention. This, however, does not devalue it as a testimony; rather, it makes it particularly relevant as a witness to the genesis of a tradition, even if it is one which may not have caught on. For in this story, we can observe how a place comes to be associated with the supernatural, by taking somewhere important for everyday work and telling a story about it which somehow relates to its name or surroundings—just as Tim Ingold highlighted how the meanings ascribed to places in the landscape are derived from the experiences that people have there. Tóftardalur, where the inhuman voice is heard, lies at the foot of Ýluskarð, which is a firmly established haunted place; Álftaskarð is surrounded by cliffs that can be interpreted as inhabited by elves, as so many other cliffs in Strandir are. To put it in a more abstract manner: the landscape is filled with supernatural associations by taking places important for everyday labor and connecting them with motifs adapted from the established stock of motifs of local traditional storytelling.

Another aspect of Guðmundur's narrative that contributes to making it an exceptionally striking example of local storytelling is how it takes up patterns already established in traditional stories located close by. From Álftaskarð, especially from the cairn that, perched on top of a massive rock outcrop, overlooks Álftaskarð, one has a wide vista in many directions. Looking south, Tóftardalur opens up, where Guðmundur's mother went to gather Iceland moss. Directly to the west, across the glen carved by the Víðidalsá River, one looks over Álftatungur, a small mountain that acts as a wedge bifurcating the valley of Víðidalur. And beyond the tip of Álftatungur on the opposite side of Víðidalur, one sees a broad, gently sloping expanse of grassland, maybe a kilometer long and a third as broad. This grassland is Púkabreið. The name Púkabreið could roughly be translated as "Devil's Broadlands." The devil of this grassland is not Satan himself, however, but rather an under-devil, a *púki*; or as Richard Cleasby and Guðbrandur Vigfússon translate the term: "a wee devil, an imp."[174]

Icelandic *púki* is essentially the same word as Irish *púca*, Welsh *pwci*, and English *puck*.[175] Etymologically, *púki* and its cognates seem to be a Germanic

---

[174] Cleasby and Gudbrand Vigfusson 1874, s.v. "púki."
[175] *eDIL* s.v. "púca"; Ó Dónaill 1977, s.v. "púca"; *OED* s.v. "puck, n.1"; Breatnach 1993.

TWELVE MOVEMENTS 143

word that spread into the Celtic languages of Irish and Welsh, though a final consensus has not yet been achieved.[176] However that may be, the figure of the *púki* has had tremendous international success in both place-names and storytelling. The Irish *púca* haunts Irish folklore,[177] with Irish places named after it, such as the Róidín an Phúca, the "Little Road of the Pooka," on the Aran Island of Inishmore,[178] and it has been immortalized in Anglo-Irish literature by many writers, including literary giants such as W. B. Yeats.[179] In England, Puck is one of the mischievous main protagonists of Shakespeare's *Midsummer Night's Dream*, and especially in southern England he is richly attested in place-names at least since the twelfth century.[180]

Púkabreið belongs to the farm Víðidalsá. When Stefán Pálsson, who had been born at Víðidalsá in 1907 and had lived there for the first fifty-three years of his life, was interviewed about his former farm in the 1970s, he stated:[181]

It was said that there was a small supernatural presence (*smáslæðingur*) in Púkabreið. There was land where grass was harvested, not worse than elsewhere in the surroundings.

A *slæðingur* is an amorphous, impersonal supernatural presence or force which does not have a specific name or personality; hence, Púkabreið emerges as a somewhat unspecific site of the supernatural.[182] Another half-century after Stefán's statement, ideas about Púkabreið become somewhat more concrete. Unnar Ragnarsson, who as a young lad, around 1970, had worked at Víðidalsá, connects the name of "Púki's Broadlands" with a tradition about how one of the farmers of Víðidalsá once made a *púki* do his bidding: this man, who had some knowledge of magic, had the work of harvesting the grass on Púkabreið done by a *púki*.[183]

If one visits Púkabreið, it is boggily obvious why anybody having to cut the grass there would either wish it on the devil or, preferably, make a devil do their work for them. A *breið* is a broad, flattish, normally grassy stretch

---

[176] Germanic origin: *OED* s.v. "puck, n.1." Sebo 2017 argues for an Irish origin.
[177] Breatnach 1993.
[178] Robinson 1996a, 31. Cf. also Hogan and Ó Corráin 2017, nos 3698, 4604, 5578, 6369, 9758.
[179] Yeats 1888, 94–107.
[180] *OED* s.v. "puck, n.1."
[181] *SÁM* Guðrún S. Magnúsdóttir 1978b, 6. Cf. *SÁM* Stefán Pálsson 1934, 7.
[182] Jón Jónsson, pers. comm.
[183] Pers. comm., 2019.

Fig. 2.12 Grassland and water mingling on Púkabreið. The water in the pools that sprinkle Púkabreið is bog water of a deep rust-red color. © M. Egeler, 2019.

of land,[184] and Púkabreið is all of that; but it is also soggy and riddled with water-filled sinkholes (Fig. 2.12). While Stefán remarks that it is "no worse than elsewhere in the surroundings," the combination of something devilish and grassland that was very wet but still had to be worked forms a recurring pattern—also "elsewhere in the surroundings." If one follows the stream that runs past Púkabreið further up into the mountains for about 3.5 km, one reaches Svartiflói. In a description of his farm that he wrote in the 1930s, Stefán Pálsson gave the following information about Svartiflói ("Black Bog"):[185]

> The name has certainly come about from the way that the grass on it seems so black, and therefore this bog is never mown as a whole. Traditional stories report that during the pagan time a child was abandoned there.

As with Púkabreið, Svartiflói, too, is a piece of grassland where grass had to be cut because it was needed, but which was unpleasantly waterlogged, which

---

[184] Jón Jónsson, pers. comm.
[185] *SÁM* Stefán Pálsson 1934, 3.

TWELVE MOVEMENTS   145

both reduced the yield of the land and, one guesses, did not make working there any more pleasant. In both places, this combination of necessity and bad conditions correlated with a connection with an uncanny supernatural presence: at Púkabreið an imp, and at Svartiflói a pagan infanticide, which often led to a haunting by the ghost of the murdered child.[186]

Similar material recurs also in other parts of Strandir. Thus, a very wet piece of land on Hlaðhamar farm in Bæjarhreppur was called Satansflói, "Satan's Bog."[187] On the lands of Stóra-Hvalsá, also in Bæjarhreppur, we meet another Púki: "Above Selbrún there is a wet bog that is called Púki. May mean that one cannot cross it anywhere."[188] At Bræðrabrekka in Bitrufjörður, there is a notably putrid bog that again is simply called Púki.[189] It seems that these places got a devilish name in order to reflect that they were a nuisance. In fact, good parallel material exists which indicates that places could be named just because they were particularly annoying. A description of the farm of Drangar in Árneshreppur by Eiríkur Guðmundsson, who had lived there for almost sixty years from 1895 to 1953, contains the following passage:[190]

> Pretty far down in the valley is a large bit of bogland that is called Óberjuflói ("Yieldless Bog"). Grass was cut there, but the piece of land will have gotten its name from the fact that it was uneven and difficult to cut. Reasonably good meadow lands without names lay to both sides of it.

There is nothing supernatural in this example. Rather, what gives this passage its importance is the seemingly offhand remark that the "Yieldless Bog" Óberjuflói was flanked by much better meadows that did not have names of their own. The land was named by the people who worked it; and what seems to have happened here is that the thoughts of these laborers focused not necessarily on the good pieces of land, but—maybe in dreading anticipation— on the bad ones; and thus the bad ones got precedence in naming and storytelling.

Returning from this detour to some of the worst grasslands of Strandir, we return to our starting point, Guðmundur Jónsson's story about "Going for Iceland Moss." Again and again throughout this story, the supernatural

---

[186] See the section "Morality."
[187] *SÁM* Guðrún S. Magnúsdóttir 1977a, 4–5.
[188] *SÁM* Guðrún S. Magnúsdóttir 1977b, 6. Cf. *SÁM* Jóhann Hjaltason s.a. (e), 4.
[189] Jón Jónsson, pers. comm.
[190] *SÁM* Guðrún Magnúsdóttir 1974b, 13.

146 LANDSCAPE, RELIGION, AND THE SUPERNATURAL

experience is set into the context of food production and agricultural labor. The occasion for the incident is a trip to gather a food supplement; and for most places involved in the story, Guðmundur explains how they are related to agriculture, especially sheep husbandry. Álftaskarð, which he idiosyncratically turns into a "Pass of the Elves" Álfaskarð, was an important place for crossing the mountains with sheep and hay, and Tóftardalur, where the ghostly voice was heard, was a place to gather Iceland moss and where milk ewes spent parts of the summer. The one key place of the story for which Guðmundur does not specify its everyday use, Ýluskarð, likewise is an important crossing place for sheep and serves this purpose to this day. And outside the story but in the immediate vicinity of its geographical setting, Púkabreið and Svartiflói provide further illustrations for how places that are a nuissance to work get stories that reflect their negative characteristics (Map 2.3).

All this material shows a direct link between practices of labor and the supernatural. Agricultural labor, it seems, is not all work and no play, but rather is interspersed with the odd imp, ghost, elf, and gruesome ancient murder. This brings us back to a few words in Guðmundur Jónsson's story that one could easily miss, but which are deeply representative of Icelandic attitudes to storytelling about the supernatural. When Guðmundur describes why his mother and her friend set out on their trip, he gives a double motivation: "to be productive and for fun" ("sér til gagns og gamans")—their outing is not just hard work driven by the necessity to stretch the farm's failing food supply a bit longer, but they also want *gaman*: fun. This Icelandic talent to see the fun in work has also been remarked on by outsiders. In 1936, Jean Young, an Icelandicist and lecturer in English at Reading University, spent a summer in Iceland and on one occasion, while everybody was waiting for the hay to dry some more, dashed off a letter in which she highlighted this Icelandic ability to find *gaman* in everything:[191]

> Then I made hay—turned over the cocks to air & dry—but there's little to do yet so I'm scribbling to you instead. They say they're going to cart the hay after dinner (it's just on 12. now). One thing I've noticed about Icelanders— they use the word "gaman" so much. It seems to mean our "fun." Everything tends to be "fun" here—washing, and hay-making, and everyday work as well as travelling about.

[191] Young 1992, 22 (letter dated 20 July 1936).

TWELVE MOVEMENTS   147

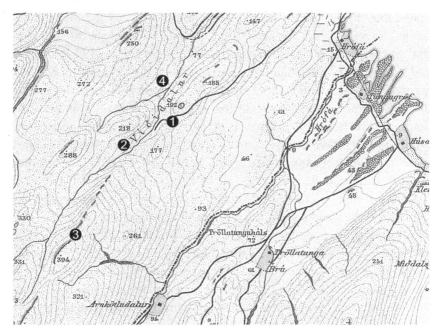

Map 2.3 The story landscape of "Going for Iceland Moss." 1: Álftaskarð/ Álfaskarð. 2: Tóftardalur/Tóttardalur. 3: Ýluskarð. 4: Púkabreið. Base map: section of *Generalstabens Topografiske Kort*, sheet *Tröllatunga—33 Óspakseyri N.V.* (drawn 1912, published 1914). Svartiflói is not marked, as it is located in a valley which is missing on the historical map. It is located c. 1.4 km west-northwest of Ýluskarð and c. 3.5 km southwest of Púkabreið, and can be reached by simply following the river that flows past Púkabreið from the southwest. This river continues for a long distance beyond the point where it ends on the map, flowing through a valley of its own.

Guðmundur's story about his mother is about work with a strong supernatural accompaniment, and maybe while the sheep and the Iceland moss are the "productive use" (*gagn*), the supernatural provides the "fun" (*gaman*). There seems to be a deep connection between everyday practices of labor and the supernatural in the landscape, but this connection does not always have to be deeply serious. Sometimes, it seems, the supernatural simply provides a mental respite from the exertion of labor, a way to add a punchline to the story of the landscape which otherwise would be a very dreary narrative that could easily be all about trying to eke a tiny bit more of food out of an unforgiving land.

*

148 LANDSCAPE, RELIGION, AND THE SUPERNATURAL

Places like the "Púki's Broadlands," the "Black Bog," or the "Pass of the Swans" turned "Pass of the Elves" show a close link between the supernatural in the landscape and practices of labor. Maybe sites like Púkabreið and Svartiflói are particularly good examples of this connection between landscape, labor, and the supernatural just because their experience is so underwhelming and so completely free of any notions of the "sublime" as it dominates the Romantic aesthetics of landscape:[192] where the supernatural is found in a sodden, boggy hayfield, supernatural storytelling seems like a direct reaction to the experience of cutting half-rotten grass while standing ankle-deep in mud.

Such storytelling can be quite drastic. Hveramýri, the "Bog of the Hot Springs" on the land of Krossness farm in Árneshreppur, was considered an *álagablettur* that one violated at one's own peril. In 1969, part of it was leveled off and integrated into the farm's home-field—and local tradition saw this as the reason for why the farmhouse of Krossness burned down in 1971.[193] The worst land can attract the most dramatic story—maybe because it is exactly this land which provokes the strongest emotional reaction if one has to work it: to hell with it!

This strong reaction to the experience of *working* the land underlines the fundamental point of this section: landscape is not only, to quote once more Schama's influential phrase, a "work of the mind" that is built up "from strata of memory," nor is it primarily—as again Schama puts it—"a text on which generations write their recurring obsessions."[194] Rather, the landscape is also the work of the hands and the stomping ground of the feet of the laborers and farmers who make their living from it: as Leslie Marmon Silko emphasized from an indigenous Pueblo perspective, the landscape is a place in which one has to survive.[195] Survival on an everyday level means farming, and the resulting work determines what parts of the land are used, how it is used and experienced, and often what it looks like. Farmland is very rarely close to its "natural" state: even on a very basic physical level, it is a creation of human culture. As Tilley and Bennett have highlighted in the passage quoted at the beginning of this section,[196] current writing on landscape—including the relationship of the landscape to religion and the supernatural—tends to be

[192] See section "Emotions."
[193] Úlfar Örn Hjartarson, pers. comm.
[194] Schama 1996, 6–7, 12. See section "Time and Memory."
[195] Silko 1996, 268, 273.
[196] Tilley and Bennett 2004, 27.

overly encephalized. The close, hands-on focus of Strandir storytelling on the minutiae of the agricultural workflow can add an important corrective to many highly abstract approaches to landscape that foreground "mental" concepts like memory or focus on textual metaphors. Approaches that take their starting point from concepts like "memory" and "text" tend to be at their most powerful when used to investigate the experience of parts of the population that are separated from the land as a basic means of existence, and it is this section of society—the urban middle class—that much theorizing has focused on.

The issue highlighted here parallels the experience that James Rebanks, a sheep farmer in the English Lake District, recently expressed in his *A Shepherd's Life* (2015). Growing up and going to school in the Lake District, it struck him already as a school boy that in the perception of the English educated public, and even in how the teacher at his local school tried to teach the children of local farmers, the Lake District has become a landscape of poets, painters, and walkers, while the sheep farmers who actually live in and have created the landscape of the Lake District are almost completely excluded from the picture. This led Rebanks, as a Lake District native, to raise the very justified question: "How come the story of our landscape wasn't about us?"[197] His experience of his landscape had much less to do with poetry than with sheep and making hay, and much the same is true of the supernatural landscape of Strandir: it is very much about sheep and making hay, or to put it more generally, about the everyday processes of labor.

One last example may illustrate the importance of this link. It again highlights the role of boggy grass fields for the experience of the supernatural but does so from a somewhat different angle. Jón Árnason's collection of folklore contains a text that Björn Björnsson of Klúka on Bjarnarfjörður wrote about an incident said to have happened on the neighboring farm of Ásmundarnes in 1855, not long before the account was written.[198] More importantly, in this year, Björn Björnsson farmed at Ásmundarnes, so his report concerns an occurrence that happened while he was at home there.[199] At Ásmundarnes, it used to be the job of a young boy to fetch the sheep from the mountain pasture in the evening—they were penned overnight to make milking easier—and one evening it got rather late and dark. The boy penned

---

[197] Rebanks 2015, esp. pp. xiv–xvi, xviii. Quotation: p. xviii.
[198] Jón Árnason 1954–1961, 3: 16, 626.
[199] Jón Jónsson, pers. comm.

150 LANDSCAPE, RELIGION, AND THE SUPERNATURAL

the sheep and then went home, and on the very last part of his way to the farmhouse he experienced the following:[200]

> The path on which he went lies by a stone there, and it is a way that is in general use. He then came a little to his right up to the stone and sees two men standing there. One of them supported himself against the stone, and the other was halfway bent over, tying his shoe, and supported himself with his backside against the stone, and they seemed to be wet on the feet and bog-red. The boy became afraid to see these men, and that so suddenly when he did not expect anybody; he therefore ran as fast as he could, until he came home and saw the couple, his parents, who were waiting for him. He was then very exhausted and crying. They asked him what ailed him. He then told the story as it appears to him. They were thought to have been men of the elves (*álfamenn*) going home from the meadows.

Not only is the experience of working the wet grass fields formative for the creation of a supernatural landscape, but it also shapes the imagined life-worlds of the supernatural beings that inhabit this landscape: in the evening, even the elves go home with their feet wet and their clothes stained by the reddish-brown water of the bogs.

6: Playfulness and Adventure

When Thomas A. Tweed formulated his spatially focused theory of religion, the first qualifier he used to describe the function of religions was that they "intensify joy": "*Religions are confluences of organic-cultural flows that intensify joy* [. . .]."[201] Tweed closely connects this focus on joy with another function he postulates, and according to which religions "confront suffering." The common denominator, he argues, lies in a close involvement of religions with emotion.[202] Such a role Tweed in turn sees as a pointer to "why religions are satisfying to adherents."[203] Among the aspects of this role that Tweed specifically highlights, one is the impact that religions have on the way human beings experience the encounter with their environment:[204]

[200] Jón Árnason 1954–1961, 3: 16.
[201] Tweed 2006, 54 (emphasis original).
[202] Tweed 2006, 69–72.
[203] Tweed 2006, 70.
[204] Tweed 2006, 72.

Religions provide ways for humans to imagine and enhance the joys associated with the encounter with the environment [...]. Humans want something to say and do in the face of wonder.

Tweed's approach to the relationship between religions, joy, and the environment has a marked focus on deeply felt, grand emotions. In some ways, this recalls Rudolf Otto's approach to religion, which was so invested in deep emotional experience that Otto even programmatically asked readers to stop reading his book unless they could recall experiences of strong religious emotions of their own.[205] Such a focus on strong emotions (Otto uses very emphatic terms like "Ergriffenheit"/"rapture" or "Erregtheit"/"excitement") reflects a romantic tradition that foregrounds extreme emotional experiences and strong feelings as the only state of life worth living. Burkhard Gladigow noted and criticized this widespread tendency in the study of religions already in the 1980s. He diagnosed a strong trend toward "reconstruction under conditions of perfection" and pointed out that in most studies, aspects such as routine, trivialization, inconsistencies, misunderstandings, or disinterest were markedly lacking, and that people, as they are described in the academic literature, constantly seem to be caught up in deep religious feelings.[206]

Tweed, when he conceptualizes the contribution of religions to the emotional life of human beings as providing "something to say [...] in the face of wonder," seems to be heading straight for the same pitfall. Yet if one strips his point of its overemphatic presentation, he is making an important observation: religion and the supernatural can be quite delightful. Certainly in Strandir, the supernatural element in the landscape can time and again seem as if its main point was to establish positive emotional responses to a place. Often, however, this is not about "wonder" or "rapture" ("Ergriffenheit"). Rather, the supernatural can appear to be aimed simply at a lightening of the atmosphere of a place; it can reflect the mere joy of storytelling, and a delight in things that are surreal and otherworldly. The supernatural in the landscape can provide those who know the stories of the land with a mental treasure map rivaling the one drawn by Robert Louis Stevenson for his *Treasure Island*, and fill the land with joy, play, and adventure, often with

---

[205] Otto 1926 (1917), 8.
[206] Gladigow 1988, 22. Original quotation: "Rekonstruktion unter den Bedingungen von Perfektion."

152 LANDSCAPE, RELIGION, AND THE SUPERNATURAL

traits of the burlesque. In the following pages, this aspect of the supernatural landscape will be highlighted by three concise examples: the miracle wrought by Guðmundur the Good in Kolbeinsvík in the face of a troll attack; the adventurous landscape of knights, outlaws, and trolls in Miðdalur; and the troll playground at Hvalsá.

*

The farm of Kolbeinsvík was located on the little bay of the same name, about halfway between the fjords of Kaldbaksvík and Veiðileysa. Today Kolbeinsvík is deserted and in ruins, but it is not forgotten. The only road that connects Árneshreppur to the southern parts of Strandir runs directly by the remains of its buildings, and by the roadside these remains are memorialized by a signpost that remembers the farm, thus turning it into an official *lieu de mémoire.*

One of the distinctive features of Kolbeinsvík is the location of the—now ruined—farm buildings, which stood directly at the foot of an old land-slide: there are mere meters between the last buildings and the edge of a towering mass of earth and stone that looks like the result of a huge collapse from the mountainside of Kolbeinsvíkurfjall. This juxtaposition of houses and the (seeming or real) landslide area suggests great drama and is one of the focal points of storytelling about Kolbeinsvík. One way that I have heard the story told is that once upon a time, a troll woman lived above Kolbeinsvík who disliked the farm, and who particularly disliked it when Guðmundur the Good stayed there. So she decided to take action, to wait for the night, and then cause a landslide to get rid of both Guðmundur and Kolbeinsvík for good. But her timing was unfortunate. During the night, Guðmundur got up to go outside for a pee, and the troll chose exactly the moment when Guðmundur was peeing to release the landslide: as he was standing outside attending to his bladder, he saw it coming before it could crush him and the farm; so he interrupted his peeing, raised his arms, and invoked the help of God with the words: "Now help, my Lord, because this is too much for poor me!" ("Hjálpa þú nú drottinn, því ei getur vesalingur minn"). The landslide stopped 20 m from the farm, and thus Kolbeinsvík was saved.[207]

Versions of the landslide story have been told for a considerable length of time, and one version is of particular value because it originated from

---

[207] Jón Jónsson, pers. comm., who could not remember where he knew the story from but only that he had been telling it in this way for at least twenty years.

TWELVE MOVEMENTS   153

somebody who not only had grown up at Kolbeinsvík but also explicitly commented on what the story meant to him. Ingi Guðmonsson (1902–1992) came to Kolbeinsvík as a four-year-old in 1906, when his parents took over the farm, and lived there until 1922.[208] The farm was later taken over by his brother Árni, who left it in 1943. After this, Kolbeinsvík was never resettled. In the early 1980s, as an old man, Ingi wrote down some of his memories about his childhood home. About the landslide, he wrote the following:[209]

Hraun ("Stone Field") [. . .] such is the name of a great chunk that has fallen from the mountain and below which the farm is located. There is the following story about how the chunk fell out of the mountain. A troll witch (*skessa*) lived on Kolbeinsvíkurfjall mountain with her two children. This troll witch had a bad character and for some reason wanted to get rid of the farmer in Kolbeinsvík, but as he was living there with good husbandry, the troll witch used tactics to wrench a piece out of the mountain and let it fall over the farm. This farmer was good and God-fearing and the troll witch was afraid of him.

One day it happened that Bishop Guðmundur the Good was travelling and came to Kolbeinsvík. He received food and drink from the farmer, and as they are sitting and eating and talking, they hear a din and a great noise from the mountain. They leave the farmhouse as fast as they can and then see the chunk of the mountain hurtling down the steep slope and heading for the farm. Guðmundur the Good then spread his arms towards the landslide and stopped it some fathoms from the farm.

About the troll witch (*skessa*), there is this to say, that she kept watch for visitors on the farm, so it would be certain that the farmer should be inside when she pushed the chunk of mountain over the farm, but it turned out differently from how she had wanted it. Guðmundur the Good stopped the landslide, but the troll witch and her two sons turned to stone, and the trinity still stands there on the mountain today, and when one goes northwards over the land of Kaldbakur, one can see her well from the road, standing on the edge of the cliffs like a statue, and her two sons to each side; equally one can easily see the combe in the rocks where the chunk was pushed out—this is all so clear and plain that one can marvel how well

---

[208] Cf. his obituary in the newspaper *Vísir*, mánudagur 18. maí 1992, p. 42 (https://timarit.is/page/2598389, last accessed 1 August 2020).
[209] Ingi Guðmonsson 1981, 99–100.

154 LANDSCAPE, RELIGION, AND THE SUPERNATURAL

that matches with the folktale, like it is with the chunk that Guðmundur the Good stopped, that no stone has ever fallen out of it in the direction of the farm, though the stone seems to be hanging loosely in its front part. It is fun (*gaman*) to go over such things and judge them calmly without superstition and mysticism (*hjátrú og hindurvitni*).

Ingi explicitly highlights the detailed, in-depth correspondences between the local landscape (landslide; combe in the mountainside; three stone pillars) and the story about the evil troll woman and the region's favorite holy man.[210] The last sentence of the account is a key statement: "It is fun (*gaman*) to go over such things and judge them calmly without superstition and mysticism (*hjátrú og hindurvitni*)." The importance of "fun" (*gaman*) is also emphasized in other testimonies,[211] but Ingi's statement makes it particularly clear how "fun" is the main factor that determined his relationship to the story about his home farm: the supernatural and the interplay of story and topography are first and foremost a source of enjoyment. Any questions of the "truth" of the story, in contrast, are emphatically left aside—which here is particularly interesting because in essence it is a classic hagiographic narrative. Ingi even explicitly underlines that pondering the story is fun independent of "superstition and mysticism" (*hjátrú og hindurvitni*): his dismissive choice of words makes clear that he does not think highly of any real belief in trolls and saintly miracles, but he nevertheless enjoys the tale. In order to work, the story did not need to be believed, and maybe it wouldn't have worked if it had been believed. And what the story did was to provide enjoyment.

Especially if the story is viewed from this perspective, it is also interesting to note how the narrative has changed since Ingi told it forty years ago. In the oral telling I heard in 2019, the story had lost its relationship to any stone pillars in the landscape as well as to the combe in the mountainside, so the "fun" that Ingi derived from his ability to point out detailed correlations between story and topography has largely disappeared. But still "fun" has remained the main point of the story: for today it is a burlesque drollery about how Guðmundur the Good's weak bladder saves the day. The details of the story have changed, but its core was preserved unaltered: it is fun.

*

---

[210] Cf. Silko's emphasis on the importance of the topographical setting as providing the inspiration for narratives in Pueblo culture: Silko 1996, 270.

[211] See especially the section "Labor."

Fig. 2.13 The western slope of Miðdalur with its panorama of trolls, knights, and outlaws, encompassing the three troll footprints of Heimstaskál, Miðskál, and Fremstaskál, the "Thieves' Hollow" Þjófalág, and the "Castle" Kastali. The distance between Heimstaskál and Kastali is c. 2.2 km. © M. Egeler, 2019.

The valley of Miðdalur, "Middle Valley," is located on the south coast of Steingrímsfjörður. To the east, it is delimited by the mountain of Kirkjubólsfjall, while to the west it is towered over by Heiðarbæjarheiði. Heiðarbæjarheiði is the highest mountain range on Steingrímsfjörður, rising to a height of over 600 m, which alone would be enough to give it a dominant position in the local landscape. This dominance is further emphasized by its sheer slopes: especially on the side overlooking Miðdalur, Heiðarbæjarheiði is characterized by steep, rocky sides that over long stretches turn into dark, sometimes near-perpendicular cliffs.

Heiðarbæjarheiði, as the largest mountain on the fjord, has attracted a rich treasure trove of stories.[212] Some of the traditions connected with it can be extremely concise, but still seem to form a coherent ensemble. Over a stretch of some 2 km in the lower part of Miðdalur, one such ensemble forms a landscape prospect that can be taken in in a single view, presenting itself as a perfect subject for a painting (Fig. 2.13).

This ensemble consists, to put it prosaically, of four hollows and one rocky hill. If one takes it in while standing in the lower part of the valley and looking up toward the upland, its first three structures form a unit: three combes or vaguely bowl-shaped hollows dug out of the mountainside

---

[212] Cf. Egeler 2021a.

156 LANDSCAPE, RELIGION, AND THE SUPERNATURAL

on roughly the same elevation and spaced maybe 300–400 m apart. These combes are Heimstaskál ("Most Homeward Bowl/Combe"), Miðskál ("Middle Bowl/Combe"), and Fremstaskál ("Furthest Bowl/Combe"). None of these three combes is particularly noticeable in and by itself, but as a sequence of three similar-sized and evenly spaced hollows on the same level of the slope their regularity makes them stand out. Furthermore, they are located in a place which is very visible from most of the inhabited part of the valley. The southernmost combe is located above the home-field or *tún* of the farm of Miðdalsgróf, and the northernmost roughly at the height of the stable buildings of Gestsstaðir on the opposite side of the valley; so these three hollows very much belong to the inhabited part of the landscape.

Given their prominence, it comes as little surprise that local storytelling should comment on them. In the late 1990s, Björn Guðmundsson and Guðfríður Guðjónsdóttir, who lived at the farm of Miðdalsgróf below these combes, explained their regular appearance: "There, a troll woman (*tröllaskessa*) was said to have put her foot down in the bowls/combes (*skálarnar*)."[213] The three dents in the mountainside become the footprints of a troll with a stride length of some 400 m. This is a big troll indeed, but its size is befitting the scale of the trolls that created the nearby island of Grímsey, which is visible from the mouth of the valley.

Less than 1 km to the southwest of the uppermost troll footstep, and much higher up on the slope, a hill protrudes from the mountainside. The dip between this hill and the slope behind it forms a sheltered hollow. If one stands at the bottom of the valley, one knows that this hollow is there, but it is one of the few places that one cannot see into: the only place from which one can look into this hollow is the top of the ridge above it. Being thus located in plain sight and hidden at the same time, it almost mocks and certainly tantalizes the viewer. This hollow is Þjófalág, the "Thieves' Hollow." Ingvar Guðmundsson, who used to live at the farm of Tindur a little further up the valley, in the late 1970s said of Þjófalág that it was "located in such a way that it was a good hiding place":[214] as such, it was perfect for thieves. A few years later, Gísli Jónatansson of nearby Naustavík wrote an article for *Strandapósturinn* in which he told the story of the "Thieves' Hollow" in somewhat more detail:[215]

---

[213] *NV* Hilmar Egill Sveinbjörnsson 1999, n. p.
[214] *SÁM* Ingvar Guðmundsson 1977, 3.
[215] Gísli Jónatansson 1989, 124.

TWELVE MOVEMENTS 157

Up below the edge of the mountain above the path that in the past used to be taken from Tindur to [Trölla-]Tunga across at the so-called Leiðaröxl ("Shoulder of the Way") is a rather deep depression, which is called Þjófalág ("Thieves' Hollow"). It was said that once smoke was seen there one spring or summer, and that was thought to be big news. It was thought that thieves had been on their way at that place and made a short stop. When people were talking about this event, the suspicion was directed towards Fjalla-Eyvindur and Halla—it was at this time that they lived. Yet no enquiries were ever made about who was to blame for the smoke in Þjófalág.

Fjalla-Eyvindur ("Eyvindur of the Mountains") and his wife, Halla, are the most famous outlaws of Icelandic folk legend. During the eighteenth century, they are said to have spent twenty years living in outlawry, which became the theme of a great many tales about their exploits.[216] Early in the twentieth century, their popularity then received yet another boost by the huge success of Jóhann Sigurjónsson's play *Fjalla-Eyvindur*, which was first staged in 1911 and soon even translated into foreign languages;[217] the lullaby *Sofðu unga ástin mín* ("Sleep, my young love") from this play is still sung today. Here in Miðdalur, these famous fugitives, who spent so much of their life in hiding, are associated with the most obvious hiding place: for the "Thieves' Hollow" is an obvious hiding place in the double sense that it is one of the only places in the lower parts of Miðdalur where one can hide—since otherwise the valley is very open and characterized by wide vistas—and that this hiding place is highly visible: the hill which hides the hollow is located high above the valley bottom, making it visible from virtually the whole settled part of Miðdalur.

The last site of our ensemble, finally, is located only about half a kilometer south of the "Thieves' Hollow," and likewise in an exposed position high up on the slope. Almost directly above the now-abandoned farm of Tindur, and at the foot of a high cliff, a rocky hill protrudes from the slope. Viewed from the right angle, this hill bears a striking resemblance to an early modern star-shaped fortress, its steep sides shaped like ramparts designed to make cannonballs bounce off them. This hill is Kastali: the "Castle."[218] Etymologically, *kastali* is indeed the same word as English "castle," both

---

[216] Jón Árnason 1961, 2: 237–245.
[217] Jóhann Sigurjónsson 1950. First English translation already 1916: Jóhann Sigurjónsson 1916.
[218] *SÁM* Ingvar Guðmundsson 1977, 3; *SÁM* Jóhann Hjaltason s.a. (f), 2.

158 LANDSCAPE, RELIGION, AND THE SUPERNATURAL

being loan words ultimately derived from Latin *castellum*.[219] There is no explicit story connected with Kastali hill, but already the name itself represents an interpretation of the landscape feature. To this day, the term *kastali* has the sound of something exotic, heroic, and chivalric; or as Jón Jónsson put it when on one occasion, and quite out of the blue, I asked him what he thought of when he heard the word *kastali*: "A building abroad. With a dragon in it." The naming of the rampart-shaped hill as Kastali points to the rich world of the Icelandic Sagas of Chivalry (*riddarasögur*), of courtly splendor, and knights in shining armor battling monsters and saving damsels in distress, all of which play an important role in Icelandic folk storytelling and later medieval literature.

Both the world of kings and chivalry represented by the "Castle" and that of the thieves represented by the nearby "Thieves' Hollow" played an important role in living folk storytelling at least until the turn of the twentieth century. This is illustrated by a passage by the Rev. Jónas Jónasson (1856–1918), in which he talks about Icelandic storytelling practice:[220]

> Where it was customary to sleep during the dusk hour, there was little activity, as may be expected, but where it was not so, people made what use they could of the time. The principal amusement was to talk, to tell stories, recite verse epigrams, chant *rímur*, or cap verses. It is incredible what a vast store of stories the people had, especially stories of outlaws and wonder-tales of kings and queens in their palaces and old men and old wives in their cottages. Then there were the stories about ghosts or fairy folk, and of those there was an inexhaustible store. I knew one old man who was able to tell three stories a night all through the winter fishing season, 2 February to 12 May, and had still not reached the end of his repertoire.

The slope of Heiðarbæjarheiði above Miðdalur allows us a glimpse of how this storytelling culture, which at home inside the farmhouse served to pleasantly while away the long hours of the evening, could be projected onto the land. On this slope, the "Thieves' Hollow" and Kastali form a toponymic Robin Hood landscape and thus stand in for the "stories of outlaws and wonder-tales of kings and queens in their palaces," while the tales of the supernatural—"the stories about ghosts or fairy folk"—are represented by the huge

---

[219] Cleasby and Gudbrand Vigfusson 1874, s.v. "kastali."
[220] Translation quoted after Einar Ólafur Sveinsson 2003, 68; for the original quotation, see Jónas Jónasson 1934, 245.

footprints of the troll. In a single landscape prospect, this slope condenses cornerstones of the storyteller's repertoire; and in doing so, it makes the entertaining stories of the evening hours constantly visible to all those out there working on the fields and pastures of the valley. The inner part of the valley was farmed by the farmsteads of Miðdalsgröf, Klúka, Gestsstaðir, and Tindur, and while all these farms had stories of their own, they share this mountainside prospect that summarizes some of the great adventures and adventurers of folk storytelling like a big mountainous cinema screen.

*

A particularly straightforward example of the playfulness of some place-lore is found on the shore of Hvalsá farm on the south coast of Steingrímsfjörður. There, immediately by the road and at the foot of the pointy triangular rock stack of the Hvalsárdrangur, at low tide a broad sheet of rock emerges from the sea. This flat stretch of intertidal ground has the name Leikvöllur: "Playground." In the late 1970s, the story behind this name was told by Ágúst Benediktsson, who had been born in nearby Steinadalur in 1900, had farmed at Hvalsá from 1929 to 1972, and was thus intimately acquainted with the area:[221]

> A short stretch of way further in is Hvalsárlending below Hvalsárdrangur, which is a very high rock stack. To the south of Hvalsárlending is a flat tongue of land or *flúra* of some size, which comes to the surface during low tide. It is called Leikvöllur ("Playground"), and it was said of it that troll women (*skessur*) reputedly used it as a playground (*leikvöllur*).

The term *flúra* denotes the flounder, and in addition to referring to this flat fish it is also a term for land that is under water during high tide but emerges during low tide.[222] Such pieces of intertidal land were occasionally named, possibly because this land betwixt and between dry land and the sea has its own economic significance: sheep like to graze on the seaweed growing there, and it is a good place to collect mussels for bait and dulse (*Palmaria palmata*) for human consumption.[223] But whatever practical use the "Playground"

---

[221] *SÁM* Guðrún S. Magnúsdóttir 1976f, 2.

[222] The second meaning is missing in most Icelandic dictionaries, though it is listed as the primary meaning of the word by Sigfús Blöndal 1920, s.v. "1. flúra." Younger Icelanders are often not aware of it, but it used to be firmly established: Jón Jónsson, pers. comm.

[223] Jón Jónsson, pers. comm.

Fig. 2.14 The intertidal rock shelf of Leikvöllur, the "Playground," which is almost smooth enough to be a ball court. The double-pointed rock stack of Hvalsárdrangur (in the foreground) has the typical geology of petrified trolls as they are found in Kollafjarðarnes or Drangsnes, but, vexingly, there is no tradition that interprets it as trolls overtaken by the sun while engrossed in their play. © M. Egeler, 2019.

may or may not have had, local tradition declared it a playground of trolls (Fig. 2.14). Here, the tongue-in-cheek character of the storytelling is directly mirrored by the games that are played inside the story: the trolls in the landscape act out whatever they are playing at with all the playfulness proper to a playground.

*

The three examples presented earlier were all, in one way or another, about trolls: we have met Guðmundur the Good defending Kolbeinsvík farm against the attack of a troll family, we have explored a landscape of outlaws and trolls in Miðdalur, and we have seen trolls playing on their playground at Hvalsá. Trolls are so prevalent in this material partly because they are generally very important in place-storytelling in Strandir, but their prominence in this particular selection of stories is also due to the specific character of trolls: they tend to be burlesque, and therefore it is commonly trolls that represent the delightful aspects of the supernatural in the landscape. While elves tend to be deeply serious, trolls are fun.

TWELVE MOVEMENTS   161

In the section on morality in the landscape, I introduced the way Keith H. Basso used the metaphor of an abandoned theater stage to describe how among the Western Apache place-lore affects the perception of the landscape: Apache stories fill the land with associations of a colorful cast of characters who once acted them out, turning the landscape into a kind of "theatre, a natural stage [...] where significant moral dramas unfolded in the past."[224] Such a heuristic conceptualization of landscape as a theater has also been addressed by Denis Cosgrove and Stephen Daniels.[225] Cosgrove and Daniels show the complexities of this metaphor by presenting a discussion of critiques of visualist metaphors and their dialectic relationship with linguistic metaphors, such as "spectacle" versus "text" or "word," and note that the gap between the two types of metaphors is to some extent bridged by the metaphor of "theater," in which word and image come together—without, however, this suspending the struggle between the visual and the verbal. Also in different forms of theater, there can be various balances between textual and visual aspects: theater can be strongly text-based and focused on intellectual aspects, or more strongly visual and spectacular, appealing to the senses more than the intellect.[226] And even if something is set in scene with a visual focus, there can still be huge variation—a panoramic, sweeping view is very different from a close-up detailed vignette.[227] Cosgrove's and Daniels's contribution thus both historicizes and shows the complex richness of the theater metaphor.

This theater metaphor, exactly because of its complexity, seems supremely fitting for natural stages like those we have encountered at Kolbeinsvík (a comparatively close-up vignette that is read in an intensely textual way), in Miðdalur (a wide, sweeping view with very little text and thus ideal for theatrical improvisation), or at Hvalsá (a vignette again, but one whose textuality is also kept to a minimum). The "playground" Leikvöllur perfectly presents itself to be viewed as a ground on which to stage the drama of the playing trolls as an almost static *tableau vivant*, while the slope of Heiðarbæjarheiði over Miðdalur contains all the props for an action-filled stage play about knights, outlaws, and monsters. These examples show that the metaphor of the landscape as a theater has the breadth to grasp much of the range of what storytelling can put on stage in this environment. This also pertains to the content

---

[224] Basso 1996, 120–121 (quotation: p. 121).
[225] Cosgrove 1998, xxvi; Cosgrove 2008, 34; Cosgrove and Daniels 1993.
[226] Esp. Cosgrove and Daniels 1993, 66.
[227] Cf. especially Cosgrove and Daniels 1993, 72–73.

162 LANDSCAPE, RELIGION, AND THE SUPERNATURAL

of the plays: while in the section on morality we saw, in a manner of speaking, performances of *King Lear* and *Macbeth*, this section has introduced us to the Icelandic landscape as Music Hall and Variety, where a holy man pisses and trolls play ball. Icelandic landscape storytelling has a ludic character that rivals that of the actual theater stage, spanning the whole spectrum from the deeply serious to the burlesque.

That being said, however, it is sometimes difficult to decide how appropriate the designation "fun" is, even for the fun part of this spectrum. In an Icelandic context, the seemingly burlesque detail of Guðmundur the Good going outside to have a piss is actually not funny in the way it would be for an Anglophone audience, as in Iceland urination (and talking about it) carries no stigma: there is an element of humor in the utterly unexpected encounter that the holy man has with the landslide, but there is no violation of social taboos about defecation. And when Ingi Guðmonsson, elaborating on the detailed correspondence between landscape and story, emphasized that "[i]t is fun (*gaman*) to review and appraise such things," it is hard to say what exactly his feelings were. His remark has to be read in its wider context. It concludes the story about Guðmundur and the trolls in an article that Ingi, then already an old man, wrote about his childhood home, where he had grown up and which at the time had been abandoned for almost forty years. The story about Guðmundur and the trolls takes up nearly a fifth of his article; that Ingi gave it so much space in his account of his childhood home suggests that it was more to him than a superficial joke, and that there might have been an undercurrent of nostalgia for the landscape of his childhood that he did not make explicit but that still underlay his narrative. Icelandic *gaman* is normally translated as "fun," and "fun" indeed seems to be at the heart of its semantic spectrum, but it is a very broadly employed term expressing a positive emotional reaction. It is exactly this aspect that seems important here: the story appears to have been an essential part of the good memories that Ingi had of his old home, and of his emotional attachment to it. To create this warm glow of affection seems to be a central aspect of what the story effects.

Nevertheless, what nostalgia there was in Ingi's article is deep in the background, and the story landscapes of Miðdalur and Hvalsá seem to be entirely about the fun and sense of adventure that forms at least an important part of Ingi's tale. This seems to be the main conclusion suggested by material like that presented in this section: stories about religious actors like Guðmundur the Good and supernatural protagonists like the troll population of Strandir do not necessarily aim to create deep emotions like Otto's "rapture" or Tweed's reaction "in the face of wonder." Rather, many of these traditions of naming the land and of telling stories about it create a positive emotional relationship to the land by employing playfulness, irony, burlesque, and occasionally the trappings of heroic storytelling. Guðmundur defeating the trolls does not create awe, but the delight that the story brings is mediated through the way it artfully connects its plot and the local landscape, and exactly the same seems to be happening in Miðdalur and at Hvalsá, even if in a less explicit way. It is the playfulness of this material, and maybe the adventure that it inscribes into the land by employing a cast of trolls, outlaws, knights, and holy men, that allows it (to use Tweed's phrase) to "intensify joy."

7: Power and Subversion

A theme that dominates much theoretical writing on landscape, and on spatial theory more generally, is power. Henri Lefebvre, who championed the tenet that "([s]ocial) space is a (social) product,"[228] argued that the category of "representational spaces," which are "lived" through the symbols and images that they are connected to and which are spaces of the arts and of storytelling, have a strong subversive potential. Later, Denis Cosgrove, who was foundational for landscape studies as one of the first scholars to champion an approach that analyzed landscape as an ideological construct, emphasized the close connection between the ideological construction of landscape perceptions as ways of seeing the world and the exercise of power.[229] "Critical place-name studies" are focused on questions of power with a near exclusivity that has led to criticism even within the field itself.[230] W. J. T. Mitchell, when formulating nine theses on landscape, argues in his sixth thesis that landscape is "a particular historical formation associated with European imperialism,"[231] suggesting that it should be seen "as something like the 'dreamwork' of imperialism."[232] In proposing this argument, however, Mitchell also notes the ambivalences in the relationship between landscape and power,

---

[228] Lefebvre 1991, 26 (emphasis original). See chapter 1, section "Living in Landscapes: Dwelling, Place, and Home."

[229] Cosgrove 1998, xxv–xxvi. Cf. Hubbard and Kitchin 2011, 121–122.

[230] Rose-Redwood et al. 2010, 466; cf. Bigon 2016, 4–5. For further examples of studies from this field, see Rose-Redwood and Alderman 2011; Berg and Vuolteenaho 2009.

[231] Mitchell 2002d, 5.

[232] Mitchell 2002d, 10 (criticized as an exaggeration by Cosgrove 1998, xix; Cosgrove 2008, 27).

164 LANDSCAPE, RELIGION, AND THE SUPERNATURAL

observing that landscape "disclose[s] both utopian fantasies of the perfect imperial prospect and fractured images of unresolved ambivalence and unsuppressed resistance."[233] Landscape is not only a place in which power becomes manifest but also a place of subversion.

The importance of the latter point—the presence of "unsuppressed resistance" in the landscape—can be illustrated by an example that Keith Hamilton Basso gives in his study of landscape and language among the Western Apache.[234] One of the great themes of his book is how in Apache culture, place-stories can be used to assert and maintain the order and the moral norms of society. In the case of the Western Apache, this entailed a strong sense of tradition and of the necessity that Apache people should not behave too much like white people, and especially that they should show solidarity in the first instance with members of their own community. One of the place-stories that Basso quotes tells the tale of an Apache policeman who arrested another Apache man for stealing and butchering a cow that belonged to a white man. But when the policeman tried to hand the cattle thief over to an officer of the U.S. military, he suddenly could not remember what he had wanted to do, because somebody had used magic to prevent him from turning the rustler in. So the story ended with the rustler going free and the Apache policeman making a fool of himself. As this story was set in the late nineteenth century, when the forced confinement of the Western Apache to the reservations demanded many lives through hunger and disease, the Apache audience of this story would have found the behavior of the rustler perfectly acceptable, while the behavior of the Apache policeman would be seen as a betrayal of his loyalties to his own starving people; that he ended up becoming a common laughingstock was merely a just punishment. This story could thus stand for a clear moral message: do not take sides with outsiders against your own people, and do not behave too much like a white person. Since this story furthermore was closely connected with a specific locality where it is said to have occurred, this specific place came to encapsulate the moral message of the tale. So telling the story could be used to chastise a person who had behaved too much like a white man and violated Apache traditions, and this chastisement would not only be effective in the moment when the story was being told, but would work on the culprit every time he or she encountered the place where the story was set. Thus, the landscape would

[233] Mitchell 2002d, 10.
[234] Basso 1996, 54–57.

TWELVE MOVEMENTS 165

embody the moral of the story and make it effective—and this moral is a subversive one that challenges the legitimacy of the dominant social hierarchies, where the Apache were a persecuted minority, and the legal norms of the state; in Mitchell's words, it embodied (em-placed?) the "unsuppressed resistance" of the Apache against their confinement to the reservations.

The humor and irony that are foundational for Basso's example of the ridiculed policeman are common (though not universal) features of such subversive place-stories. The largest settlement and main administrative center in Strandir is the town of Hólmavík. In the late 1970s, Óli E. Björnsson (1926–2013) wrote down some memories about places and place-names in Hólmavík and its surroundings. In this document he also mentions a "Kattegat" that had been a location at sea somewhere close to the town:[235]

> In the northern part of the sound of Hólmasund was (and is) a very big skerry. With rowing boats it was possible to sail between the skerry and the headland of Höfði when it was high tide. Jokers called this "sailing the Kattegat," and it existed for a long time. Now the sound has silted up and the days of the "Kattegat" are obviously numbered.

Elsewhere, the Kattegat is the sea between Denmark and Sweden, a quite considerable stretch of ocean some 25,000 km^2 in size that connects the North Sea and the Baltic Sea. Yet in the old Hólmavík that Óli remembered—which will have been the Hólmavík of the Danish rule of Iceland and its immediate aftermath after Iceland declared its independence in 1944—the Kattegat was a tiny stretch of sea between a skerry and the mainland that could only be sailed at high tide and even then only by small rowing boats, but not by bigger motorized vessels. As Óli himself noted, the Icelandic place-name was a joke and it was taken as a joke, and enjoyed wide popularity. It mocked the Danish stretch of sea, and in doing so it mocked the Denmark that ruled Iceland and asserted its own Icelandic perspective on Danish-Icelandic relations. The Kattegat thus illustrates how power and, especially, the subversion of power structures play a prominent role also in the landscape of Strandir: time and again, an "unsuppressed resistance" is formulated that simply laughs power off.

While the Kattegat, both in Denmark and in Iceland, is entirely of this world, Christopher Tilley highlights the presence of forms of power also in

---

[235] *SÁM* Óli E. Björnsson 1978, 4.

166   LANDSCAPE, RELIGION, AND THE SUPERNATURAL

mythological landscapes.[236] The rest of this section returns to such super-natural landscapes and places, and to the representation of the Lutheran-Protestant Icelandic national Church in Strandir place-lore. To this end, the following pages will focus on two examples that illustrate typical traits of the Strandir approach to power and subversion in the landscape. These examples will be Oddshóll hill and the abandoned farm of Feykishólar, both of which are located on the land of Stóra-Hvalsá farm in Bæjarhreppur, and both of which talk about priests to whom there is more than strikes the eye.

*

The Hvalsá ("Whale River") has its source in the mountains to the west of Hrútafjörður in the southern part of Strandir, and it flows into the fjord less than 7 km north of the church of Prestbakki. About 1.4 km north of the mouth of the Hvalsá, on land belonging to Stóra-Hvalsá farm, the road runs directly along the coast and passes the rock ridge of Oddshóll or Oddshólar, "Oddur's Hill" or "Oddur's Hills." Oddshóll is a narrow wall of rock with a knife-edge ridge that runs in a straight line for some 50 m; a cleft in its middle may be the reason for why its name has a singular and a plural variant ("Oddur's Hill" or "Hills"), as one may equally well view it as one or two cliffs. On its seaward side, it still forms a near-perpendicular cliff face several meters in height. On the landward side, however, the construction of the modern road has rendered Oddshóll somewhat indistinct: the new road embankment has been raised almost to the height of the top of Oddshóll, virtually obliterating the dip to its north that once made it an unmissable landmark.

Not only was Oddshóll a prominent landmark by the roadside, but it is also connected with a roadside tale about the odd behavior of the priest Oddur, which is said to have given this rock formation its name. Writing at some point around the middle of the twentieth century, Jóhann Hjaltason told this tale in the following, minimalist way:[237]

> [. . .] two hills (*hólar*) that are called Oddshólar. It is said that they have their name from a certain priest who once, a long time ago, was priest at Prestbakki. And it happened with him, that he sat on this hill during mass time and plucked lice from himself.

---

[236] Tilley 1994, 22.
[237] *SÁM* Jóhann Hjaltason s.a. (e), 1–2.

The way Jóhann Hjaltason tells the tale, this rock formation got its name from a priest who missed his own mass because he sat on this rock and was engrossed in delousing himself. The priest—one of the most prominent local authority figures—thus not only made a joke of himself, but by giving a name to a prominent landmark, this joke was also inscribed into the landscape in one of the most public locations possible. To make matters worse, many members of the congregation of the church at Prestbakki would cross this landmark every time they went to attend divine service there. Thus, the way to church would itself entail a ridiculing of the authority of this very Church.

The story was popular enough to be told in different versions. A very detailed variant was published by Skúli Guðjónsson in the 1970s. It runs as follows:[238]

By the sea midway between Stóra-Hvalsá and Borgir stands a hill (*hóll*), or rather a cliff, that is called Oddshóll. The following story tells about how this place-name came into being.

At some time in the past, the priest was the incumbent in Staður in Hrútafjörður. He was called Oddur and was said to have some knowledge of magic. He also served Prestbakki and Óspakseyri in Bitra.

It happened one summer, when Oddur had to officiate in Óspakseyri, that a group of people from the inner part of Bæjarhreppur intended to make a special day for themselves and to listen to their pastor officiating there.

This [group] was now riding as the lie of the road was, northwards along Hrútafjörður, and nothing worth telling happened until they came to the hill between Stóra-Hvalsá and Borgir. Then they saw that the cleric's horse was standing on a pasture by the hill, and the cleric himself was sitting up on the hill and was busy seeking out lice on himself. The people did not address the cleric, nor he them, and they continued on their way and didn't rush, because they assumed that the priest would come shortly and join them. When they reached Skálholtsvík, the priest had still not caught up with them. The people therefore decided to wait for him there. In the end it came to this, that their patience ran out, and now they set off over Stikuháls, and besides they had not given up all hope that the priest would soon catch up with them.

So there is no need to dwell on it that at a late hour at last the people come all the way to Óspakseyri, without having become aware of the priest, but

---

[238] Skúli Guðjónsson 1974, 95–96.

168 LANDSCAPE, RELIGION, AND THE SUPERNATURAL

as soon as they came to the church, Pastor Oddur appeared in the door of the church and had then concluded the celebration of the service, and not many greetings were exchanged.

The priest then went to the farm [at Óspakseyri], together with those people from Bitra who had listened to the mass, but the people from Bæjarhreppur thereupon turned homewards, and they thought that their trip had been a great mockery.

Now nothing worth telling happened until they came to that hill that has been mentioned earlier. There they saw Pastor Oddur sitting on the hill, and he was still seeking out lice on himself, and his horse was standing on the pasture by the hill. Now they seemed to understand that the priest through his magic (fjölkynngi) had made the funniest illusions (hinar skemmilegustu sjónhverfingar) for them.

Then this hill was named Oddshóll.

Finally, one may tell this, that there is another version of this story that is identical apart from this, that the Oddur who played his tricks on the people from Bæjarhreppur is said to have been Bishop Oddur Einarsson on a trip of inspection or visitation through Strandir.

This account reports two versions of the story, in which the lice-ridden priest is turned into either a parish priest or a bishop with magical abilities and a very particular sense of humor: for his congregation, a trip to church turns into a trip to have the mickey taken out of them. While Jóhann Hjaltason's version of the tale humiliates the priest, this version manages to both aggrandize and mock him, while at the same time—and this is the decisive point—bringing the sincerity of the visit to church as a religious exercise into question.

Such mocking of church attendance in Strandir had a firm place in social life. The Icelandic lack of reverence toward formal religion has been much commented on by foreign visitors. As Ida Pfeiffer famously put it in a description of a service she participated in in Reykjavík in the 1850s: "Most of the congregation sat with their faces turned towards the altar; but this rule had its exceptions."[239] This lack of religious ardor could even be put to good social use. Many vagrant paupers made their living by providing entertainments such as storytelling, dancing, or performing a kind of stand-up comedy in exchange for board and lodging. An established set piece in the repertoire

---

[239] Pfeiffer 1853, 88; cf. Auden and MacNeice 1937, 62, 68.

TWELVE MOVEMENTS 169

of a number of these paupers was the parodying of the characteristic style of language used by parsons, of religious song, and of other elements of religious services; for instance, a certain Halldór Hómer (1845–1895) developed a comedy routine in which he dressed up in priestly garb to chant, baptize bottles, and perform "marriage" ceremonies between agricultural workers.[240] The stories about Oddshóll can be understood in this context of the pervasive irreverence that people had for the Church. The Lutheran-Protestant Church of Iceland was one of the great institutions of the (until 1944 Danish) state, and none the more respected for that.

*

A fifteen-minute walk south of Oddshóll, the "Whale River" Hvalsá flows into the fjord, coming down from the uplands through the valley of Hvalsárdalur. While the river mouth itself is still flanked by the two farms of Stóra-Hvalsá and Litla-Hvalsá, the once-rich settlement landscape of the valley has long been abandoned. Already the map of the Danish General Staff from 1912 shows the valley's farms and shielings as deserted:[241] Árbakki, about 2 km from the mouth of the river as the crow flies; Helgukot some 3 km further into the mountains; Gíslakot some 600 m on from there; and finally Feykishólar another 1.5 km upvalley from Gíslakot (Map 2.4). All these abandoned farms now lie in swampy land that already the Danish maps mark as boggy, which may have been one of the reasons they were given up.

The ruins of their buildings are still well preserved and quite visible, and have invited the genesis of a rich tradition of naming and storytelling. Thus, the bog Púki, discussed earlier, is located above Árbakki.[242] More elaborate is a tradition recorded in 1977, which tells that Gíslakot and Helgukot, "Gísli's Smallholding" and "Helga's Smallholding," came into being through marital discord: when the difficulties between Helga and her husband, Gísli, became insurmountable, Helga simply moved out and founded her own little farm a little further down the valley.[243] This story is particularly interesting because it shows how keen local storytelling was to give explanations for the remains found in the abandoned valley, and what liberties one was prepared to take to get such explanations. For in the older Danish maps, Helgukot appears as

---

[240] Jón Jónsson 2018c, 107–124, esp. pp. 112–121. On Halldór Hómer: pp. 110–114.
[241] *Generalstabens Topografiske Kort*, sheet *Tröllatunga—33 Óspakseyri N.V.* (drawn 1912, published 1914).
[242] *SÁM* Jóhann Hjaltason s.a. (e), 3–4. See section "Labor."
[243] *SÁM* Guðrún S. Magnúsdóttir 1977b, 7.

170 LANDSCAPE, RELIGION, AND THE SUPERNATURAL

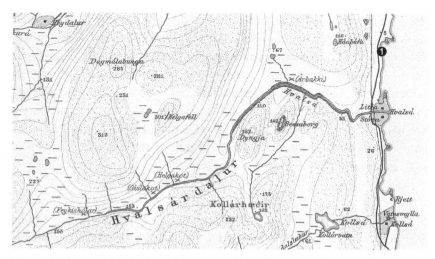

Map 2.4 The story landscape of Stóra-Hvalsá in the maps of the Danish General Staff. 1: Oddshóll. Note the spelling of Helgakot, which by the 1970s had turned to Helgukot. Litla- and Stóra-Hvalsá are interchanged. Base map: section of *Generalstabens Topografiske Kort*, sheet *Tröllatunga—33 Óspakseyri N.V.* (drawn 1912, published 1914).

Helgakot, which is a name that sounds very similar but has a completely different meaning. Helgakot could be based on the male personal name Helgi ("Helgi's Smallholding"), but more likely it originally meant "Holy/Blessed Smallholding," as this older name mirrors and is probably based on the name of the mountain Helgafell ("Holy Mountain") that rises directly above it; so Helgakot can be assumed to be the original name of the farm. It appears that at some point between 1912 and 1977,[244] somebody came up with the idea that by changing Helgakot to Helgukot one could get a (funny? educational?) origin story for one of the abandoned farms by creating a female founder figure that could have been the wife of the male founder of the neighboring croft. On the ground, this story furthermore is enriched by the artful mutual mirroring of story and topography: there is no line of sight between the two ruins, so the dislike of the former partners is reflected by (or rather: the narrative about this dislike may be inspired by) the impossibility of seeing the one place from the other.

---

[244] The form Helgukot is used already in the undated but probably mid-twentieth-century account of *SÁM* Jóhann Hjaltason s.a. (e), 4.

At Feykishólar, the uppermost ruin of the valley, this creation of origin stories has been performed to grand subversive effect. There, among other things, the engagement with gender roles and the relationship between the sexes that we just met at Gíslakot and Helgukot is taken onto the plane of the supernatural. In the 1970s, local opinion had it that Feykishólar was probably abandoned at some point in the second half of the nineteenth century;[245] yet the abandonment of the farm is taken for granted already by a story collected by Jón Árnason in the mid-nineteenth century.[246] The bulk of the ruins of Feykishólar is distributed over three small hills (hólar)[247] that roughly form a triangle with sides around 100 m in length. By the middle of the twentieth century, these hills had the names Bæjarhóll ("Farm Hill"), Húsahóll ("Hill of Houses"), and Hesthúshóll ("Horse-House Hill"); about the last one of these three it was still remembered that it had formerly been called Kirkjuhóll ("Church Hill").[248] From each of these hills, one has a good view of the other two; and from Kirkjuhóll one also has a good overview of the fairly flat grassland that was probably the home-field or tún of the farm.

Of these three settlement mounds, Kirkjuhóll is the one with the most distinctive appearance: it is a low but prominent circular hillock crowned by the ruins of a small rectangular building (Fig. 2.15). These ruins are exactly the right size for an old Icelandic turf-built church. An interior wall inside the building and the sloping of its walls show that this is not what it really was (and may have formed the basis for the later reinterpretation as a horse stable), but for the sake of a story it comes close enough. The most important feature that prompted the interpretation of this hill as a "Church Hill," however, is probably the structure of the tussocks at its foot. In Iceland, if grassland is left to itself, then processes of freezing and thawing and a concomitant rising of the ground lead to the formation of very marked tussocks. At the foot of Kirkjuhóll, these tussocks have a striking resemblance to old burials, which on old Icelandic cemeteries are marked by raised sections of ground (Fig. 2.16). Thus, "Church Hill" has both church-sized ruins and grave-like tussocks, and in Jón Árnason's story about Feykishólar, these very features have been made the centerpiece of an etiology of why Feykishólar was abandoned.[249]

---

[245] SÁM Guðrún S. Magnúsdóttir 1977b, 8.
[246] Jón Árnason 1954–1961, 1: 276–277, 678.
[247] Cf. SÁM Jóhann Hjaltason s.a. (e), 6–7.
[248] SÁM Jóhann Hjaltason s.a. (e), 6–7.
[249] Jón Árnason 1954–1961, 1: 276–277, 678. On aspects of the portrayal of gender relations in this and similar narratives, cf. Dagrún Ósk Jónsdóttir 2020.

Fig. 2.15 Kirkjuhóll, "Church Hill," at Feykishólar, crowned by a small rectangular ruin just the right size for an old Icelandic turf church. Kirkjuhóll is located at N 65°21.164' W 021°19.414'. © M. Egeler, 2019.

Fig. 2.16 One of the "graves" (grave-shaped tussocks) at the foot of Kirkjuhóll. A section of ground at the foot of the hill is formed by a whole series of such tussocks. They are oriented radially toward the center of the hill, where the ruin of the "church" is located, like the spokes of a sepulchral wheel. © M. Egeler, 2019.

The story begins with the statement that "in the past" ("í fyrndinni") there was a parsonage farm (*kirkjustaður*) in Feykishólar: this is the basic premise that constitutes the starting and end point of the whole story, and while the story does not make this explicit, this premise is based on the appearance of Kirkjuhóll. The farmer at Feykishólar, the tale continues, was a rich and learned man, and he had a daughter who would make a good catch. Soon enough, a young man who was living on the farm developed a strong interest in her. The woman, however, rebuffed his advances. One day the young man drowned during a fishing expedition that had set out from the mouth of the Hvalsá, but his body was recovered from the sea and buried in the churchyard at Feykishólar. He then started to haunt the farm, and the farmer's daughter in particular thought that he often visited her during the night.

One day the following spring, almost all members of the household left Feykishólar to attend a wedding. Only the daughter and a new maid stayed at home, and while the daughter went to bed, the maid took her knitting and sat down by the church, because from there she had a good view over the home-field and could keep an eye on the livestock to prevent it from grazing on the hay fields. (During the height of the Icelandic summer, it does essentially not get dark at night; therefore, the maid can still work on her knitting even while the farmer's daughter goes to bed.) When the maid had just sat down with her knitting needles and her ball of yarn, she saw that one of the graves was standing open. It seemed to her that this might herald big news, and so she came up with a plan. She let her ball of yarn roll into the open grave, keeping the end of the thread in her hand. After this, she did not have to wait long until she saw a man returning from the farm. This man did not spare her a glance and tried to enter the grave; yet as soon as he saw the yarn he hesitated, looked at the maid, and asked her to remove the yarn. She refused to do so if he did not first talk to her, and even though the ghost refused, she did not budge and eventually got her way. Before the dead man could return to his grave, he first had to explain himself: who was he? How had it come about that he walked? Cornered, the ghost said:

> "I am the young man from here who drowned on the Hvalsá last autumn. While I was alive, I was in love with the daughter of the farmer here and wanted to live together with her, but she always refused. Since I died I have often visited her, but now tonight I have for the first time gotten my way with her, because she was inside alone. She will be pregnant by my power

174 LANDSCAPE, RELIGION, AND THE SUPERNATURAL

and give birth to a son and thereupon die in childbed. Her son will be brought up with grandfather and grandmother and will resemble me very much in his looks. He will be splendidly gifted; his grandfather will set him on a scholarly career; as a twenty-year old he will be ordained a priest and will celebrate his first service here in Feykishólar, and he will succeed at that so well that it will be worth listening to. But when, after the sermon, he has to bless the congregation from the altar, he will turn the words of the blessing into the bitterest curse, and that with such power that the church with the whole congregation will sink into the ground."

Hearing this, the young maid immediately grasped the seriousness of the situation and kept her wits about her: having the ghost, who wanted to return into his grave, at her mercy, she forced him to tell her whether this catastrophe could be averted. The ghost replied:

"Yes," says the ghost (*draugur*), "there is one way to escape that, to thrust my son through with a blessed iron in that moment when he turns from the altar and wants to begin the curse instead of the blessing; for immediately as he begins to intone the curse, all those who are listening will become so paralyzed and apathic that nobody will be able to do anything. But if he is pierced through so before that, then he will disappear and nothing else remain behind in the chasuble but three drops of blood, which are the remains of the baptism. Some time afterwards the farm and the church here will burn down to ashes without anybody knowing the reason. Then the settlement here will be abandoned, and never again will there be a settlement here except one little cottage."

This, or so the story says, all came true. The maid secretly had everything written down that had occurred, so the prophecy would not be lost even if she herself should die. Yet this precaution turned out to be unnecessary: she watched the son of the farmer's daughter grow up and be ordained a priest, and she attended when he performed his first service at Feykishólar. But the woman kept a close watch over him, and by then she also had a husband, who served as the sacristan of the church. He had brought an iron tool to the fateful service that had been hardened in holy water, and in the decisive moment he ran the priest through with it; after this, the story ends with the words: "he [the priest] then completely disappeared, and nothing else remained behind but three drops of blood. Somewhat later the farm and the church in Feykishólar burned, and the settlement was then abandoned during the Black Death."

The story never tells us the names of any of the persons involved. It is extremely specific in its reference to a particular place and its topographical features: one can still visit the place "where it happened" and trace, step by step, the locations, the sight lines, the buildings, and even the "graves" that feature in the narrative. The names of the protagonists, however, remain open, as does the time in which it is set. The heroine of the tale is only ever called a *vinnukona* or a *stúlka*: a "woman in service" or a "girl." Maybe this makes the occurrences all the more archetypical: the tale of the *Feykishóladraugur*, the "Ghost of Feykishólar," is not told as happening to a specific named person, but could have happened to any young woman who might have found herself in service at the wrong place at the wrong time.

If this is so, however, it is particularly interesting to consider the role that the maidservant plays, especially if one contrasts her social role and her role in the narrative. Her social role is almost as low as it can be: as a young maid in service, she would have been very close to the bottom of the farm's social hierarchy. Within the narrative, however, she is the heroine who saves the whole congregation in the church from death and maybe worse. One of the lowest of the low becomes the savior of the community, inverting and subverting normal power relations and social hierarchies.

At the same time, the story also inverts power relations on the opposite end of the social spectrum. One of the most drastically victimized protagonists of the story is the farmer's daughter, who is raped by the specter and ultimately dies as the result—even though she had started off from a comparatively strong social position, as her father was both wealthy and knowledgeable and should thus have been able to guarantee her a safe and sheltered life. So the socially high are depicted as falling deep and cruelly. And in parallel to their fall, they also become morally corrupt: the grandson of the rich farmer becomes a priest, which should put him into a position of moral superiority, power, and high status. Yet the priest turns out to be a monster that threatens the whole community, and this high-status monster is brought down through the agency of somebody who used to be one of the lowest members of the household. The story of the Ghost of Feykishólar thus performs a kind of social transvaluation of values: the low are elevated, the rich are shown their vulnerability, and the morally superior are demonstrated to be morally corrupt. The story subverts social hierarchies and power relations, and makes this subversion visible in the landscape by tying it closely to

176 LANDSCAPE, RELIGION, AND THE SUPERNATURAL

the microtopography of Feykishólar and presenting it as the reason for the
abandonment of the valley.

*

When Mitchell in the early 2000s looked back over almost a decade's worth
of research on the relationship between landscape and power, one of his first
conclusions was that the power exerted by the landscape is a relatively "weak"
one, at least compared to the kind of power that is wielded by armed or police forces, governments, or big companies. The power of the landscape, he
emphasized, is a subtle one, whose basic mechanism Mitchell identifies in
the landscape's ability to elicit a broad spectrum of emotional responses; he
calls this an "indeterminacy of affect," which he considers to be crucial for
the influence exerted by the landscape.[250] This indeterminate weakness also
comes into play where the landscape of Strandir seems to be commenting on
questions of social power such as political structures and social hierarchies.
The Kattegat could be understood as a subversive mocking of the Danish
rule of Iceland, but for those less politically inclined it could just as well have
been a simple joke. The lice-picking sorcerer-magician Oddur and his an-
tics at Oddshóll can be understood as a mocking of the Church's claim to
social supremacy and moral superiority; but it could also be perceived as
simply a roadside tale that alleviates the boredom of a tedious journey. The
"Church Hill" Kirkjuhóll, surrounded by its tussock-graves, can be taken
to manifest the injustice of the power claims of the rich and the clergy, to
denounce the violent power exerted by men over women, and to celebrate
laborers and service staff, thus narratively empowering them; but likewise
it can be perceived as just a good horror story that offers a distraction from
the hardships of agricultural work in the upper parts of a long-abandoned,
boggy valley. For it is worthwhile remembering that until very recently nobody would have visited a place like Feykishólar for fun. Places were visited
because one lived there or because one had work to do. A place thus was always either "home" or "labor" (or both). A story connected to such a place
would add an additional level of "meaning" and emotion to it, but whether
this additional level would be perceived as subversive or escapist could often
lie in the eye of the beholder. Also, emphases can shift over time. The historic nineteenth-century narrative about the ghost of Feykishólar, as it was
recorded by Jón Árnason and as I have discussed it earlier, strongly suggests

[250] Mitchell 2002b, vii.

a moral, subversive interpretation. Yet on the one occasion on which I was told a story about the ghost by a farmer from the region, it emphasized the ghost's continuing presence, but had no moral thrust: it simply related that two young men recently went to Feykishólar on brand-new quad bikes, both of which broke down at the haunted farm; and since it is not possible that the engines of two new bikes would fail simultaneously, this must reflect the continuing activity of the ghost.[251]

In storytelling in Strandir, it virtually never happens that the moral of a story is made explicit: nobody ever says "this story means this and that." This understated implicitness of the "message" of Strandir place-lore reflects the "indeterminacy of affect" that Mitchell identified as a central feature of how the landscape works, but it constitutes a major methodological problem when interpreting individual instances of place-storytelling. How can one grasp how a historical audience understood a story when this audience has left no record of its reactions? The answer, one has to admit, is: in many cases one can't. Yet even if individual instances of place-lore may elude clear interpretation, the collective bulk of the storytelling tradition provides guidance: if a single story seems to subvert social hierarchies, it may mean nothing; but if such subversion is a pervasive feature of local storytelling, it becomes significant. In Strandir, a critical view of power structures seems to have been extremely widespread, and the landscape was one arena in which it was articulated: be it by the side of a busy road, along the sea routes, or in the upper reaches of mountain valleys, again and again the power of places is used to subvert power structures and social hierarchies.

8: Sound

The landscape is not only a "geographical" space, a space of the "description of earth," but also a "soundscape,"[252] a space filled with acoustic phenomena. Much like other aspects of the landscape, its sonic aspects can be natural and human-made, real and imagined, or real-and-imagined like Soja's Thirdspace. Here belongs the natural howling of the wind as much as the ringing of human bells, the real sounds of the weather as much as imaginings

---

[251] Ingþór Ólafsson, pers. comm.

[252] On the term "soundscape" cf., for instance, Samuels et al. 2010; Hackett 2016, 323; Hackett 2012, 17–18; Schulz 2008. The term was first established by R. Murray Schafer 1994 (1977). Recently on the analogy between "soundscape" and "landscape," cf. Samuels et al. 2010, 330.

178   LANDSCAPE, RELIGION, AND THE SUPERNATURAL

of "a dark and unspeakable" inhuman voice heard in the fog.[253] All these different sounds, whatever their origin or their "objective reality" (or lack thereof), are a central part of how religion and the supernatural are present in the land.

Auditory approaches to space, and to the study of religions more generally, have long played a comparatively marginal role in research. In recent years, however, sonic perspectives on religions are becoming increasingly more prominent. Thus, Marleen de Witte, using the example of the city of Accra in Ghana, has investigated how religions can use sound to sacralize the urban landscape, to compete over public presence, and to occupy public space. Her study, among many other things, shows how religious practices of creating sound can establish auditory sacred spaces that are not contained within the physical boundaries of the places of worship; and that this spilling over of sound beyond the confines of the cult place into the wider (in her case, urban) landscape is not only used as a way to establish symbolic control of spaces on a political level but also aims to control the spiritual power balance: the aggressive use of loud sound by charismatic Pentecostalist churches is both a political move against the representatives of traditional religion and part of a struggle against the presence of the devil.[254] Charles Hirschkind, in a study of cassette sermons in modern-day Cairo, has focused on the "ethical soundscape" that such sermon tapes create, which the audience uses as a means of moral self-improvement.[255] Rosalind I. J. Hackett, surveying the state of research on sound and religions, has emphasized that the role of sound in religions is vastly understudied and has highlighted the value that an expansion of such research could have for the discipline.[256] Recently, she has even argued for a "sonic turn" in the study of religions.[257]

While in studies of the relationship between religions and sound the topic of sacred music has often taken center stage,[258] Hackett rightly points out that "sound" should be studied as a complex phenomenon that goes far beyond the specific case of music: "sound" includes all audible events, and furthermore it not only includes actual sonic events but also ideas about sound

---

[253] See sections "Morality" and "Labor."

[254] de Witte 2008, esp. pp. 706–707.

[255] Hirschkind 2006.

[256] Hackett 2016; Hackett 2012.

[257] "Sound in/as Religion: Time for a Sonic Turn?" Lecture delivered in Munich on 5 November 2018. Cf. Hackett 2018 and the "call for an aural reflexive turn in the discipline [of anthropology]" by Samuels et al. 2010, 330, 339.

[258] Cf. Schulz 2008, 172; for instance, the special issue "Music and Transcendence" of *Temenos* 48, no. 1 (2012).

as well as sounds that are not "real," but imagined by individual persons—just as one can "see things" in a vision, one can also "hear things."[259] We have encountered such auditory visions previously, as in the story of how the mother of Guðmundur Jónsson from Selbekk heard a terrifying voice below Ýluskarð. Here also belong the stories about how somebody hears the crying of a dead exposed child: such an *útburður* inscribes a moral message into the landscape by literally making its suffering heard. To use Hirschkind's phrase, it creates an "ethical soundscape": just like Hirschkind's cassette sermons, it makes a moral message audible.[260] At an *útburður* site, the howling of the wind can become a "real-and-imagined" sound in which the physical acoustic phenomenon combines with complex overlays of cultural, religious, and moral interpretations.

In the following pages we will pursue the theme of sound in the supernatural landscape of Strandir through two clusters of examples. These encompass both "real" and "imagined" sounds: they focus, on the one hand, on how certain human-made sounds—specifically the ringing of church bells—are interpreted in stories of the supernatural and, on the other hand, on imaginings of sounds emanating from the otherworld inside the rocks.

*

Mókollsdalur is an upland valley located in the mountains south of the fjord of Kollafjörður. It forms an elongated shallow bowl only a few dozen meters below the level of the surrounding plateau. In its shape, with a gently sloping bottom and framed by a ring of steep cliffs, it recalls a kylix, the shallow but steep-rimmed wine-drinking cup of ancient Greece; or a vastly oversized amphitheater. Near its eastern end, set before the background of a perpendicular rock face, a rocky hill rises from the rim of this bowl. The main section of this hill is about 20 m high, and its shape seems to emulate the Bent Pyramid of Dahshur: a pyramid that ends in a clear point, but whose edges, which otherwise form ruler-straight lines, change their angle about halfway up its slope. This hill is Mókollshaugur: "Mókollur's Burial Mound" (Fig. 2.17). It is a massive, prominent structure that became an object of antiquarian and folkloristic interest early on. In 1780, Olaus Olavius in his account of northern Iceland published the following description and discussion:[261]

---

[259] Hackett 2016, 317–318.

[260] See section "Morality."

[261] Olaus Olavius 1780, 1: 154–155 (Danish edition); Olaus Olavius 1787, 101–102 (German edition). For other testimonies about Mókollshaugur, in addition to those quoted below, cf. *SÁM* Guðrún S. Magnúsdóttir 1976a, 4; an interview with Sigríður Gísladóttir recorded on 13 July 1970

180 LANDSCAPE, RELIGION, AND THE SUPERNATURAL

Fig. 2.17 Mókollshaugur ("Mókollur's Burial Mound") in the valley Mókollsdalur ("Mókollur's Valley"), south of Kollafjörður. The foot of this hill, which is c. 20 m high, is located at an elevation of around 390 m above sea level. © M. Egeler, 2019.

Right at the top of Mókollsdalur lies a very large mound, which is steep on all sides, and in which they wished to assert that one of the first inhabitants of the place, by the name of Mókullur or Kollur, was in his time buried with his whole inheritance, under a large hill of stones. But such a report does not seem credible, for however much stronger one wants to imagine the heroes of Antiquity to have been in comparison to the people of this time, it would without the help of mighty machines still have been impossible for them to move such mightily big stones as this hill consists of. The whole report is thus a mere fancy of the imagination, as probably is that, that this man had himself buried precisely here so that he should not be disturbed by the ringing of the bells in the nearest church, and the sun should also not

(SÁM 91/2368 EF—19, https://www.ismus.is/i/audio/id-1013221, 14 August 2020); an interview with Þorvaldur Jónsson recorded on 4 December 1973 (SÁM 92/2587 EF—30, https://www.ismus.is/i/audio/id-1015062, 14 August 2020); an interview with Þórður Bjarnason recorded on 7 July 1970 (SÁM 90/2355 EF—4, https://www.ismus.is/i/audio/id-1013036, 14 August 2020); or the newspaper article by Árni Óla 1956, 280. Mókollshaugur already appears in the writings of Jón Guðmundsson the Learned (1574–1658): Viðar Hreinsson 2016, 145–146.

TWELVE MOVEMENTS 181

end up shining on the hill; which last-mentioned thing, however, at times happens during summer.

In this tradition, a very striking—but also very obviously natural—hill is interpreted as the burial mound of a local founding hero. Directly drawing on Olaus Olavius, Jón Árnason also told this story in the mid-nineteenth century.[262] Jón's version highlights the historical roots of this tradition by emphasizing that the Kollur or Mókollur ("Brown-Kollur") of this legend is the same man whom the medieval *Book of Settlements* mentions as the first and eponymous settler of Kollafjörður.[263] Here, as with other legendary founders' burial mounds, the eponymous founding hero of a fjord, who appears already in medieval literature, receives a monumental "grave" in the mountains above the fjord. In this way, he is forever after enshrined above the fjord that he is said to have settled during the Icelandic Settlement Period of the ninth and tenth centuries.

Such founders' burial mounds come close to Mikhail Bakhtin's concept of the "chronotope" as it has been adopted and transformed in landscape research.[264] Bakhtin (1895–1975) developed this concept specifically for the study of literature and explained that his intention was to "give the name *chronotope* (literally, 'time space') to the intrinsic connectedness of temporal and spatial relationships that are artistically expressed in literature. [. . .] [I]t expresses the inseparability of space and time." The term aims to capture a literary intersection and fusion of time and space. In the chronotope, "spatial and temporal indicators are fused into one carefully thought-out, concrete whole. Time, as it were, thickens, takes on flesh, becomes artistically visible; likewise, space becomes charged and responsive to the movements of time, plot and history."[265] Originally, this concept was intended for the analysis of literature and literary motifs, such as historical literary genres and characteristic kinds of historical spaces in literature. In landscape research it has been adapted to refer to places in which time is felt to take on concrete form, and where in this way "time takes on flesh." Ingold, for

---

[262] Jón Árnason 1954–1961, 2: 91, 570.

[263] *Landnámabók*, ed. Jakob Benediktsson 1968, ch. S164=H133. There, the name of the settler appears in the form *Kolli* rather than *Kollur* (which represent a weak and a strong declension respectively); linguistically the older form shows a better congruence with the name of the fjord that allegedly is derived from it, since only the older form "Kolli" forms a genitive singular *Kolla* leading to Kollafjörður, "Kolli's Fjord."

[264] Bakhtin 1981; cf. Tally 2013, 54–58, 155. On its applicability in research on supernatural folk storytelling, see Asplund Ingemark 2006.

[265] Quotations: Bakhtin 1981, 84.

182 LANDSCAPE, RELIGION, AND THE SUPERNATURAL

instance, applies it to the examples of a mature tree or an old church,[266] whereas Basso uses the concept to approach places in the landscape of the Western Apache that have names and are connected with deeply important historical stories.[267] In Strandir storytelling, the concept of the chronotope seems particularly opportune to grasp a marked characteristic of the regional tradition of founders' burial mounds: they are consistently connected with specific types of stories that locate their creation in a deep past. In the founder's burial mound as a chronotope, the past takes on material form in the landscape, and this is connected with a storytelling tradition that is so fixed it can almost be described as a genre. Correspondingly, Mókollshaugur is connected with the same miracle story as other such founders' burial mounds. Commonly, at such mounds would-be grave robbers are deterred by fire illusions: once upon a time, when an attempt was made to break into the mound, everything suddenly seemed to stand in flames, and the work was stopped.[268] According to a version still told today, when some people tried to break into Mókollshaugur, the church at Fell seemed to be burning, which put an immediate end to the mound-breaking attempt. The only thing that was retrieved from the treasure in the mound was a ring, which afterward served as the door ring of the church at Fell—just as the door ring of the church of Staður likewise came from the local founder's burial mound Steingrímshaugur, the traditional burial place of Steingrímur the Troll, who is viewed as the founding settler of Steingrímsfjörður and the first person/troll to live at Staður.[269]

What makes Mókollshaugur and the chronotope of the founder's burial mound particularly interesting in the current context are the parameters that Olaus Olavius and Jón Árnason give for its choice of location: "this man had himself buried precisely here so that he should not be disturbed by the

---

[266] Ingold 1993, 169.

[267] Basso 1996, 62. Basso has had a particularly strong impact as he provides a reformulation of Bakhtin's term, which was designed for studying literature, for the study of physical story landscapes, but unfortunately presents this reformulation as if it were a direct quotation from Bakhtin. This has created a "pseudo-Bakhtinian" passage that itself has been quoted widely.

[268] For Mókollshaugur cf. the interview with Þorvaldur Jónsson recorded on 13 December 1973 (SÁM 91/2573 EF—24, https://www.ismus.is/i/audio/id-1014865, 5 July 2020). The same story is also attested multiple times for the founder's burial mound Steingrímshaugur above the church of Staður, e.g., SÁM Magnús Steingrímsson 1929, 10; SÁM Magnús Steingrímsson 1953a, 33–34; SÁM Magnús Steingrímsson 1953c, 5. Cf. Egeler forthcoming a, with further attestations.

[269] Gunnhildur Halldórsdóttir, pers. comm.; cf. the interviews with Þorvaldur Jónsson recorded on 4 December 1973 (SÁM 92/2587 EF—30, https://www.ismus.is/i/audio/id-1015062, 14 August 2020) and on 13 December 1973 (SÁM 91/2574 EF—25, https://www.ismus.is/i/audio/id-1014866, and SÁM 91/2573 EF—24, https://www.ismus.is/i/audio/id-1014865, 14 August 2020).

ringing of the bells in the nearest church," and so that the sun should never shine on his hill. To a certain extent, these parameters are based on stock motifs of local storytelling rather than on topographical reality. The church at Fell would indeed have been too far away for its bells to be heard—it was located on the other side of a mountain ridge—but the sun very much does shine on Mókollshaugur. So the story was told in this way not because it reflects physical reality, but in order to conform with established themes of local folklore. There, the avoidance of sunlight and—especially—the ringing of church bells is closely associated with paganism, magic, and the world of the trolls. The parsonage of Hvammur in the neighboring district of Dalir is connected with a founding story in which the malevolent pagan witch Gullbrá plays a central role. After this being of pagan evil has been driven from the valley by the power of Christianity, Gullbrá withdraws into a deep chasm in the mountain to lead a kind of undead existence: "She said she wanted to lie where she would never see the sun and would never be able to hear the ringing of bells."[270] These are exactly the same specifications as those stipulated by Mókollur, which indicates that the mode of his burial puts the primeval founder squarely into the world of the pagan past. What is important here is that the chronotope of the ancient pagan grave seems to include a horror of the sound of Christian bells.

An association between ancient paganism and a dislike of church bells also recurs in other types of narratives. The founding story of the church at Staður closely connects the history of the church there with the troll woman Kleppa. Kleppa particularly hated it when she heard the church bells ring while she was on her way to her temple at Hofstaðir ("Temple-Steads"). What is more, the church at Staður itself was built from driftwood that had been procured from the troll by the ringing of church bells: on one occasion, when Kleppa was transporting driftwood past the site of the church, she suddenly heard the bells chiming, and this startled her so much that she dropped the wood where she stood, rushed home, packed her stuff, and left the district for good.[271] The church bells at Staður also play a similar—if more burlesque— role in a story about the troll woman Þjóðbrók. This troll lusted after a farmhand; so she abducted the man and kept him prisoner. In the end, however, he managed to escape from her cave and was saved from her pursuit by ringing the bell in the portico of the church at Staður, as its sound drove the

---

[270] Jón Árnason 1954–1961, 1: 140–144, quotation: p. 142.
[271] Jón Árnason 1954–1961, 1: 144–145.

184   LANDSCAPE, RELIGION, AND THE SUPERNATURAL

troll away, who otherwise would just have dragged him back to her lair.[272] Furthermore, a story connected with Drangsnes illustrates the vanity of any trollish attempt to stand up against the might of the bells. Once upon a time, a troll lived on the mountain above the village. This troll was greatly vexed by the ringing of the bells of the monastery of Þingeyrar. Yet when his patience snapped and he in the end decided to go and silence them, he merely ended up getting caught out by the sun and turning to stone, and to this day he can be seen as the sea-stack of Hvítserkur.[273]

The sound of church bells banishes the hostile supernatural world of trolls, witchcraft, and paganism. Their chiming marks out a Christian space in which such remnants of the pre-Christian period—or what was felt to be remnants of this period—literally had no place. Where this principle is applied to the grave mound of the founding hero of the fjord, a marked ambivalence becomes evident: according to local tradition, Kollafjörður was founded and named from (Mó-)Kollur; but the coming of Christianity pushes the ancient pagan hero to the margins of the space that he himself had established. Like other founding heroes, he is a figure somewhere betwixt and between veneration for antiquity and suspicion of its pagan ways. He is the venerated embodiment of the foundational time of the Settlement Period; and yet his flight from the chiming of the bells brings him close to the trolls, the prehuman inhabitants of Iceland.

We can observe exactly the same kind of marginality also in the person of Steingrímur the Troll, even though there it is expressed in a slightly different way. Steingrímur as well is a venerated founder, and while his trollishness is not indicated by a flight from the church bells, he carries his troll-like nature in his very name: Steingrímur *trölli*, Steingrímur the Troll. Maybe the first generation of settlers and founders had to be imagined as taking up an ambivalent position between human and troll to be able to mediate between the prehuman land of the trolls and the post-Settlement landscape of human beings. In the landscape, storytelling then compressed this temporal distinction into a spatial one, much as Bachelard proposed: "In its countless alveoli space contains compressed time. That is what space is for."[274] In this spatial compression of time, the reach of the Christian church bells marked

[272] E.g., *SÁM* Magnús Steingrímsson 1953c, 7–8; *SÁM* Magnús Steingrímsson 1929, 11–12; Jón Árnason 1954–1961, 1: 183.
[273] See the local Strandir webpage: http://strandir.saudfjarsetur.is/af-skessum-bofum-og-drau gum/, 18 August 2020.
[274] Bachelard 1994 (1958), 8.

TWELVE MOVEMENTS   185

the Christian present, while the silence of the mountains remained the space of a pagan past. Thus, the location of Mókollshaugur, as well as the flight of the trolls from the ringing bells more generally, asserts the Christian identity of Iceland while at the same time allocating a space to its older heritage. In this way it facilitates the coexistence of both without having to forgo the self-definition of the island as a Lutheran-Protestant Christian country.

*

Integration through sound, in a way which almost inverts the fate of the trolls, also seems to play a central role for another type of supernatural beings—though not necessarily in a straightforward or overly serious manner. One prime example that we have encountered already is the hill Álfhóll ("Elf Hill") or Nónhóll ("3 O'Clock Hill") at Kleifar.[275] Some people are said to have thought the hill a dwelling place of elves and to have heard singing from there on holy days—yet one of the farmers at Kleifar nevertheless put a flagpole on top of it, and his successor found this so ridiculous that he in turn renamed the hill Gálgahóll, "Gallows' Hill." With its name changes, its hymnal music, and how it was not exactly taken seriously by everybody, this Elf Hill/3 O'Clock Hill/Gallow's Hill is a good example of its kind. A few farms further east, it finds a remarkably close parallel in the Stórusteinar ("Big Stones") or Nónsteinar ("3 O'Clock Stones") over the farm of Geirmundarstaðir in Selárdalur. Like the elf hill at Kleifar, these stones were prominently visible from the farmhouse; they likewise derived one of their names (Nónsteinar, "3 O'Clock Stones") from the position of the sun at 3 o'clock; and they were both supernatural and yet not really taken that seriously. As Sigurður Gunnlaugsson wrote of them:[276]

> It is said that hidden folk (*huldufólk*) live in these stones. Often one can see light, one can hear speaking, singing, rattling, and ringing; yet the one who is writing this has still never become aware of anything and considers it likely that everything of that sort is a figment of the imagination, and nothing else.

Both Nónhóll/Álfhóll/Gálgahóll hill and the boulders of the Nónsteinar/Stórusteinar are places said to be inhabited by elves without this arousing the

---

[275] See section "Time and Memory."
[276] *SÁM* Sigurður Gunnlaugsson 1929b, 2. Cf. *SÁM* Sigurður Gunnlaugsson 1929a, 20–21.

186 LANDSCAPE, RELIGION, AND THE SUPERNATURAL

awe of contemporaries: Sigurður tells the stories but doesn't believe a word of it, and the elf hill at Kleifar has a history of use and reuse where the hill could shift from a place of the supernatural to a foundation for a flagpole and from there to an object of a contemptuous joke, though it seems it could be a combination of any or all of these things for different people at the same time.

Another aspect that connects these two elven places is their use of sound. In what seems like an inversion of the story told about Mókollur's place of burial, which is located in silence and sunless darkness, these places of the elves emanate light and, especially, sound: around them, one hears all the sounds of human life—"speaking, singing, rattling, and ringing"—of which the singing in particular plays a recurring role. This singing was (claimed to be) heard especially on holy days, indicating that it emanated from a Christian divine service that was being celebrated by the elves.

Throughout Strandir, prominent rocky hills served as the churches of the elves, and time and again the music and the bells of their services could be heard there. Thus, the rock Hestur in Goðdalur was considered such a place, of which "[i]t was said that this rock was the church of the hidden people (*huldufólk*) [. . .]. There is a story about that, that the people who once lived in Goðdalur had heard the ringing of church bells from there, and all the inhabitants of the farm heard it, so one could not speak of mishearing."[277] On the land of the farm of Skjaldabjarnarvík in Árneshreppur, not far from the farmhouse, there were rocks inhabited by elves that had the name Kórklettar: "Choir Rocks."[278] It seems as if the singing of the elven church choir here provided the name for the place in which they were thought to have their abode. When Ingimundur Ingimundarson wrote about his farm of Svanshóll in Bjarnarfjörður in the late 1970s, furthermore, he noted with particular affection (Fig. 2.18):[279]

> Neðri-Hamar ("Lower Crag") [. . .] The crag was an abode of the hidden people (*huldufólksbyggð*) and from there one could hear the sound of butter churns and spinning wheels, and also singing. Hopefully the homestead is there still, and I have from an early age had particularly fond feelings towards this place of the hidden people (*huldufólksstaður*) and been careful not to do any damage there.

---

[277] Guðrún Níelsdóttir 1976, 68.
[278] *SÁM* Haukur Jóhannesson s.a. (b), 5.
[279] *SÁM* Ingimundur Ingimundarson 1978, 9.

Fig. 2.18 The elf-rock Neðri-Hamar ("Lower Crag") on the land of Svanshóll farm, from where "one could hear the sound of butter churns and spinning wheels, and also singing." © M. Egeler, 2019.

Sound—or the imagining of sound—here becomes a central part of what establishes the emotional connections between the farmer and the supernatural on his or her land; or in other words: imaginings and cultural interpretations of sound appear as a central means through which the affective relationship to the landscape is shaped. In the case of elf rocks and elf hills, this relationship can span a broad spectrum, covering everything from acerbic humor via polite disbelief to deep fondness. Elves create the same sounds as their human neighbors, including the sounds of work as much as those of religious observances, and end up being viewed with much the same range of attitudes that human neighbors might be. The human and Christian sound world of the elves marks their integration into the order of a human and Christian society.

*

R. Murray Schafer, in his foundational *The Soundscape*, did not specifically focus on religion and the supernatural; but given the central role that religious sounds can play for a community, some aspects of religious sound

188 LANDSCAPE, RELIGION, AND THE SUPERNATURAL

still formed part of his discussion. Thus, he remarked on the role of church bells:[280]

> The most salient sound signal in the Christian community is the church bell. In a very real sense it defines the community, for the parish is an acoustic space, circumscribed by the range of the church bell. The church bell is a centripetal sound; it attracts and unifies the community in a social sense, just as it draws man and God together. At times in the past it took on a centrifugal force as well, when it served to frighten away evil spirits.

Schafer's approach has been criticized as being based on a somewhat romantic worldview,[281] and his simplistic equation of the boundaries of the parish with the range of the bells of the parish church is certainly romantic more than realistic. Yet this only makes it the more interesting that his romantic, idealist view of the ringing of church bells actually finds a close counterpart in the story of Mókollur's burial mound: for according to the Mókollur legend, the old pagan founding hero wanted to be buried outside the new Christian world, at a place where the ringing of the church bells would never reach him, and thus the location of Mókollshaugur, "Mókollur's Mound," was chosen. Also all other aspects of Schafer's musings on bells are mirrored in the material discussed earlier. The imagined bells of the elves in their mounds have a centripetal force in that they mark the common bond between human and elven society, both of which are part of Christendom and connected by the shared sacred sounds of bells and hymns; and the real bells of the human churches are ascribed a centrifugal force when they drive away trolls and thus offer protection against the pagan past that is still lurking in the mountains.[282]

Sound in this storytelling tradition is a central part of a construction of contrasting spaces that represents the difference between the safe, inhabited human world of the coastline and the valley bottoms, on the one hand, and the dangerous world of the mountains that surrounds it, on the other hand. In this construction of the world, the elves are part not of the threatening outside, but of the human inside of the cosmos. Their belonging to the human world is marked not least through their sounds. The abodes of the elves are not only located in close proximity to the human farmhouses, but they also

---

[280] Schafer 1994 (1977), 54. Cf. Hackett 2016, 321.
[281] Samuels et al. 2010, 331.
[282] Cf. de Witte 2008, 707.

Table 2.1 The Supernatural Landscape and Soundscape of Lowland versus Upland Areas

Intensely Farmed Lowland	Extensively Farmed Upland
Soundscape of bells, Christian liturgy, and productive work	Silence of the mountains outside the range of the bells
Humans and elves	Trolls and pagan heroes
Safety	Danger

utter the same sounds of Christian worship and productive agricultural work as human houses and human churches do. The closest that trolls ever come to farming is rustling sheep from upland pastures; but from an elf rock, one can hear the homely sound of a butter churn. The differences between the intensely farmed lowland and the extensively farmed upland are thus reflected in differences between the supernatural actors located there and the sounds shunned or emitted by them (Table 2.1).

The soundscape of Strandir thus forms part of how the landscape is filled with specific meanings. Within this construction of a humanized space, the soundscape makes clear how the central opposition that characterizes this system is not an opposition between "natural" and "supernatural" or between "human" and "supernatural," but between the intensely farmed lowland close by the farmhouses and the upland areas of the mountains, where extensive farming is practiced. Comparatively remote and removed from human beings, this highland space is a dangerous place to be. There, the weather is at its most extreme, and in the case of accidents, help is far away. Storytelling mirrors the very real dangers of the upland areas in the form of man-grabbing trolls that, closer to home, within the range of the church bells, would pose no threat. Home is safety, and this safety is marked by sound.

9: Emotions

Emotions have always played a major role in the study of religions, even, indeed, in its fundamental conceptualization; with the current "emotive turn" of the arts and humanities their role in research is increasing even more.[283]

---

[283] For overviews, cf. Corrigan 2016; Corrigan 2008a; Stubbe 1999.

190 LANDSCAPE, RELIGION, AND THE SUPERNATURAL

A focus on emotions was deeply embedded already in those strands of Protestant theology that were to exert a formative influence on the creation of the study of religions as a nontheological discipline.[284] One proponent of a particularly influential view of religion as founded on emotions was Friedrich Schleiermacher (1768–1854), who identified the essential core of religion with feeling and the perception of the universe: "Ihr Wesen ist weder Denken noch Handeln, sondern Anschauung und Gefühl" ("Its inner essence is neither thinking nor action, but perception and feeling").[285] Specifically, he came to argue that the central core of religion is to be seen in a feeling of absolute dependency.[286] Rudolf Otto, whose *Das Heilige* ("The Sacred," first edition 1917) was to become tremendously influential in spite of its essentially theological thrust, developed Schleiermacher's emphasis on a feeling of dependency into his own notion of the "Kreaturgefühl" ("creature feeling"), which—or so he argued—is experienced in the face of the "numinous." The numinous he defined as the sacred minus any ethical or rational elements; in this concept he saw the core of all religions. For Otto, the experience of the numinous, which engendered the "creature feeling," was an experience of a *mysterium tremendum* and a *mysterium fascinans*: a feeling of absolute inferiority in the face of a mystery that both inspires fear and exerts fascination.[287]

Otto's two-pronged *mysterium tremendum* and *mysterium fascinans* in some respects closely parallels the category of the "sublime." Since the eighteenth century, the "sublime" has become established as one of the most central, and most enduring, conceptualizations of an attractive landscape in Western culture. In 1757, Edmund Burke published his *A Philosophical Enquiry into the Origin of Our Ideas of the Sublime and Beautiful*, which was to become a milestone of (thinking about) the perception of landscapes in Europe. Burke explored how "terrible objects" exercise an attraction through the "sublime," which is experienced when something terrible is observed at a safe distance: something terrifying that is looked at without danger to oneself, so the argument goes, creates a strong feeling of delight, and this is what is described by the "sublime."[288] This sublime, as something whose

---

[284] Cf. Gladigow 1988, 7.

[285] Schleiermacher 1969 (1799), 35.

[286] Corrigan 2016, 512.

[287] Otto 1926 (1917), 5–7 ("Das Numinose"), 8–12 ("Kreaturgefühl"), 13–30 ("Mysterium tremendum"), 43–54 ("Fascinans"). Cf. Yelle 2019, 10; Corrigan 2016, 512; Mariña 2008.

[288] Esp. Burke 1887, 1: 110–111 (Part 1, Section VII). Cf. Macfarlane 2008, 74–77; Pavord 2016, 13–14, 28; Doran 2015; Tuan 2013, esp. p. 96; Schama 1996, 447–462.

fascination is fueled by a sense of terror, has entered landscape painting through features such as soaring cliffs, raging torrents, or deep ravines, and has remained a central element of the popular representation of landscape to this day; it would not be a difficult task to base a textbook on the sublime on contemporary advertisements for "adventure travel" and outdoor gear. In its emotional composition as a blend of terror and delighted attraction, the sublime in its basic outlines is much the same as Otto's *mysterium tremendum et fascinans*. Otto indeed identifies the sublime (in German: "das Erhabene")[289] as the most effective way of representing his "numinous" in the arts. He even uses landscape painting, specifically landscape painting from classical China, as one of his examples for particularly potent artistic expressions of the "numinous."[290]

Against this background, when approaching landscape and emotions in the study of religions, one might expect that the sublime would play a major role in the enquiry. In many contexts, indeed it would—I have already mentioned its pervasiveness in the iconography of (urban) advertising. The growth of the study of emotions in the study of religions has, however, created an awareness of the huge range of emotions that can play a role in this field. Emotions in religions are not just the feelings created by the sublime or Otto's "creature feeling" but also hope, melancholia, or the complex emotional cocktail associated with sexuality and the erotic.[291] Thomas A. Tweed highlights especially the intensifying of joy and the confronting of suffering as important emotional aspects of religions.[292] Also in the field of geography, more emotions than just the experience of the "sublime" have been investigated. Especially the foundational studies of Yi-Fu Tuan should be mentioned here. Thus, Tuan pioneered topics such as the study of landscapes of fear;[293] the concept of "topophilia" as "the affective bond between people and place or setting";[294] or the concept of "geopiety," which he defines as a mutually respectful, pious, and reverent relationship between the land, its supernatural entities, and its human beings.[295] In the philosophical discourse,

---

[289] Cf. the discussions of "das Erhabene" by Friedrich von Schiller (1759–1805): Schiller 1980, 5: 489–512, 792–808.
[290] Otto 1926 (1917), 88, 91. Cf. Kieschnick 2008, 226.
[291] On hope in religions, cf. Miller 2008; Tweed 2006, 71; on melancholia: Rubin 2008; on sexuality: Kripal 2008.
[292] Tweed 2006, 54, 69–72. See section "Playfulness and Adventure."
[293] Tuan 2013 (1979); more recently, cf. Felton 2018; Egeler 2021a.
[294] Tuan 1990 (1974), quotation: p. 4.
[295] Tuan 1976. Further cf., for instance, Cosgrove 1998, xx; Cosgrove 2008, 27.

192 LANDSCAPE, RELIGION, AND THE SUPERNATURAL

Angelika Krebs has even proposed that experiencing the atmosphere of beautiful landscapes is an essential part of "the good human life."[296]

Looking at the Icelandic material not only justifies but actually demands such a breadth of analytical approaches; for even though the iconography of Icelandic tourism marketing liberally draws on an imagery based on the sublime, the sublime appears to play hardly any role in the traditional farming landscape of Strandir. Emotions are culturally specific and historically contingent,[297] and the sublime is just not articulated as part of the traditional emotional repertoire of the supernatural landscape of the region. Rather, the dominant building blocks of Strandir's "emotional topography"—to use Camilla Asplund Ingemark's and Dominic Ingemark's term[298]—are expressions of the close relationship that people have with the agricultural land, and the importance of creating a feeling of safety. On the following pages, I will pursue these themes through three clusters of examples: love affairs between humans and the spirits of the farmland, the "elves"; the song *Sveitin mín*, "My Country," which is the unofficial hymn of the Icelandic countryside; and the wells and watercourses blessed by Guðmundur the Good.

*

The inner part of the valley of Selárdalur used to be farmed by Gilsstaðir farm. A prominent, large boulder sits low on the slope above the home-field of the former farm, not far from the farmhouse. In the late 1920s, in an issue of the local journal *Viljinn*, Sigurður Rósmundsson told the following story about this boulder:[299]

> In front of [the old night pen] is a big stone, which is called Ekkjusteinn ("Stone of the Widow"). In connection with its name this is told, which I shall relate now:
>
> A man was called Eyúlfur. He lived at Gilsstaðir in the second half of the eighteenth century. It is said that he disappeared every New Year's Eve, so that nobody knew what became of him. Yet the tradition had it that he visited that stone, and reputedly an elf woman (*huldukona*) was there that he had an acquaintance with, and she was a widow. And the stone has its name from that. In like manner, this Eyúlfur reputedly went into some other

---

[296] Krebs 2014.
[297] Cf. Corrigan 2016, 513.
[298] Asplund Ingemark and Ingemark 2020, esp. pp. 167–171, 248–250. See chapter 1, section "Living in Landscapes."
[299] *SÁM* Sigurður Rósmundsson s.a., 12–13.

TWELVE MOVEMENTS   193

stones (*steina*) and cliffs (*kletta*) that exist in many places in Selárdalur valley.

The nature of Eyúlfur's "acquaintance" (*kunningsskapur*) with the elf woman is not spelled out, but the story type is common enough to make clear that it was of the biblical variety: erotic love relationships between elves and humans are a very common topic of Icelandic folklore.[300] The following story is set somewhere on nearby Selströnd, the section of the north coast of Steingrímsfjörður onto which the Selárdalur valley opens. This tale was put into writing in 1902:[301]

> A man is called Kristinn, and some years ago he was at home at Selströnd on Steingrímsfjörður. There, he often met a girl of the race of the elves (*álfakyn*), and they became so dear to each other that she sometimes visited him, and they agreed to meet under a certain cliff (*klettur*) not far from the farm every New Year's Eve. Kristinn moved from Selströnd into a different district, but the elf woman (*huldukona*) promised him beforehand to meet him at the next turn of the year. He was betrayed, and Kristinn became very melancholy (*þunglyndur*) from that.

Both these stories tell of how a farmer had a love affair with the spirit of his land, bringing Tuan's concepts of "topophilia" and "geopiety" together in a way evocative of the Song of Songs:[302] living with the supernatural is imagined as cohabitation in both senses of the word. While Sigurður Rósmundsson's account of the "Widow's Stone" at Gilsstaðir, taken by itself, might have suggested the erotic fantasies of a lonely bachelor, comparison with the roughly contemporary and geographically nearby account of Kristinn at Selströnd suggests that something more complex is going on here. When Kristinn moves away from his farm, he also loses his elven beloved and sinks into depression. Arguably, what brings Kristinn down is his longing for home: homesickness is expressed in the image of a farmer's pining for his supernatural lover. This ties in with the typical location of elf rocks. The cliff where Kristinn met his supernatural lover was "not far from the farm" ("skammt frá bænum"); the "Widow's Stone" at Gilsstaðir is located not only

---

[300] Cf. the collection of stories of love between elves and human beings assembled by Ólafur Davíðsson 1978–1980, 1: 40–59.
[301] Ólafur Davíðsson 1978–1980, 1: 43.
[302] Tuan 1990 (1974); Tuan 1976.

194 LANDSCAPE, RELIGION, AND THE SUPERNATURAL

less than 300 m from the farmhouse as the crow flies but also directly above an old night pen; and also on other farms, the farm's elf hills and elf rocks are typically located in the direct vicinity of the human habitations. At Gilsstaðir, the detail that Ekkjusteinn was located directly above a former night pen is both typical and important. This night pen would have been used to hold the milk-giving ewes overnight so one would be able to milk them; this means that people would have worked and spent much time there on a daily basis. The rocks and cliffs of the hidden people belong closely to the farms and their everyday life, and have done so for a very long time: a story about a marriage between the farmer at Stóra-Fjarðarhorn in the parish of Fell and an elf woman was recorded already by Jón Guðmundsson the Learned (1574–1658).[303] It seems that one important aspect of storytelling about the rocks of the hidden people was to describe the close connection between the land and the human beings working it: the dwellings of the elves give a physical shape to how people can fall in love with their home.

*

Gaston Bachelard, one of the pioneers of spatial theory, entitled his foundational study of the experience of space as *La poétique de l'espace*, "The Poetics of Space."[304] The influence of his work has reached far beyond poetics, but poetic texts that address the relationship between people and space still offer important insights into perceptions of space and landscape. In Iceland, and certainly in Strandir, a special place is here taken by Sigurður Jónsson's poem *Sveitin mín*, "My Country." Sigurður Jónsson (1878–1949) was a farmer, teacher, and poet who was born and spent his life in the district of Mývatnssveit.[305] He wrote *Sveitin mín* as a very young man at some point around 1900.[306] In 1904, Bjarni Þorsteinsson set *Sveitin mín* to music as a choral song in four parts in the Romantic style.[307] Poem and setting struck a chord and quickly became one of the most popular songs of Iceland. To

---

[303] Jón Árnason 1954–1961, 1: 99–100; Viðar Hreinsson 2016, 146–147; Einar Ólafur Sveinsson 2003, 107.

[304] Bachelard 1994 (1958).

[305] *Ísmús* s.v. "Sigurður Jónsson á Arnarvatni" (https://www.ismus.is/einstaklingar/1001359, 11 April 2022).

[306] I have not been able to locate for certain where the poem was first published. Today, the text circulates in all manner of forms, including web pages, sheets of music, and reprints in newspapers, with no source ever being given. It was published by 1902 at the latest, when it was printed in the Icelandic literature periodical *Eimreiðin* 8, no. 2 (1902): 107–108.

[307] *Petrucci Music Library* s.v. "Sveitin mín (Þorsteinsson, Bjarni)" (https://imslp.org/wiki/Sveitin_m%C3%ADn_(%C3%9Eorsteinsson%2C_Bjarni), 20 August 2020).

this day, it is regularly performed in everything from the original Romantic choral setting to the jazzy reinterpretation by Kjass in her album *Rætur* (2019).

Sveitin mín is something like the unofficial hymn of the Icelandic countryside. The term *sveit* can denote a district or region, and thus "sveitin mín," "my *sveit*," has undertones of a very local specificity; but it also has connotations of being rural and agricultural. *Sveitin mín* is "My local rural home area," and the poem lets an unnamed speaker describe his relationship to his rural home in the following way:

Queen of mountains, my mother!	Fjalladrottning, móðir mín!
So beloved to me and close to my heart,	mér svo kær og hjartabundin,
Full of bliss do I live at your breast,	sæll ég bý við brjóstin þín,
My blessed foster mother of the hills.	blessuð aldna fóstra mín.
Here the soul has all its homelands	Hér á andinn óðul sín
That are found on earth.	öll, sem verða á jörðu fundin.
Queen of mountains, my mother,	Fjalladrottning, móðir mín,
So beloved to me and close to my heart.	mér svo kær og hjartabundin.
Blessed be you, my country,	Blessuð sértu, sveitin mín,
Summer, winter, year, and days.	sumar, vetur, ár og daga.
Your pasture, mountains, river	Engið, fjöllin, áin þín,
—My wonderful country!—	—yndislega sveitin mín!—
Enchant me and pull my mind	heilla mig og heim til sín
Home to itself from the distance.	huga minn úr fjarlægð draga.
Blessed be, my country,	Blessuð sértu, sveitin mín,
Summer, winter, year, and days.	sumar, vetur, ár og daga.
Everything that I loved and love most	Allt, sem mest ég unni og ann,
Is enveloped in your embrace.	er í þínum faðmi bundið.
Everything that I found most beautiful,	Allt það, sem ég fegurst fann,
Fight for and love most ardently,	fyrir berst og heitast ann,
Everything that made a man of me	allt, sem gert fékk úr mér mann
And gave me strength to work,	og til starfa kröftum hrundið,
Everything that I loved and love most	allt, sem mest ég unni og ann,
Is enveloped in your embrace.	er í þínum faðmi bundið.
My beautiful, dear mother,	Fagra, dýra móðir mín,
Refuge of my cradle,	minnar vöggu griðastaður,

When life's day dwindles,	þegar lífsins dagur dvín,
My dear, beloved foster mother,	dýra, kæra fóstra mín,
Prepare for me a place by your heart.	búðu um mig við brjóstin þín.
There, glad, I dwell forever.	Bý ég þar um eilífð glaður.
My beautiful, dear mother,	Fagra, dýra móðir mín,
Refuge of my cradle.	minnar vöggu griðastaður.

This poem is a declaration of love for a rural home and its landscape. The "queen of mountains" (*fjalladrottning*), which in Strandir was explained to me as a personification of nature,[308] is here described as the "mother" of the speaker, and as his *fóstra*. The latter term means a "foster mother," but not in a specific institutional sense but as the person who brought somebody up and taught them to know right from wrong and how to tackle life. This mother guides and accompanies the speaker from the cradle to the grave and beyond.

The most iconic stanza of the poem is the second one, "Blessuð sértu, sveitin mín"/"Blessed be you, my country." In abridged musical performances, the second stanza is always performed, whereas the remaining stanzas are sung more rarely. The first verse of this stanza is so strongly felt to encapsulate people's relationship to their home that one may, for instance, find it in elegant, large lettering in a meters-long scroll running along the living-room wall of a farmhouse, where it seems to express the relationship to home in the most intimate space of the home. Even more poignantly, this stanza is one of the most frequently used pieces of music that are sung at funerals. Especially at the funerals of farmers, and here in particular at the funerals of those farmers that had not been particularly close to the Church, "Blessuð sértu, sveitin mín" is part of the stock repertoire of songs sung at the graveside.[309]

The vocabulary used by the poem has a certain inherent ambivalence that allows a broad span of readings. It can be understood as a secular (if poetic) declaration of love to one's homeland, where "homeland" is not the nation, but the concrete land farmed by oneself and one's neighbors. Equally, it can be interpreted as an expression of an agricultural nature mysticism,

---

[308] Jón Jónsson, pers. comm.; Sigurður Jónsson may have meant something different—maybe a particular mountain belonging specifically to his personal home district—but the success of the poem is based on its openness, which allows every Icelander to interpret it as a reference to his or her own home county. Cf. also the motif of the *Fjallkona* ("Mountain Woman"), an image for Iceland coined in nineteenth-century Romantic poetry; on the *Fjallkona*, see Gunnell 2016.

[309] Jón Jónsson, pers. comm.

which elevates, venerates, and loves the land it works (the working relationship to the land is made very explicit in the verse "And gave me strength to work"). The blessing at the beginning of the poem's most famous verse, "Blessuð sértu"/"Blessed be you," uses the verb *blessa*, "to bless." This verb reached Iceland as a loanword from Old English when Iceland became Christian; so in its earliest usage in Icelandic it was a specifically Christian religious term designating a Christian blessing. Yet while it is still used in this sense, its usage has broadened to include greetings and even the polite opening of letters, so the verse can be understood in as much a strictly "religious" sense as it pleases singers and audience.[310] Similarly, when the home country "enchants" the speaker, the verb *heilla* can, used in the strict sense, have strong magical-supernatural connotations ("to bewitch, enchant, spellbind"); but metaphorically it can also be used for amorous infatuation, for being in love.[311] So the language of the poem is ambivalent. The way it is used, however, is much less so. When the poem is found as an inscription in a farmhouse in the same way in which in the Alpine countries one would find an invocation of God and the saints, and even more when it is sung at funerals, it becomes clear that both emotionally and spiritually, the poem is understood in just as emphatic a way as a first reading of the text suggests. It hints at a sublimation of one's farmland and an infatuation with one's home landscape just as strong as the one that made Kristinn at Selströnd "melancholy" for the rest of his life when he was separated from his elven lover, the spirit of his farm.

*

"Topophilia" is not the only central theme of the *ménage à trois* of emotions, landscape, and religion but also the thematic field of contingency, safety, and protection is important in this context. John Corrigan highlighted contingency as a core theme of the study of religion and emotion in the very first sentence of his handbook on religions and emotion,[312] and Bachelard in his classic *The Poetics of Space* put a feeling of being protected at the heart of what creates a positive emotional bond between people and places.[313] Even though elsewhere in this book coping with contingency, given its fundamental importance, is the topic of a chapter of its own, it is so important in the context

---

[310] Cf. Cleasby and Gudbrand Vigfusson 1874, s.v. "bleza."
[311] Cleasby and Gudbrand Vigfusson 1874, s.v. "heilla."
[312] Corrigan 2008b, 3. Cf. already Simmel 1885.
[313] Bachelard 1994 (1958), xxxv–xxxvi.

198 LANDSCAPE, RELIGION, AND THE SUPERNATURAL

of the field of emotions in religion that it would be a grave omission not to consider approaches to contingency here as well.

In Strandir, in this context a central position is taken by the figure of Guðmundur the Good; he is the favorite holy man of the region.[314] Some of his most typical places of activity are springs, wells, and watercourses, most often those that provide the main water supply of farms and which Guðmundur is said to have blessed throughout the region, thus ensuring that they never fail. Such springs are often simply called *Gvendarbrunnur*, "Guðmundur's Well," or *Heilsubót*, "Recovery of Health"; the latter name implies a healing function that indeed is often made explicit.

A typical, concise example is found in a description of Hrófberg farm by Halldór Sigurbjörn Halldórsson (1925–2013), who lived there for most of his life. Of a spring that welled up by the old enclosure of the home-field he noted:[315]

> This spring, Heilsubót ("Recovery of Health"), was blessed by Guðmundur the Good. Its water is especially fresh and good. It has so happened that it has been used for people's various illnesses, and according to the account of those who drank it, it has proved itself well.

We see here the typical recurrent features of springs blessed by Guðmundur: it was located in the central part of the farm by the home-field; it provided particularly good water; and it was even ascribed healing powers.

Today, probably the most-frequented Gvendarbrunnur in Strandir, and the only one which in any way is architecturally marked for devotional use, is that at Kálfanes. It is located within walking distance of the village of Hólmavík and directly opposite the gate of the farm of Kálfanes. Physically, it consists of a rivulet that emerges from under a small scree slope in a nook between two hills; access is provided by a footpath. A few steps from the source of the water, a section of an old utility mast has been erected on which cheerfully patterned cups hang on nails, to be used by whoever visits the holy well (Fig. 2.19). The water is ascribed healing powers (though it is impossible to quantify who, if anybody, believes in these healing powers with any conviction), and the well is still regularly visited. One old man from Hólmavík is said to have taken the waters of this Gvendarbrunnur every day until very

---

[314] In general on Guðmundur the Good, see chapter 1, section "The Church in Strandir."
[315] *SÁM* Halldór S. Halldórsson 1989, 4–5.

Fig. 2.19 The Gvendarbrunnur of Kálfanes. Next to the spring, a section of an old utility pole has been erected on which cups are suspended from simple nails. © M. Egeler, 2019.

recently, when his failing health began to make his daily walk to the spring too difficult.[316]

Yet while at Kálfanes a Gvendarbrunnur is developing into a kind of pilgrimage destination, this is exceptional: much more typically, the extant sources explain that the water of a Gvendarbrunnur simply provides the drinking water of a farm. In at least one case, the historic practice of using such water as the source of the daily drinking water is still alive. At Steinadalur farm in Kollafjörður, Guðmundur the Good applied his miracle-working powers to Góðilækur, "Good Brook": "Guðmundur the Good is said to have blessed it. It never freezes there."[317] To this day (2019), Góðilækur supplies the drinking water for the farm, which via a set of hoses is directly led from the upper part of the watercourse, only a few meters below the spring, down to the farmhouse (Fig. 2.20). It never freezes, never dries up, and its water is thought to be eminently healthy; thus, it is outstandingly suitable as a drinking water source.[318] Also, it makes good coffee.

---

[316] Dagrún Ósk Jónsdóttir and Ester Sigfúsdóttir, pers. comm.
[317] *SÁM* Guðrún S. Magnúsdóttir 1976b, 8.
[318] Jón Jónsson, pers. comm.

Fig. 2.20 Góðilækur ("Good Brook") above the farm of Steinadalur. The two hoses visible in the water are the beginning of the water line to the farmhouse, as the drinking water of the farm is to this day (2019) supplied by the brook blessed by Guðmundur the Good. © M. Egeler, 2019.

In Strandir, I have become aware of fifteen examples of sources of drinking water—both springs and brooks—that have been blessed by Guðmundur, though historically there were certainly more examples: the Gvendarbrunnur of Kálfanes today is the most prominent Gvendarbrunnur in Strandir, but it is not mentioned even once in the historical documentation which has yielded the other fourteen instances and thus illustrates the incompleteness of this historic documentation (Map 2.5). In this corpus, incomplete as it may be, the normal case seems to be represented by the drinking water brook at Steinadalur: most commonly, a Gvendarbrunnur appears to have been the most reliable source of drinking water for a particular location. To cite just two final examples, at the fishing station of Búðarvogur on the land of Kolbeinsá farm in Hrútafjörður, there was "Gvendarbrunnur, a wetland area that has been dug up and shored up inside. There is excellent drinking water there, and there was the well used by the fishermen."[319] At Ljótunnarstaðir, the holy man was connected with "Neðstibrunnur ('Bottom Well'). It was

---

[319] Jón Kristjánsson and Björn Kristmundsson 1977, 12.

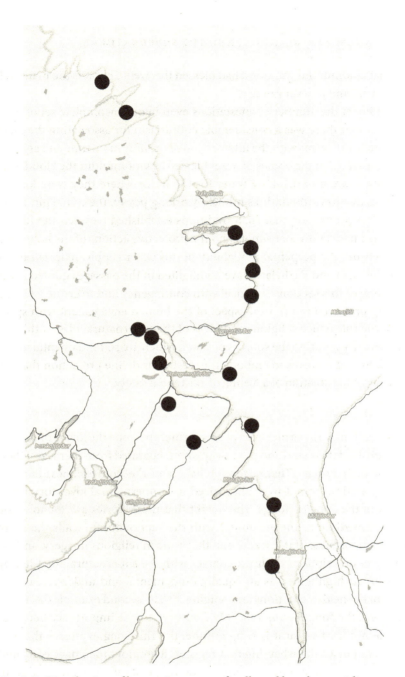

Map 2.5 Distribution of known instances of wells and brooks providing drinking water that are said to have been blessed by Guðmundur the Good. Such bodies of water are attested for (following the coastline from north to south) Skjaldabjarnarvík, Drangar, Kambur, Byrgisvík, Kaldbakur, Eyjar, Grímsey, Staður, Hrófberg, Kálfanes, Tröllatunga, Steinadalur, Skriðnesenni, Búðarvogur, and Ljótunnarstaðir, though this list is certainly incomplete. Location accurate to the level of individual farms. Base map created on Inkatlas. com; © OpenStreetMap contributors (openstreetmap.org), Inkatlas.

202 LANDSCAPE, RELIGION, AND THE SUPERNATURAL

said that Guðmundur the Good had blessed this well. That was the main well of the farm, and it never ran dry."[320]

Looking at the number of attestations even in our incomplete set of data, it is clear that there was a considerable enthusiasm for associating the main water supply of farms with the intercession of the holy man: time and again, it is emphasized that the bodies of water blessed by Guðmundur the Good were the main sources of drinking water for the farms where they were located and that, due to Guðmundur's miracle-working power, their vital gift never failed. The connection that such traditions established between the fundamentally important water supply and the protective actions of the holy man, which ensure the perpetual availability of this water supply, reflects exactly what Corrigan and Bachelard have highlighted in the passages quoted at the beginning of this section:[321] to deal with contingency and to create a feeling of being protected is a central aspect of the human engagement with space and of the role which religions and ideas of the supernatural play in this engagement. By securing the sources of water, which are so fundamental to any life, Guðmundur seems to embody this desire for divine protection that is a mainstay of the creation of a feeling of existential safety.

*

In this section, we have met tales of how farmers become the lovers of the resident spirits of their land and pine away when separated from them, as if their love for their home—Tuan's "topophilia"—and the homesickness ensuing from separation from it were allegorized in a supernatural love story reminiscent of the Song of Songs. The weight that these stories ascribe to erotic love as a medium of the encounter with the supernatural recalls the more general importance of the sexual and the erotic in religious imagery, and especially in descriptions of direct contact with the supernatural, that Jeffrey J. Kripal has highlighted as an equally fundamental and under-researched aspect of the field of emotions and religion.[322] The second example discussed earlier was the song *Sveitin mín*, "My Country," whose importance becomes tangible not least when it is sung at funerals. This song expresses the love for the land in a somewhat different register: it employs the image of a child at the breast of the motherly figure of Nature personified as the "Queen of the Mountains." Again, love of the land is expressed through the image of

[320] *SÁM* Skúli Guðjónsson 1978, 6.
[321] Corrigan 2008b, 3; Bachelard 1994 (1958), xxxv–xxxvi.
[322] Kripal 2008, 168–169.

love between persons, though here a different kind of love is referenced. In this second example, it is also acknowledged more clearly that the relationship is not one of equals, but a submission of the human partner to Nature personified.

The springs and water courses blessed by Bishop Guðmundur the Good, finally, add a third, more explicitly protective take on the close relationship between the people and their land: the intervention of the holy man creates sources of drinking water that never fail and even actively further the health of those who partake of their waters, turning the land into a source of everyday succor in a part of the farm's economy that is of fundamental importance for its survival. This aspect—protection—is not made explicit in the stories of elven lovers or the song *Sveitin mín*, but it is implied there as well: many stories of elven revenge show how the well-being of a farm is dependent on the goodwill of the local elves, which conversely means that an outright love relationship between the farmer and the resident elf will, as a side effect, ensure the farm's safety and prosperity; and in the countryside hymn "My Country," nature is described as a "refuge" and "enveloping in its embrace," again suggesting a view of the land as fundamentally protective.

In his discussion of the importance of material culture for the relationship between religions and emotion, John Kieschnick emphasizes that unworked, "natural" landscape features are not "material culture," as the term, strictly applied, only refers to artifacts and landscape features that have been the object of physical human intervention.[323] In Strandir, this excludes many, maybe most, important sites of the supernatural from the category of "material culture." A site such as Ekkjusteinn, where the elven lover of the farmer at Gilsstaðir had her abode, is almost by definition untouchable and natural rather than shaped by physical intervention. The transformation of such a site into a place of the supernatural does not happen on the material plain, but through an intense intellectual engagement through storytelling.

Nevertheless, aspects of what Kieschnick highlights about the role of material culture for the field of religions and emotion also seem to apply to such "natural places."[324] One point of particular importance is the comparatively "subdued" role that material culture plays for emotional experience.[325] While religion is a context where extreme emotions can occur—here belong

---

[323] Kieschnick 2008, 224.
[324] Sensu Bradley 2000.
[325] Kieschnick 2008, 232–233; cf. Gladigow 1988, 22.

204 LANDSCAPE, RELIGION, AND THE SUPERNATURAL

the ecstasies of a visionary as much as the anger that can drive religious violence—much of religious emotion is set in everyday contexts and remains well within the range of everyday, "ordinary" feelings. Kieschnick introduces this through a photograph of a room in the house of a rural American family.[326] Among other furnishings, this photograph shows the various pictures that are used to decorate the room. They include prints of Jesus as well as an *Infant Samuel*, but in addition to these two religious images also a calendar image of a child playing with a dog. This example illustrates that even sacred images do not always have to be set apart in a way that suggests a deep emotional impact: an image hung in a room used on a daily basis, and side by side with purely "secular" pictures, is not normally a vessel of sacred power. Integrated into the pedestrian decoration of the household and other everyday contexts, such elements of religious material culture are not constant focuses of intense religious feelings, but rather contribute to a subdued emotional experience that may not even be very clearly defined, though it may have a consistent effect on the lived-in environment. Kieschnick speaks of a "vague sense of spiritual comfort" that the everyday material culture of religions can provide.[327]

This perfectly dovetails with W. J. T. Mitchell's observation of what he calls the "weak power" of the landscape: talking not about material culture in general but about landscape in particular, he highlights how the emotional impact of landscape can be broad, difficult to specify, and indeterminate[328]— much like that of the religious decoration in the American home cited by Kieschnick. The same holds true also for the supernatural landscape of Strandir. Not every elf hill inspires (imaginings of) otherworldly erotic experiences; not every cup of coffee brewed from the water of a spring blessed by Guðmundur the Good is a holy communion. Mostly, the hill is a hill and the coffee is just good coffee. But the connotations are there, people are aware of them (as I was, if jokingly, told in Steinadalur: "this is coffee from holy water"), and they contribute to an emotional experience of the land that mostly remains diffuse. Yet at times, this diffuse emotional experience can crystallize to the depth and emphasis expressed by the lyrics of *Sveitin mín*, "My Country."

---

[326] Kieschnick 2008, 233; McDannell 1995, xii.
[327] Kieschnick 2008, 233.
[328] Mitchell 2002b, vii.

TWELVE MOVEMENTS 205

10: Coping with Contingency

In his *Natural History of Religion*, the Enlightenment philosopher David Hume argued that "the first ideas of religion arose [. . .] from a concern with regard to the events of life, and from the incessant hopes and fears, which actuate the human mind."[329] Thus, as Hume saw it, one of the central tasks that religion was meant to fulfill was to cope with the fears that are part of everyday life. In various ways and from a broad range of perspectives, the importance of this point has been highlighted again and again, also beyond the field of the study of religions. In theorizing on space, Gaston Bachelard emphasized the central connection between the human engagement with space and the dispelling of fear: as a core feature of space that has been lived in and that "has been seized upon by the imagination," he noted that it creates a positive attraction because it is felt to protect.[330] Another classic theorist of space, Yi-Fu Tuan, explicitly emphasized the role that ideas of the supernatural play in dealing with the uncertainties that people face in confronting their environment. He argues that ideas about the supernatural contribute to coping with the fears that result from such uncertainties:[331]

> Superstitions are the rules by which a human group attempts to generate an illusion of predictability in an uncertain environment. Rules are effective in tempering anxiety; and the numerous rules themselves cease to be a conscious burden once they become habit.

Tuan, a geographer, in using the term "superstition" employs a language that is theologically loaded and unintentionally judgmental, but while in other contexts the term may be polemic, he does not use it so. For Tuan, ideas about rules imposed by supernatural circumstances ("superstitions") play an important role in that they help to cope with contingency. This, he argues, they do by "generat[ing] an illusion of predictability," and they manage to dispel fears without actually imposing much of a burden on human beings.

Also in recent theorizing in the study of religions proper a role of religions in dealing with fears and uncertainty, and with the suffering that follows if fears come true, is still a prominent theme.[332] To name just one example,

---

[329] *The Natural History of Religion* (1757, 1777), Section 2.4, in Merivale and Millican s.a.
[330] Bachelard 1994 (1958), xxxv–xxxvi.
[331] Tuan 1980, 9.
[332] Cf. Auffarth and Mohr 2006, 1613.

206   LANDSCAPE, RELIGION, AND THE SUPERNATURAL

Thomas A. Tweed, himself drawing on classics like Hume and Max Weber, makes it a central point of his theory that religions "confront suffering," and specifically that they "interpret and ease suffering: disease, disaster, and death."[333]

Fears of disaster, and ways to cope with the contingency that governs it, form a central aspect of place-lore and spatial practices in Strandir. Especially Tuan's argument that rules serve as a way of tempering anxiety seems almost as if it had been developed for this region. On the following pages, the themes of anxiety and coping with contingency will be pursued through a group of examples taken from the vast corpus of Strandir *álagablettir*, which are one of the most common types of supernatural places in the region.

*

Etymologically, the term *álagablettur* (plural: *álagablettir*) means simply "place/spot (*blettur*) of enchantments (*álög*)," but the word is used to refer to a very specific type of "enchanted" places: places that are set apart from normal agricultural use and which are connected with the belief that some kind of misfortune happens if they are violated.[334] The concept of such *álagablettir*, while beyond its heyday, is still alive today, but it rarely manifests itself in any kind of elaborate storytelling. An *álagablettur* does not need a story. Primarily, such a place is constituted not by a narrative with a beginning, a middle, and an end, but by a simple belief statement that such and such a place is an *álagablettur* whose disturbance will lead to punishment. In an account of Kolbeinsvík farm, where he had grown up and lived between 1906 and 1922, Ingi Guðmonsson described the farm's *álagablettur* simply in the following manner:[335]

> There is a wetland (*mýri*) by the river, which is called Dalholtsmýri. It is an *álagablettur*, where one may not cut the grass.

This account contains no "story" in the sense of a narrative with a plot where something actually happens; it is a simple belief statement. Even where people give systematic descriptions of the *álagablettir* of their home region,

---

[333] Tweed 2006, 54, 71.
[334] For a general discussion of and literature on *álagablettir*, see chapter 1, section "Common Elements and Story Patterns of the Supernatural Landscape."
[335] *SÁM* Ingi Guðmonsson 1973, 3.

such descriptions tend toward this same brevity. A compilation of *álagablettir* in the district of Árneshreppur by Símon Jóh. Ágústsson simply reads:[336]

1. Reykjafjörður: Búhóll *no grass cutting*
2. Naustvík: Grænaflöt *no grass cutting*
3. Finnbogastaðir: Kleppa *no grass cutting*
4. Melar: Álfhóll & Stórhóll
5. Krossnes: Hveramýri *no grass cutting*
6. Stóra-Ávík: Skyrkollusteinn (do not disturb)
7. Byrgisvík: by Torfholt, a place where one may not cut the grass
8. Kaldbakur: on top of Torfholt a place with nard grass where one may not cut the grass
9. Kleifar: Gullhóll, do not disturb
10. Drangar: Kerlingartóft

In Símon's list, just as in Ingi Guðmonsson's account of Kolbeinsvík, there is virtually no narrative—because there is nothing to tell beyond the belief statement that the place is an *álagablettur*.

Probably by accident rather than design, Símon's list is illustrative also of two other important characteristics of the *álagablettir* tradition. The first point is made by its lack of comprehensiveness: Símon's list is incomplete. This is illustrated already by Ingi Guðmonsson's description of the *álagablettur* of Dalholtsmýri in Kolbeinsvík, as this place is located within the geographical area that Símon covers and therefore should have been on his list. Its absence is probably due to a typical trait of *álagablettir*: they are features of individual farms that are not told about for the sake of storytelling—after all, there is often very little in terms of actual "stories" connected with them—but that are part of the process of agricultural work on the farm. They are talked about when they are encountered in the landscape, which for the most part would be in the context of working the land; and consequently they are known primarily to the people who actually have to do work in their vicinity and therefore have to be aware of the injunctions connected with them. That one is not allowed to cut the grass at a particular spot is important to know only for those who make the hay. So even somebody like Símon, who himself was a native of Árneshreppur, would not be aware of all the *álagablettir* of the region.[337]

---

[336] *SÁM* Símon Jóh. Ágústsson s.a. (a).
[337] Cf. Gunnell 2018a, 32.

208   LANDSCAPE, RELIGION, AND THE SUPERNATURAL

The other feature illustrated by this list is how *álagablettir* can acquire stories, even though they do not have to have them. Símon's list dates from the 1960s.[338] About the farm of Krossnes, it simply reads: "Krossnes: Hveramýri *no grass cutting*." Hveramýri, the *álagablettur* where no grass may be cut, is an area that abuts a group of hot springs; this is also the origin of its name, which means "Wetland of Hot Springs." In 1969, a few years after Símon had worked on collecting place-traditions from the area, the owner of Krossnes decided to expand his home-field, where most of the farm's hay is produced. As part of this work, a section of Hveramýri was leveled off and incorporated into the home-field. To expand a farm's home-field in this way was a very common thing to do, so in and by itself it would not have been particularly memorable—except that two years later, in 1971, the farmhouse of Krossnes burned down. Ever since, Hveramýri has had a story: it had become the *álagablettur* whose violation was followed by the burning of the farm.[339]

This pattern for the emergence of *álagablettur* stories—or at least for how they are told—is very typical. Where an *álagablettur* has a story, it generally follows the pattern: PROHIBITION—VIOLATION OF PROHIBITION—PUNISHMENT. Another good example from the region has been recorded by Ingimundur Ingimundarson (1911–2000), who was the farmer at Svanshóll farm in Bjarnarfjörður and made extensive notes about the toponymy, topography, and lore of his farm. When he comes to talk about *álagablettir* on his land, he gives a detailed account of Kvíjaklettabrekka, the "Slope of the Rocks of the Sheep Pen." Kvíjaklettabrekka is a slope abutting low but very marked cliffs some 3 m in height. About this site, Ingimundur wrote down the following reminiscences:[340]

> Nothing is known about other *álagablettir* on the land of Svanshóll than Kvíjaklettabrekka, and indeed also the cliffs.
>
> The smell of buffalo grass rises from the slope, and it always lies waste, and is all stony. The sacred prohibition (*bannhelgi*) only reaches down to the old country road, which in places can still be seen.
>
> As far as I can remember, it was twice mown a tiny bit up into the slope. The earlier time was summer 1925, when it was mown by accident. Then in autumn, or in a heavy snowstorm on 28 November, the main draught horse

---

[338] The list itself is undated, but most of his work on toponymy dates from the 1960s, and the list is included in Árni Óla 1968.

[339] Úlfar Örn Hjartarson, pers. comm.

[340] *SÁM* Ingimundur Ingimundarson s.a. (a), 1.

died in Bjarnarfjarðará river, and that is the only horse that I know to have died in dangerous circumstances here.

Some years later a similar indiscretion happened during grass cutting, without being on purpose.

When the hay was used, then, for feed during the winter, suddenly an excellent milk cow died. Both these incidents were linked with the sacred prohibition (*bannhelgi*).

I am telling these things I have mentioned here more for fun (*gaman*) than that I would really believe in such stuff.

Still, I do want to preserve this belief (*átrúnaður*), and I do not see cause to knowingly go against it.

I have the wish that the next generations should see no reason to dig around in the slope or the rocks.

However, I can add one point here that has almost been forgotten. When the men who were working on the electricity line were taking care of setting up the masts here at Neðri tún, they were fetching stones up in Húsahjallabrekka, and everything went like normal.

But then I saw that they had expanded to the Kvíjaklettar for stones, and then one accident after another happened to these lads and their gear, which did not seem to be of the normal kind.

I got going at once and asked them to leave the Kvíjaklettar in peace, and they did too.

This note tells three stories of how violations of the *álagablettur* were punished: two instances of grass cutting on the margins of the slope were connected with the death of livestock by accident or disease, and collecting stones for the foundations of power poles led to an inordinate number of puzzling accidents that befell the workers.

In all instances quoted by Ingimundur, the violation of the *álagablettur* happened unintentionally but still led to punishment. In another type of story, people who violate an *álagablettur* are let off with a caution. Examples of such traditions are connected with Kross at Kaldrananes on Bjarnarfjörður and Gullhóll ("Gold Hill") on the land of Þorpar farm on Steingrímsfjörður, where in both cases the culprits that violate the place are warned off by a dream vision.[341] Common, and very much alive to this day, are also stories where an *álagablettur* is violated in spite of prior warnings. The most

---

[341] See section "Repeating Patterns."

210 LANDSCAPE, RELIGION, AND THE SUPERNATURAL

infamous representative of this type is the way the story of the Goðdalur tragedy was told after it had happened: that Jóhann Kristmundsson had willfully ignored all warnings, built his new farmhouse on an *álagablettur*, and thus provoked the avalanche in which almost his whole family was killed.[342] Mostly, however, the punishment is rather less severe. Huldufólksbrekka, "Slope of the Hidden People," is a small, very steep section of the bank of the Víðidalsá River; it is located on the land of the farm of the same name, only some 50 m from the farmhouse. In the summer of 2019, two local museums organized a history walk around Víðidalsá that was meant to introduce local people to the stories and history of what essentially was the land of their neighbors. Such history walks are the modern-day equivalent of what in the early twentieth century was done through articles contributed to the local journal *Viljinn*, where farmers described the lore of their farms to their neighbors; both the old and the contemporary practice show the deep interest that people took and take in the minutiae of the local landscape. In any case, on that summer evening in 2019, one of the participants of the tour was Unnar Ragnarsson, a lively old man well into his seventies, who as a young lad used to work on the farm. When the group had assembled at Huldufólksbrekka and was surveying the various historical and legendary structures that cluster around it—ruins of old outbuildings, the remains of a derelict footbridge over the river, the reputed grave of a suicide shepherd— Unnar chimed in that around 1970 he had told the farmer who then owned Víðidalsá that he was not allowed to cut grass at Huldufólksbrekka. Yet the farmer did not believe him, cut the grass there, and shortly afterward his favorite horse fell down the slope of Huldufólksbrekka, broke its back, and died.

Huldufólksbrekka not only shows how *álagablettir* are still part of living oral tradition but also illustrates how sometimes the concept of the enchanted place can be reflected in material culture. Most *álagablettir* are entirely natural places that have not been physically altered by human intervention. In some instances, however, the attempt to avoid violating the enchantment can be grasped physically. Thus, at the foot of the slope of Huldufólksbrekka the remains of a drystone wall are still clearly visible. The practical purpose of this wall is obscure; but since Huldufólksbrekka is inviolable, one wonders whether this wall was erected to ensure that it was not touched (Fig. 2.21).

---

[342] See the "Prelude" and chapter 1, section "Home and Unhomeliness."

Fig. 2.21 Huldufólksbrekka, "Slope of the Hidden People," a steep section of the riverbank of the Víðidalsá River in the immediate vicinity of the farmhouse of Víðidalsá. At some point, a wall was erected at the foot of the slope. © M. Egeler, 2019.

In addition to being walled off, Huldufólksbrekka also represents another aspect that recurs in *álagablettir* in Strandir but is not always made very explicit: an association with elves. The name Huldufólksbrekka means "Slope of the Hidden People" and Páll Gíslason, who at the time farmed at Víðidalsá, in 1945 made a statement in which he explained that Huldufólksbrekka was a dwelling place of the elves and that this was the reason why it was prohibited to cut the grass there:[343] this grass is owned by the elves. Likewise, the aforementioned Gullhóll at Þorpar is inhabited by an elf woman, whose threats put an end to quarrying work that was about to destroy her home (Fig. 2.22).[344] The *álagablettur* of Torfholt in Kaldbaksdalur is crowned by a house-shaped rock,[345] which suggests a dwelling place of elves. In a glen above Ljúfustaðir farm in Kollafjörður, there is an *álagablettur* called Kirkjuhvammur, "Grassy Hollow of the Church," which is located directly above the rock outcrop Álfakirkja, "Church of the Elves":[346] so this piece of land, where cutting the grass was prohibited, again belonged to the elves, if as a kind of church green.

Such an association of *álagablettir* with elves is by no means universal, but recurs with reasonable frequency. Where it is made explicit, it seems to

---

[343] Árni Óla 1968, 125.
[344] *NV* Hilmar Egill Sveinbjörnsson 1999, n. p. (Þorpar).
[345] *SÁM* Guðrún S. Magnúsdóttir 1975d, 5.
[346] *SÁM* Þórður Bjarnason s.a., 3–4.

Fig. 2.22 The rock outcrop Gullhóll ("Gold Hill") overlooking the farm of Þorpar on the south coast of Steingrímsfjörður. © M. Egeler, 2019.

rationalize why a place may not be put to human use: because it is elf property. A story from Munaðarnes farm in Árneshreppur takes this property concept to its logical conclusion. There, Jón Elías Jónsson, who farmed at Munaðarnes from 1928 to 1953, once cut the grass of an *álagablettur*. Yet this *álagablettur* belonged to an elf woman; so she appeared to the farmer's wife in a dream vision and requested that the farmer should feed her two goats through the winter, because normally she would have fed these animals from the grass growing on the *álagablettur*. To avoid otherworldly retaliation, the farmer did so; and throughout the whole winter, there was an empty space in his sheep house that matched the size of two goats and was never entered by any of his sheep, and all the hay he put into the feeding trough in front of it disappeared.[347]

Yet not all *álagablettir* are based on an age-old tradition: it is a central characteristic of the concept of *álagablettir* that new places of this type can be found "empirically." If work at a place is accompanied by unusual problems, this can be interpreted through the lens of *álagablettur* lore and understood as a consequence of having stumbled upon a "place (*blettur*) of enchantments

---

[347] *SÁM* Haukur Jóhannesson and Guðmundur G. Jónsson 1992, 19–20.

(álög)." Such "discoveries" can, for instance, be made during road-building work. In an interview conducted in 1999, Bragi Guðbrandsson remembered such an incident from the small headland of Sauðabólshöfði on the south coast of Steingrímsfjörður. There, tenacious problems during the construction of the coastal road led to its interpretation as a place under an enchantment (*álög*):[348]

> Sauðabólshöfði. Was blasted during road-building work. Working on the headland went poorly. Probably some enchantment (*álög*). Wheelbarrows broke or got stuck and men got unbelievably limp.

The most famous such case of the finding of an *álagablettur* in Strandir is connected with a little gravel hill on Kálfanesskeið in Hólmavík, immediately north of the parking lot of the cemetery. The events purported to have occurred there would have taken place in the summer of the year 1961. When they were first written down in 2006, the story had long been reshaped in the mold of traditional storytelling, including the stock motif of a dream vision.[349]

The report of the discovery of this *álagablettur* begins with an outline of the topography of the scene. The *álagablettur* is a small hill of gravel. This hill is not natural, however, but has come into being because the material around it was artificially removed: it represents the remains of a quarried, formerly much larger gravel bank. The quarrying that created this hill was part of the construction of a new pier in the harbor of Hólmavík, which was begun shortly before 1960. This new pier consists of rockfill between steel walls, and the rockfill came from Kálfanesskeið. In 1961, quarrying was at its height and reached the site of the *álagablettur*. The main machine that was used to quarry the material and load it into trucks was a large rope crane, which was operated by a certain Baldur. When the crane began its work at Kálfanesskeið, Baldur's health suddenly started declining, and he began to suffer from sleeplessness, loss of appetite, and a feeling of overwhelming weakness. Yet still he carried on working. Then, one day, a larger boulder emerged from the otherwise easily manageable material of the gravel bank, and Baldur got out of the crane to ascertain that he could move it safely.

---

[348] *NV* Hilmar Egill Sveinbjörnsson 1999, n. p. (Heydalsá).
[349] *ÞS* Stefán Gíslason 2006. The report runs to three pages of typed text, so I refrain from a full translation and merely summarize the main points.

214   LANDSCAPE, RELIGION, AND THE SUPERNATURAL

Having satisfied himself that he could, he went back to his crane—but found that he could not enter the driver's cab. With considerable effort, Baldur finally managed to get back into the crane and started to work on moving the boulder onto the platform of a truck. But when he lifted the stone, the crane's claw suddenly opened, and the boulder fell right on top of the driver's cab of the truck, with the driver inside. Luckily, the cabin was protected by a special frame, so the driver escaped, terrified but unharmed. The incident left everybody shaken and Baldur wanted to move the crane and quarry material elsewhere, but the foreman insisted on continuing on site. Further problems followed. Not long afterward, the load-bearing cable of the crane broke, even though it was new and designed to carry much heavier loads than it did during the work on Kálfanesskeið. When a new cable had been procured, this brand-new steel cable already broke before Baldur had even resumed work, snapping just from the burden of the crane's claw. Then a third steel cable was brought and installed; but in the night before he was to resume work with the repaired crane, Baldur had a dream in which a man approached him: this man told Baldur that if he did not leave this part of the gravel alone, he would be the worse off for it. Baldur then telephoned the port authority and managed to get the excavation work moved elsewhere. Now his health, which had been declining steadily until this point, suddenly greatly improved, and the rest of the work proceeded without any trouble. When the work was stopped on Kálfanesskeið, a hill was left behind, around which the ground had been dug down to a much lower level. The edges of this hill were smoothed off, and while an industrial area was developed to its north and east, it was generally left alone. Tools and equipment were stored around it, but never on it.

As a coda, the report mentions that there are indications that there were some thanks for the protection of the hill. An area close by the hill is used for repair work on big trucks. On one occasion, Kristján Guðmundsson was working on a truck engine, and to be able to access the engine, he had to fold the driver's cab forward (which otherwise sits right over the engine). To make sure the cabin would not fall back and crush him, he tied it down securely. Yet somehow, while Kristján was right under it, the cabin came loose and fell back and on top of him—except that for no apparent reason it stopped short just before it hit him. Witnesses were present when this happened, and nobody was ever able to figure out what had arrested the fall of the cab and saved Kristján.

This *álagablettur* still exists and indeed forms a topic of town politics (Fig. 2.23). The space could be usefully employed to store the extensive vintage car

Fig. 2.23 The *álagablettur* of Hólmavík, a low hill that resisted quarrying. Considerable amounts of junk (mostly wrecked cars and mechanical parts) are distributed around, but by and large not on top of the hill. The white wooden fence in the background encircles the parking lot of the town cemetery. The hedge in the right-hand middle ground of the picture hides some of the traffic (but not the noise) of the main road no. 61, arguably the busiest road of the area. © M. Egeler, 2019.

collection of one of the residents of Hólmavík, which is now (2019) distributed throughout the village. When Sigurður Marinó Þorvaldsson, one of the employees of the community, proposed this to the owner of the cars, however, this elderly citizen was horrified: he pointed to the danger posed by the enchantment of the place and refused to move even a single car onto this dangerous terrain.

Storytelling in Strandir, of course, never ascribes a "function" to *álagablettir*. They are not said to be there for a purpose; they are just said to be there, and if you find a new one, you rather wish you hadn't. But looking at *álagablettir* from the outside, there seems to be a pattern to what they do: they rationalize accidents. Farming work is dangerous work, and the well-being of the livestock is both crucial and to a certain extent always beyond the control of the farmer. However good the care is for one's animals, they can always fall victim to accidents and disease—and if they do, this is a direct blow to the economy of the farm. An *álagablettur* gives a rationale to such occurrences and makes the unpredictable predictable. It says: "If you cut the grass here, something bad will happen"—which conversely seems to whisper: "If only you keep away from this one spot, everybody and everything else will be safe." An *álagablettur* controls accidents, and this means that it not only causes them but also offers a way to avoid them by following very simple precautions. This latter aspect, the "protective" function of *álagablettir*, seems crucial, even though it is hardly ever made explicit. It seems directly implied by the concept of a place that has control over accidents, and time and again we see this control being actively used on a farm: the wall in front of Huldufólksbrekka is a way to "use" the *álagablettur* to proactively prevent accidents.

One reason why the "effects" of *álagablettur* lore are explicated to such a small extent is that generally so little about them is put into words. Most *álagablettir* are connected with no stories, at least not with stories in the sense of a narrative with a beginning, a middle, and an end. Rather, in most cases there is simply the belief statement that "this place may not be violated, otherwise accidents will happen." Everything else tends to remain wholly implicit. More detailed narratives are rare and then mostly follow a simple pattern of crime and punishment. But in the one case in Strandir where we have a detailed account of an *álagablettur*—the report about that next to the cemetery of Hólmavík—the two-way working of the enchanted place is actually made explicit: it "caused" accidents when it was being violated, but when it was respected, it "saved" Kristján Guðmundsson from being crushed by the driver's cab.

The *álagablettir* of Strandir thus help to cope with contingency on at least two different but interlinked levels. They help to rationalize accidents and disasters that have already occurred by identifying a reason for something that had no reason and thus making it intelligible and quasi-controllable ("one could have avoided this"); and they provide a simple way of preventing further accidents. This is a double function that looks both forward and backward in time: it explains and thus helps to cope with things that have happened in the past, and it gives guidance for how to create a feeling of safety in the future. In this way *álagablettir* transform contingency into controllability.

In Strandir, *álagablettir* have an extremely wide distribution.[350] The material collected so far suggests that in the early decades of the twentieth century probably nearly every farm had at least one *álagablettur* on its land. We

---

[350] An unpublished corpus has been prepared by Jón Jónsson and Dagrún Ósk Jónsdóttir, of which a selection has been published as Dagrún Ósk Jónsdóttir and Jón Jónsson 2021.

do not have detailed descriptions of all farms of Strandir—too many were abandoned before such accounts were drawn up—but those existing accounts suggest that whether an *álagablettur* is attested may largely depend on whether enough information exists about a farm. This extremely wide distribution of *álagablettir* indicates that they fulfilled a positive function: if they had primarily been places of danger, people would not have been so eager to identify them on their own land. Yet *álagablettir* do not *pose* a danger, but *control* danger; and thus they contribute to creating the feeling of safety that is crucial for how human beings construct their environment.[351]

*

Not too long ago, Susan Kwilecki emphasized that research into religious coping strategies largely lacks a historical perspective.[352] Examples like the many sites of the *álagablettur* type show that historical material certainly has much to contribute to the discourse on religious coping. The *álagablettir* or "places of enchantment" are a large, immensely productive category of sites that is widely attested throughout Strandir and to which new instances are added through "empirical" correlations between accidents and places that have been worked on. Thus, *álagablettir* are not stable, but react to the concerns of the day: if certain work needs to be done and problems occur, an *álagablettur* can be diagnosed and thus encouragement can be gained that the problems will go away. In this way, long-established *álagablettir* directly mirror Tuan's argument that "[s]uperstitions are the rules by which a human group attempts to generate an illusion of predictability in an uncertain environment."[353] At the same time, the possibility of identifying new *álagablettir* "empirically" shows how dynamic such a system can be, directly and quickly responding to evolving circumstances and offering a way to rationalize (if not solve) problems.

The clear focus on local people and their needs is very much evident from the distribution across the landscape of *álagablettir* as manifestations of ways of coping. Most *álagablettir* are connected with farm work, especially hay-making, locating them squarely in the heart of the space and economy of their farmsteads and connecting them closely with where people are at home. Even knowledge about them tends to be restricted to people directly

---

[351] Cf. Bachelard 1994 (1958), xxxvi.
[352] Kwilecki 2004, 482–483.
[353] Tuan 2013, 9.

218 LANDSCAPE, RELIGION, AND THE SUPERNATURAL

connected to the specific individual farm who were at one point or another at home there.

In this context, "home" may be a keyword. A central aspect of Tuan's definition of "home" as an analytical term of geographical research is that "home" is "a unit of space organized mentally and materially to satisfy a people's real and perceived basic biosocial needs."[354] One of the "basic needs" that Tuan put at the heart of his definition of "home" is basic safety and security, what Bachelard in his study of *The Poetics of Space*, which focuses on the intimate spaces of home, identified as the attraction that lived-in spaces develop because they protect.[355] Home is nothing so much as the place where one is safe from unpleasant surprises. Much of the contribution that the supernatural in the landscape makes to coping with contingency seems to be focused on home and its immediate surroundings. Its effects, therefore, are strictly local and a central part of the construction of "home" in Tuan's sense: it helps to make home homely.

Is it, however, always a good thing to have a feeling that home is safe? The vast numbers of Strandir *álagablettir* all help to make people feel safe by specifying with great exactness which places have to be avoided to make sure no misfortune happens. This can help create a feeling of control—but ultimately, of course, this control is not as firm as its underlying cosmological idea seems to suggest. The recurring inability of the supernatural landscape to make good on its promises will form the focus of the next section.

11: Home and Unhomeliness

In his famous essay "Paris: Capital of the Nineteenth Century," Walter Benjamin (1892–1940) discussed, among other topics, the developments of living and the home in nineteenth-century Paris. He located the rise of the Parisian private individual in the context of the July Monarchy, that is, the reign of King Louis Philippe I (1830–1848), a period characterized by far-reaching economic change and the beginning of industrialization. The changes of this time deeply affected the way people worked and lived:

---

[354] Tuan 1991, 102. See chapter 1, section "Living in Landscapes: Dwelling, Place, and Home."
[355] Bachelard 1994 (1958), xxxvi.

TWELVE MOVEMENTS   219

Under Louis Philippe the private individual enters the stage of history. [...] For the private individual, the space of living for the first time comes to stand in contrast to the space of work. The first is constituted in the interior. The business office is its complement. The private individual, who in the business office takes account of reality, demands from the interior to be entertained in his illusions. This necessity is the more urgent, as he does not intend to expand his business considerations into social ones. In the design of his private environment, he suppresses both. From this emanate the phantasmagorias of the interior. For the private individual, it constitutes the universe. In it, he assembles the distance and the past. His salon is a loge in the theatre of the world.[356]

What Benjamin observes here is a construction of the home as a counterworld: the lived-in space of the home becomes a refuge from the public spaces outside it and from the economic and social realities that these spaces reflect. This anticipates an observation about the idea of home that Gaston Bachelard was to formulate a generation after Benjamin, when he identified the root of the human attachment to the places that form the home in the safety they offer. As Bachelard phrased it, they "concentrate [...] being within limits that protect."[357] Much more recently, this potential of home to offer a protective safe space within a hostile environment was also put center stage by the Black feminist author bell hooks, who from an African American perspective described home as a place of shelter and resistance that offered a measure of safety within racist surroundings filled with oppression and hate.[358]

At a cursory glance, Benjamin's description of the interior of the private home seems to recall Martin Heidegger's account of dwelling that he developed in the image of an age-old farmhouse in the Black Forest:[359] for

---

[356] Benjamin 2011, 2: 841–842 (my translation; original: "Unter Louis-Philippe betritt der Privatmann den geschichtlichen Schauplatz. [...] Für den Privatmann tritt erstmals der Lebensraum in Gegensatz zu der Arbeitsstätte. Der erste konstituiert sich im Interieur. Das Kontor ist sein Komplement. Der Privatmann, der im Kontor der Realität Rechnung trägt, verlangt vom Interieur in seinen Illusionen unterhalten zu werden. Diese Notwendigkeit ist um so dringlicher, als er seine geschäftlichen Überlegungen nicht zu gesellschaftlichen zu erweitern gedenkt. In der Gestaltung seiner privaten Umwelt verdrängt er beide. Dem entspringen die Phantasmagorien des Interieurs. Es stellt für den Privatmann das Universum dar. In ihm versammelt er die Ferne und die Vergangenheit. Sein Salon ist eine Loge im Welttheater.").
[357] Bachelard 1994 (1958), xxxvi.
[358] hooks 1990.
[359] Heidegger 1993, 361–362. See chapter 1, section "Living in Landscapes: Dwelling, Place, and Home."

220 LANDSCAPE, RELIGION, AND THE SUPERNATURAL

Heidegger, the archetypal image of home was the shelter offered by a traditional farm building. Heidegger imagined this idea of home as one of absolute, even spiritual harmony, where "the self-sufficiency of the power to let earth and sky, divinities and mortals enter *in simple oneness* into things ordered the house."[360] Reading Benjamin attentively, however, it is quite clear that his account of the Parisian home reveals cracks that in Heidegger's account are thoroughly plastered over. For Heidegger, his imaginary (Black Forest) home is one of perfect harmony; Benjamin, in contrast, notes that the (Parisian) home he observes is an escapist illusion filled with phantasmagorias that tries to deny the realities of life instead of being harmoniously integrated into them. This lack of integration, of course, makes the home a brittle place. Later in his discussion, Benjamin goes on to observe that this new interior living space is also where the first detective novels are set—Benjamin terms Edgar Allan Poe "the first physiognomist of the interior"—in which the criminals are bourgeois private individuals.[361] In this development, the home becomes the archetypal place of (if imaginary) murder and horror. Structurally, in pointing out the unhomely aspects of the home, Benjamin here foreshadows the criticisms that many white feminist writers have raised against the idea of home as a place of safety: writers such as Gillian Rose foreground the home as a major site of the oppression of women.[362]

In the acuity and multifacetedness of his observations, Benjamin, even though he wrote some twenty years earlier than Heidegger, is strikingly more modern than Heidegger and his Romantic idealization of home. As a one-time supporter of the Nazi regime, Heidegger, it seems, had a much less clear view of the brittleness of home and safety than Benjamin, a Jewish intellectual from Berlin who from 1933 onward had to live in exile in Paris and who in 1940 committed suicide when it became clear that he would not be able to flee from Nazi-occupied France.[363]

Such brittleness is a central trait of home, and it also extends to its supernatural landscape (homescape?). This book began with the interview that Jóhann Kristmundsson gave on New Year's Eve of the year 1948, in which he told of the events at his home in Goðdalur whose consequences were to lead to his suicide in 1953, two years after Heidegger gave his lecture on "Building Dwelling Thinking." To complete the circle, it is time to return to

---

[360] Heidegger 1993, 362.
[361] Benjamin 2011, 2: 843.
[362] Rose 1993, 54–56.
[363] Vogt 2020.

the concept of dwelling in Goðdalur. I will first sketch how Goðdalur was viewed from the outside. Then I give a short survey of the rich assembly of supernatural places in Goðdalur as viewed from the inside perspective of the farm, and follow this with a discussion of how the exceptional spatial distribution of these places suggests that they were used to create a feeling of a protected home. Finally, I return to the theme of the brittleness of home as it was brought to our attention by Benjamin, and as it manifested itself in Goðdalur in the inability of even the most elaborately constructed supernatural landscape to physically deliver the safety that it spiritually promised. Thus, the section will conclude with a classic fallacy of the supernatural landscape as home.

*

We begin this return to Goðdalur at a place of remembrance: a memorial consisting of a black plaque mounted on a rough stone (Fig. 2.24). The memorial is placed on a tiny, inconspicuous elevation covered in heather and bare, stony soil. It is oriented in such a way that whoever faces it to read the inscription looks directly toward the mouth of Goðdalur, where in 1948 an

Fig. 2.24 The memorial to the victims of the Goðdalur avalanche of 1948, about 5 km from the farm of Goðdalur, without direct road access at N 65°46.962" W 021°34.771." © M. Egeler, 2019.

222 LANDSCAPE, RELIGION, AND THE SUPERNATURAL

avalanche killed almost all inhabitants of the farm. Yet it is not actually close to either valley or farm. The memorial looks toward the mouth of the valley from a distance of some 2 km; and from the memorial to the farm ruins deep inside Goðdalur valley it is almost 5 km as the crow flies. To memorialize memory is not always welcome at the place where something occurred; sometimes, it has to be enough that a memorial is oriented toward the place whose remembrance it serves.

The inscription on the plaque lists the victims of the avalanche that hit the farm in Goðdalur on Sunday, 12 December 1948, with their names, age, and relationship to each other. The horror of not only the dead but also the survivor is indicated in some few sparse words. The plaque lists the six people who died and then concludes: "The farmer, Jóhann Kristmundsson, 42 years, was rescued out of the avalanche after four days. Blessed be their memory." Explicit and implicit in this memorial is an abyss of horror. It mentions the deaths and the ordeal of the survivor that had been a consequence of the extreme isolation of the farm; but it does not mention Jóhann's suicide, which took place less than five years later. It mentions, among the victims, the old woman "Jónina Jóhannsdóttir, 75 years" and "her daughter: Guðrún Jóhannsdóttir, 53 years." What remains unspoken is that mother and daughter share the same patronymic because they are also sisters. A victim of meningitis, Jónina was deaf and mute. She was abused by her father, Jóhann Pálsson, which led to her pregnancy and the birth of her daughter, and subsequently to one of the first convictions for child abuse to be secured in Iceland and for which Jóhann in 1896 was condemned to six years of penal labor.[364]

Both the crime and the natural disaster were facilitated by the remoteness of the farm of Goðdalur. While already the memorial stone is located far from everything, the former farm itself lies another 5 km further up the valley and has not seen permanent habitation since 1948. Also from the perspective of the local population, its remoteness was exceptional and invited comment. In the mid-1970s, the isolation of Goðdalur featured prominently in an account which Guðrún Níelsdóttir published in the regional journal *Strandapósturinn*: there, she described Goðdalur as one of the last refuges of a sinister paganism in Iceland, a place where pagan cult allegedly survived longer than in other, more accessible parts of the country, and where its supernatural impact reverberates to this day and—she even

---

[364] *Landsyfirréttardómar* 1901, 310–313 (https://timarit.is/page/3524751#page/n359/mode/2up, 9 February 2022) and Jón Jónsson, pers. comm.

goes on to say—will reverberate as long as people live in Strandir.[365] As in Robin Hardy's classic horror movie *The Wicker Man* (1973), where a remote Scottish island is painted as the place of a revival of a homicidal pre-Christian paganism, in Guðrún's account the isolated distant farm becomes the place of survival of something imagined as ancient evil. After the widely publicized catastrophe of 1948,[366] Goðdalur became firmly connected with associations of bad things happening,[367] and its remoteness became part and parcel of the valley's alleged sinister pagan character. This remoteness, which in both the eyes of the local community and in historical reality seems to have drawn so much harm on the farm, makes it particularly interesting from the perspective of a specific question: How is "home" organized in the supernatural landscape of such a remote location, where it has to be stripped down to its bare essentials?

*

Since the nineteenth century, much that was written about Goðdalur reflected outside perspectives that viewed the valley as a place of abject poverty, sorcery, and evil things happening.[368] Yet there are also accounts of the farm that have originated with people stemming from or closely connected with it on a personal level.[369] These latter texts paint a picture much closer to the farm's living cosmos than to outside prejudice: perceptions of a landscape by the people actually living there are often very different from those by outsiders. Arguably the most important of these testimonies is a description dated to the year 1949, written by Rósmundur Jóhannsson (1883–1971), who in his youth had for a while lived in Goðdalur and worked there as a shepherd.[370] From his and similar accounts, it becomes clear that Goðdalur had

---

[365] Guðrún Níelsdóttir 1976, 66.

[366] The avalanche made the title pages of a who's who of Icelandic newspapers of the time: *Tíminn* (19 December 1948); *Vísir* (18 December 1948); *Alþýðumaðurinn* (21 December 1948); *Alþýðublaðið* (18 December 1948).

[367] Cf. the many recordings of interviews about Goðdalur accessible on *Ísmús* (https://www.ismus.is/) under the shelf numbers SÁM 92/2685 EF—2; SÁM 91/2360 EF—11 and 8; SÁM 92/2768 EF—7; SÁM 93/3500 EF—3; SÁM 90/2134 EF—36; SÁM 92/2597 EF—10; SÁM 88/1513 EF—13; SÁM 91/2452 EF—14; SÁM 90/2295 EF—18; SÁM 91/2357 EF—12; SÁM 91/2367 EF—10 and 12; as well as (likewise at *Ísmús*) *Magnús Rafnsson—Minningar úr Reykjavík og Bjarnarfirði* (10:58–14:45) and *Minningar úr Bjarnarfirði* (29:06–34:37). Rather the exception is Emil Als 2003, who in loving colors desribes a summer he spent in Goðdalur as a young lad in 1938.

[368] An early example is the mid-nineteenth century story about a poor farmer-necromancer at Goðdalur in Jón Árnason 1954–1961, 1: 590.

[369] Esp. *SÁM* Matthías Helgason, s.a. (b); *SÁM* Ingimundur Ingimundarson 1976; *SÁM* Rósmundur Jóhannsson 1949.

[370] *SÁM* Rósmundur Jóhannsson 1949.

224   LANDSCAPE, RELIGION, AND THE SUPERNATURAL

a rich supernatural world inscribed into its land that focused on a number of key places: the hill Goði; the rock Hestur; the fateful "places of enchantment" Bólbali and Bólbarð; and the waterfall Goðafoss (Map 2.6).

Visually the most dominating of the storied places of Goðdalur is Hestur, the "Horse." Hestur is a towering rock outcrop maybe 8 m high that juts out of a ledge in the western side of the valley and that, if viewed from the right angle, looks remarkably like a horse rearing up on its hind legs. Guðrún Níelsdóttir describes it in the following manner:[371]

> In the northern part of Hraun is a very big rock that is called Hestur ("Horse"). It was said that this rock was the church of the hidden people (*huldufólk*), and should people be on the road by it, they travelled completely quietly, for nobody wanted to offend the hidden people with unnecessary noise or groundless prattle. There is a story about that, that the people who once lived in Goðdalur had heard the ringing of church bells from there, and all the inhabitants of the farm heard that, so one could not speak of mishearing.

From Hestur, one looks over virtually the whole valley of Goðdalur, just as conversely it can be seen from everywhere in the valley. If, standing at Hestur, one looks up the valley, one sees a river running down the opposite mountainside in a series of impressive cascades (Fig. 2.25): this series of waterfalls is extremely picturesque, and it plays no role whatsoever for the local landscape of storytelling and belief. Having reached the foot of the mountain, its waters merge with the Goðdalsá River that runs the length of the valley. At a point almost exactly equidistant from the Horse and the former farm, some 600 m away as the crow flies, the Goðdalsá takes an inconspicuous, stepped drop into a low narrow gorge. After this, it disappears from view between the rocks. This half-hidden fall is Goðafoss.

It is not a long walk from the farm to Goðafoss. For a modern observer primed in the preconceptions of the Romantic landscape tradition, which have now been naturalized throughout Western societies by their mass marketing in outdoor advertising, it is tempting to just walk past it without much more than a passing glance. There is none of the height that in Western mainstream aesthetics has been canonized as the hallmark of a "beautiful" waterfall; nor does it in any way visually dominate its surroundings. The modern

---

[371] Guðrún Níelsdóttir 1976, 68.

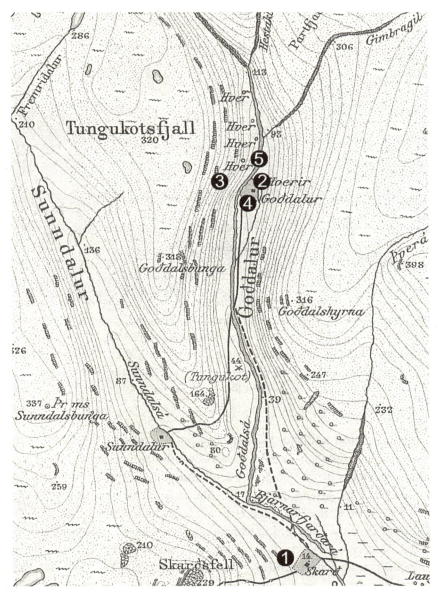

Map 2.6 The remote farm of Goðdalur in the valley of the same name. 1: The memorial for the victims of the avalanche of 1948. 2: Bólbali and Bólbarð with the ruins of the farmhouse destroyed in 1948. The old farmhouse that predated this fateful new building had been located less than 100 m to its southwest. 3: Hestur. 4: The ship-shaped founder's burial mound Goði. 5: Goðafoss. The farm of Skarð has now disappeared; Sunndalur exists only as a summer house. The map illustrates not only the remoteness of the farm of Goðdalur but also the unusual clustering of its supernatural sites around the farm. Section of *Generalstabens Topografiske Kort*, sheet *Hrófberg—32 Kúvíkur S.V.* (drawn 1912–14, published 1915).

Fig. 2.25 Hestur seen from the mountainside just south of it. This towering spur of rock both overlooks and is visible from almost everywhere in the valley of Goðdalur. On the valley bottom visible in the distance, the Goðdalsá River disappears in a gorge at the waterfall Goðafoss. The distance between Hestur and Goðafoss is c. 600 m as the crow flies. © M. Egeler, 2019.

Romantic rambler would be tempted to just push on straight north, where the river gorge of Gimbragil pours its waters down the steep mountain slope in a series of cascades that would do any Romantic painting proud. At Goðafoss, the river simply narrows between two low spurs of rock and, speeding up in the confines of this restricted channel, in two steps pours into a basin surrounded by low cliffs, within which the river remains caught for the next stretch of its course. The total drop height of the water over the two steps of Goðafoss may be in the region of a mere 2.5 m. Yet this is Goðafoss: this is the waterfall which has been singled out by story and tradition as one of the focal points of the mental map of the valley.

Guðrún Níelsdóttir not only wrote about Hestur but also discussed one of the main traditions about Goðafoss. According to this story, there once stood a pagan temple in Goðdalur, the "Valley of the Gods." After Iceland became Christian, the statues from this temple were sunk into the depths of the waterfall, and this drowning of the divine images gave it the name Goðafoss,

"Waterfall of the Gods."[372] This story was certainly a traditional one, as it was mentioned already by Rósmundur Jóhannsson in 1949.[373] Expanding it in a different direction, however, Guðrún in the 1970s also told a tale which seems to etymologize the name of the waterfall as "Goði's Waterfall," which grammatically likewise is perfectly possible. According to this alternative version of the valley's history, the driving force behind the naming of its places was a certain Goði, who here appears as the first settler and founding hero of the farm:[374]

A man was called Goði. He was a great strongman and not easy to have dealings with. He had been on military campaigns widely through the lands and was very wealthy. When he gave up campaigning, he set up a farm in the valley that goes off from Bjarnarfjörður towards northwest and that he called Goðadalur ("Valley of the Gods" or "Goði's Valley"). When Goði felt his death drawing near, he placed all his gold into a big chest and sank it under the waterfall in Goðdalsá river which is called Goðafoss ("Waterfall of the Gods" or "Goði's Waterfall") and arranged it thus, that nobody should succeed in getting the gold, for such was his temperament that he was unable to not begrudge somebody else's enjoyment of the gold.

While Goði lived in Goðdalur, he had some fishery and from that had great wealth.

In Guðrún's account, this story about the waterfall and its name stands side by side with its explanation as the waterfall where the divine images were drowned; there is no attempt to address or even acknowledge a tension between the two stories and their competing explanations of the toponym Goðafoss as "Goði's Waterfall" or "Waterfall of the Gods." It does not seem to matter which of these stories is "true" or thought to be "true." In a way reminiscent of Niels Bohr's remarks about Hamlet's presence in Kronberg Castle,[375] the only thing that matters is the presence of the story, not the presence of historical reality; and if this is so, the juxtaposition of alternative narratives may be desirable rather than being a problem.

The way Guðrún Níelsdóttir told her tale about Goðafoss ties her storytelling back to the everyday economic use of the land. In her account, the

---

[372] Guðrún Níelsdóttir 1976, 66.
[373] *SÁM* Rósmundur Jóhannsson 1949, 6.
[374] Guðrún Níelsdóttir 1976, 67.
[375] See chapter 1, section "Living in Landscapes: Dwelling, Place, and Home."

228 LANDSCAPE, RELIGION, AND THE SUPERNATURAL

story of how Goði hid his gold in his waterfall is immediately followed by the statement that Goði had become rich through his fisheries. Here it is important to remember that Goðdalur is completely landlocked: located in an inland mountain valley, it has no direct access to the sea. In 1949, however, Rósmundur Jóhannsson in his description of Goðdalur remarked about Goðafoss that "*silungur* will often stay there all year round."[376] The word *silungur* denotes a group of sweet-water fish of the *salmonidae* family covering both trout and Arctic char; it is fish to eat, and the juxtaposition of the treasure tale with the remark about Goði's fisheries makes one wonder whether this is the fish that made Goði rich. If so, this also goes a long way toward explaining why the waterfall with the story is not one of the high cascades of Gimbragil a bit further north, but rather the inconspicuous waterfall of Goðafoss: the reason may be that this is the waterfall which is most important for the fish of the Goðdalsá River. Goðafoss is a particularly good spot to make a catch, and viewed from a fishing perspective, furthermore, it is also of particular importance because it is the highest point in the river that fish can reach. Goðafoss is the first fall in the river that is too high for fish to cross; thus, it marks the upper end of the fish run in the river. Being the defining point for the river's fisheries, it is a natural place for a good part of the valley's wealth to be symbolically hidden.

Goðafoss is located less than 500 m upriver from the location where both the old and the new farmhouse stood close by each other. A mere 200 m south of the farmhouses, one meets the next traditional site: a low but sharply delineated and almost completely symmetrical hill that looks like a ship turned bottom-up. This is the hill Goði. About this hill, which has been attested since at least 1817,[377] Rósmundur Jóhannsson wrote in 1949:[378]

> If one goes home on the track of the path that leads out of the gate of the enclosure homewards into the boundaries of the home-field (*tún*), to one's right is a small hill which is called Goði. That is an overgrown gravel hill with very big stones here and there. It is said of this hill that one may not move anything there; also nobody has done that. It is said that the man is buried there who in all likelihood lived in Goðdalur and was maybe the overseer or owner of Goðahof ("Goði's Temple" or "Temple of the Gods").

---

[376] *SÁM* Rósmundur Jóhannsson 1949, 2.
[377] Sveinbjörn Rafnsson 1983, 441.
[378] *SÁM* Rósmundur Jóhannsson 1949, 5.

The hill is rocky and rugged, but the home-field (*tún*) is extra green and even, on both sides of the hill.

More concisely but still adding new detail, Guðrún Níelsdóttir almost thirty years later described this hill with the following words:[379]

> There is a hill pretty far down on the old home-field (*tún*) in Goðdalur, and Goði is said to be buried there in his ship. This hill had a hollow in its top just as if there had been some empty space that had collapsed, and in rainy weather one could see water coming from under the hill.

Furthermore, also Guðrún notes "that one was not allowed to move anything there."[380] The latter injunction, as it happens, early on was turned into law: Goði received a status of legal protection as a historical monument in the early 1930s.[381] The hill, however, clearly is not a real grave mound, but rather a natural hill created by the flow of the river; at least one Icelandic author pointed this out as early as the 1940s.[382] In this, as in almost all its features, Goði is a very typical example of a founder's grave mound as we have already encountered them several times. Such mounds are generally natural hills which, just like Goði, can be connected with the story of a ship burial if their shape evokes that of a ship, as is the case with one of the Önundarhaugar ("Önundur's Mounds") in Kaldbaksdalur, or with Skiphóll ("Ship Hill") in Brunngil.[383] Time and again, their natural origin is so obvious that local people comment on it.[384] Typical, too, is the claim that there is a hollow on top of this hill (which, quite typically again, today [2019] cannot be made out anymore): the only deviation from the usual pattern is that in this case, Guðrún Níelsdóttir reads the supposed hollow as an indication of a collapsed burial chamber, whereas normally it is interpreted as the traces of a past attempt to break into the mound to rob it of its treasure.[385]

---

[379] Guðrún Níelsdóttir 1976, 67.

[380] Guðrún Níelsdóttir 1976, 67.

[381] Valtýr Stefánsson 1949, 25.

[382] Valtýr Stefánsson 1949, 25.

[383] Önundarhaugar: *SÁM* Guðrún S. Magnúsdóttir 1975b, 2. Skiphóll: *SÁM* Guðrún S. Magnúsdóttir 1977c, 6.

[384] Sigurður Franklínsson, who for more than half a century (from 1905 to 1964) lived at nearby farms, about "Ljúfa's Hill" Ljúfuholt at Ljúfustaðir in Fellshreppur: *SÁM* Guðrún S. Magnúsdóttir 1976e, 6; Guðmundur Gísli Sigurðsson, who was the incumbent priest at Staður in the middle of the nineteenth century, about "Steingrímur's Grave Mound" Steingrímshaugur: Jón Árnason 1954–1961, 4: 36.

[385] Cf. section "Repeating Patterns" (example of Gullhóll at Tröllatunga).

230 LANDSCAPE, RELIGION, AND THE SUPERNATURAL

Goði hill lies within the heart of the agricultural compound: as mentioned by both Rósmundur Jóhannsson and Guðrún Níelsdóttir in the quotations given earlier, it is located within the boundaries of the home-field, the *tún* that was specially cared for and produced much of the farm's hay. Immediately to the west of Goði one can still see the ruins of a tiny building that reputedly served as a stable for two rams. On its northern end, furthermore, the hill abuts the ruins of an old sheep house, and a wall that helped to channel the sheep when they were driven into the building may even slightly cut into the hill.

Another traditional site of folk belief in Goðdalur was the alleged remains of the pre-Christian temple. In the 1940s, this temple was identified with ruins of a length of c. 40 m that lay "about 60 m east of the farm."[386] These ruins were considered an *álagablettur* that one was not allowed to meddle with.[387] Yet thirty years later they had (or were thought to have) disappeared: Guðrún Níelsdóttir mentioned in the 1970s that "[o]n the hill, where the temple stood, one could see ruins of buildings until a short while ago,"[388] implying that at her time of writing this was no longer the case.

From the various extant reports, it never becomes quite clear where exactly the ruins of the temple were thought to have been located. There is reason to believe, however, that, at least in the opinion of some, it was located on Bólbali, the most tragic of the story places of Goðdalur. According to a close relative of his, when Jóhann Kristmundsson worked on expanding his home-field, he found the foundations of a wall which he identified with the ruins of the temple; in consequence, he gave his new farmhouse the name Hof, "Temple."[389] The implication seems to be that the "place of enchantment" (*álagablettur*) of the temple site is identical with Bólbali; but this is neither certain nor do the exact spatial relationships become clear. Likewise difficult to determine is the exact relationship between Bólbali and Bólbarð, which in accounts of Goðdalur appear as its premier "places of enchantment." The one appears to have in some way been part of the other, but details remain hazy, and occasionally the names seem to be used almost synonymously.

---

[386] Valtýr Stefánsson 1949, 25. Cf. *SÁM* Rósmundur Jóhannsson 1949, 2.
[387] Guðrún Níelsdóttir 1976, 66, 67.
[388] Guðrún Níelsdóttir 1976, 66.
[389] Ingimundur Ingimundarson 1983, 2. The remark is found in an obituary that Ingimundur wrote for his sister Svanborg, who was the wife of Jóhann Kristmundsson and died in the avalanche. Ingimundur Ingimundarson lived on Svanshóll farm, which is one of the closest farms to Goðdalur; he was thus a particularly well-informed source.

It is certain that these places were located in close spatial association with each other, and however they may relate to each other exactly, they became associated with stories that emphasized their dangerous power. In an undated but probably early description of Goðdalur, Matthías Helgason simply and succinctly states:[390]

> There are places of enchantment (*álagablettir*) on Ból and Bólbarð. It's best not to move anything there. That is said to cause mishaps and great difficulties. There is talk that things have gone this way somewhat.

After the disaster of 1948, the accounts became vastly more expansive. The catastrophe provides an outstanding example of how tragedy can enliven a belief and bring it to the fore of people's minds. In the wake of the avalanche, especially Rósmundur Jóhannsson wrote down a number of stories about how through the generations, violations of Bólbali again and again led to repercussions. One of these stories tells of the death of two ewes after Jóhann Pálsson and his son Kristmundur cut the grass at Bólbali, which in this narrative was considered "a dwelling place of the hidden people (*huldufólk*) or of other hidden spirits (*dularvættir*)" and therefore untouchable.[391] In another story, Rósmundur tells how a certain Níels Hjaltalín, who was a farmer in Goðdalur, against the explicit wishes of his wife, violated the *álagablettur* and was punished for this by the death of a cow from mastitis.[392] These narratives show the standard pattern found again and again in stories about *álagablettir*: after a WARNING or the PRONOUNCEMENT OF A PROHIBITION follows a VIOLATION OF THE PROHIBITION; this leads to PUNISHMENT, after which a REFORM of the behavior of the perpetrator may occur. This narrative pattern also came to be applied in stories about the avalanche of 1948. Rósmundur Jóhannsson told the events in the following words:[393]

> In the year 1938, Jóhann Kristmundsson started erecting a new farmhouse on this much-spoken-about Bólbali, even though his relatives by marriage, father, and brother were much against it; he said that he was not afraid at all of such superstition, and he did not let himself be swayed. At the same time he started cultivating and enclosing Bólbarð. He also built a cowshed there

---

[390] *SÁM* Matthías Helgason s.a. (b), 2.
[391] *SÁM* Rósmundur Jóhannsson 1949, 6.
[392] *SÁM* Rósmundur Jóhannsson 1949, 6–7.
[393] *SÁM* Rósmundur Jóhannsson 1949, 7.

232 LANDSCAPE, RELIGION, AND THE SUPERNATURAL

and a barn as well. He was a most energetic and hard-working man, and the couple both, and he was married to Svanborg Ingimundardóttir from Svanshóll, a most excellent woman. Then Jóhann demolished the old farm, and lived in the new house made from concrete on Bólbali. That was a most splendid dwelling, [and] the husbandry of the couple was in full bloom until 12 December 1948, but then the tragic events happened that a snow avalanche fell on top of the house and all the people perished, except that Jóhann alone got away with his life.

In this telling of the events, we encounter yet another repetition of the established story pattern: WARNING/PRONOUNCEMENT OF PROHIBITION—VIOLATION OF PROHIBITION—PUNISHMENT [—REFORM]. This illustrates how our testimonies are never "objective" reports of things "how they really happened," but rather narratives which cannot help but follow the established storytelling patterns of the culture which has brought them forth. This drive to make the narrative conform to the received cultural pattern is so strong that it even colors the newsprint reporting about the accident. In the interview quoted in the prelude at the beginning of this book, the story is told in a way that conforms to the standard pattern WARNING/PRONOUNCEMENT OF PROHIBITION—VIOLATION OF PROHIBITION—PUNISHMENT—REFORM: in this telling of the events, Kristmundur knew of the supernatural injunctions, knowingly acted against them, was punished, and in the end was "reformed" by publicly accepting his responsibility for the death of his family.

The interview in *Vísir*, however, was not the only long interview with Jóhann that was published after the accident. Another, even longer (and rather more sympathetic) one appeared in a supplement of the newspaper *Morgunblaðið*.[394] In this interview as well, the journalist probingly enquired about supernatural traditions; but here, Kristmundur insisted firmly that there were no old traditions about an enchantment on the place where he built his house. While also in this interview, Kristmundur told of an *álagablettur* on his land, he located it elsewhere and emphasized that its "holiness, if one may call it that" ("helgin, ef um nokkuð slíkt er að ræða") was transferred to Bólbali only secondarily. The way this interview reported him as telling the story, Bólbali had throughout his life never been treated as particularly special in a supernatural sense; rather, its geothermal heat had made it a good spot to grow potatoes.[395] While today it is irrecoverable what

---

[394] Valtýr Stefánsson 1949.
[395] Valtýr Stefánsson 1949, 24–25.

Kristmundur really said on which occasion, this second interview makes one wonder whether the clear causality and ascription of guilt in the interview in *Vísir* may be not so much based on what Kristmundur said or did, but on what the journalist wanted to hear and how, consciously or unconsciously, he forced the statements of his interviewee into the mold provided by established Icelandic storytelling patterns about *álagablettir*.

*

Goðdalur farm shows a broad selection of the most typical supernatural places found on farms in Strandir:[396] it has at least one, maybe two dwelling places of elves (in Hestur and at Bólbali), one of which was also interpreted as their church; it has a founder's grave mound; treasure hidden by the founder; and the *álagablettur* which in 1948 made it notorious throughout Iceland. Furthermore, it is also connected with some rarer but still recurring motifs: the waterfall that is connected with a story; temple ruins; and a Christian conversion narrative. These places are all found within a triangle whose points are marked by the founder's burial mound Goði, the elf-church Hestur, and the waterfall Goðafoss. What is remarkable about this arrangement is its density (Map 2.6). For elf dwellings it is typical that they are located close to the farms to which they belong, but founders' burial mounds and storied waterfalls are often several kilometers from the farm buildings. The aforementioned Önundarhaugar, the burial mounds of Önundur Wooden-Foot, the founding hero of the farms of Kaldbakur and Kleifar in Kaldbaksdalur, are around 4.7 km from the farms.[397] Mókollshaugur is 4.3 km as the crow flies from the nearest farm, the now-abandoned farmstead of Hamar.[398] The two founders' burial mounds of Haugvatnshólmi and Lön, which belong to Hellar farm on Steingrímsfjörður, are, as the crow flies, respectively 4 km and 3 km from their farms; on the ground, the distance is much bigger, as the mounds are up on the mountain plateau, whereas the farm is down on the coast.[399] The typical situation seems to be that founders' burial mounds are comparatively far removed from the farm that was founded by their incumbent. Yet in Goðdalur, the pre-1938 farm buildings were located less than 200 m from Goði, and in 1938 the farmhouse was

---

[396] Cf. chapter 1, section "Common Elements and Story Patterns of the Supernatural Landscape."
[397] *SÁM* Guðrún S. Magnúsdóttir 1975b, 2. Cf. Egeler 2022.
[398] Cf. section "Sound."
[399] *SÁM* Jóhann Hjaltason and Ingimundur Guðmundsson s.a., 5–6; Sveinbjörn Rafnsson 1983, 441.

234 LANDSCAPE, RELIGION, AND THE SUPERNATURAL

moved by only about 100 m, retaining its closeness to the mound. A sheep house even directly abutted Goði, leaving no distance whatsoever between the farm buildings and the legendary founder's burial site.

Similar is the situation of the story-waterfall. The waterfall Gullfoss in Miðdalur,[400] where the founding hero Gestur hid his treasure, is 2.3 km from Gestsstaðir farm that bears his name. The waterfall Kerlingarfoss, in which the troll woman Þömb committed suicide,[401] is 6 km from Þambárvellir farm that has her as its founding heroine. The two waterfalls Rönkufoss and Laugufoss,[402] where the two troll women Ragnheiður and Guðlaug committed suicide, are 3.8 km and 5.4 km from the nearest (abandoned) farm, the farm of Vonarholt. So again, a substantial distance seems to be common— yet from Goðafoss to the area where the various farm buildings of Goðdalur stood over time, it is a stroll of less than 500 m.

Of course, there are always exceptions; the trends I have just outlined about the relative locations of founders' burial mounds and story-waterfalls to farmsteads are just trends, not rules. Also the founder's burial mound of Gestur in Miðdalur is located almost on the doorstep of the farm.[403] Yet even acknowledging that trends are just trends, it is worth highlighting how strongly the ensemble in Goðdalur deviates from these trends. There, all the story places described earlier are contained in a triangle of roughly 600 m × 400 m × 600 m: where on other farms the founder's burial mound may be an hour's walk or even further away, in Goðdalur it is barely a matter of minutes. What makes this striking is not only the markedly different trends observable at other farms, but especially also the contrast between this proximity of sites to each other on the farm and the general remoteness of the farm establishment in the landscape. As mentioned at the beginning of this section, the memorial to the victims of the accident of 1948 is some 5 km from the farm, and its next neighbors in Sunndalur were never much closer. The farm in Goðdalur has a huge amount of space at its disposal in which to locate its supernatural places; yet they huddle together around the farm as if they were denying this space.

It is tempting to correlate this huddling together of the standard types of supernatural places with the remarkable number of story places of a very specific other kind that is found on the land of the farm: reading the extant

---

[400] Þorsteinn Erlingsson 1954, 348–349.
[401] See section "Repeating Patterns."
[402] *SÁM* Guðrún S. Magnúsdóttir 1978a, 2.
[403] Cf. Þorsteinn Erlingsson 1954, 349.

TWELVE MOVEMENTS 235

accounts of Goðdalur, one gets the impression that places of tragic deaths were unusually common there. At the small muddy pool Sigríðartjörn, "Sigríður's Pond," a shepherdess of that name is said to have died.[404] Another girl was thought to have died at Gljúfravað ford; already in the 1950s, her name was not widely remembered,[405] though one local farmer identified her as Jónína Strandfeld, who lived during the nineteenth century.[406] Rönkuvað, "Ragnheiður's Ford," was said to be called so because a girl called Ragnheiður drowned in the river and her body washed up there.[407] Þorbjarnarhóll, "Þorbjörn's Hill," is named from a murder. Þorbjörn, so the story goes, was a man who a long time ago worked as a farmhand for a farmer in Goðdalur—the name of the farmer is forgotten now—and who was murdered and buried by his employer at the place that henceforth bore his name: Þorbjarnarhóll.[408] At Tungukot, south of the farm buildings of Goðdalur, a whole farm is said to have been buried by an avalanche and all its inhabitants killed.[409] Remains of a building on a small island in the river within the home-field of Goðdalur were connected with a story that they had once been the home of a poor loner. On one occasion, he had to borrow a pot from the farmer's wife at Goðdalur. During that night, an avalanche hit his hovel, killing him and destroying the house and everything in it; only the borrowed iron pot remained unscathed.[410] One of the ravines that open into Goðdalur—Svartagil, "Black Ravine"—is connected with a tradition according to which twenty men are destined to die there. At the time when this tradition was put down in writing by Guðrún Níelsdóttir, the actual body count was said to have reached eighteen or nineteen,[411] who had found their deaths through a combination of the difficult terrain and bad weather; one of the victims, a certain Ari, was said to have given his name to a ford close to the farm buildings in Goðdalur, which has been called Aravað ("Ari's Ford") ever since his body washed up there. It was also said that one could often catch a glimpse of the dead men,

---

[404] *SÁM* Ingimundur Ingimundarson 1976, 1; *SÁM* Ingimundur Ingimundarson s.a. (c).

[405] *SÁM* Rósmundur Jóhannsson 1959, 1.

[406] *SÁM* Ingimundur Ingimundarson s.a. (c).

[407] *SÁM* Rósmundur Jóhannsson 1949, 1.

[408] *SÁM* Rósmundur Jóhannsson 1949, 3. In 1817, it is attested as Þorbjarnarhaugur, "Þorbjörn's Burial Mound": Sveinbjörn Rafnsson 1983, 441. In this account, Þorbjörn's master is identified with Goði.

[409] *SÁM* Rósmundur Jóhannsson 1949, 5.

[410] *SÁM* Rósmundur Jóhannsson 1949, 6.

[411] Guðrún gives the number of the dead as eighteen; a variant of the story told in an interview by Ingimundur Ingimundarson gave their number as nineteen: SÁM 91/2367 EF—10, interview with Ingimundur Ingimundarson, recorded 12 July 1970. On the significance of this, see later discussion.

236 LANDSCAPE, RELIGION, AND THE SUPERNATURAL

especially before bad weather. This mostly manifested itself as a knocking on the doors, which was sometimes so substantial that the door broke.[412]

This litany of death is probably a complex mixture of the historical and the legendary. While a tradition like the one about the death of Jónína Strandfeld has a down-to-earth specificity that just might indicate that it has a historical basis, other tales of death are clearly based on stock motifs. Virtually the same tradition that is connected with the "Black Ravine" Svartagil recurs in connection with the "Threshold Ravine" Þröskuldagil, somewhat further north in Strandir, in Skjaldabjarnarvík in Árneshreppur: while there the deaths of two people and one cow were remembered as historical, it was also said that twenty people were destined to die in this ravine, of which nineteen had already died.[413] Even the numbers of the dead tally exactly, as one variant of the story about Svartagil likewise claims that of twenty destined to die, nineteen had already found their end. In the same way, the detail of the weather-sensitive ghosts recurs. In Guðrún's narrative about Svartagil, the basic elements of the story are as follows: men have died through a tragic combination of difficult terrain and bad weather, even though they already were relatively close to the farm; and ever since, their ghosts have visited the farm when the weather was about to turn bad. Much the same, only transferred to a maritime context, is told about the skerries Skottar off Broddanes in Kollafjörður: they are inhabited by the ghosts of men from Broddanes farm who died at sea, and who return to the farm whenever the weather is about to turn cold or bad.[414] So the litany of death that is connected with the land surrounding the farm buildings of Goðdalur is not all "factual"; much of it is the stuff of folktales. If anything, however, this makes this litany the more telling for the way this land was perceived. The surroundings of the remote and isolated farm were seen as a terrain that was extremely dangerous and indeed, as Svartagil exemplifies, cursed. The farm was surrounded by a circle of accidents, murder, and malevolent destiny.

*

The storytelling landscape of Goðdalur overall appears to be characterized by two trends that seem to form a counterpoint to each other: on the one hand, the land of Goðdalur was perceived as fraught with danger well beyond its normal share; and on the other hand, the typical set of supernatural

---

[412] Guðrún Níelsdóttir 1976, 68.
[413] *SÁM* Jóhann Hjaltason s.a. (d), 10.
[414] Ólafur Davíðsson 1978–1980, 2: 60.

story places was located much closer to the farm than the general tendencies observable elsewhere would lead one to expect. This makes one wonder whether there is a correlation between the closeness of the supernatural places and the intensity of the danger felt to surround the farm, and it raises the question of what this tells us about the construction of "home." As quoted in the introduction of this section, already Bachelard emphasized the protective aspect that in his view typically characterizes the space of "home," and so did Heidegger in his imaginings of a sheltering Black Forest farmhouse as an archetypal place of home. Whatever else traditional storytelling places like the burial mound of the farm's founder may be, they are certainly part of the creation of home, and at Goðdalur this effort to construct home through the elaboration of a supernatural landscape appears to have been especially focused and dense. In view of the emphasis that classic theorists placed on the importance of shelter and safety for the creation of home, maybe in this remote farm we can observe a contraction of the main places that define it as "home" just because it was so isolated, and perceived as such a dangerous place to live in. Maybe Goði, Hestur, Goðafoss, and the *álagablettur* which elsewhere serves to control and thus contain accidents[415] are localized in such a way as to form a close-knit protective cordon around the farm, providing an emotional shield against the pervasive dangers of the valley and its suffocating isolation, which, in one way or another, led to so much suffering and death.

Except that in the end, the failure of this attempt to gain safety tragically illustrates the brittleness of human constructions of home, even where the medium of this construction is the supernatural landscape. In the long run, the home that was elaborately and laboriously created around the farmhouse of Goðdalur proved to be quite like Benjamin's salon of the Parisian private individual: filled with illusions and phantasmagorias, but ultimately a mere attempt to lock out reality. It was a space whose dreams could quickly turn into nightmares, just as the homeliness of the salon did when Poe transformed it into a space of horror, and that was unable to withstand the realities that the Parisian private individual tried to leave behind (and probably equally failed to leave behind) in the business office. Filled with supernatural imaginaries, the supernatural landscape as home promised a safety it could not deliver. Instead, Goðdalur became a tragic illustration of how far the human perception and the "real" properties of the landscape can diverge,

---

[415] See section "Coping with Contingency."

Fig. 2.26 The ruins of the farmhouse destroyed in 1948. The power of the impact of the avalanche appears to have shifted the whole upper structure of the house, whose remains are offset from its foundations by around two meters. © M. Egeler, 2019.

also when it comes to the creation of home: no ascription of meaning moves the boundaries of what is physically possible, and faith certainly does not move a mountain to spare its victims. The case of Goðdalur is typical in how this extreme divergence happened at a mountain farm. As Robert Macfarlane observed, a "disjunction between the imagined and the real is a characteristic of all human activities, but it finds one of its sharpest expressions in the mountains."[416] Even today, hardly anywhere else do so many people get themselves killed—though today these deaths do not occur in an attempt at subsistence farming, but in the pursuit of leisure, be it hiking, climbing, or mountaineering. Against the very real danger of the mountains, an Alpine summit cross is as little help as the blessings offered by the bells heard ringing from a church of the hidden people, and however close one draws one's sacred places, they do not stop an avalanche (Fig. 2.26).

[416] Macfarlane 2008 (2003), 17–19 (quotation: p. 19).

12: Nature and Environment

Landscape is not the same as "nature" or "the environment," but in both the history of environmentalism and in its present-day manifestations, these concepts overlap. This overlap includes religious and supernatural interpretations of the landscape, which are inseparable from how human beings treat the part of the environment that is represented by the landscapes they engage with. As Daniel Sävborg and Ülo Valk have highlighted from the perspective of folkloristics, place-lore can move people to action to protect special places;[417] thus, it can directly feed into landscape conservation and environmental protection. Therefore, a book on the supernatural landscape also has to touch on the closely interrelated topic of religion and the environment.

In the academic debate about the relationships between religions and the environment, a central touchstone has long been the "Lynn White thesis," which the historian Lynn White Jr. published in *Science* in 1967.[418] In White's view, one of the central historical roots of the current ecological crisis was to be found in attitudes to the environment that came to dominate Occidental, Latinate Christianity, that is, its Catholic and Protestant rather than its Orthodox forms. This form of Christianity, White argued, considered the whole of creation as destined by God for the benefit and use of human beings. In its fundamentally anthropocentric cosmology, human beings were not part of nature, but stood above a nature that existed solely to serve their every need. This legitimized the unfettered exploitation of nature which in combination with scientific and technological progress led to the ecological crisis that in the course of the twentieth century became so unmistakable. In this view, a specific—and specifically Occidental—form of religion was one of the central reasons for environmental degradation, showing the impact of religious attitudes to the environment at its most destructive.

The Lynn White thesis has been widely debated and widely criticized for its generalizations,[419] some of which White himself consciously highlighted in his equally famous and short paper. Later research has emphasized the complexities of the relationship between religion and nature, including, for instance, Mark R. Stoll's analysis of the contributions that various strands

---

[417] Sävborg and Valk 2018b, 10.
[418] White 1967.
[419] For instance, Hunt 2019; LeVasseur and Peterson 2017; Berner 1996.

240 LANDSCAPE, RELIGION, AND THE SUPERNATURAL

of American Protestantism made to the rise of different kinds of environmentalism and environmental legislation in North America.[420] Of particular importance in this later research has been a shift of focus from the damage allegedly done by specific forms of religion to the potential that other forms of religion might have to address the environmental crisis.

In this more recent research, Bron Taylor's concept of "dark green religion" played a central role. Researching the contemporary Western religious scene, Taylor has noted a "greening" of religions: in present-day religious discourses, environmental concerns are increasingly important. A common form of such discourses in the West is that of "dark green religion." Taylor defines dark green religion as a religious attitude that views nature as inherently sacred and in need of protection; given the basic assumption of the sacrality of all nature, within dark green religion this protection indeed becomes a central religious obligation.[421] As an analytical category, dark green religion covers a range of attitudes in which Taylor noted distinct subtypes, covering both worldviews that have supernatural referents and worldviews that are purely materialist. The materialist end of the spectrum even includes meaning systems based on science that see themselves as decidedly antireligious.[422] What connects these sometimes very different meaning systems, however, is the way they allocate agency: generally, dark green religions see nature as threatened and in need of protection by humans. They discard the idea that nature exists in order to serve human beings, as White identified it within mainstream Occidental Christianity; but they maintain a dominant position of humanity in the sense that nature by itself is unable to avert its imminent destruction and has now to be saved by humans taking the necessary environmentalist action.

However, as Taylor has likewise highlighted, any analysis of the relationship between religion and nature does well to consider the environmental context of the religion it studies,[423] and the same holds true for analyses of the religious and supernatural landscape. Dark green religion is a phenomenon that seems to belong primarily to the period after the invention of the internal combustion engine, which gave human beings a power over the land that previously had been unimaginable.[424] This innovation decisively

---

[420] Stoll 2015.

[421] Taylor 2010; Taylor 2020.

[422] For instance, Taylor 2020, 498. On science-based meaning systems as a source for an ecologically oriented spirituality see also Sideris 2015.

[423] Taylor 2005b, x.

[424] Taylor 2005b, xi.

shifted the power balance between nature and human beings, toppling nature from its position as the most powerful force. In contrast to this modern, technology-driven assessment of power hierarchies, scholars such as Rayson K. Alex and S. Susan Deborah postulated that "indigenous" cultures sacralize their land by viewing it with a mixture of fear, awe, and reverence. Alex and Deborah imagined this process as being centered on a concept they called "indigenous reverential eco-fear" and postulated that "traditional indigenous communities" use this eco-fear to manage the relationship between humans and ecology.[425]

The concept of "indigenous reverential eco-fear" is not without its problems. Alex and Deborah employed the category of "indigeneity" in a vague and undefined fashion that appears to owe more to common clichés of the "ecological Indian"[426] than to a close engagement with primary sources. The way they imagined sacralization, furthermore, strikingly recalls Rudolf Otto's Protestant conceptualization of religion as focused on a *mysterium tremendum et fascinans*.[427] Yet even if their analysis seems marred by Protestant projections, it highlights how the power hierarchies assumed by dark green religion are not universal. While the modern, typically urban environmentalists that are among the most ardent adherents of dark green religion see nature as a victim that needs saving, assigning themselves the agency of the crusading savior in contrast to the powerless passivity of the environment, other views may well be dominated by worries about what nature does when you push it too far.

The two concepts of "dark green religion" and "indigenous referential eco-fear" can stand for two fundamentally different ways of viewing the distribution of power and agency between human beings and the land. I will draw here on three concise case studies to pursue how this power balance can be imagined in the supernatural landscape. Then I conclude with an outlook on the potential contributions and limitations of the supernatural landscape in landscape conservation.

*

The discussions sparked by the Lynn White thesis to a very large extent focused on the question of whether, and to what extent and in which ways,

---

[425] Alex and Deborah 2019.
[426] See Garrard 2012, 129–137; Taylor 2005b, xvii.
[427] See section "Emotions."

different religions are either detrimental to or beneficial for the human relationship with the environment, and specifically for environmental conservation. For Icelandic folk belief and folk storytelling, it has been argued repeatedly that it is particularly closely in touch with environmental factors or even has an outright environmentalist thrust. A research project on resource management in the Mývatn district concluded that local troll stories of the area reflect the ambiguities of local relationships between human beings and nature, and are based on the necessities of local water and soil management. In consequence, the project argued that Icelandic folklore could be interpreted as "traditional ecological knowledge."[428] Along similar lines, Ólína Þorvarðardóttir proposed that Icelandic folk storytelling has a didactic aspect that threatens dire punishment for those who overstretch the resources of their land: in her view, *álagablettir* in particular have an essentially conservationist function that protects specific places from overuse.[429]

In some cases, one is indeed tempted to think that practices based on traditional concepts of the supernatural landscape aim at environmental conservation. Maybe the most suggestive such site in Strandir is located at Snartartunga farm in Bitra. There, not far from the farm buildings, the hollow of Rauf ("Gap") is considered an *álagablettur* whose grass is never cut. After living and farming there for more than six decades, Ásmundur Sturlaugsson (1896–1980) stated this about Rauf in an interview he gave in 1976:[430]

In the home-field is a deep hollow, which is called Rauf ("Gap"). It is adorned with flowers and particularly beautiful. There are stories about how the hidden people (*huldufólk*) live there, and the grass is never cut in the hollow together with the home-field.

To this day, Rauf is famous and much loved for its flowers. In early summer, it transforms from a shaggy green hollow into a little sunken lake of blue, when an abundant plant population of wood cranesbill (*Geranium sylvaticum*) starts flowering and turns Rauf into one of the most colorful and unique flower gardens of the district. Half a century after Ásmundur had foregrounded these flowers in his interview, they are still one of the first things that people mention when the conversation turns to Rauf.[431]

---

[428] Ragnhildur Sigurðardóttir et al. 2019, esp. pp. 94–95 (quotation: p. 95).
[429] Ólína Þorvarðardóttir 2002, 159–160.
[430] *SÁM* Guðrún S. Magnúsdóttir 1976d, 7.
[431] I would like to thank Gunnhildur Halldórsdóttir, Sigurkarl Ásmundsson, and Svavar Sigurkarlsson for their hospitality at Snartartunga. For a collection of material on Rauf, see Dagrún

This natural flowering garden is set aside from the agriculturally used land on several levels. Ecologically, it is the habitat of a uniquely splendid assembly of flowers. Mythologically, it is inhabited by the hidden people: the elves were mentioned not only by Ásmundur, but even today are explicitly said to inhabit Rauf, and testimonies for this tradition go back at least to the mid-nineteenth century, when it seems to be implied by a story in Jón Árnason's *Icelandic Folk- and Fairytales.*[432] Topographically, it consists in a sharply demarcated hollow that is clearly set apart from the adjoining grass fields.[433] And as if all this were not enough, Rauf is also enclosed by a strong wire-mesh fence whose corners are formed by massive sections of old telegraph poles (Fig. 2.27). This fence does not have a gate or any other kind of entrance. The enchanted place is thus set apart not only by nature and belief but also by a remarkably sturdy enclosure.

But is Rauf a nature reserve in miniature? At first glance, the fence certainly suggests so, and on some practical level it is, because its exceptional plant population of wood cranesbill *is* protected by this fence. Yet if one considers the stories connected with Rauf, the picture shifts in a subtle but important way. Rauf is connected with much the same range of narratives as other *álagablettir.* These narratives follow the familiar pattern of PROHIBITION— VIOLATION—PUNISHMENT that generally characterizes such stories: it is prohibited to violate the place, which belongs to the hidden people; this prohibition is violated nonetheless; and punishment follows swiftly. There are stories that in the past, before the fence was erected, it happened that the grass was cut in Rauf, and then in the following winter a favorite cow or a favorite horse died. One tradition even ascribes a human death to Rauf, when a boy froze to death in a storm in the early twentieth century after the grass had been cut there.[434]

Ósk Jónsdóttir and Jón Jónsson 2021, 60–62 (with color photographs of the flowering field of wood cranesbill).

[432] Gunnhildur Halldórsdóttir, pers. comm.; *SÁM* Guðrún S. Magnúsdóttir 1976d, 7; Jón Árnason 1954–1961, 3: 24. The story in Jón Árnason does not explicitly mention Rauf: it tells how elves react when they are annoyed by children playing nosily by a stable building. However, the ruins of this stable building are only about 70 m from Rauf—close enough that noise made in front of it can still irritate the inhabitants of Rauf.

[433] Rauf appears to be the only place in Strandir where the hidden people are said to live in a hollow sunken into the landscape, rather than the usual hills, cliffs, or rocks protruding from the landscape. Its identification as an elf dwelling is unambiguous, however.

[434] Dagrún Ósk Jónsdóttir and Jón Jónsson 2021, 60. The death is also mentioned by *SÁM* Gísli Þ. Gíslason 1977, 7 with further details about the historical accident, which occurred in 1925; in this source, however, no connection is made with Rauf.

244 LANDSCAPE, RELIGION, AND THE SUPERNATURAL

Fig. 2.27 The fenced-in *álagablettur* of Rauf ("Gap") on Snartartunga farm in Bitra. © M. Egeler, 2019.

Particularly telling is the tradition connected with the construction of the fence.[435] As the story goes, people built a road that ran past Rauf in order to make it easier to transport the hay from the farm's home-field to the farm buildings. Yet the roadwork got too close to Rauf, and as a punishment, the horse of the man who was in charge of the work died. The fence was then built to ensure that further accidents of this kind would not happen.

This little story treats Rauf as a typical Strandir *álagablettur*: it is a place that is not so much protected for its own sake as for the sake of protecting the people who had to work in its surroundings. In the material discussed in this book so far, it has its closest parallel in the *álagablettur* of Huldufólksbrekka at Víðidalsá: there, a wall seems to have been built to prevent violations of a section of the river bank such as had allegedly taken place in the past— and, just as at Rauf, had led to the death of at least one horse.[436] The comparison between the wall at Huldufólksbrekka and the fence at Rauf is particularly telling because the environmental aspects of these places are so different: while at Rauf the fence can be seen as protecting special flowers,

---

[435] Jón Jónsson, pers. comm., and Dagrún Ósk Jónsdóttir and Jón Jónsson 2021, 60.
[436] See earlier section "Coping with Contingency."

at Huldufólksbrekka there is nothing in the vegetation that sets this place apart from miles of other sections of the riverbank. Comparing Rauf and Huldufólksbrekka suggests that they share almost all core elements of their respective traditions—except the special status of Rauf as a plant habitat. Yet the aspects of Rauf that make it a typical and representative *álagablettur* are not the ones that are peculiar to it, but the ones which recur at other such sites. Environmentalism as such is not among those. The typical, recurring characteristic of an *álagablettur* is not that the place is protected as an environmental site, but that the place is set apart to protect the humans living nearby. In practice, the environmental effect can be the same. But the underlying main motivation is not the feeling at the heart of dark green religion that nature is vulnerable and in need of protection. Rather, at its heart is a nagging worry that nature is dangerous and that humans need protection from it.

*

Dark green religion as it was studied by Taylor to a very large extent appears to be a consequence of the environmental costs of technological development and excessive resource exploitation. In Iceland, one of the most contentious forms of such exploitation is the construction of hydroelectric plants. Such construction projects first led to a major conflict in the 1960s and 1970s, when the farming community of the Mývatn district fought tooth and nail against the damming of the Laxá River, and in the end averted the construction of a dam that threatened the agricultural viability of their land by strategically blowing up an older dam with dynamite liberated from the electricity company.[437] More international attention was drawn by the controversy over the construction of the Fljótsdalur Power Station in the 2000s. For this project, about a thousand square kilometers of land in the heart of what until then had been the largest wilderness area in Europe were flooded, and sustained protests that also reached an international audience proved useless.[438]

Development of hydroelectric power also happened in Strandir. Hólmavík draws its electricity from the Þverárvirkjun hydroelectric plant, which

---

[437] See Haraldur Ólafsson 1981 and the interviews in the documentary *The Laxá Farmers* (dir. Grímur Hákonarson, 2013).

[438] See the book *Draumalandið* (English edition: *Dreamland*) by the Icelandic activist Andri Snær Magnason (2008), which was also turned into a feature-length documentary film *Dreamland* (dir. Þorfinnur Guðnason and Andri Snær Magnason, 2009).

246   LANDSCAPE, RELIGION, AND THE SUPERNATURAL

was first constructed between 1951 and 1953.[439] The water pressure that powered (and still powers) its turbines was created by damming the gorge of the Þverá River by the construction of a 17 m long and 10 m high arched dam, the first of its kind in Iceland. This dam raised the water level of the lake Þiðriksvallavatn in the valley of Þiðriksvalladalur.

Before the construction of the dam, there had been two working farms in Þiðriksvalladalur: Vatnshorn and Þiðriksvellir. The rise in water level that resulted from the damming forced the abandonment of both. Both farms had a rich heritage of landscape storytelling and of places of the supernatural. Some of these places were submerged in the new reservoir, and others nearly so. A site which was nearly submerged but not quite is Stúlkuhóll hill. This hill is located roughly halfway between the former farmhouses of the two now-abandoned farms, and while it used to lie far up the valley from the lake, the waters of the reservoir now lap against its base.

Stúlkuhóll, the "Hill of the Girl," is said to be named from an elf woman who has her residence in it. With a size of about 130 m × 200 m, this hill is rather larger than the average elf hill, which tends to be roughly the size of a human house (though there are exceptions in either direction). But while it may be a little large, it does share other typical characteristics of elf hills: it is clearly set apart from its surrounding landscape, and it has a marked cliff face on one section of its slopes, where a dome-shaped rock outcrop measuring some 30 m across protrudes from the northern side. This dome of rock, if taken by itself, even has a very typical elf-hill size; it has probably played a major role in the identification of Stúlkuhóll as a hill inhabited by the hidden people (Fig. 2.28).

The idea that Stúlkuhóll is named from and inhabited by an elf woman goes back at least to the 1930s, when it is first attested in a description of Þiðriksvellir by Jóhann Hjaltason.[440] Already then, it was connected with an unusually detailed storytelling tradition, which focused on how this elf woman provided help with shepherding in exchange for a poem. The most detailed of several recordings of this tradition runs as follows:[441]

---

[439] Major renovation and enlargement works were undertaken from 1999 to 2001. In general on this power plant, see "Þverárvirkjun" on *Orkubú Vestfjarða*, https://www.ov.is/orkubuid/starfssemi/virkjanir/thverarvirkjun/, 7 September 2020.

[440] *SÁM* Jóhann Hjaltason 1934, 6.

[441] *SÁM* Stefán Pálsson 1953, 4–5. Cf. *SÁM* Guðrún S. Magnúsdóttir 1978c, 6; *SÁM* Jóhann Hjaltason 1934, 6; Sigurður Bergsteinsson and Þór Hjaltalín 2012, 7.

Fig. 2.28 A view of Þiðriksvallavatn from Þiðriksvalladalur. Stúlkuhóll is the hill in the center of the photograph. The ruins of Þiðriksvellir and Vatnshorn farms are located respectively on the right-hand and the left-hand shore of the lake. © M. Egeler, 2019.

At the front of Flói ("Wetland") is a very peculiar hill, which is called Stúlkuhóll ("Hill of the Girl"). I have heard that a woman of the hidden people (*huldukona*) lives there. The shepherd at Þiðriksvellir reputedly once composed this stanza:

Good woman, get under way;	Faldaskorðin farðu á ról
Your honor does not dwindle;	fremd þín ekki dvínar;
Good girl in Girl's Hill (*Stúlkuhóll*)	stúlkan góða í Stúlkuhól
Make my sheep stop.	stöðvaðu kindur mínar.

And the story tells that after that the shepherd no longer had to search for the pen ewes (*kvíær*) in front of Stúlkuhóll.

This story is very much a story of the dairy economy of the late nineteenth and early twentieth centuries. In this period, milk-giving sheep were penned overnight so the lambs would not drink their milk and one would be able to milk them. The term "pen ewes" (*kvíær*) describes this specific type of

248 LANDSCAPE, RELIGION, AND THE SUPERNATURAL

dairy sheep and thus summarizes the context that the story has in everyday practices of labor.[442] Such sheep were not constantly kept in a pen, but during the day they were left to roam to find their own feed—which means that they had to be driven together every day anew. This Sisyphean task so much exasperated the anonymous shepherd of Þiðriksvellir that in the end he sought supernatural succor, turning to the closest supernatural presence on his land: the elf woman in the hill near the farm. The elf here fulfills much the same function as elsewhere a patron saint might: she is the go-to supernatural entity to help with everyday issues, a figure that is respected and whose power is recognized but who is too familiar to awe the people of the farm. She is a neighbor from the parallel society in the rocks, and she helps much like a powerful and benevolent human neighbor might.

Yet at the same time, there is also a threatening power lurking there that one disrespects at one's own peril. Today, when the water level in the lake is high, its waters reach as far as the lower edge of Stúlkuhóll. The threat that the reservoir poses to the elf hill has long been noted with some anxiety. The power generated by the Þverárvirkjun hydroelectric plant in the first instance serves to electrify Hólmavík, which lies less than 2.5 km to the northeast of the lake. There is a story that in 1954, shortly after the dam had been constructed, a woman in Hólmavík had a prophetic dream: this dream told her that something would happen to Hólmavík if Stúlkuhóll should ever be surrounded by water on all sides. The elf in the hill will behave as a good, helpful neighbor if treated properly, but good neighborly relations are based on the proper behavior of both parties involved, and the elf woman would not stand by idly if her dwelling were about to be destroyed.[443] Beliefs about supernatural entities in the landscape can thus also have a conservationist effect. A story about a supernatural presence seems to give some added value, or at least added significance, to a place. This added significance may not provide it with absolute protection, but it seems that it raises the inhibition

---

[442] See section "Labor."

[443] Jón Jónsson, pers. comm. Further on Stúlkuhóll cf. also the interviews with Magnús Gunnlaugsson recorded on 17 September 1970 (SÁM 85/593 EF—10, https://www.ismus.is/i/audio/id-1024673, 9 September 2020) and with Svava Pétursdóttir recorded on 17 September 1970 (SÁM 85/596 EF—10, https://www.ismus.is/i/audio/id-1024695, 9 September 2020). No tradition seems to preserve the name of the woman who had the dream. Given the intense interest of Strandir storytelling in individual persons, this may suggest that the "old woman" is an imaginary spokesperson of the fears of the original storytellers rather than a historical individual. This is the more likely as her gender tallies with typical role models in Strandir folktales, where it typically is a woman who warns against the violation of an álagablettur.

threshold for destroying such a site by inspiring something like what Alex and Deborah termed "eco-fear."

*

At least at one place in Strandir, such eco-fear appears to have turned into full-blown eco-terror. In 2013, the local Sheep Farming Museum opened an exhibition on *álagablettir*, the emic category of supernatural places where a violation of the place threatens punishment. Some months afterward, the Folklore Institute in Hólmavík received a letter in which a local person detailed their experiences with such a site on their family farm. The letter contains too much sensitive personal information about still-living or recently deceased persons to be quoted in full, but in anonymized form and to such an extent as they are important for this discussion, its contents are as follows:[444]

> Thoughts about elves at _____
>
> It was around the year?, when hay-making was being done at full stretch and there was a lot of livestock on the farm. Every available space was then used to house the animals. Somebody then had the idea to wall off a small ravine under the rocks west of the farm. And there is a big dwelling place of the elves (*álfabyggð*). They wanted to build a wall in order to lock the livestock in overnight. No consultation was held with the elves in the rock, and they became very angry and destroyed the drystone wall three times. One night a sheep was dead up on the rock. That was the end of the undertakings at that place. The brothers were not happy with how this matter had ended. They took an old rotary rake [a piece of agricultural machinery, in this context effectively scrap iron] and let it roll down from the rock and down onto the shore [which is located just a couple of meters in front of the elf rock]. The elves were not amused and became very angry and put an enchantment (*álög*) on all the brothers of _____ at _____. The first of the brothers, _____, died from a terminal illness in the year 1960, the next was _____. Then _____ fell ill, and dies of Alzheimer's. _____ dies in the year 1980. _____ falls ill and is very ill today, _____ is very sick and his wife _____ also has Alzheimer's.
>
> I emphasize that these are my thoughts about the elves at _____.

---

[444] My anonymized translation.

250 LANDSCAPE, RELIGION, AND THE SUPERNATURAL

> I developed a strong desire to remove this machine from the shore, and I pulled it up to the road, and there it is now.

This letter presents an openly subjective, personal engagement with a traditional site. The place in question was documented as a traditional folklore site some fifteen years before the letter was written,[445] which shows that the subjectivity of the letter is restricted to the causal chains it constructs, rather than the underlying belief in the status of the place as an elf dwelling. The story starts off harmlessly enough, and indeed at first is almost humorous. In order to create more space to pen the animals of a thriving farm, a wall is constructed that turns a natural rock formation into a sheep pen. Yet the elves living in the rocks take offence and destroy the wall several times. To get back at the elves, the farmers then dump trash at the shore in front of the elf dwelling. After this escalation, things spin out of control entirely and the elves kill off one family member after another, until the narrator (and survivor) removes the trash from the shore (Fig. 2.29).

One of the peculiarities of the chains of causation constructed by the author of this letter is their time frame: after the first death in 1960, the author keeps ascribing deaths and illnesses to the curse of the elves that happen decades and in some cases more than half a century after the environmental offence. Here, supernatural explanations are construed for the death and illness of some very old people indeed. Assuming that we can take the author's statements at face value, this suggests that in this case, some old trash on the shoreline created an abyss of fear that for decades to come pulled every major misfortune that befell the family into its field of gravity.

In the way this abyss of "eco-fear" is narrated, it is worth noting how the chain of events that was construed by the letter systematically denied the human farmers any effective agency. The humans try to act on the environment and its powers; but at turn after turn, they are thwarted and punished: their wall is broken down again and again, their livestock dies, and when they resort to wanton pollution of the environment, they themselves die. This letter reveals feelings toward the environment that could not be further from dark green religion: this nature does not need saving or protecting; it needs appeasing.

*

---

[445] I have to refrain from giving references, as this would void the anonymization of the letter.

Fig. 2.29 The elf-inhabited rocks and the remains of the wall constructed to create a sheep pen but destroyed by the elves. The old rotary rake was dumped on the shore immediately in front of this rock formation, but it has now been removed to put an end to the elves' vengeance. © M. Egeler, 2021.

In modern Western environmentalism, the idea that the land strikes back in a way that is driven by a supernatural, conscious will is today probably very much the exception. The predominant attitude now seems to be that the human suffering that results from environmental damage is the consequence of human exploitation in a rather more mechanical way: by destroying the resources that sustain us, we threaten to deprive ourselves of the material basis of our survival. In this modern Western discourse, the figures of supernatural folklore still appear, but often they are used more as symbols for loss and a better past than as something that is actually believed to have a power and agency of its own. In the controversy that resulted from the construction of the Kárahnjúkar Dam that was opened in 2009, the Icelandic environmentalist Andri Snær Magnason expressed his anguish about the environmental cost of such projects by lamenting the disappearance of Tröllkonuhlaup in the Þjórsá River. The name Tröllkonuhlaup means "Run of the Troll Woman": it was a well-known local story place that was connected with a troll tale and formed part of the course of the Þjórsá River. But then the hydroelectric plant

252 LANDSCAPE, RELIGION, AND THE SUPERNATURAL

of Búrfellsstöð was constructed. Andri Snær described the impact that the construction work had on the river in the following words:[446]

> Places disappear. On the way out to the natural hot pools at Landmannalaugar, my family always used to stop at the Tröllkonuhlaup falls on Þjórsá and our parents told us the story of the place—about how the rocks in the middle were stepping stones set there by a troll woman so she could visit her sister on the other side. Then one year there was a fence up, and the river was gone and the falls had disappeared. Even so, you can still find the place listed in the guides and textbooks. Visiting a primary school one day I saw a poster on the wall where a child had written: "Tröllkonuhlaup is on Þjórsá." Perhaps the place-name committee could issue a list of places that no longer exist.

Andri Snær here uses the supernatural landscape of Icelandic folklore to express his sense of loss, but in the way he uses it, it is stripped of any "real" (supernatural) power and reduced to the nostalgic symbol of a paradise lost. His perspective is worlds apart from the eco-terror expressed by the local from Strandir who saw a rotary rake that polluted some land owned by the hidden people as the cause of half a century's worth of death and misery, or of the old woman who prophesied the downfall of Hólmavík if ever the elf-hill Stúlkuhóll should be fully surrounded by the waters of the reservoir of the Þverárvirkjun hydroelectric plant. For Andri Snær, the land was filled with significance, but it was not filled with power.

In this, Andri Snær's comments on the impact of hydroelectric development are representative of a broader trend in modern environmentalism. This trend even widely applies in cases where activists invoke a supernatural that—in difference to Andri Snær's troll women—is still believed in. This is exemplified by another and much more famous case of an environmentalist debate about the construction of a dam.[447] Here, the main champion of the supernatural landscape had been John Muir (1838–1914), the Scottish-born American environmentalist and nature mystic whose enormously successful environmental activism played a crucial role for the establishment of the US National Parks. In the 1910s, a heated debate arose over the question

---

[446] Andri Snær Magnason 2008, 206. After the completion of the building work, the Tröllkonuhlaup falls today are again a working local attraction.
[447] Stoll 2015, 110–111, 149–150, 159.

TWELVE MOVEMENTS   253

of damming Hetch Hetchy Valley in the Yosemite National Park, for whose foundation Muir's work had been fundamental. The proponents of a dam pointed to San Francisco's need for clean drinking water and hydropower; opposing them, Muir pointed to the sacrality of the valley as a cathedral of Nature in which the greatness of God could be encountered:[448]

> Hetch Hetchy Valley [...] is a grand landscape garden, one of Nature's rarest and most precious mountain temples. [...] The proponents of the dam scheme bring forward a lot of bad arguments that the only righteous thing to do with the people's parks is to destroy them bit by bit as they are able. Their arguments are curiously like those of the devil, devised for the destruction of the first garden [...]. These temple destroyers, devotees of ravaging commercialism, seem to have a perfect contempt for Nature, and, instead of lifting their eyes to the God of the mountains, lift them to the Almighty Dollar.
>
> Dam Hetch Hetchy! As well dam for water-tanks the people's cathedrals and churches, for no holier temple has ever been consecrated by the heart of man.

For Muir, the mountain valley is an image of the Garden of Eden, endangered by satanic persecution; it is a place which lifts the gaze of human beings up to God, if only they are prepared to look. In another passage, he compares the proponents of the dam to the money changers in the temple in Jerusalem.[449]

For all we can say, Muir and Andri Snær had a fundamentally different outlook on the varieties of the supernatural (God and two troll women) that they referred to, but both of them used a form of the supernatural as a rallying cry in a fight against what they perceived as unbridled development at too high a cost. What is important here is that both these modern environmentalists used the supernatural landscape in exactly parallel ways, even though the one appears to have believed in his supernatural and the other, we can assume, did not: the supernatural of Christian faith and the supernatural of folklore are both equally used as mere symbols that lend force to an emotional appeal for conservation, but they are not invoked

---

[448] Muir 1912, 255, 260, 261–262.
[449] Muir 1912, 257.

254 LANDSCAPE, RELIGION, AND THE SUPERNATURAL

as something that is actually expected to act in the way that a traditional Strandir *álagablettur* would. Differing from traditional Strandir folk belief, in modern Western environmentalism the agency lies firmly with humans rather than with supernatural entities. The landscape of this environmentalism is not disenchanted; but it is deeply disempowered. This highlights a basic analytic distinction between two fundamentally different types of views of the environment as represented by the supernatural landscape: one that ascribes to it its own power and agency, and another that sees it as a passive victim; one that assumes humans need protecting from the powers of the land, and another that assumes the land needs protecting from humans.

How much of a difference does this distinction make for the amount of effective protection that religions and systems of belief and folk belief offer the environment? And how different is the situation in "modern" versus "indigenous" or "traditional" contexts? This is a point on which more empirical research is needed that, instead of repeating stereotypes akin to the "ecological Indian," would develop in-depth analyses of concrete data sets.[450] Yet research to date already allows us valuable glimpses. Writing from within Pueblo culture, Leslie Marmon Silko noted about the importance of Pueblo storytelling for the relationship to the environment: "The narratives linked with prominent features of the landscape [. . .] delineate the complexities of the relationship which human beings must maintain with the surrounding natural world if they hope to survive in this place."[451] Her emphasis on practical survival is a crucial reminder that the land is not what human beings want it to be, but the place where, for better or worse, human beings have to live. This means that spiritual concerns tend to lose out against practical necessities, irrespective of whether these necessities are perceived or real. Muir's fight for the preservation of "one of Nature's rarest and most precious mountain temples" ended in defeat: the damming of Hetch Hetchy Valley was approved in December 1913. Similarly, whatever the nameless old woman dreamed in Hólmavík in the 1950s, during renovation and modernization works undertaken between 1999 and 2001 the Þiðriksvallavatn dam was raised, and so was the water level of the lake (though it still does not surround the hill on all sides). Since then, San Francisco has had sufficient clean water, and Hólmavík sufficient clean electricity. It seems that, however much the

---

[450] Such studies have already been called for by Garrard 2010, 30–31.

[451] Silko 1996, 273, cf. p. 268. Cf. the remarks by Cladis 2018, 849, on the pragmatism that underlies the relation of Navajo farmers to their land (and which is radically different from how the same land is seen by tourists).

supernatural landscape may (in the minds of some) attempt to protect itself by the promise of spiritual uplifting and the threat of curses, an apparently even more fundamental aspect of "home" prevails: "to satisfy a people's real and perceived basic biosocial needs."[452] Whoever needs its water, it seems, does not much care about the sacrality of a river valley.

---

[452] Tuan 1991, 102, from his definition of "home" as a critical term. See chapter 1, section "Living in Landscapes: Dwelling, Place, and Home."

3

Coda

Theses on the Supernatural Landscape

There is a qualitative difference between the perception of the landscape by the inhabitants of the city and by those of the country. This difference largely coincides, but is not identical, with the difference between landscape as a place of labor and everyday life and landscape as a view.

Transferred to urban contexts, place mythology loses its entanglement with concrete specific localities in the landscape.

In the countryside, the landscape is its own medium. In the city, this medium is remediated through representations in other, second-degree media, which here become the primary way of engaging with the landscape.

The sublime reduces the landscape to something two-dimensional.

The urban view of landscape finds one of its primary expressions in art.

In its mediated form, the supernatural landscape is an object of consumption in contexts of leisure.

Transformations between the Country and the City

The preceding chapters have grappled with the mechanisms through which the supernatural landscape is constructed by those that inhabit it and closely engage with it in their everyday life and work. These chapters have attempted to offer a panorama of current and classic theorizing through a series of vignettes that contrasted theoretical perspectives with thick descriptions and analyses of the historical experience of the countryside of Strandir.

Yet, of course, landscapes are perceived not only by the people who inhabit them but also by those who pass through, who visit them, or who for other reasons look at them from the outside. In theorizing on landscape, such an

Landscape, Religion, and the Supernatural. Matthias Egeler, Oxford University Press. © Oxford University Press 2024.
DOI: 10.1093/oso/9780197747360.003.0004

outside perspective has probably been most influential through the writings of Denis Cosgrove.[1] He championed an approach to landscape as a "way of seeing" that reflects how the urban bourgeoisie look upon it as their property and subject to their domination: in this perspective, landscape is looked at both from the outside and, in terms of social hierarchy, from above. More recently, an outside perspective was enacted by the wildly successful works of Robert Macfarlane, who today is probably the most prominent representative of the "New Nature Writing." An important rhetorical and structural figure in his work is that of the urban first-person narrator leaving the city, exploring different facets of the landscape, and then returning.[2] Even though this author-centered structure was criticized scathingly by Kathleen Jamie,[3] it seems representative of a very prominent way of experiencing the landscape: by visiting it as an outsider.

In Iceland, the pre-COVID-19 tourism statistics dramatically illustrate the prevalence of this experience. In 2019 (when most of the fieldwork for this book was conducted) Iceland registered just over 2 million foreign visitors, which is more than five times the number of its inhabitants.[4] According to a survey from 2007/2008, about 5 percent of these tourists visit the Westfjords.[5] This may look like a low number, but the Westfjords are disproportionately thinly populated; if 5 percent visited the Westfjords in 2019, the resulting number of visitors would have been about fourteen times the number of local inhabitants. The people who perceive and experience the landscape of Strandir from the outside vastly outnumber those who experience it from the inside.

To engage with some features of such an outside experience of the land, the present chapter will approach the representation of the Strandir countryside in the town of Hólmavík. This is the largest settlement in Strandir and the one most firmly established on the tourist circuit. Studying the way the landscape is represented there for outside visitors opens up some broader perspectives on the urban or outside engagement with the landscape in contrast to the rural experience of it. These two experiences form two contrasting types of engagement that differ markedly; they form the focus of the last two chapters of this book.

*

[1] Cosgrove 1985.
[2] E.g., Macfarlane 2007.
[3] Jamie 2008.
[4] Icelandic Tourist Board, https://www.ferdamalastofa.is/en/research-and-statistics/numbers-of-foreign-visitors, last accessed 3 February 2021.
[5] Statistics Iceland Travel Survey 2007–2008, https://statice.is/statistics/business-sectors/tourism/travel-survey, last accessed 3 February 2021.

258   LANDSCAPE, RELIGION, AND THE SUPERNATURAL

Hólmavík in many ways is the center of Strandir. Almost all the infrastructure for trade, schooling, and medical care is located here, and it is also where more than half of the district's inhabitants live. Finding Hólmavík is very simple: whether one comes from the north or from the south, one only has to follow the coastal road. Today, all roads in Strandir lead to Hólmavík.

The road that connects Hólmavík with the rest of Strandir is constantly being improved. Driving along its smooth strip of tarmac, over large stretches of the way one passes exactly the same landmarks and story places that were located by the old coastal road. Many of them have been mentioned in the preceding chapters: the two trolls that were turned to stone in Kollafjörður when daybreak interrupted their attempt to separate the Westfjords from the rest of Iceland; the Sesselja skerry that memorializes the death of a young pauper; or the petrified trolls and the landfall that was halted by Guðmundur the Good just behind the farmhouse at Kolbeinsvík. Yet while a century ago the traveler would walk or ride immediately past these places and have plenty of time to recall and retell their stories, today, driving past at normal Icelandic speed (which is generally a bit too fast), one barely gets a glimpse of them.

In fact, knowledge of many of these places is fading today even among local inhabitants, and from roadside landmarks they are turning into specialist knowledge that is shared by few beyond the members of the families on whose farm they are located. While before the arrival of motorized traffic the roadside was thickly filled with narrative associations, it is now becoming a "non-place." This concept was first developed by Marc Augé (b. 1935) in his book of the same name.[6] Augé proposed that in the "supermodern" world of the contemporary West, we can observe an increasing proliferation of what he calls "non-places." Such "non-places" form the counterpoint to "anthropological place." For Augé, "anthropological place" was the deeply meaningful, familiar, historically grown, and dwelt-in place as it is focused on by the humanistic geography of Yi-Fu Tuan or Heidegger's philosophical thoughts on dwelling. This anthropological place Augé put into direct contrast to the concept of the "non-place," which is characterized by a lack of identity, history, or meaningful relations; as core examples for non-places, Augé named the infrastructure of high-speed travel (motorways and motorway intersections, airports), the means of transport of modern-day high-speed travel themselves, or shopping centers.[7] For Augé, transport and being in transit were

---

[6] Augé 2014; cf. Merriman 2011; Cresswell 2015, 78, 81–82, 108, 146; Günzel 2013, 94–98.
[7] Augé 2014, 42, 83.

CODA 259

particularly typical non-places: he even called the space of the traveler the archetype of a non-place.[8] Such non-places can be full of individuals, but they convey no meaning: at a non-place, the transitory, the ephemeral, the socially disconnected, and the meaningless has become em-placed. If we drive along the Strandir coastal road instead of walking it, we indeed make a big step toward implementing the change that Augé postulated. As a place passed too quickly, the road is turning into a place with no intrinsic meaning that is passed by many people but means nothing much to most of them.[9]

This is particularly the case for anybody who comes in from the outside and is not familiar with the Strandir landscape to begin with. Hardly any of the traditional sites of Strandir storytelling are signposted or mentioned in guidebooks, so outside visitors never even gauge how much they miss by traveling along the road to Hólmavík at automobile speed. For such visitors, chances are good that their first encounter with the supernatural landscape of Strandir only happens when they reach Hólmavík and drive into the center of the little town in search of parking space.

Most parking is located by the harbor basin, and there the first structure that strikes the eye is a large stainless-steel fountain that is all edges and abstract geometrical shapes (Fig. 3.1). Whatever the weather, its polished metal somehow always seems to take up and magnify the essence of the light and the colors of the sea at any given moment. In Icelandic folklore, Strandir has long been the home of sorcery, and the triangles that form the fountain's main structure seem to hint at the geometrical shapes of magical signs from Icelandic grimoires.[10] At the same time, the rows of jagged triangular teeth that crown these steel triangles evoke the steep coastal mountains of Árneshreppur, which is the home of magic in Strandir as Strandir is the home of magic in Iceland. The fountain thus brings together the land, magic, and the sea. It is a creation of Einar Hákonarson (b. 1945), a resident of Hólmavík and an acclaimed artist, who for decades has played an important role in the Icelandic art scene; in 2012, he gave the fountain as a gift to the people of Strandir. Einar named his creation *Seiður*, "Witchcraft," which has been a term for sorcery since the medieval literature of Iceland. In this fountain, art achieves two seemingly contradictory effects all at once: it makes magic part of urban public space, and at the same time, through its references

---

[8] Augé 2014, 90.

[9] Augé 2014, esp. pp. 42, 83, 90, 98–101. See chapter 1, section on "Living in Landscapes: Dwelling, Place, and Home."

[10] E.g., Magnús Rafnsson 2018a, 2018b.

Fig. 3.1 The fountain *Seiður* ("Witchcraft"), given to the people of Strandir by the artist Einar Hákonarson in 2012.

to the mountains, it represents this magic as part of a rural landscape that is not present, but that is looked at beyond the fjord, where miles and miles of thinly inhabited shoreline are visible in the distance.

From the fountain, diagonally across a corner of the harbor basin, one can see the museum Galdrasýning á Ströndum, the "Museum of Sorcery and Witchcraft." This museum is the reason why most visitors come to Hólmavík. Over the last two decades it has put the settlement firmly on the Iceland circuit of international tourists: it is listed in every guidebook, and it is the first place whose name is displayed if one zooms into Hólmavík on Google Maps. Strandir sorcery here enters international travel routes and cyberspace.

The Witchcraft Museum was established and is being run as a local initiative.[11] Its exhibition, where pop art meets folklore, presents both Icelandic and international visitors with an introduction to folk belief and witchcraft in Strandir. It puts a particular focus on the seventeenth century, when Strandir was the center of the Icelandic witch craze. Witch trials in Iceland peaked between 1654 and 1680, and most of the trials were held in the Westfjords.

---

[11] *Strandagaldur—Galdrasýning á Ströndum* (http://www.galdrasyning.is, 23 December 2020).

CODA   261

When in the late 1990s local people started toying with the idea of creating a local museum—which in Iceland are very numerous—this historical fact became the basis for the choice of topic for this new museum, and in this way local Strandir witchcraft has come to be presented to an eager international audience of tourists.

In the museum's exhibition, traditional ideas of the supernatural are developed in a new direction by being musealized.[12] In the exhibition strictly speaking, landscape is not explicitly addressed, as it focuses on the history of the witch craze and on magical spells and beings from Icelandic grimoires and folktales. A connection to local place-lore is established only indirectly, through the Goðdalur "sacrificial bowl."[13] The landscape aspect of this object is not developed, however, and the bowl itself, which ten years ago still had an exhibition room all of its own, is now (2019) placed in a marginal position next to a door in a small foyer.

The "sacrificial bowl" of Goðdalur is a very rough stone bowl hewn from a piece of natural rock, about the size and shape of half a honey melon. It was first found in the early 1960s during building work in Goðdalur, when foundations were being dug for a new summer house, the predecessor of the current summer house in the valley. Not long afterward, the bowl was lost again. Yet it resurfaced when the present summer house was erected, turning up when a wooden terrace was removed. This happened to be around the time when the Witchcraft Museum was opened. Inga Ingibjörg Guðmundsdóttir and Gunnlaugur Pálsson, who together were building the new summer house, felt that this coincidence was a sign that the bowl was destined for the museum, so they donated it. A forensic study undertaken by Thora S. Steffensen and Omar Palmason indicated that the bottom of the bowl contains a residue of blood.[14] In the light of the folklore connected with Goðdalur, which closely associates the valley with pre-Christian cult,[15] the museum exhibition now presents an interpretation of this residue which views it as the remains of pagan blood sacrifices. Thus, the presentation of the bowl in the museum is essentially based on the place-legend of Goðdalur: it is place-myth turned stone. In the process of musealization, however, the bowl and its story are largely stripped of their connection to the landscape.

[12] Cf. the special issue "Museality" of the *Journal of Religion in Europe* 4, no. 1 (January 2011).

[13] The following account is based on pers. comm. by Jón Jónsson, a visit by the author in 2011, the current museum exhibition, the museum's catalogue brochure, and Kári Pálsson 2019, 40–42.

[14] Thora S. Steffensen and Omar Palmason 2005.

[15] See chapter 2, section "Home and Unhomeliness."

262 LANDSCAPE, RELIGION, AND THE SUPERNATURAL

The story's character as a place-legend is lost, and it never becomes clear to the visitor just how much every aspect of the story of the "sacrificial bowl" breathes the place-legends of Goðdalur. Instead, the exhibition focuses on the scientific evidence for blood, which is then interpreted as sacrificial blood, leaving the visitor to either shiver in delighted horror or to wonder how one knows that the bowl wasn't simply used to transport a nice cut of lamb.

*

We encounter another kind of distancing from the land if, after the visit to the exhibition, we enjoy a coffee in the museum restaurant, which is the only restaurant in Hólmavík that is open all year round. There, the wall space to the left of the entrance is taken up by a large oil painting. This painting shows a symbol resembling an hourglass in front of a coastal landscape painted in warm terracotta tones and light blues. The symbol is completely disconnected from its landscape background and is hovering in an undefined foreground space. Having just visited the exhibition of the Witchcraft Museum, we have seen enough representations of traditional Icelandic magical signs to recognize the strange symbol as probably another example of them. The painting, then, seems to represent magic superinscribed over the landscape.

This intuition would be correct. The painting was created in 2019 by Guðlaugur Jón Bjarnason, who painted it as a cover image for that year's issue of *Strandapósturinn* (Fig. 3.2). It is one of a series of covers that Guðlaugur Jón designed for the journal, all of which follow the same pattern: a magic sign superimposed over a Strandir landscape view (Fig. 3.3).[16] The painting in the museum café is entitled *Himinbarna hjálmur* ("Helmet of the Children of Heaven," i.e., of the angels),[17] and it shows the magic sign "Helmet of Angels," which is meant to provide protection against one's enemies.[18] The design for the "Helmet of Angels" is taken from a magical manuscript that Magnús Steingrímsson hand-copied in 1928—the same Magnús Steingrímsson who was also one of the most prolific collectors of place-names and place traditions from Steingrímsfjörður in the early twentieth century.[19] The

---

[16] *Strandapósturinn* 50 (2018): *Ægishjálmur* superimposed over the mountain Lambatindur; *Strandapósturinn* 51 (2019): *Himinbarna hjálmur* superimposed over Ófeigsfjarðarflói; *Strandapósturinn* 52 (2020): a magic sign for successful fishing superimposed over a shark drying hut in the landscape of Steingrímsfjörður.

[17] Information about the painting with a reproduction of the pertinent manuscript page: imprint section of *Strandapósturinn* 51 (2019), 6.

[18] Imprint section of *Strandapósturinn* 51 (2019), 6.

[19] Magnús Rafnsson 2018a, 5, 55.

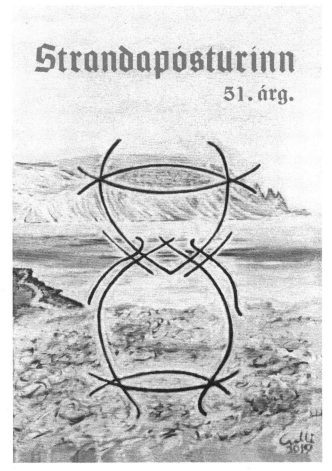

Fig. 3.2 The cover of *Strandapósturinn*, "The Strandir Post," 51 (2019). It reproduces the painting *Himinbarna hjálmur* ("Helmet of the Angels") that Guðlaugur Jón Bjarnason created for *Strandapósturinn*. In 2019, the original was displayed prominently in the restaurant of the Witchcraft Museum. Original: oil on canvas, 70 cm × 50 cm. Reproduced with permission of *Strandapósturinn* and Guðlaugur Jón Bjarnason.

painting superimposes this magic sign over a landscape prospect from Árneshreppur, the northernmost community of Strandir. The landscape represents the view across the bay of Ófeigsfjarðarflói to the rock pinnacles of Drangaskörð. This is an iconic landscape: the Drangaskörð ("Notches of the Rock Pinnacles") are a sequence of impossibly jagged rock teeth that form the

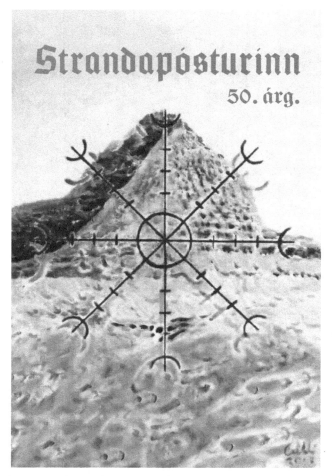

Fig. 3.3 The cover of *Strandapósturinn*, "The Strandir Post," 50 (2018). This anniversary edition was the first of a sequence of issues whose covers show a landscape prospect superimposed with a magic sign. This cover features the magical sign *Ægishjálmur*, a sign of protection, superimposed over a view of the mountain Lambatindur. With a height of 854 m, Lambatindur is the highest mountain in Strandir. The image thus combines the best known magic sign with the highest peak of the district. Reproduced with permission of *Strandapósturinn* and Guðlaugur Jón Bjarnason.

end of a peninsula and one of the most famous views in Árneshreppur. They are so iconic of northern Strandir that they can even be quoted. For instance, they form the background of the logo of the search and rescue association Björgunarsveitin Strandasól, the "Rescue Team 'Sun of Strandir'," which is based in Árnes. This logo in fact uses the same pattern that Guðlaugur Jón also adopted for his painting: it shows a magical sign suspended in space in front of the landscape prospect of the pinnacles of Drangaskörð. In this case, the magical sign used in the logo is the protective sign Ægishjálmur ("Helmet of Ægir," who is a supernatural being of Old Norse mythology).

In Strandir, such magical signs are ubiquitous. In Icelandic magic as described by the extant grimoires, they form a core element of magical practice: the central act of a magic "spell" generally consists in carving or painting the design of such a magical sign on a specific kind of material.[20] At the same time, because of Strandir's importance for the history of witchcraft and the Icelandic witchcraft trials, such signs have also acquired a close association with Strandir identity: since 1930, even the crest of arms of the district of Strandir is a red Ægishjálmur on a white shield. The Ægishjálmur can thus stand for magic and protection, but it can also stand for Strandir. This has made the Ægishjálmur the most prominent magic sign by far, and it is widely used even by public bodies in public space. I have already mentioned the example of the logo of the rescue association Björgunarsveitin Strandasól, and more examples could be added; thus, also the Reforestation Association of the Strandir District (Skógræktarfélag Strandasýslu) uses the Ægishjálmur on its signposts. But it is not only public bodies that have made the magic signs their own. On the concrete wall of the disused water tank above the church of Hólmavík, the use of such a sign as a graffito motif shows their wide presence in Strandir society at large (Fig. 3.4).

With their explicit symbolism, Guðlaugur Jón's paintings of Strandir landscapes and magic signs very bluntly pronounce an interlock between landscape and the supernatural as a central feature of the district. Especially given their use as cover images for the region's yearbook, they emphatically showcase an amalgamation of landscape, identity, and the supernatural expressed through the medium of painting. Guðlaugur Jón's decision to represent magic signs as free-floating entities in the foreground of his paintings makes this amalgamation exceptionally clear; but expressing it through painting and photography is not new. Many issues of Strandapósturinn show

---

[20] Cf. the two grimoires edited by Magnús Rafnsson 2018b.

Fig. 3.4 An Icelandic magical sign as a graffito on a disused concrete water tank above the church of Hólmavík. The tip of the church steeple and the roof of the church are just visible to the left of the tank. © M. Egeler, 2019.

photographs or watercolors of sites of legends, Christian worship, or folk belief, ranging from the region's churches to petrified trolls. We have already met the watercolor of the enchanted piece of driftwood atop Kross that is featured on the cover of issue 3 (1969).[21] As W. J. T. Mitchell has pointed out, landscape itself is a medium;[22] but this medium can easily be transferred into other media, most traditionally that of painting. Thus, in the museum café in Hólmavík, we finally encounter Cosgrove's landscape as a "way of seeing" that manifests itself first and foremost through representations.[23] Guðlaugur Jón in his paintings marks the Strandir way of seeing landscape as characterized by looking at the land through magic and enchantment. In his art, the landscape is something that is not so much lived in but looked at, and this way of experiencing landscape replaces the physical land by its artistic representation in an image that is highly charged with symbolism. In the urban environment of the museum café, landscape as a way of seeing

---

[21] See chapter 2, section "Repeating Patterns."
[22] Mitchell 2002c, 2; Mitchell 2002d, 5, 13–15.
[23] See chapter 1, section "Looking at Landscapes," and Cosgrove 1985, 45, 46, 47, 55; Cosgrove 2008, 20; Cosgrove 1998, xiv, xx, xxv, 1, 13; Kühne et al. 2018, 11–12; Lilley 2011, 122.

replaces landscape as a place of dwelling. For the experience of the lived-in landscape of the countryside that we had encountered in the preceding chapters, such representations played a strikingly small role: on a Strandir farm, the supernatural landscape is experienced through this concrete hill or that concrete rock, but not as something represented. In the urban environment, by contrast, the symbolically charged representation of landscape takes center stage. There, the *representation* of landscape becomes the primary way of experiencing the supernatural in the landscape. Guðlaugur Jón's painting in the museum café thus stands for a fundamental transformation of the experience of landscape between the country and the city.

Experiencing the landscape as a symbolic space that is accessed through representations has a long history. In Strandir, where painting is a comparatively new form of artistic expression, an early pioneer of approaching the landscape through its artistic representation was an outsider: the British traveler William Gershom Collingwood (1854–1932). Collingwood was a prominent figure of British cultural life in the late nineteenth and early twentieth centuries: he was an antiquarian, author, and artist, who translated medieval Icelandic saga literature into English, played a key role in research on the Norse heritage of northern England, and for many years was the secretary of John Ruskin. Collingwood was also a founding member of at least two artistic and academic associations (the Viking Society for Northern Research and the Lake Artists Society), and Professor of Fine Arts at Reading University.[24]

In 1897, Collingwood's enthusiasm for the Icelandic sagas led him to undertake a journey to Iceland, during which he and his Icelandic friend Jón Stefánsson spent ten weeks traveling through the country. At the time, this was a major undertaking. In most of the country touristic infrastructure was still nonexistent, and hospitality was provided by the local farmers. For Collingwood and Jón, this journey had an ulterior motif: their aim was to publish a volume of Icelandic landscape art which reproduced sketches and watercolors of places in which main events of medieval Icelandic saga literature were set. To use their own—rather understated—words, they wanted to create "a picture book to illustrate the sagas of Iceland."[25] The book which they published two years after their trip in fact was a lavish, large-format art volume that contained a total of 151 illustrations, of which 13 were printed

---

[24] Lea and Lea 2013, 6. For a detailed study of his life and influence, see Townend 2009.
[25] Collingwood and Jón Stefánsson 1899, v.

268 LANDSCAPE, RELIGION, AND THE SUPERNATURAL

in color—which for a late nineteenth-century publication meant a major expense. Their *Pilgrimage to the Saga-Steads of Iceland* (1899) became a milestone of Iceland travel writing and one of the classic books about Iceland in English.

The travels of Collingwood and Jón Stefánsson also led them to Strandir, where they passed through Bitrufjörður. In one of the letters that Collingwood wrote to his family, he describes how wet the two men got on the pass that led them into Bitra ("river after river, snow after snow, bog after bog, rock after rock").[26] From there they got to Snartartunga, which was mentioned earlier for its *álagablettur* and the folktales connected with it.[27] Collingwood was intrigued by Snartartunga primarily because it was the home of one of the protagonists of the medieval *Kormáks saga*, the saga of Cormac the Skald, of which he and Jón later published an English translation.[28] The next day, the two travelers rode round Bitrufjörður and past Þambárdalur,[29] which was discussed earlier for its troll stories, while Collingwood again got excited by the associations that this farm had with *Kormáks saga*: according to the saga, Cormac killed some men there who had abducted his daughter. Along the way, Collingwood painted a watercolor with a view of Þambárdalur and Bitrufjörður. This painting is still extant and part of the collection of Abbot Hall in the English Lake District;[30] a black-and-white version of it was printed in the *Pilgrimage* (Fig. 3.5).[31]

The object of Collingwood's paintings and sketches was not just topography, but, as he himself put it, "romantic scenery enriched with noble memories."[32] This focus on the Romantic not only allowed Collingwood to exaggerate the vertical axis in some of his paintings—every now and again, Collingwood's rock formations are rather more impressive than the originals[33]—but also charged the Icelandic landscape with such an intensity of meaning that for him and his friend Jón, the journey there became a *Pilgrimage*, as they entitled their book. In his extreme enthusiasm for the story places of Iceland, Collingwood stands in a long tradition of British

---

[26] Lea and Lea 2013, 80 (letter dated 29 July 1897).
[27] See chapter 2, section "Nature and Environment."
[28] Lea and Lea 2013, 81; Collingwood and Jón Stefánsson 1902.
[29] Þambárdalur ("Valley of the river of [the troll woman] Þömb") is today's Þambárvellir ("Fields of the river of [the troll woman] Þömb"): in the place-name, *dalur* ("valley") has become replaced by *vellir* ("fields"). On Þambárvellir see earlier, especially chapter 2, section "Repeating Patterns."
[30] For a color reproduction, see Lea and Lea 2013, 82.
[31] Collingwood and Jón Stefánsson 1899, 148 (fig. 126).
[32] Collingwood and Jón Stefánsson 1899, v.
[33] Cf. Egeler 2015b, unpaginated introduction.

Fig. 3.5 Bitrufjörður with Þambárdalur on the left. Watercolor by W. G. Collingwood from his and Jón Stefánsson's *Pilgrimage to the Saga-Steads of Iceland*. Reproduced after Collingwood and Jón Stefánsson 1899, 148 (fig. 126).

travelers and travel writers. Already Lord Dufferin in his *Letters from High Latitudes* (1857) declared that an Icelandic place connected to an old story is "consecrated" by that story;[34] and William Morris—founder of the Arts and Crafts movement, one of the founders of British socialism, and thus one of the most prominent British lovers of Icelandic saga literature—in his Icelandic travel journals from the 1870s called himself a "pilgrim to the holy places of Iceland,"[35] which for him were the country's historic and saga sites.

Icelandic literature, however, is only part of the reason why traveling the Icelandic landscape could become a "pilgrimage." Collingwood the painter, and later Professor of Art, practiced his trade in a tradition that was firmly rooted in the concept of the sublime and employed natural scenery to express sacrality and moral values. I have already mentioned the concept of the sublime for its striking absence from the treatment of the landscape in

---

[34] Lord Dufferin 1857, 140.
[35] Morris 1911, 67. Collingwood, of course, knew Morris and repeatedly quoted him in the *Pilgrimage*; even the description of his mountain crossing on the way to Snartartunga refers to Morris, quoting his *The Story of the Glittering Plain*: Collingwood and Jón Stefánsson 1899, 148; Morris 1912.

Fig. 3.6 A classic sublime landscape: Collingwood's sketch of the Horn, the sea cliff that marks the northwestern point of Hornstrandir. Reproduced after Collingwood and Jón Stefánsson 1899, 112 (fig. 95).

traditional, rural Strandir storytelling.[36] I mentioned that the fundamental conceptualization of the sublime consists in something terrifying or overwhelming that is observed without danger to oneself and thus creates a strong emotional reaction of delight. Classic tropes for representing the sublime in painting are rough mountain sceneries, waterfalls, spectacular rock formations, and high cliffs—of which Collingwood included many examples in the *Pilgrimage* (Fig. 3.6).[37] In a detailed study of the history of the "sublime," Robert Doran has made clear that the various conceptualizations of the sublime in the history of Western thought not only share the double focus on terror and delight but also a common concern: they reflect a striving for the preservation of a notion of transcendence, especially in the face of the perceived secularization of modern Western culture.[38] In approaches to landscape like that of Collingwood, this transcendence is pervasive and forms the implicit base layer on which the additional associations of Icelandic literature

---

[36] See chapter 2, section "Emotions."
[37] Schneider 2011, 181–183. Collingwood's "The Horn": Collingwood and Jón Stefánsson 1899, 112 (fig. 95).
[38] Doran 2015.

are superinscribed, to create the heady mixture that made travelers like Lord Dufferin, Morris, and Collingwood feel like pilgrims in a holy land.[39]

As an academic and artist, Collingwood was intimately familiar with contemporary reflections about the significance of landscape painting. For many years, Collingwood was the personal secretary of the immensely influential Victorian art critic John Ruskin (1819–1900), and after Ruskin's death, Collingwood became his biographer. Ruskin was the first art critic and art historian to focus primarily on self-conscious European landscape art.[40] He treated landscape as a text in which the order of a divine design could be recognized. According to Ruskin, landscape paintings, if executed by masters of the genre, could be treatments of questions of truth and morality, and bear witness to the omnipotence of God.[41] In the preface to the second edition (1844) of his epoch-making *Modern Painters*, Ruskin declared programmatically:[42]

> I shall proceed [...] to analyse and demonstrate the nature of the emotions of the Beautiful and Sublime; to examine the particular characters of every kind of scenery; and to bring to light, as far as may be in my power, that faultless, ceaseless, inconceivable, inexhaustible loveliness, which God has stamped upon all things, if man will only receive them as He gives them. Finally, I shall endeavour to trace the operation of all this on the hearts and minds of men; to exhibit the moral function and end of art; to prove the share which it ought to have in the thoughts, and influence on the lives, of all of us; to attach to the artist the responsibility of a preacher, and to kindle in the general mind that regard which such an office must demand.

In Ruskin's highly influential idea of the role of landscape and landscape art,[43] the beauty and sublimity of the landscape become the work of God, and through its appropriate representation the artist has to act as a preacher who brings the divine moral lessons of the landscape to the hearts and minds of his fellow human beings.

---

[39] Cf. Egeler 2020b, 37, with further examples for such perceptions of Iceland.

[40] Cosgrove and Daniels 1988, 4.

[41] Stoll 2015, 78–79, 99; Cosgrove and Daniels 1988, 4–6.

[42] Cook and Wedderburn 1903, 48.

[43] Arguably the most influential activist of landscape and the environment who was directly inspired by Ruskin was John Muir, who read some of Ruskin's books several times over: cf. Stoll 2015, 149. See chapter 2, section "Nature and Environment."

272   LANDSCAPE, RELIGION, AND THE SUPERNATURAL

In the history of Western art,[44] the idea that representations of landscape can express the human relationship to the divine has had a huge influence. In Collingwood's paintings of Strandir landscapes this idea remains largely implicit and is present mostly through the emphasis on classically "sublime" prospects, which is the same type of landscapes from which a direct line can be drawn to representations of landscape in modern-day glossy magazines and advertisements for travel or outdoor gear.[45] Other painters, however, have been just as explicit in their painting as Ruskin was in his critical writing. Here belongs the German Romantic painter Caspar David Friedrich (1774–1840), with paintings like *Mönch am Meer* ("Monk by the Sea," 1808/1809)[46] or *Kreuz und Kathedrale im Gebirge* ("Cross and Cathedral in the Mountains," 1812)[47] but also many of the works of Iceland's most famous painter, Jóhannes Sveinsson Kjarval (1885–1972).

Kjarval's art makes it particularly clear how landscape painting can serve as a medium for illustrating the relationship between the viewer, the land, and ulterior realities. Kjarval, who through his extensive *œuvre* in the course of his long life established himself as *the* painter of the Icelandic landscape, liberally peopled many of this landscape views with beings from Icelandic legend and folk belief. The poet Matthías Johannessen, who was closely acquainted with Kjarval, described him as a man deeply connected to both the natural environment and traditional Icelandic folklore:[48]

He listened to the breathing of the deep ocean, listened to the land that no one had seen before, listened to the folkloric light of the fantasies which are supremely Icelandic in the half-foreign setting of this day and age, where the lights in the mossy lava rocks still flicker like pallid stars, unextinguished.
And cast their light into the world of old elfin rocks.

This attitude that Kjarval had to the land and to reality at large found its expression in a vast number of paintings that combine landscape views with supernatural presences. His early oil painting *Gljúfrabúi*, "Glen-Dweller,"

---

[44] On North America, see Stoll 2015.

[45] Cf., for instance, the travel section of *The Reykjavík Grapevine*, which almost seems like a textbook of classic representations of the sublime in landscape photography (https://grapevine.is/travel/, 28 December 2020).

[46] Schneider 2011, 193–195.

[47] Cf. Koerner 2009; Busch 2003.

[48] Matthías Johannessen 2005, 547.

CODA 273

shows a luminous being in a brightly lit cave between two waterfalls,[49] reminiscent of the recurrent connection between trolls and waterfalls in Strandir. The oil painting *Andar öræfanna* ("Spirits of the Wilderness")[50] shows four spirits in the shape of floating body-less heads in a mountainous wasteland; one may think of the Útburðarhraun, "Rock Field of the Infant Ghost," at Veiðileysa, or the spectral crying on the "Pass of Howling," Ýluskarð. A recurring subject of Kjarval's art is elf churches; most of his paintings of such churches depict exactly the kind of rocks that would typically be identified as elf rocks in Strandir folklore.[51] His paintings of elf churches sometimes show only the rock, whose identification as an elf church is indicated merely by the title of the work; or they show both the church rock and a luminous, semi-translucent congregation of elves, who appear as beings of human shape that are represented only in outline and often have no distinct facial features.[52] Kjarval also produced several paintings of elf dwellings.[53] His *Álfastapar* ("Rocks of the Elves") look like a textbook example of typical Strandir elf rocks, or indeed typical elf rocks anywhere in Iceland (Fig. 3.7).

In other paintings, Kjarval focused more generally on the presence of elves in natural environments. His oil painting *Álfkonur við Vífilsfell* ("Elf Women at Mt. Vífilsfell")[54] depicts three tall elf women in front of what seems to be a lava field, with Vífilsfell mountain in the background; the bodies of the elf women show the same patterning as the landscape in front of which they are standing, suggesting a deep connection between them and the land. The watercolor *Álfar og blóm* ("Elves and Flowers")[55] seethes with an exuberant tangle of flowers and seemingly free-floating faces with long, flowing hair,

[49] *Gljúfrabúi*, oil on canvas, 45.5 × 57 cm, before 1908, Reykjavík Art Museum—Kjarval Collection. Einar Matthíasson et al. 2005, 29.

[50] *Andar öræfanna* ("Spirits of the Wilderness"), oil on canvas, 54 × 131 cm, 1929, private collection. Einar Matthíasson et al. 2005, 228.

[51] The exception to this pattern is the painting *Álfakirkja* ("Elf Church"), oil on canvas, 49 × 38 cm, about 1920, Davíð Stefánsson Museum, in which the elf church is represented like a wooden Icelandic church of the nineteenth century. Einar Matthíasson et al. 2005, 127.

[52] *Álfakirkja* ("Elf Church"), watercolor on paper, 26 × 28 cm, about 1912, Westman Islands Art Museum; *Álfakirkja* ("Elf Church"), oil on canvas, 42 × 49 cm, about 1916, private collection; different versions of *Álfakirkja í Borgarfirði eystri, Islandsk eventyr* ("Elf Church in Borgarfjörður eystri, Icelandic Fantasy"), lithograph on paper, 30.5 × 40.5 cm, 1919, private collection. Einar Matthíasson et al. 2005, 54, 129, 136–137.

[53] *Álfabyggð* ("Elf Settlement"), oil on canvas, 32.5 × 52 cm, about 1920, ÞG/IG Art Collection; *Álfaberg* ("Elf Cliffs"), oil on canvas, 27.5 × 35.5 cm, about 1920, private collection; *Álfastapar* ("Elf Rocks"), oil on canvas, 50.5 × 89 cm, 1935, Reykjavík Art Museum—Kjarval Collection. Einar Matthíasson et al. 2005, 126, 128, 263.

[54] *Álfkonur við Vífilsfell* ("Elf Women at Mt. Vífilsfell"), oil on canvas, 100 × 144 cm, 1936, private collection. Einar Matthíasson et al. 2005, 296.

[55] *Álfar og blóm* ("Elves and Flowers"), watercolor on paper, 16.5 × 16.5 cm, about 1930, private collection. Einar Matthíasson et al. 2005, 363.

Fig. 3.7 Jóhannes S. Kjarval: *Álfastapar* ("Rocks of the Elves"). Oil on canvas, 50.5 × 89 cm, 1935, Reykjavík Art Museum—Kjarval Collection. Reproduced with permission.

as if the flowering of nature and the presence of the *álfar* were flowing into one. In Kjarval's most famous treatment of an elf rock, the elven aspect remains wholly implicit, but it would have been immediately obvious to the picture's intended audience: Kjarval's altar piece for Bakkagerði church in Borgarfjörður eystri has Christ hold the Sermon of the Mount on top of the local elf hill Álfaborg,[56] localizing a central moment of the history of salvation right in the center of the supernatural landscape of local folklore.

Kjarval's art was not exclusively focused on "elves," however. As in the case of Bakkagerði church, he also took on ecclesiastical work, designed church windows, and painted saints and angels.[57] Particularly striking is his oil painting *Engill við foss* ("Angel by a Waterfall"),[58] in which the waterfall—reminiscent of his earlier painting of the "Glen-Dweller"—is inhabited by an angel that is painted in the same colors and similar semi-translucent patterns as the water of the fall itself: the angel here almost seems represented

[56] Fjallræðan ("The Sermon on the Mount"), oil on canvas, 112 × 91 cm, 1914, Bakkagerði church, Borgarfjörður eystri. Einar Matthíasson et al. 2005, 74–76; cf. Egeler 2020b, 26, 32–33.

[57] Angels: *Engill* ("Angel"), oil on plywood, 44 × 54 cm, 1934, private collection; *Svarti Engillinn* ("The Black Angel"), oil on canvas, 40 × 60 cm, about 1940, private collection; *Engill vorsins* ("Angel of the Spring"), oil on canvas, 102 × 146 cm, 1939, private collection (Einar Matthíasson et al. 2005, 261, 271, 299). For other ecclesiastical work, see Einar Matthíasson et al. 2005, 216, 220, 269, 511.

[58] *Engill við foss* ("Angel by a Waterfall"), oil on canvas, 40.5 × 50.5 cm, 1936, National Gallery of Iceland. Einar Matthíasson et al. 2005, 268.

as a spirit of the element water. Kjarval's work encompasses the whole supernatural cosmos of Iceland in the early twentieth century, including both Lutheran Protestantism and traditional folk belief, though he put a stronger focus on the latter than on the former. In Kjarval's work, elves and angels are both welded together with the landscape, and landscape and the supernatural have their connection expressed through the medium of painting. Kjarval's landscape art may be preaching not quite the kind of amalgamation of landscape and spirituality that Ruskin had had in mind; but preach it does.

Guðlaugur Jón Bjarnason's painting "Helmet of Angels" in the café of the Witchcraft Museum in Hólmavík stands in the same tradition: it treats landscape as a way of seeing the supernatural in the representations of the land. The lived-in supernatural landscape as we encountered it on the farms of Strandir here is transformed into a stylized representation in a different medium, and having been separated from the actual land, it becomes portable and can be consumed by the urban viewer. In the importance they give to mediation, such representations function much like a modern-day Claude Glass. This was a contraption that was fashionable among affluent landscape aesthetes in Europe and North America throughout much of the eighteenth and nineteenth centuries: a portable, dark-tinted convex mirror, often bound like a pocket book, that allowed its user to view a prospect behind their back, and through the distortion and coloring of the mirror gave it a look approximating that achieved by the French landscape painter Claude Lorraine (1600–1682). The Claude Glass was both wildly popular and widely ridiculed: the irony that it required the viewer of a landscape to turn their back on the object of their appreciation was not lost on some contemporary observers. Yet proponents of the aesthetics of the Claude Glass sometimes went to great lengths to make the most of its effect. When the poet Thomas Grey visited the English Lake District in 1769, he wanted to have the best possible experience of a famous view from a certain ferry landing on Lake Windermere. So during the ferry crossing he put on a blindfold, and after his arrival at the spot of the famous view he turned his back to it and first looked at the celebrated landscape through his Claude Glass. As Anna Pavord observed, it was as if "the view did not properly exist until it had been mediated."[59]

*

---

[59] Pavord 2016, 16; cf. Schama 1996, 11–12.

276 LANDSCAPE, RELIGION, AND THE SUPERNATURAL

This chapter has followed an arc that took its starting point from how in Hólmavík the supernatural landscape is represented to the touristic visitor, and from there it gradually expanded its focus to a broader discussion of the representation of the supernatural landscape in art, which is a cultural product that has its primary home in affluent urban contexts. Pursuing this arc has made clear that there is a continuum in such outside perspectives that seamlessly connects the representation and experience of the landscape of travelers, of Icelandic artists like Kjarval and Guðlaugur Jón Bjarnason, and of foreign artists and art critics such as Collingwood or Ruskin. Common to these perspectives is that they experience the supernatural landscape in a mediated form.

Mediating the landscape seems to be a central aspect of how it is experienced in a modern urban context. In recent years, the research field of material religion has highlighted the importance of material objects for practices of religious mediation that help create a feeling of the presence of the ("supernatural") entities postulated by religious cosmologies.[60] Birgit Meyer goes so far as to make such processes of mediation a central feature of her concept of religion: she sees "religion as a practice of mediation, through which a distance between the immanent and what lies 'beyond' is posited and held to be bridged, albeit temporarily. From this angle, religion may well be analyzed as a technique of reaching out to—and by the same token generating a sense of—an 'otherworld' via various kinds of media."[61] Here, the discourse on the materiality of religion comes very close to conceptualizations of the landscape such as that proposed by W. J. T. Mitchell, when he described landscape as "a physical [=material] and multisensory medium [...] in which cultural meanings and values are encoded."[62] In both approaches, mediation plays a central role: materiality is used to mediate realities imagined to exist beyond it, be it "cultural meanings" more generally or an "otherworld" more specifically.

What has changed between the countryside of Strandir and the urban context of the Witchcraft Museum is the degree of mediation. The landscape of the countryside could be described as a "first-degree" mediation: the rock needle "is" a petrified troll; the hill "is" a dwelling place of the hidden people; the land of the farm "is" haunted by a ghost. In Hólmavík, we meet this landscape through the mirror of another mediation that could be called

---

[60] E.g., Meyer and Houtman 2012.
[61] Meyer 2012, 24.
[62] Mitchell 2002d, 14.

a "second-degree" mediation: we see a painting that *depicts* a landscape that "is" filled with magic. In both cases, landscape is a medium that serves supernatural mediation; but whereas in the countryside perspective it does so directly ("first-degree"), in the urban perspective it is experienced through a second mediation of the medium ("second-degree").

For this, the specifics of the medium appear to be secondary. What is happening in Guðlaugur Jón's painting in the museum café is much the same as what is happening at the fountain by the harbor basin, and functionally similar examples could be quoted from landscape photography or film. In this process of mediation, a connection between the land and the supernatural is constructed through artistic representation rather than through the direct experience of being in and working on the land. For all that they engage with the land, these artistic representations mark a fundamental disjuncture: the transformation of the countryside landscape as a place of dwelling into the mediated urban experience of landscape as a way of seeing.

This change also appears to be entangled with other shifts. Thus, while the countryside perspective is deeply shaped by the everyday experience of working the land, the example of a museum visit during a holiday stands in for a typical urban framework for experiencing the landscape: namely, in contexts of leisure. In the next, concluding chapter, we will come back to the range of changes that are concomitant with the change from "first-degree" to "second-degree" engagement with the landscape.

4

Encore

Theses on the Supernatural Landscape

The landscape can be used to express ideological claims.

The landscape can be used to ridicule ideological claims.

The supernatural landscape is a landscape of storytelling: patterns of narratives are a central means through which the supernatural landscape is constructed.

The central place of the supernatural landscape is the individual locale. Place-names can play a prominent role in engaging with these individual sites, but the main importance does not lie with the name, but with the physical place.

The supernatural landscape consists of a dense network of meaningful places which constitute a discourse on a broad range of themes.

The country and the city represent an insider and an outsider perspective on the rural landscape: "being-in-a-place" and "looking-at-a-place." These different perspectives largely reflect the basic differences between the landscape as a place of dwelling and the landscape as a way of seeing, which are entangled with different interests, priorities, social claims, and ways of engagement with the land.

The urban experience of the landscape is a mediated experience. It still works like a Claude Glass, even though the world at large has long forgotten the Claude Glass.

Viewed through the Claude Glass, elves and trolls are both cute. No need to beware of the troll.

Landscape, Religion, and the Supernatural. Matthias Egeler, Oxford University Press. © Oxford University Press 2024.
DOI: 10.1093/oso/9780197747360.003.0005

Being-in-a-Place? Retrospect and Prospects

Landscape: A Vignette

The lighthouse at Gjögur is the most rickety working lighthouse I have seen in my life. Perched on a craggy rock outcrop above the "Shark Bay," Hákarlavogur, it is the tallest light on the mainland of Árneshreppur, the northernmost part of Strandir (Fig. 4.1). Its lantern is mounted inside an iron-and-glass capsule that sits atop an iron latticework tower, like a miniature Eiffel Tower, or like a large electricity pylon. Even at the base of the structure, where its ironwork is at its most massive, a number of the cross struts that hold this latticework together are rusted clean through. Where the feet of this pylon are cemented into the ground, there are places where the metal of its massive struts flakes off like puff pastry. The floor of the gallery that runs around the lantern at a height of 15 m or so is so rusted that even from the ground one can see the sky through the holes. I cannot help but wonder who goes up there to maintain the lamp. Yet at the same time, this lighthouse is magnificent even in its decay. Árneshreppur is literally at the end of the road: it is the northernmost inhabited district of Strandir. The light at Gjögur speaks of its will to keep going, to make do with what is available, and not to be daunted. There is an anecdote that an old farmer from Gjögur took a trip to Reykjavík. Since this was the old man's first trip to the capital, some

Fig. 4.1 The lighthouse at Gjögur. © M. Egeler, 2021.

280   LANDSCAPE, RELIGION, AND THE SUPERNATURAL

friends who knew the city showed him the sights. The highlight of the tour was Hallgrímskirkja, the soaring city church of Reykjavík. The spire is 74.5 m high and both crowned and flanked by concrete columns that imitate the structure of columnar basalt, evoking one of the most characteristic rocks of the Icelandic landscape. At its completion in 1974, the tower was the highest building in Iceland, and it has been a national monument ever since. When the old farmer from Gjögur saw it, he looked up the tower and said: "Not bad. But it's nothing compared to the lighthouse at Gjögur."

Whether or not this anecdote is true, it picks up several of the main themes discussed in the preceding chapters. One is the theme of power and subversion. Many theorists have highlighted the importance of power structures for both the representation and the perception of landscape; thus, among those discussed earlier, Denis Cosgrove viewed landscape first and foremost as a bourgeois ideological construct, and in his analyses he emphasized that landscape perceptions were ideologically constructed ways of seeing the world that were closely connected with the exercise of power.[1] W. J. T Mitchell took this one step further by describing the landscape as "something like the 'dreamwork' of imperialism," which, however, at the same time was also a place of resistance against this imperialism.[2] The way the farmer from Gjögur allegedly viewed the great city church of his national capital can be read along very similar lines. Hallgrímskirkja was never just a place of worship: its monumental size is a statement of power. By integrating symbols of Icelandic nature in the form of the typical columnar basalt, this power can be read as Icelandic power in the face of the national struggle for independence, as the church was designed in the 1930s, when Iceland still belonged to Denmark. Yet it can also be read as a statement of power within Iceland. By its monumentality in combination with its references to Icelandic nature, Hallgrímskirkja represents and "naturalizes" the domination of the national Icelandic Lutheran Protestant Church as the dominant faith in Iceland. Either way, furthermore, the church stands for the hegemony of Reykjavík within Iceland, be it as the seat of national government or as the seat of the Lutheran bishop of Iceland.[3] The farmer's nonchalance implicitly makes both claims void. His comment indicates that he saw right through the attempt of the builders of the church to express their status as they saw it, and that their self-aggrandizement did not really impress him.

[1] Cosgrove 1998, xxv–xxvi.
[2] Mitchell 2002d, 10.
[3] This holds true even though Hallgrímskirkja is not the episcopal church. One of the motivations for its size was that it was to be bigger than the Catholic Basilica of Christ the King, which until then had been the largest church in Reykjavík: Benárd 2018, 89.

ENCORE 281

Another prominent theme of the preceding discussions was identity. The importance that landscape can have for the construction of regional and national identities has been highlighted by Diana L. Eck in her study of the sacred geography of India.[4] Here also belongs the emphasis that Thomas A. Tween puts on the interlinked importance of home, homemaking, and the construction of identity as some of the things that play a central role for religions.[5] In Strandir, one of the examples that I highlighted was that of Hvítarhlíð farm. There, the local farming family viewed their home farm as the foundation of the troll woman Hvít, who in their opinion had also given her name to Hvítarhlíð farm, "Hvít's Slope." When the road authority put up new road signs, they "corrected" the name of the farm and turned Hvítarhlíð ("Hvít's Slope") into Hvítahlíð ("White Slope"). This led to considerable consternation on the part of the locals, but the road sign was never changed back: the authorities saw it as their right to overrule local feelings of identity. Also in this light, the comment of the farmer from Gjögur makes sense. Hallgrímskirkja was designed as a symbol of and an attempt to express Icelandic national identity in architectural form,[6] combining the country's traditional Lutheran Protestantism with typical forms of its natural landscapes. But who wants to have their identity dictated by the same authorities that have not the slightest interest in how the local farming families view the identities of their homes? Citing the lighthouse by his farm as superior, the old farmer made a point about what the most important point of reference was for himself—and for that, he preferred the lighthouse that ensured the safe homecoming of the local fishermen over the great architectural gestures of the nation state.

A third point that I highlighted as central for the relationship between landscape and religion is everyday labor. The importance of work is probably one of the most understudied aspects of the interpretation of landscape in contemporary landscape theory. Tim Ingold has seen this lacuna and tried to fill it by discussing "*landscape* [. . .] *as the taskscape in its embodied form*,"[7] that is, as a place of everyday work; but few researchers have followed his lead. In large areas of landscape theory, labor is still a blind spot. This has roots that go back all the way to the very origin of the modern English word "landscape." The word was borrowed into English in the sixteenth century, when the Dutch term *landschap* was adopted as a technical term of painting that reached Britain together with the Dutch landscape paintings that at the

[4] For instance, Eck 2012, 6.
[5] For instance, Tweed 2006, 75, 97.
[6] Benárd 2018.
[7] Ingold 1993, 162 (emphasis original).

time were imported in large numbers. This has given the term "landscape" a start in the culture of those wealthy parts of society that, rather than getting their hands dirty while working the land, imported foreign representations of the land as a means of displaying their social and economic status. These roots of "landscape" still reverberate today in the predominance of research that treats it as something that is looked at from the outside by somebody who is too wealthy to do any actual manual work there. The anecdote about the farmer from Gjögur in Reykjavík reflects exactly this tension between those who hold power over the land and represent it through abstract symbols and those who hold little power and experience the land as the place of their everyday labor. The facade of Hallgrímskirkja with its faux-basaltic columns is a symbolic representation of the Icelandic landscape by and for the wealthy bourgeoisie of Reykjavík and the members of the national government in Reykjavík. Its construction was a national project supported by the Icelandic parliament and major political players like Jónas Jónsson,[8] who served as Minister for Justice and Religion from 1927 to 1932 and was one of the founders of the "Progress Party," Framsóknarflokkurinn, which for decades to come was one of the leading Icelandic parties. The farmer's ironic view of this political statement piece may well have reflected not only his preference for the real land over its urban symbolic representation but also a pointed awareness of the concomitant tension between the perspectives of those in power and those who actually do the work.

The way the farmer expressed his criticism likewise takes up an important theme. He did not complain about the towering power claims of Hallgrímskirkja. Rather, he turned them into a joke, and that is how this anecdote has survived and how it was told to me: as a funny anecdote about the lighthouse and the good folk of Gjögur. Representations of landscapes can voice anger and moral outrage, as the story of the drowned pauper Sesselja exemplified in the preceding discussion. Just as important, however, is the humor that often infuses cultural engagements with the landscape. The landscape can be ironic, funny, and a way to bring some playfulness into the hard work of everyday life—which may be even more important to the farmer for whom the land is actually a place of work than for the urbanite, who uses it as a projection screen for his or her ideas about cultural constructs like the "sublime" or "nature."

*

[8] Bénard 2018, 90.

The remainder of this chapter will consist of two parts that will progress in a kind of counterpoint movement. The first part continues from the vignette of the lighthouse of Gjögur to present a *summa* of the main points highlighted and the main conclusions drawn in the discussion so far. This synopsis will cover both themes whose importance for the construction of a supernatural landscape was an object of dedicated chapters—such as the importance of everyday labor or playfulness—and aspects that were pervasive but never formed the focus of a chapter of their own, such as the role of place-names. The second part of this chapter then concludes this book by moving toward a more abstract synthesis. It presents an analysis of the different forms and elements of the supernatural landscape in order to propose a heuristic pair of ideal types: "being-in-a-place" versus "looking-at-a-place." This complementary pair of concepts serves to highlight some crucial differences between respectively the countryside view of the landscape and its urban perception.

Landscape: A Panoramic View

The main aim of this book was to present a cross-section of some current and classic thinking in landscape theory and spatial theory more generally, and to highlight some of the aspects of this thinking that in the application to both historical and contemporary religious landscapes I found most useful. In doing so, I also tried to highlight a number of aspects which in research to date have been particularly under-researched, and which, from my personal experience, seemed especially worth investigating in greater depth. This selection does not claim general intercultural validity. In a way, it is pragmatic rather than systematic: what I am trying to offer is not a unified theory of the religious or supernatural landscape, but a toolbox that for me has stood the test in its application to those data sets that I have some familiarity with, which for the most part means medieval and contemporary Iceland, Ireland, and Germany, and aspects of the classical Mediterranean.[9] To give this book unity and coherence, I have presented this toolbox on one single example of a landscape: that of the Icelandic district of Strandir. I hope that drawing my examples from this restricted area has allowed me to cumulatively show how much we can deepen our understanding of religious landscapes by paying detailed attention to certain themes. My hope is that some readers

---

[9] For instance, Egeler 2019a; Egeler 2018a; Egeler 2017; Egeler 2015a.

will find these themes, or variations thereof, useful for the analysis of different contexts in the study of religions, not least where such study intersects with the fields of folkloristics and ethnography. I take it for granted that such future analyses of different contexts will add important new themes to the toolbox I have proposed here.

Looking back over the discussions of the preceding chapters, one pervasive theme was the importance of narratives. Narratives permeate the way the religious and supernatural landscape is interpreted, given meaning, and used in social discourses. Such narratives can be quite extensive, such as the story of how the pauper Sesselja drowned because of the unwillingness of the rich and powerful to fulfill their legal and moral obligations. Yet equally such "narratives" can be extremely terse. The various stories of ghosts of dead babies can be so concise that in their extreme brevity they are no more than belief statements that the ghost of a murdered child can be heard crying at such and such a place. To contribute to the creation of a supernatural landscape, a narrative does not need to be extensive.

Another aspect that pervaded the material discussed earlier was the role of place-names. Many of the stories through which the mythological landscape of Strandir is constructed show an intense engagement with place-names in which a name's meaning directly correlates with the story of the place it relates to, as in the case of the Sesselja skerry, named from the pauper who allegedly died there. Such an emphasis on place-names also recurs in some other cultural contexts: not only was it a central point of Keith H. Basso's analysis of landscape storytelling among the Western Apache,[10] but it is also fundamental for the landscape mythology of Ireland[11] or of ancient Greece, where playing with place-names pervades Pausanias's *Description of Greece* from the second century AD. On a more fundamental level, however, what is of central significance here is the importance of the specific local place. The story of Sesselja is not significant because this pauper died somewhere in the region, but because she died in *this specific place* that would recall her fate to passersby forever after. For the presence of religion and the supernatural in the landscape, it is not the general, but the specific that takes center stage.

These specific places, at the same time, are everywhere. One of the remarkable lessons from the Strandir data set is the sheer density of places connected with supernatural and religious traditions. Such traditions are inscribed into

[10] Basso 1996.
[11] Egeler 2019a; Murray 2017; Baumgarten 1986/87; Egeler and Ruhland 2023.

the landscape not on the level of areas or regions, but on that of the specific small-scale locality; yet these localities saturate the landscape. Often, it is only a couple of hundred meters between individual sites, and sometimes considerably less. A single view can take in a whole string of such places. One example discussed earlier was the valley of Miðdalur, where an ensemble of half a dozen interrelated story sites can be taken in with one view. The sites of the local tradition of storytelling and folk belief form a dense network that entails a near-comprehensive coverage of the inhabited parts of the region.

The density of this data set makes unusually clear the extent to which it is structured by the repetition of fixed patterns. In her outline of the "grammar of sanctification" that governs the sacred geography of India, Diana L. Eck highlighted repetition as one of the central elements of this sacred geography: whatever is important in this system is repeated widely and reduplicated again and again.[12] In folkloristic research on Scandinavian supernatural storytelling, similar observations had been made in the 1940s by Albert Eskeröd,[13] and the supernatural landscape of Strandir supplies a cornucopia of examples: repetition here is an integral part of the system. The mythological landscape of Strandir is characterized by an ultimately comparatively limited number of recurrent motifs and story types that mostly remain clearly recognizable even though they are adapted to local circumstances and combined in different ways to form new interpretations of individual places. Thus, the *álagablettir* or "places of enchantment" that have come up again and again throughout this book are a type of site that recurs so often that a century ago probably every farm had at least one, and even today many have several. Extreme repetition in such cases means importance: the repetition of an element of the local system lends it importance, and this importance moreover forms the basis of its continued repetition; the more something is repeated, the more necessary it is to pay close attention to it. Sometimes, this can hint at hierarchies of importance that at first glance seem deeply counterintuitive: there are many more places in Strandir that are associated with elves than there are places associated with the Christian holy man Guðmundur the Good, and there are many more *álagablettir* than there ever were churches or chapels. Strandir is traditionally Lutheran Protestant; but if we look at what recurs again and again, what was important in the cosmology of everyday life in this local variety of Lutheran Protestantism was not quite what the higher

[12] Eck 2012, 5, 17–41.
[13] Eskeröd 1947.

286 LANDSCAPE, RELIGION, AND THE SUPERNATURAL

echelons of the church, or Lutherans in other countries, would have viewed as Lutheran orthodoxy.[14]

Another theme was that of identity, which I have just mentioned in connection with the farmer from Gjögur. The main part of this book pursued the theme of identity through the example of three stories of trolls. One of these was the founder of a farm and as such a central element of this farm's identity, whereas the two other troll tales were connected with very public places that allowed them to become established as parts and symbols of a regional identity. What was particularly important for the latter example was the public location of the places in question. The Kollafjörður trolls, for instance, are two stone pillars that until comparatively recently were located directly next to a major road. This location ensured that they were seen and visited on a regular basis by many people, and every such visit evoked their story, which was a story about the creation of the region's landscape. The constant encounters that travelers had with this story through its main physical monument helped to establish it firmly as a shared and deeply naturalized regional founding narrative. Just as the landscape of the immediate home can carry meanings and associations connected with the identity of this home, also larger regions can draw part of their identity from elements of the physical landscape that are connected with pertinent narratives and have a strong presence in the public life of the region's population.

The theme of morality is a classic topic of the study of landscape, not least as a consequence of the landmark study that Basso conducted among a community of Western Apache; in particular, he was able to show the complex and elaborate ways in which landscape storytelling was used to uphold the values of the community.[15] In Strandir, similar mechanisms are at work in tales about the abuse of the very old, the very young, and the very poor: time and again, places are connected with stories about the wrongs done to the weakest members of society, and the hauntings that resulted from these crimes. In such stories, the ghosts of the mistreated populate the landscape, to remind society of the need for social justice.

This aspect of the landscape, as so many others, is closely linked with the role of everyday labor for the experience of the land. The farmers and farm

---

[14] While it has not been studied as much as maybe it should, a discrepancy between local lived everyday belief and practice (often including the belief and practices of the lower local clergy) and the doctrines of the higher parts of the Church hierarchy is quite normal; on an Irish example, see Naughton 2003, 23–27.

[15] Basso 1996.

laborers of Strandir did not hear the crying of the ghosts of murdered children during leisurely hikes into the wild, but when they had to herd sheep and cut the grass on the mountain pastures. As Ingold observed, the landscape is a taskscape. The tasks performed there color how the land is experienced, and this in turn leaves its impression on how the land is seen through the lens of religion and the supernatural: they determine what blessings are sought from holy men, or which ghosts and devils one tries to exorcize. This importance of labor is pervasive in the makeup of the supernatural and religious landscape of Strandir: over and over again, one can observe that those places that have supernatural associations are the very ones that are also important for everyday land use, and these places are turned into something that transcends their mere laborious physicality by connecting them with stories and motifs taken from the established stock of local traditional storytelling.

At the same time, the landscape is not just work and no play. In proposing a spatially focused theory of religion, Tweed emphasized that one of the functions of religions is that they "enhance the joys associated with the encounter with the environment."[16] The phrasing he employs in his discussion often comes dangerously close to the fallacy of taking intense states of emotional involvement for granted as the standard way of being for religious people. Such an assumption was fundamental for Protestant theorists such as Friedrich Schleiermacher or Rudolf Otto, but its problems have long been recognized. The religious and supernatural landscape of Strandir confirms this criticism, but at the same time it also highlights how Tweed's emphasis on joy was making an important point: the supernatural landscape is fun. Examples like the story of Guðmundur the Good in Kolbeinsvík, where the holy man saved a farm because he had to relieve his bladder at just the right moment, illustrate how this landscape contributes to filling the lives of its inhabitants with deeply playful joy in a way which does not reflect the stereotype of sober Protestant interiority. This landscape is one whose holy and supernatural beings have burlesque adventures and do not preserve their dignity. Just as in the comparison that the farmer from Gjögur made between his lighthouse and Hallgrímskirkja, it is a landscape that is not above the occasional joke.

The people who invested this landscape with meaning nevertheless were well aware of the gravity of some situations, especially where hierarchies and social power relations were concerned. Power is one of the core themes

---

[16] Tweed 2006, 72.

288 LANDSCAPE, RELIGION, AND THE SUPERNATURAL

of current landscape theory and has stood at the center of many eminent contributions to this field. I have taken this point up again in my discussion of the Gjögur anecdote. There I highlighted especially the contribution of Mitchell, who drew attention to the ambivalence that characterizes the presence of power in the landscape: it reflects power relations as seen from the perspective of the established social hierarchies, but often also reflects resistance to these hierarchies. Engaging with the material from Strandir, it becomes clear very quickly that such subversive uses of the landscape are pervasive. In this, the Strandir data set strikingly parallels the ethnographic material collected by Basso among the Western Apache, where the subversion of official state hierarchies also formed a central theme of storytelling about the land. In Strandir, one element of subversion that is particularly prominent is a gentle (and sometimes not so gentle) mocking of ecclesiastical aspirations to moral and spiritual superiority: taking the pastor down a peg or two is a favorite theme among Strandir storytellers. Such stories not only criticize ecclesiastical claims to a particularly elevated status, but sometimes even go on to question the spiritual status of local parsons, depicting one pastor as a sorcerer and another as a deeply evil entity that was closer to the devil than to divine grace. Thus, such tales not only illustrate the importance of subversion for the way power structures are addressed through the medium of landscape, but this material with its (anti-)ecclesiastical focus also brings to the fore how right Birgit Meyer and Dick Houtman were to demand new case studies of all varieties of Protestantism in order to challenge those "facile understandings of Protestantism" that follow, without question, the mainstream views promulgated by the Churches concerned.[17] The local folk tradition does not present us with the views of the Church, but with everyday perspectives of the local population on the Church, which makes glaringly obvious that lived everyday religion even in this traditionally Lutheran region was sometimes not at all what the Church hierarchies might have wanted it to be. As proposed by Ülo Valk, popular storytelling about encounters with the supernatural indeed constitutes a counterdiscourse to the official institutional discourse as it is represented by societal authorities like the Church.[18]

One of the great themes of landscape theory is landscape as a view. Often, in the academic discourse landscape is treated as something that is looked

[17] Meyer and Houtman 2012, 13.
[18] Valk 2012, esp. p. 26.

at. One of the main innovative focuses of this book is to expand on and away from such a visual focus. I have already highlighted the importance that paying attention to everyday labor has for this refocusing. Another important but long-neglected aspect of the religious and supernatural landscape is sound. In recent years, the term "soundscape" has gained increasing currency in the research discourse, and Rosalind I. J. Hackett has even called for a "sonic turn" in the study of religions. Viewing (or rather: listening to) the landscape as a soundscape has the potential of opening up almost unstudied layers of meaning. For as soon as one starts to look out (listen out?) for auditory layers of meaning in the landscape, it turns out that sounds across a broad spectrum play central roles in how the supernatural landscape is constructed. There are human-made sounds such as the sound of church bells, whose ringing time and again forms a crucial point in traditions about the supernatural landscape. There are natural sounds like the howling of the wind, in which one may hear the plaintive crying of a ghost that makes the injustice it has experienced literally audible. There are real sounds like the resounding of the church bell in Fell or Staður; or imagined ones like the ringing of bells and the singing of psalms that time and again has been heard inside rocks inhabited by the hidden people. An analysis of these human-made as well as natural, real as well as imagined soundscapes showed clearly how sound is a central part of the mechanisms of structuring the supernatural landscape. It also suggested that there are clear patterns to how different kinds of sound are associated with different parts of the landscape: sound forms a central means for how these various parts are differentiated from each other. In a close analysis, the use of different kinds of sound indeed appears to be so systematic that it suggests that maybe the basic distinction in the landscape of Strandir was not so much the distinction between "human" and "supernatural," but rather between lowland and upland areas. These correlate with different types of inhabitants (humans and elves vs. trolls and pagan heroes) and with different religious affiliations (Christianity vs. paganism), and they are clearly marked off by their different soundscapes. Thus, paying attention to sound and soundscapes can add important pieces to the puzzle of how different spaces are filled with meaning. A "sonic turn" could indeed help us to see (hear?) things we had never noticed before.

While sound has rarely received the attention it deserves, emotions form a theme that has long been a classic in the study of religions. In the wake of the current "emotive turn," this topic is now receiving increased attention again, but it was central already for the rise of the study of religions in the

290 LANDSCAPE, RELIGION, AND THE SUPERNATURAL

nineteenth and early twentieth centuries. At the time, the study of religions was deeply influenced by Protestant theology, and this Protestant heritage has left far-reaching—and highly problematic—traces in our terminology to this day.[19] A typical trait of this early and lingering legacy was an overemphasis on strong emotional experiences, such as Otto's "creature feeling" that he conceptualized as a feeling of absolute inferiority in the face of a mystery that is both terrifying and deeply fascinating.[20] In the engagement with landscape, this Protestant theological tradition of thought had a direct parallel in the concept of the "sublime." Since the eighteenth century, the "sublime" has become established as one of the most enduring Western ideas of what makes an attractive landscape. Like Otto's "creature feeling," the sublime is two-pronged. In its most influential formulation by Edmund Burke, it was understood as a combination of horror and attraction: something terrifying that is viewed without danger and consequently engenders a uniquely strong feeling of delight.[21] The parallelism between the two concepts, of course, did not go unnoticed, and Otto himself foregrounded the sublime as one of the best possible artistic expressions of religious emotional experience as he saw it. In Western visual culture, variants of the sublime to this day play a major role for expressing and representing religious and spiritual experiences of "nature." Yet a crucial insight in the study of emotions is that emotions are culturally specific and historically contingent, and while the sublime has played a central role for many approaches to landscape, in recent decades researchers have also tackled other emotions. The material from Strandir contributes to this questioning of the prevalence of the sublime. In Iceland, the sublime is pervasive in tourism marketing and the advertising of products for an international market, but in the traditional rural supernatural landscape of Strandir it plays virtually no role. Examples such as stories of love affairs between farmers and the spirits of their land, the popular song *Sveitin mín* ("My Country"), and the mythology of the Christian holy man Guðmundur the Good bring to the fore how feelings are crucial for the local relationship to the landscape, but they are used in a way which is very different from notions like the sublime that outsiders tend to project onto the rugged landscapes of Strandir. In this local tradition, the elements of the supernatural landscape help create feelings of belonging and safety, which strike a markedly different chord from the sublime; and the emotional connotations of this supernatural

---

[19] Meyer and Houtman 2012, 9–13; Ruel 1997.
[20] Otto 1926 (1917).
[21] Esp. Burke 1887, 1: 110–111 (Part 1, Section VII).

landscape have nothing like the ecstatic intensity of the feelings postulated by Otto or Burke, but mostly remain low-key and diffuse. In this way, they illustrate the need to analyze emotions by asking how things are experienced by specific people in specific cultural contexts: the universals that Otto and Burke tried to capture do not exist, and the importance of emotions for the supernatural landscape only becomes accessible through the analysis of their historically contingent use in specific cultural situations.

Another important theme of this book, and of much theorizing in the study of religions, has been the human need to cope with contingency. For David Hume, a desire to deal with contingency was even the very origin of religion.[22] The topic remains prominent in recent theories of religions, and similarly also in theorizing on space. In Strandir, this theme is particularly important for understanding what probably is the most numerous class of local supernatural places: *álagablettir*, a hugely productive type of supernatural sites that were typically connected with the prohibition that their violation led to accidents and ill luck—which conversely made them a prime (if fallible) way of controlling the vagaries of farming life, as all one had to do to avoid ill luck was to leave such places well alone. The typical close connection between these sites and the immediate surroundings of the farm also suggested a more general conclusion: the supernatural landscape concepts that control contingency (or, rather, create a feeling of control over contingency) are closely tied to where the people whom they serve are at home, and they perform their service of helping to deal with contingency at or in the immediate surroundings of this home. This highlights a point repeatedly made by theories of space: home is a place where we feel safe. By helping to cope with contingency, the supernatural landscape is one of the media through which this feeling of safety is established that is so essential for the feeling of being at home.

Not always, however, does this work equally well: even when the supernatural landscape throws everything at life that it has at its disposal, there is only so much that it can do. As already observed by Walter Benjamin,[23] cultural constructions of home time and again do not integrate living into the world as it is, but try to create counterworlds: in such cases, the space of home becomes a refuge from the social and economic realities surrounding it. Recurrently, such developments aim to offer a protective safe space within

---

[22] *The Natural History of Religion* (1757, 1777), Section 2.4, in Merivale and Millican s.a.
[23] Benjamin 2011, 2: 841–842.

292 LANDSCAPE, RELIGION, AND THE SUPERNATURAL

a hostile environment, and some constructions of home are very successful in achieving this aim. Others, however, are little more than escapist fantasies that deny rather than resolve challenges, and that consequently can be eminently brittle and in practice fail to deliver the safety that they promise. The Goðdalur tragedy provides a brutal reminder of the potential brittleness of the supernatural landscape and its construction of home. The specific and unusual arrangement of the supernatural places in the valley of Goðdalur seemed to form something like a protective cordon against the multiple fears and threats that encircled one of Strandir's most isolated farmsteads. Yet for all that the supernatural landscape of Goðdalur gave a spiritual promise of safety, in real life it was unable to deliver on this promise: the cordon of supernatural places that surrounded the farmhouse in Goðdalur with a feeling of homeliness failed to stop the avalanche that destroyed the farm in 1948. Thus, the Goðdalur tragedy highlighted a classic fallacy of the supernatural landscape as home: it creates a disjunction between the imagined and the real that may promise more than it can deliver. The cultural overlays that turn the landscape from empty space into "home" can paint even the most deadly space as benevolent and thus make one's presence there emotionally bearable; but they may well turn out entirely unable to stop the physical realities of this space from striking back and crushing even the most elaborate construction of home.

The case of Goðdalur shows that human beings and the land sometimes need protecting from each other. Tackling this from a different angle brings us to the human relationship to nature and the environment in landscape conservation. As highlighted by Daniel Sävborg and Ülo Valk, place-lore can move people to action to protect special places,[24] thus contributing directly to environmental conservation. Also on a level of abstraction separated from specific places in the landscape, conceptions of religion and the supernatural have long played an important role in ongoing discussions about human attitudes to the environment and its protection. A central touchstone has been the "Lynn White thesis" (1967) which posits that attitudes to the environment developed in Occidental Christianity are one of the roots of the current environmental crisis. In recent years, much of the academic discourse has focused on phenomena like "dark green religion" (Bron Taylor), that is, movements which see "nature" as having an intrinsic sacrality and as being both worthy and in need of protection. If such modern environmentalist

---

[24] Sävborg and Valk 2018b, 10.

discourses are contrasted with traditional storytelling and active protection measures for places of the supernatural in Strandir, one difference in particular emerges as fundamental: the different ascription of agency. Modern "dark green religion" ascribes sacrality to nature, but not agency: it views nature as in need of being protected *through human agency*, with humans being the only ones who have the necessary capacity to act and to implement conservation measures. In contrast to this virtually exclusive ascription of agency to human beings in the modern environmentalist discourse, traditional sites of the supernatural in Strandir as described in local storytelling are perfectly able to look after themselves through their own agency: the *álagablettir* of Strandir are "places of enchantments" whose use by humans is prohibited or at least strongly regulated, and which themselves take vengeance on their human violators if those prohibitions are ever disregarded. They do not need to be protected from humans, but humans need to be protected from them. Thus, examples from the supernatural landscape of Strandir highlight a fundamental difference between views of the land in modern Western environmentalism and in at least some traditional folk storytelling: while the one ascribes agency exclusively to the human actors and posits the land as in need of protection, the other ascribes the most dangerous agency to the land and posits its human inhabitants as in need of protection.

At the same time, in spite of the far-reaching differences between modern environmentalist and "traditional" views of the sacrality of nature and the environment, both seem to have a common denominator where they have their limitations: both the protection of an environment by the ascription of an abstract inherent sacrality and its protection by the ascription of a concrete inherent vengeful power fail to enforce protection of this environment where there is an overriding practical need for the resources it has to offer. Whatever reservations the supernaturalization of the land puts in the way of its exploitation, it seems that pragmatic considerations defeat them with remarkable ease. Once again, the supernatural landscape is ultimately governed by land use rather than the other way around.

Country and City: Being-in-a-Place and Looking-at-a-Place

In the preceding section, I have tried to synthesize some main characteristics of how the landscape is experienced from the inside perspective of the countryside. Yet this is not the only way human beings encounter the

294 LANDSCAPE, RELIGION, AND THE SUPERNATURAL

landscape: they also approach it from the outside perspective of urban contexts. In Strandir, the mechanisms of the urban experience of the landscape become clear in its one structurally urban space: the small town of Hólmavík. There, something new can be seen emerging that I have tried to grasp in the section "Transformations between the Country and the City": representations of the supernatural landscape which offer an experience of it that is separate from the direct encounter with the land. The clearest example was a painting by Guðlaugur Jón Bjarnason, which showed the magic sign "Helmet of Angels" superimposed over an iconic landscape prospect from northern Strandir. Here, for the first time in the book we met with a variety of landscape that has dominated much of the landscape theoretical discourse to date: the landscape as a "way of seeing" that becomes manifest through representation in different media. Guðlaugur Jón's painting expresses a way of seeing the land through the enchantment of magic—and importantly, the Strandir landscape here is not a place that is lived in, but one that is looked at. Experientially, the direct engagement with the physical land is here replaced by an artistic representation that conveys its meaning through abstract symbolism. The present, concluding section of this book will discuss the relationship between this "way of seeing" and the characteristics of the countryside experience of the landscape in order to formulate them as a contrasting and complementary pair of ideal types.

The shift from direct experience to mediated representation of the landscape, far from being specific to Guðlaugur Jón's painting, is a general characteristic of landscape representations in art, be it in the medium of painting, photography, or film. In urban contexts, the direct experience of the landscape fades from the spotlight in favor of symbolically charged abstract representations, which replace the actual physical landscape as the primary medium through which the supernatural landscape is experienced. This shift of focus from the actual physical landscape to its representation is arguably one of the most fundamental shifts in the way the landscape is experienced between the country and the city. In research to date, most of the focus has been on the urban experience. By their very nature, the vast majority of representations have originated from social contexts that were urban or at least structurally urban, that is, representations that were created by and for a more or less affluent middle and upper class that had both the desire and the means to purchase paintings and books, but did not themselves engage in any physical labor on the land. This does not mean that the rural populace does not own paintings (they do, of course) or does not write about the land (they do that as well), but the core markets for the sort of cultural production that has traditionally been the focus of research are urban. While both wrote about the country and represent much the same period, the poet John Clare (1793–1864, son of an agricultural laborer) never had the kind of readership that was mustered by William Wordsworth (1770–1850, son of a lawyer). In research to date, this urban perspective has long been so dominant that for classic theorists like Cosgrove it seemed entirely unproblematic to reduce landscape to a "way of seeing" that reflected the ideology of bourgeois culture—which in his data set, of course, it did, because this data set consisted of representations of the landscape that had been produced for exactly the bourgeois culture that he treated as the creator and main audience of landscape. This focus on (bourgeois) landscape representations has undoubtedly created deep insights into bourgeois views of the landscape, but it has also entailed an inadvertent silencing of the rural perspective.

A full analysis would need to give due consideration to both views of landscape; it is not something in and by itself, but is viewed and treated in different ways by different people. As Daniel Sävborg and Ülo Valk have emphasized, there are marked differences in the perception of places, especially between locals and outsiders.[25] In Strandir it is striking how these different perspectives are not so much in conflict but sit side by side in blissful ignorance of each other. Over the course of my fieldwork, I time and again talked to both tourists and artists, both locally and in other parts of Iceland as well as during an artists' conference about Iceland. One thing that struck me with virtually absolute consistency was that the travelers and artists I talked to or heard talking about their approaches to Iceland were fascinated by the "emptiness" of the country. Vast openness—and its aesthetic appreciation—is a classic part of the concept of the sublime and has long played a central role in representations of northern landscapes in Western art.[26] This "emptiness," however, is something that one is only able to see if one is unable to perceive the extremely dense semanticization of the local landscape that is such a typical and fundamental characteristic of the local culture. Ironically, it seems that outsiders often love Iceland because of their lack of knowledge about the local culture, and how deeply it has shaped the land. This blissful ignorance allows them to use the Icelandic landscape as a projection screen for ideas like the sublime or, more recently, the "pristine nature" that is foregrounded by much of Icelandic tourism marketing.

As an aside, by focusing on this kind of tourism, Iceland is unwittingly repeating a pattern that was characteristic already for major parts of

---

[25] Sävborg and Valk 2018b, 9.
[26] Cf. Dietrich 2014, 10.

tourism—specifically hunting tourism—in nineteenth-century Scotland. There, one of the motivations of the Highland Clearances, which emptied large stretches of the Highlands through the systematic ruthless eviction of tenant farmers, had been the creation of deer parks for aristocratic blood sport. The upper-class fashion for deer stalking found its most iconic representation in Sir Edwin Landseer's oil painting *The Monarch of the Glen* (1851), which shows a twelve-pointer stag in an empty mountain landscape.[27] This and similar works by Landseer became exceptionally popular, and it has been argued that they have acted as one of the most effective contemporary advertisements for deer stalking as a sport.[28] Yet they were only able to achieve their advertisement effect by presenting the Scottish Highlands as a natural wilderness—and not as a country whose inhabitants had very recently been forcefully evicted to create space for privileged upper-class entertainment. For the wealthy tourist, time and again an empty sublime landscape is more attractive than one filled with local human beings and culture.

What, in sum, characterizes the landscape experience of the inhabitants of the countryside versus that of the inhabitants of the city when they visit or represent this countryside? I propose that the countryside and the city perspective on the landscape can be summarized as two ideal types, which can serve as heuristic tools to analyze different attitudes to the supernatural landscape; they could be called "being-in-a-place" versus "looking-at-a-place."[29] Of these, the rural perspective or "being-in-a-place" is characterized by direct experience, an inside perspective, long-term presence, a primarily physical engagement with the land in contexts of everyday labor, a shared and in this sense collective way of perceiving the land, and a focus on networks of small-scale individual sites that facilitate a complex and diverse presence of a broad range of varieties of the supernatural. The city perspective ("looking-at-a-place"), in contrast, is characterized by mediated experience, an outside perspective, short-term presence, a primarily visual engagement with the land in contexts of leisure, an individualist perception of the land, and a focus on sweeping landscape prospects that foreground simple abstract blanket concepts such as the sublime or "nature" over more complex and diversified interpretations.

---

[27] Worthing 2006, 206–207, 247–248, 268, plate 77.

[28] Butler 1985, 379.

[29] The term "being-in-a-place" is not intended to allude to Heidegger's concept of *In-der-Welt-sein* ("Being-in-the-world"; cf. McManus 2021, Stapleton 2014), which has a much more fundamental ontological focus and pointedly does not refer to spatial experience (see McManus 2021, 104).

Of the differences between "being-in-a-place" and "looking-at-a-place," maybe one of the most fundamental is that of mediation. Between the experience of rural people and that of the city population, there is a shift in how and which media are used to convey meanings. Mitchell has famously defined landscape as a "physical and multisensory medium,"[30] highlighting how the landscape is, as it were, its own medium. This is particularly true for the people living in and working the land, for whom the landscape itself carries its meanings. In urban contexts, experiencing the landscape as its own medium recedes in favor of representations of it, be they literary descriptions, art installations like the fountain by the harbor of Hólmavík, photography, or painting. In the city, the landscape is not experienced directly, but is mediated through a broad range of representations. This naturalizes what Cosgrove called a "way of seeing" and leads to the view of the landscape that has been put center stage by theorists such as Raymond Williams or Tim Cresswell:[31] that landscape is intrinsically something that is looked at from the outside by an observer who remains separate from it. The ideal type of the urban view of landscape maintains this way of seeing also when the viewer directly encounters the physical landscape: the urban tourist in the countryside typically engages with the landscape as a sequence of views, as something to look at. Historically, the Claude Glass maybe was the most extreme expression of this way of engaging with the landscape that tried to turn it into a framed view even when the observer was himself or herself out there and could have experienced it directly. Today, the selfie plays much the same role: it enacts a deep habit of experiencing the landscape as something that is mediated. The landscape experience of the inhabitants of the countryside versus that of the inhabitants of the city is thus characterized by the opposition of direct experience versus mediated experience.

This difference between direct and mediated experience is not the same as, but it is linked with, the equally important contrast between inside and outside perspective. The ideal type of the countryside experience of the landscape takes a perspective from the inside that is based on intense everyday movement through the land. Whoever works the land knows it inside out, from all kinds of angles and in all kinds of conditions. This repeated mundane experience creates a crucial awareness of not just famous views, but of the individual character of places as well as the intricate relationships between

---

[30] See chapter 2, section "Morality."
[31] See chapter 1, section "Looking at Landscapes: Ideology and Way of Seeing."

298 LANDSCAPE, RELIGION, AND THE SUPERNATURAL

them. I introduced the story of the "Pass of Howling," Ýluskarð, where one could hear the crying of the ghosts of children where Keralín had left his offspring to die. Only an observer who is intimately familiar with the lie of the land, and the whereabouts of its different sites, would notice that during the descent from the "Pass of Howling" one continuously looks toward the entrance of the valley where Keralín allegedly had his farm, creating the association between Ýluskarð and Keralín that underlies the story. Urban views of the landscape, in contrast, hardly ever convey this feeling that one is truly inside the places. Even works as famous and deeply knowledgeable as W. G. Collingwood's paintings of Icelandic landscapes are sequences of views of outside observers who do not much care what is behind their back while they are looking in a particular direction. Even out in the country, such observers look at the landscape as if they were still structurally outside it.

This spatial opposition of inside versus outside view has a temporal counterpart in an opposition of long-term versus short-term perspective. The dense and complex supernatural landscape of the traditional Icelandic countryside has been built up not just over individual lifetimes but over generations. For many Strandir traditions—the folktale of the family ghost Þorpa-Gudda is just one of several examples mentioned in the preceding chapters—their intergenerational character is not incidental, but essential for their significance: Þorpa-Gudda is important not as a poltergeist who does some one-off mischief, but because she is firmly attached to a family and their farm and has remained so for well over a century, becoming part and parcel of the identity of the place and its people. This time depth is foundational for the creation of a lived supernatural landscape: new things are created constantly, but if everything was new, it would lack the legitimacy of tradition and people would just feel as if they had wandered into the set of a fantasy movie instead of an everyday landscape. If one watches some of the myriad of films about Iceland, or reads travelogues written by outsiders, this feeling of having wandered into a film set indeed seems to be what outside visitors appear to be looking for: a short-term stay in a world which is not taken seriously as a world of the everyday, but which presents an exotic, escapist fantasy laced with a colorful set of supernatural beings. In this world, elves and trolls are equally cute and delightful; they no longer reflect the loneliness and the dangers of this land but are reduced to quaintness. The perspective of the urban visitor is a short-term one, which sets it in opposition to the long-term world of work and the everyday and allows it to become escapist and illusionary in the sense that it disregards everyday necessities in favor of exotic exaggeration, even while at the same time it allows it to be much shallower and more two-dimensional than the way the landscape is experienced from the rural perspective.

Another aspect that gives the rural experience a quality different from the urban is the primary way people engage with the land: while the rural experience is of the landscape as a "taskscape" and place of physical work, the urban experience is a primarily visual one of the landscape as a "way of seeing" in contexts of leisure. An *álagablettur* is not something that is defined by how it looks, but by its place in the workflow of the farm; and Ýluskarð is not visited for the views it offers, but when people are herding sheep. Conversely, for the landscape experience of painters like Collingwood or Guðlaugur Jón Bjarnason, what is central is the visual appearance of the land, whereas the land as taskscape plays no intrinsic role and appears, if at all, only as a prop in genre scenes where some picturesque shepherds are added to the sublime mountain scenery. An aspect that is worth highlighting here is that the opposition is not a simple one of physical versus visual engagement with the landscape, but that also the intention behind the act is important. A shepherd who scans a mountain vista for stray sheep is taking a visual approach, but not an urban one; whereas Collingwood's travels through Iceland entailed an eminently physical effort, but he undertook this effort for reasons that had never occurred to the population of the local countryside. The physical engagement that characterizes the ideal type of the countryside approach to the landscape is one that is fundamentally colored by the necessities of everyday work, whereas the ideal type of the city approach is one that engages with the landscape in contexts of leisure—which means mostly: looking at it. To be able to look at it, the urban viewer may accept considerable hardships; many travelogues written by travelers to Iceland make a point of emphasizing that, including the one written by Collingwood and Jón Stefánsson. But the end of these hardships is not a necessary job well done, but the leisurely enjoyment of a series of views: looking-at-a-place.

Another difference is entangled with some of the preceding points, especially (but not only) the importance of labor: the contrast between the collective character of rural being-in-a-place versus the individual character of urban looking-at-a-place. The labor that shapes so much of everyday countryside engagement with the landscape is essentially a collective effort: a farm, especially a traditional twentieth-century one, is not a one-man enterprise but is able to cope with all the different tasks at hand only through the close cooperation of all family members, often supported by hired laborers. Tasks like rounding up the sheep in autumn, when a place like the "Pass of Howling" is visited to this day, are virtually impossible to do

300 LANDSCAPE, RELIGION, AND THE SUPERNATURAL

alone, and the cutting of grass that gave the "Imp's Broadlands," Púkabreið, its name and story was done by whole workgangs of people. Such collaborative work establishes a shared experience, and only within such a framework does the supernatural landscape emerge as something of social, and not just individual, importance. This mirrors the emphasis that Leslie Marmon Silko, writing from an indigenous Pueblo perspective, puts on the collective character of (Pueblo) tradition, which is part of a fundamentally communal process.[32] In marked contrast to this, the ideal typical Romantic landscape experience as it is represented by Caspar David Friedrich's *Wanderer above the Sea of Fog* (1818)[33] is focused virtually exclusively on the isolated individual: Friedrich's wanderer is a well-dressed man who clearly is not of the working class, and standing alone on a solitary rock outcrop, he looks out over a landscape so shrouded in mist that—in a fitting irony—he actually does not even see particularly much of it. But what he sees, he enjoys in solipsistic isolation. In writing about Iceland, this focus on the individual becomes particularly striking in some early mountaineering literature. One example is provided by the first ascent of Hvannadalshnúkur, the highest peak of Iceland, by Frederick W. W. Howell in 1890.[34] In the popular account he published soon afterward, Howell—an outspoken Free Church Protestant—described this first ascent as a deeply religious experience, and even included a long quotation from the prayer that he spoke as he led his mountaineering party onto the snowfields, and in which he praised his God as the creator of the wonders of nature. In his account, Howell did mention local Icelandic companions, but he also emphasized in no uncertain terms that he alone was the hero and driving force behind the ascent. More importantly, his account of the ascent and of the religious significance that Howell ascribed to it remained entirely within the conventions of his Free Church Protestantism; local Icelandic views of the mountain did not enter the picture at all. Howell thus presented his experience very much as that of—to use Kathleen Jamie's phrase—a "lone enraptured male"[35] overlooking a rugged mountainscape he has conquered and where he finds spiritual uplifting, without needing to listen to the stories of the local farmers. For it is quite noticeable that the way Howell ascribed spiritual significance to the Icelandic landscape showed no impact whatsoever from his Icelandic companions or their culture. He

---

[32] Silko 1996, 268–269.
[33] Schneider 2011, 190 (fig. 143).
[34] Howell 1893, 72–75.
[35] Jamie 2008.

represents a type of urban Romantic individual who feels no need to integrate himself into the local ways of experiencing the land.

There is a difference of scale in the countryside experience of being-in-a-place versus the urban experience of looking-at-a-place not only in the subject of this experience (group versus individual) but also in its object. While the countryside experience focuses on a network of small-scale individual sites, the urban "way of seeing" tends to focus its gaze on the broad panorama of a sweeping landscape prospect. The supernatural landscape of farming is a patchwork consisting of predominantly small-scale structures: a small corner of a hay meadow that is set aside as an *álagablettur*, a stone inhabited by elves, or a small spring of sweet water that has been blessed by Guðmundur the Good. All of these places tend to be small, and all of them have their own specific contexts in which they make sense. The spring, for instance, would not have been (thought to have been) blessed by Guðmundur the Good if it was not the farm's most reliable source of drinking water. The intricate small-scale structuring of the landscape in this rural perspective stands in marked contrast to the most common urban ways of seeing the land. Since the eighteenth century, the most prominent bourgeois way of ascribing religious and spiritual significance to the landscape has been the sublime, and depictions of the sublime do not put small-scale places center-stage: its most traditional topoi, which in popular film and photography survive virtually intact to this day, are motifs like thundering waterfalls, high cliffs, or rugged mountains. Here also belong the aesthetic preferences of the many tourists who are drawn to the "emptiness" of Iceland. Rural being-in-a-place means a zooming in, while urban looking-at-a-place stands for a corresponding zooming out.

This difference in focus between local detail and broad panorama goes hand in hand with an equally characteristic difference in how these respective places, viewed at such different scales, are filled. The supernatural landscape of the countryside perspective typically shows a complex and diverse presence of a broad range of varieties of the supernatural that are connected with a range of different concrete places: in addition to an *álagablettur*, an elf hill, and a spring blessed by Guðmundur the Good, there may be a founder's burial mound, the grave of two shepherds, a crying baby ghost, a Paradís, a place where a parson made a fool of himself, or a place where a lethal accident happened and that has been haunted ever since.[36] This landscape is made

---

[36] See especially chapter 1, section "Common Elements and Story Patterns of the Supernatural Landscape" and Map 1.1.

colorful by a complexity born out of diversity. The typical urban perspective, in contrast, is quite monochrome. In a way, it is much like the Claude Glass: the tinted mirror of the Claude Glass allowed one to view a landscape with the reduced color range that had been made popular by the works of the painter Claude Lorraine and thus created a simplified near-monochrome. This preference of the Romantic urban landscape enthusiasts of the eighteenth and nineteenth centuries for simplification is also mirrored in the typical content of the supernatural landscape as seen in the urban perspective. In most cases, it was reduced to the simple vague religious semantics of the sublime. Some viewers were more specific, but only by giving the generalizing blanket interpretation of the landscape a slightly different emphasis. Thus, John Ruskin saw the aim of landscape painting in revealing the beauty of God's creation and the Victorian morals of his day. More recently, scholars like Bron Taylor have traced the increasing prominence of environmentalist spiritualities that, driven primarily by sections of the urban population, make "nature" itself the object of religious veneration; Taylor summarized this development with his term "dark green religion."[37] The Claude Glass, the sublime, and dark green religion all exemplify the typical monochrome of urban looking-at-a-place, which, in poignant contrast to the modern association of the city with sophistication, seems rather impoverished if compared with the colorful complexity of rural being-in-a-place (Table 4.1).

Table 4.1 Being-in-a-Place and Looking-at-a-Place

Countryside Perspective	City Perspective
Direct experience	Mediated experience
Inside perspective	Outside perspective
Long-term	Short-term
Primarily physical and focused on labor ("taskscape")	Primarily visual and focused on leisure ("way of seeing")
Collective	Individual
Focus on network of small-scale individual places	Focus on sweeping landscape prospect
Complex and diverse presence of a broad range of varieties of the supernatural connected with concrete places (e.g., saints; elves; trolls; *álagablettir*; ghosts)	Foregrounding of simple abstract blanket concepts (the sublime; nature)
Being-in-a-place	Looking-at-a-place

[37] Taylor 2020; Taylor 2010.

Bibliography

Note: In keeping with Icelandic convention, Icelanders are listed by their first name.

Abbreviations of Archives

ÞS = Rannsóknasetur Háskóla Íslands á Ströndum—Þjóðfræðistofa
NV = Náttúrustofa Vestfjarða á Hólmavík
SÁM = Stofnun Árna Magnússonar í íslenskum fræðum

Archival Sources

Rannsóknasetur Háskóla Íslands á Ströndum—Þjóðfræðistofa

Letter [anonymized] about the revenge of elves at [anonymized], 2013.
Stefán Gíslason. 2006. *Álagablettur á Kálfanesskeiði við Hólmavík*. Heimildarmaður: Jóhann Guðmundsson.

Náttúrustofa Vestfjarða á Hólmavík

Hilmar Egill Sveinbjörnsson. 1999. *Kirkjubólshr.* Two unpaginated notebooks of fieldnotes, with maps.

Stofnun Árna Magnússonar í íslenskum fræðum

Collection of files of the former Place-Name Institute of the Icelandic National Museum, first consulted through the copies held at Rannsóknasetur Háskóla Íslands á Ströndum—Þjóðfræðistofa, now largely digitized at Nafnið.is, https://nafnid.is/, last accessed 12 January 2021.

Einar Magnússon. 1999. *Örnefnaskrá fyrir jörðina Hvítarhlíð í Broddaneshreppi Strandasýslu.* Skráð af Einari Magnússyni bónda í Hvítarhlíð, https://nafnid.is/orne fnaskra/17744.
Gísli Þ. Gíslason. 1977. *Örnefnaskrá Brunngils (Óspakseyrarhreppur, Strandasýsla)*, https://nafnid.is/ornefnaskra/17735.
Grímur Benediktsson, s.a. *[Kirkjuból (Kirkjubólshreppur, Strandasýsla).]* Svör við spurningum Örnefnastofnunar, https://nafnid.arnastofnun.is/ornefnaskra/17652.
Guðmundur Jóhannsson; Guðrún Magnúsdóttir. 1975. *Kleifar á Selströnd (Strandasýsla, Kaldrananeshreppur).* Heimildarmenn: Guðmundur Jóhannsson og Guðbjörg Torfadóttir, https://nafnid.is/ornefnaskra/17503.
Guðmundur P. Valgeirsson. 1979. *Örnefni Finnbogastaða í Árneshreppi, Strandasýslu,* https://nafnid.is/ornefnaskra/17321.
Guðrún S. Magnúsdóttir. 1979a. *Finnbogastaðir (Strandasýsla, Árneshreppur).* Heimildarmenn: Guðjón Magnússon, Gyða Guðmundsdóttir og Pálína Þórólfsdóttir, https://nafnid.is/ornefnaskra/17323.

304   BIBLIOGRAPHY

Guðrún S. Magnúsdóttir. 1978a. *Vonarholt (Strandasýsla, Kirkjubólshreppur).* *Athugasemdir og viðbætur.* Heimildarmaður: Karl Guðmundsson, https://nafnid.is/ornefnaskra/17680.

Guðrún S. Magnúsdóttir. 1978b. *Víðidalsá (Strandasýsla, Hólmavíkurhreppur).* *Athugasemdir og viðbætur.* Heimildarmaður: Stefán Pálsson, https://nafnid.is/orne fnaskra/17619.

Guðrún S. Magnúsdóttir. 1978c. *Þiðriksvellir (Hólmavíkurhreppur, Strandasýsla).* Heimildarmaður: Jóhann Hjaltason, https://nafnid.is/ornefnaskra/17621.

Guðrún S. Magnúsdóttir. 1978d. *Vatnshorn (Strandasýsla, Hólmavíkurhreppur).* Heimildarmaður: Jóhann Hjaltason, https://nafnid.is/ornefnaskra/17615.

Guðrún S. Magnúsdóttir. 1978e. *Hrófá (Strandasýsla, Hrófbergshreppur). Athugasemdir og viðbætur.* Heimildarmaður: Þorgeir Þorgeirsson, https://nafnid.is/ornefnaskra/17597.

Guðrún S. Magnúsdóttir. 1977a. *Hlaðhamar (Strandasýsla, Bæjarhreppur).* Heimildarmaður: Þorsteinn Ólafsson, https://nafnid.is/ornefnaskra/17805.

Guðrún S. Magnúsdóttir. 1977b. *Stóra-Hvalsá (Strandasýsla, Bæjarhreppur).* Heimildarmaður: Eiríkur Sigfússon, https://nafnid.is/ornefnaskra/17846.

Guðrún S. Magnúsdóttir. 1977c. *Brunngil (Strandasýsla, Óspakseyrarhreppur).* Heimildarmaður: Sigríður Gísladóttir, https://nafnid.is/ornefnaskra/17734.

Guðrún S. Magnúsdóttir. 1976a. *Þrúðardalur (Strandasýsla, Fellshreppur).* Heimildarmaður: Alfreð Halldórsson, https://nafnid.is/ornefnaskra/17724.

Guðrún S. Magnúsdóttir. 1976b. *Steinadalur (Strandasýsla, Fellshreppur).* Heimildarmaður: Sigurður Franklínsson, https://nafnid.is/ornefnaskra/17716.

Guðrún S. Magnúsdóttir. 1976c. *Broddanes (Strandasýsla, Fellshreppur).* Heimildarmaður: Guðbrandur Benediktsson, https://nafnid.is/ornefnaskra/17698.

Guðrún S. Magnúsdóttir. 1976d. *Snartartunga (Strandasýsla, Óspakseyrarhreppur).* Heimildarmaður: Ásmundur Sturlaugsson, https://nafnid.is/ornefnaskra/17753.

Guðrún S. Magnúsdóttir. 1976e. *Ljúfustaðir (Fellshreppur, Strandasýsla).* Heimildarmaður: Sigurður Franklínsson, https://nafnid.is/ornefnaskra/17710.

Guðrún S. Magnúsdóttir. 1976f. *Hvalsá (Kirkjubólshreppur, Strandasýsla).* Heimildarmaður: Ágúst Benediktsson, https://nafnid.is/ornefnaskra/17647.

Guðrún S. Magnúsdóttir. 1975a. *Veiðileysa (Strandasýsla, Árneshreppur).* Heimildarmenn: Guðbrandur Sveinn Þorláksson og Annes Þorláksson, https://nafnid.is/ornefnaskra/17423.

Guðrún S. Magnúsdóttir. 1975b. *Kleifar í Kaldbaksvík (Strandasýsla, Kaldrananeshreppur).* Heimildarmaður: Páll Guðjónsson, https://nafnid.is/ornefnaskra/17505.

Guðrún Magnúsdóttir. 1975c. *Tröllatunga (Kirkjubólshreppur, Strandasýsla).* Heimildarmaður: Ásgeir Jónsson, https://nafnid.is/ornefnaskra/17672.

Guðrún S. Magnúsdóttir. 1975d. *Kaldbakur (Strandasýsla, Kaldrananeshreppur).* Heimildarmaður: Páll Guðjónsson, https://nafnid.is/ornefnaskra/17496.

Guðrún Magnúsdóttir. 1975e. *Drangsnes (Strandasýsla, Kaldrananeshreppur).* *Athugasemdir og viðbætur.* Heimildarmenn: Magndís Aradóttir og Jón Pétur Jónsson, https://nafnid.is/ornefnaskra/17462.

Guðrún Magnúsdóttir. 1974a. *Reykjarfjörður (Árneshreppur, Strandasýsla).* Heimildarmaður: Guðmundur Ágústsson, https://nafnid.is/ornefnaskra/17404.

Guðrún Magnúsdóttir. 1974b. *Drangar (Strandasýsla, Árneshreppur).* Heimildarmaður: Eiríkur Guðmundsson, https://nafnid.is/ornefnaskra/17304.

Guðrún S. Magnúsdóttir; Guðjón Guðmundsson. 1976. *Grímsey (Strandasýsla, Kaldrananeshreppur)*, https://nafnid.is/ornefnaskra/17487.

BIBLIOGRAPHY   305

Halldór S. Halldórsson. 1989. *Hrófberg (Hólmavíkurhreppur, Strandasýsla)*, https://naf nid.is/ornefnaskra/17553.

Haukur Jóhannesson. 2008. *Drangsnes*. Heimildarmaður: Bjarni Elíasson, https://nafnid. is/ornefnaskra/17463.

Haukur Jóhannesson. 1988. *Örnefnalýsing Ófeigsfjarðar*. Ófeigur— Reykjavík: [Örnefnastofnun Þjóðminjasafns], https://nafnid.is/ornefnaskra/17430.

Haukur Jóhannesson, s.a. (a). *Örnefni í og við fjöru á Krossnesi í Árneshreppi*, https://naf nid.is/ornefnaskra/17366.

Haukur Jóhannesson, s.a. (b). *Skjaldabjarnarvík (Strandasýsla, Árneshreppur). Uppkast*, https://nafnid.is/ornefnaskra/17414.

Haukur Jóhannesson; Guðmundur G. Jónsson. 1992. *Munaðarnes. Örnefni og hlunnindi*, https://nafnid.is/ornefnaskra/17383.

Haukur Jóhannesson; Helgi Jónsson. 2007. *Örnefni á Reykjanesi í Árneshreppi 1*, https:// nafnid.is/ornefnaskra/17401.

Ingi Guðmonsson. 1973. *Kolbeinsvík (Árneshreppur, Strandasýsla)*, https://nafnid.is/orne fnaskra/17357.

Ingimundur Ingimundarson. 1978. *Svanshóll (Strandasýsla, Kaldrananeshreppur)*, https:// nafnid.is/ornefnaskra/17520.

Ingimundur Ingimundarson. 1976. *Örnefnaskráning Goðdals*, https://nafnid.is/ornefnas kra/17476.

Ingimundur Ingimundarson, s.a. (a). *Álagablettir og huldufólkstrú*, https://nafnid.is/orne fnaskra/17522.

Ingimundur Ingimundarson, s.a. (b). *Frekari skýringar um nokkur örnefni í Svanshólslandi í Kaldrananeshreppi*, https://nafnid.is/ornefnaskra/17521.

Ingimundur Ingimundarson, s.a. (c). *Athugasemdir mínar og viðauki við örnefnalýsingu Rósmundar Jóhannssonar á Goðdalslandi*, https://nafnid.is/ornefnaskra/17478 (p. 8).

Ingvar Guðmundsson. 1977. *Tindur (Kirkjubólshreppur, Strandasýsla)*, https://nafnid.is/ ornefnaskra/17669.

Jóhann Hjaltason. 1934. *Örnefni og sagnir í landi jarðarinnar Þiðriksvellir í Þiðriksvalladal*. Skráð af Jóh. Hjaltasyni, https://nafnid.is/ornefnaskra/17622.

Jóhann Hjaltason, s.a. (a). *Finnbogastaðir í Trékyllisvík (Strandasýsla, Árneshreppur). Örnefni og sagnir*. Skráð af J. Hj. eftir handriti G. Þ. Guðmundssonar, skólastj. á Finnbogastöðum, https://nafnid.is/ornefnaskra/17324.

Jóhann Hjaltason, s.a. (b). *Hrófá (Strandasýsla, Hrófbergshreppur). Örnefni og sagnir*, https://nafnid.is/ornefnaskra/17598.

Jóhann Hjaltason, s.a. (c). *Reykjarfjörður (Strandasýsla, Árneshreppur). Örnefni og sagnir*. Skráð af J. Hj. eftir sögn Jakobs Saubekks fyrrum bónda í Reykjarfirði, https://nafnid.is/ ornefnaskra/17405.

Jóhann Hjaltason, s.a. (d). *Skjaldabjarnarvík (Árneshreppur, Strandasýsla). Örnefni og sagnir*. Heimildarmaður: Bergur Jónsson, https://nafnid.is/ornefnaskra/16820.

Jóhann Hjaltason, s.a. (e). *Stóra-Hvalsá (Strandasýsla, Bæjarhreppur). Örnefni og sagnir*. Skráð af J. Hj. eftir sögn Vigfúsar Guðmundssonar bónda að St. Hvalsá, https://nafnid. is/ornefnaskra/17847.

Jóhann Hjaltason, s.a. (f). *Tindur (Strandasýsla, Kirkjubólshreppur). Örnefni og sagnir*. Skráð af J. Hj. eftir handriti Guðjóns bónda Halldórssonar í Heiðarbæ í Miðdal, https:// nafnid.is/ornefnaskra/17670.

Jóhann Hjaltason; Ingimundur Guðmundsson, s.a. *Hella (Kaldrananeshreppur, Strandasýsla)*, https://nafnid.is/ornefnaskra/17492.

306 BIBLIOGRAPHY

Jóhannes Jónsson, s.a. *Asparvík (Strandasýsla, Kaldrananeshreppur)*, https://nafnid.is/ornefnaskra/17443.

Jón Jóhannsson. 1930. *Víðivellir (Hrófbergshreppur, Strandasýsla)*, https://nafnid.is/orne fnaskra/17585.

Magnús Kristjánsson. 1977. *Þambárvellir (Strandasýsla, Óspakseyrarhreppur). Örnefni og sagnir*, https://nafnid.is/ornefnaskra/17760.

Magnús Steingrímsson. 1929. "Örnefni og sagnir um benefisið Stað í Steingrímsfirði, skrásett á Gvendardag 16. mars 1929," in: *Viljinn* VII/7: 1–12.

Magnús Steingrímsson. 1953a. *Örnefnatal allra jarða í Hrófbergshreppi hinum forna*. Samantekið eftir bestu heimildum af Magnúsi Steingrímssyni, https://nafnid.is/orne fnaskra/17595.

Magnús Steingrímsson. 1953b. *Vatnshorn (Strandasýsla, Hrófbergshreppur [recte leg. Hólmavíkurhreppur])*, https://nafnid.is/ornefnaskra/17618.

Magnús Steingrímsson. 1953c. *Staður (Hrófbergshreppur, Strandasýsla)*, https://nafnid.is/ornefnaskra/17576.

Matthías Helgason, s.a. (a). *Drangsnes (Strandasýsla, Kaldrananeshreppur)*, https://naf nid.is/ornefnaskra/17465.

Matthías Helgason, s.a. (b). *Goðdalur (Strandasýsla, Kaldrananeshreppur)*, https://nafnid.is/ornefnaskra/17477.

Matthías Helgason, s.a. (c). *Kaldrananes (Kaldrananeshreppur, Strandasýsla)*, https://naf nid.is/ornefnaskra/17500.

Óli E. Björnsson. 1978. *Nokkur nöfn og athugasemdir frá Kálfanesi og Hólmavík*, https://nafnid.is/ornefnaskra/17611.

Pálína Þórólfsdóttir. 1980. *Finnbogastaðir (Árneshreppur, Strandasýsla). Athugasemdir og viðbætur*, https://nafnid.is/ornefnaskra/17325.

Pétur Guðmundsson; Guðmundur Guðmundsson, s.a. *Jörðin Ófeigsfjörður, Árneshreppi í Strandasýslu*, https://nafnid.is/ornefnaskra/17434.

Rósmundur Jóhannsson. 1959. *Letter to an unnamed addressee dated 15 July 1959*, https://nafnid.is/ornefnaskra/17478 (p. 1).

Rósmundur Jóhannsson. 1949. *Goðdalur í Bjarnarfirði. Örnefni og sagnir*, https://nafnid.is/ornefnaskra/17478 (pp. 2–8).

Sigurður Gunnlaugsson. 1929a. *Örnefni og sagnir jarðarinnar Geirmundarstaða í Selárdal*. 6 pp. (pp. 19–24 of a ledger), https://nafnid.is/ornefnaskra/17540.

Sigurður Gunnlaugsson. 1929b. *Geirmundarstaðir (Hrófbergshreppur, Strandasýsla)*, https://nafnid.is/ornefnaskra/17541 (typewritten transcript of an article originally published in *Viljinn* VII/5 (1929)).

Sigurður Rósmundsson, s.a. *Kolbjarnarstaðir og Gilsstaðir (Hrófbergshreppur, Strandasýsla)*, https://nafnid.is/ornefnaskra/17572 (typed transcript of a description first published in *Viljinn* VII/3 (1928) and VII/4 (1929)).

Símon Jóh. Ágústsson. 1964. *Örnefni: Kjós (Árneshreppur, Strandasýsla)*, https://nafnid.is/ornefnaskra/17354.

Símon Jóh. Ágústsson, s.a. (a). *Álagablettir (Árneshreppur, Strandasýsla)*, https://nafnid.is/ornefnaskra/17427.

Símon Jóh. Ágústsson, s.a. (b). *Örnefni. Kambur (Árneshreppur, Strandasýsla)*. Heimildarmaður: Páll Sæmunðsson, https://nafnid.is/ornefnaskra/17349.

Símon Jóh. Ágústsson, s.a. (c). *Örnefni. Norðurfjörður og Steinstún (Árneshreppur, Strandasýsla)*. Heimildarmaður: Eyjólfur Valgeirsson, https://nafnid.is/ornefnaskra/17398.

BIBLIOGRAPHY 307

Skúli Guðjónsson. 1978. *Ljótunnarstaðir (Strandasýsla, Bæjarhreppur)*, https://nafnid.is/ornefnaskra/17825.

Stefán Pálsson. 1953. *Þiðriksvellir (Hrófbergshreppur, Strandasýsla)*, https://nafnid.is/orne fnaskra/17624.

Stefán Pálsson. 1934. *Víðidalsá (Hrófbergshreppur, Strandasýsla)*, https://nafnid.is/orne fnaskra/17620.

Þórður Bjarnason, s.a. *Ljúfustaðir (Strandasýsla, Fellshreppur)*, https://nafnid.is/ornefnas kra/17713.

Secondary Literature and Printed Sources

Adler, Carolina E.; McEvoy, Darryn; Chhetri, Prem; Kruk, Ester: "The Role of Tourism in a Changing Climate for Conservation and Development. A Problem-oriented Study in the Kailash Sacred Landscape, Nepal," in: *Policy Sciences* 46/2 (2013): 161–178, http://www.jstor.org/stable/42636467, last accessed 16 September 2023.

Ahn, Gregor: "Religion. I. Religionsgeschichtlich," in: Gerhard Müller (ed.): *Theologische Realenzyklopädie. Band XXVIII: Pürstinger—Religionsphilosophie.* Berlin—New York: Walter de Gruyter 1997, 513–522.

Alcock, Susan E.; Osborne, Robin (eds.): *Placing the Gods. Sanctuaries and Sacred Space in Ancient Greece.* Oxford: Clarendon Press 1994.

Alex, Rayson K.; Deborah, S. Susan: "Ecophobia, Reverential Eco-fear, and Indigenous Worldviews," in: *ISLE: Interdisciplinary Studies in Literature and Environment* 26/2 (Spring 2019): 422–429, https://doi.org/10.1093/isle/isz032.

Andri Snær Magnason: *Dreamland. A Self-Help Manual for a Frightened Nation.* London: Citizen Press 2008 (Icelandic original ed.: *Draumalandið: Sjálfshjálparbók handa hræddri þjóð.* Reykjavík: Mál og menning 2006).

Anonymous: "Harmleikurinn í Goðdal: Gekk í berhögg við álögin—og nú er bærinn í rúst. Viðtal við Jóhann Kristmundsson bónda frá Goðdal," in: *Vísir*, 11. janúar 1949: 5–6.

Ármann Jakobsson: *The Troll Inside You. Paranormal Activity in the Medieval North.* [Santa Barbara—The Hague]: Punctum Books 2017.

Ármann Jakobsson: "Beware of the Elf!: A Note on the Evolving Meaning of Álfar," in: *Folklore* 126 (2015): 215–223.

Ármann Jakobsson: "Identifying the Ogre: The Legendary Saga Giants," in: Annette Lassen; Agneta Ney; Ármann Jakobsson (eds.): *Fornaldarsagaerne, myter og virkelighed. Studier i de oldislandske fornaldarsögur Norðurlanda.* Copenhagen: Museum Tusculanum Press 2009, 181–200.

Ármann Jakobsson: "A Contest of Cosmic Fathers. God and Giant in Vafþrúðnismál," in: *Neophilologus* 92 (2008): 263–277.

Ármann Jakobsson: "Where Do the Giants Live?" In: *Arkiv för nordisk filologi* 121 (2006): 101–112.

Ármann Jakobsson: "The Good, the Bad, and the Ugly: *Bárðar saga* and Its Giants," in: *Mediaeval Scandinavia* 15 (2005): 1–15.

Árngrímur Fr. Bjarnason; Helgi Guðmundsson: *Vestfirzkar sagnir.* 3 vols. (Helgi ed. vols. 1–2; Árngrímur ed. vol. 3), Reykjavík: Bókaforlagið Fagurskinna—Guðm. Gamalíelsson 1933–1949.

Árni Óla: *Álög og bannhelgi. Sögur og sagnir um fjölmarga álagastaði í öllum landshlutum.* Reykjavík: Setberg 1968.

Árni Óla: "Kollafirðir og Kollabúðir," in: *Lesbók Morgunblaðsins*, sunnudagur 20. maí 1956, 18 tbl., XXXI. árg., 277–282.

308 BIBLIOGRAPHY

Asplund Ingemark, Camilla: "The Chronotope of Enchantment," in: *Journal of Folklore Research* 43/1 (2006): 1–30.

Asplund Ingemark, Camilla; Ingemark, Dominic: *Representations of Fear. Verbalising Emotion in Ancient Roman Folk Narrative.* (=Folklore Fellows' Communications 320), Helsinki: Suomalainen Tiedeakatemia (Academia Scientiarum Fennica) 2020.

Asprem, Egil: *The Problem of Disenchantment. Scientific Naturalism and Esoteric Discourse 1900–1939.* (=Numen Book Series 147), Leiden: Brill 2014.

Assmann, Aleida: *Erinnerungsräume. Formen und Wandlungen des kulturellen Gedächtnisses.* München: C.H. Beck 1999.

Assmann, Jan: *Religion und kulturelles Gedächtnis. Zehn Studien.* 4. Auflage, München: C.H. Beck 2017.

Assmann, Jan: *Das kulturelle Gedächtnis. Schrift, Erinnerung und politische Identität in frühen Hochkulturen.* 6. Auflage, München: C.H. Beck 2007 (original edition 1992).

Auden, W. H.; MacNeice, Louis: *Letters from Iceland.* London: Faber and Faber 1937.

Auffarth, Christoph; Mohr, Hubert: "Religion," in: Kocku von Stuckrad (ed.): *The Brill Dictionary of Religion. Volume III: M–R.* Revised edition of *Metzler Lexikon Religion* edited by Christoph Auffarth, Jutta Bernard, and Hubert Mohr. Translated from the German by Robert R. Barr. Leiden—Boston: Brill 2006, 1607–1619.

Augé, Marc: *Nicht-Orte.* Aus dem Französischen von Michael Bischoff. Um ein Nachwort erweiterte Auflage, 4. Auflage, München: C.H. Beck 2014.

Bachelard, Gaston: *The Poetics of Space.* Translated from the French by Maria Jolas. With a new foreword by John R. Stilgoe. Boston: Beacon Press 1994. (Originally published as *La poétique de l'espace*, 1958.)

Backhaus, Gary; Murungi, John (eds.): *Symbolic Landscapes.* n.p.: Springer 2009.

Bakhtin, Mikhail: "Forms of Time and the Chronotope in the Novel," in: Mikhail Bakhtin: *The Dialogic Imagination. Four Essays by M. M. Bakhtin.* Ed. by Michael Holquist, translated by Caryl Emerson and Michael Holquist. (=University of Texas Press Slavic Series 1), Austin: University of Texas Press 1981, 84–258.

Basso, Keith H.: *Wisdom Sits in Places. Landscape and Language among the Western Apache.* Albuquerque: University of New Mexico Press 1996.

Bätzing, Werner: *Das Landleben. Geschichte und Zukunft einer gefährdeten Lebensform.* München: Beck 2020.

Baumgarten, Rolf: "Placenames, Etymology, and the Structure of Fianaigecht," in: *Béaloideas* 54/55 (1986/1987): 1–24.

Beinhauer-Köhler, Bärbel; Franke, Edith; Frateantonio, Christa; Nagel, Alexander (eds.): *Religion, Raum und Natur. Religionswissenschaftliche Erkundungen.* (= Marburger Religionswissenschaft im Diskurs 1), Berlin—Münster—Wien—Zürich—London: LIT Verlag 2017.

Benárd, Aurél: "Hallgrímskirkja, Reykjavík: A Late Example of Expressionist Church Architecture," in: *YBL Journal of Built Environment* 6/1 (2018): 86–102, doi: 10.2478/jbe-2018-0006.

Bender, Barbara: "Time and Landscape," in: *Current Anthropology*, special issue "Repertoires of Timekeeping in Anthropology" 43/S4 (August/October 2002): S103–S112.

Beneš, Jaromír; Zvelebil, Marek: "A Historical Interactive Landscape in the Heart of Europe: The Case of Bohemia," in: Peter J. Ucko; Robert Layton (eds.): *The Archaeology and Anthropology of Landscape. Shaping your Landscape.* (=One World Archaelogy 30), London—New York: Routledge 1999, 73–93.

BIBLIOGRAPHY   309

Benjamin, Walter: *Gesammelte Werke*. 2 vols., Frankfurt a. M.: Zweitausendeins 2011.

Benozzo, Francesco: *Landscape Perception in Early Celtic Literature*. (=Celtic Studies Publications 8), Aberystwyth: Celtic Studies Publications 2004.

Berg, Lawrence D.; Vuolteenaho, Jani (eds.): *Critical Toponymies: The Contested Politics of Place Naming*. Farnham—Burlington, VT: Ashgate 2009.

Berner, Ulrich: "Religion und Natur: Zur Debatte über die historischen Wurzeln der ökologischen Krise," in: Hans Kessler (ed.): *Ökologisches Weltethos im Dialog der Kulturen und Religionen*. Darmstadt: Wissenschaftliche Buchgesellschaft 1996, 33–57.

Bigon, Liora: "Introduction: Place Names in Africa: Colonial Urban Legacies, Entangled Histories," in: Liora Bigon (ed.): *Place Names in Africa. Colonial Urban Legacies, Entangled Histories*. [n. p.]: Springer 2016, 1–25.

Bosworth, Joseph; Toller, T. Northcote: *An Anglo-Saxon Dictionary*. Based on the manuscript collections of the late Joseph Bosworth, edited and enlarged by T. Northcote Toller. London: Oxford University Press 1898 (reprint 1972).

Brace, Catherine; Bailey, Adrian R.; Harvey, David C.: "Religion, Place and Space: a Framework for Investigating Historical Geographies of Religious Identities and Communities," in: *Progress in Human Geography* 30/1 (February 2006): 28–43.

Bradley, Richard: *An Archaeology of Natural Places*. London: Routledge 2000.

Breatnach, Deasún: "The Púca: A Multi-Functional Irish Supernatural Entity," in: *Folklore* 104 (1993): 105–110.

Brink, Stefan: "Myth and Ritual in Pre-Christian Scandinavian Landscape," in: Stefan Brink; Sæbjørg Walaker Nordeide (eds.): *Sacred Sites and Holy Places. Exploring the Sacralization of Landscape through Time and Space*. (=Studies in the Early Middle Ages 11), Turnhout: Brepols Publishers 2013, 33–51.

Bühler, Benjamin: *Ecocriticism. Grundlagen—Theorien—Interpretationen*. Stuttgart: J. B. Metzler 2016.

Burke, Edmund: *The Works of the Right Honourable Edmund Burke in Twelve Volumes*. Vol. 1. London: Nimmo 1887.

Busch, Werner: *Caspar David Friedrich: Ästhetik und Religion*. München: C.H. Beck 2003.

Butler, Richard: "Evolution of Tourism in the Scottish Highlands," in: *Annals of Tourism Research* 12 (1985): 371–391.

Cancik, Hubert: "Rome as Sacred Landscape. Varro and the End of Republican Religion in Rome," in: *Visible Religion: Annual for Religious Iconography* 4–5 (1985–1986), thematic issue "Approaches to Iconology," 250–265.

de Certeau, Michel: *The Practice of Everyday Life*. Berkeley: University of California Press 1984.

Chadbourne, Kate: "The Knife Against the Wave: Fairies, Fishermen, and the Sea," in: *Béaloideas* 80 (2012): 70–85.

Chadwick, Adrian M.; Gibson, Catriona D. (eds.): *Memory, Myth and Long-Term Landscape Inhabitation*. (=Celtic Studies Publications 17), Oxford: Oxbow Books 2013.

Chidester, David; Linenthal, Edward T. (eds.): *American Sacred Space*. Bloomington—Indianapolis: Indiana University Press 1995.

Christiansen, Reidar Th.: *The Migratory Legends. A Proposed List of Types with a Systematic Catalogue of the Norwegian Variants*. (=Folklore Fellows' Communications 175), Helsinki: Suomalainen tiedeakatemia (Academia Scientiarum Fennica) 1958.

Ciklamini, Marlene: "Folklore and Hagiography in Arngrímr's *Guðmundar saga Arasonar*," in: *Fabula* 49 (2008): 1–18, doi:10.1515/fabl.2008.002.

310 BIBLIOGRAPHY

Ciklamini, Marlene: "Folklore and Hagiography in Arngrímr's *Guðmundar saga Arasona*," in: John McKinnell; David Ashurst; Donata Kick (eds.): *The Fantastic in Old Norse/Icelandic Literature. Sagas and the British Isles. Preprint Papers of the Thirteenth International Saga Conference, Durham and York, 6th–12th August 2006*. 2 vols., Durham: Centre for Medieval and Renaissance Studies 2006, 171–179, http://sagacon ference.org/SC13/SC13.html, last accessed 3 December 2020.

Ciklamini, Marlene: "Sainthood in the Making: The Arduous Path of Guðmundr the Good, Iceland's Uncanonized Saint," in: *Alvíssmál* 11 (2004): 55–74, http://userpage. fu-berlin.de/~alvismal/11gudmun.pdf, last accessed 30 June 2020.

Cladis, Mark: "Radical Romanticism and its Alternative Account of the Wild and Wilderness," in: *ISLE: Interdisciplinary Studies in Literature and Environment* 25/4 (2018): 835–857.

Cleasby, Richard; Gudbrand Vigfusson: *An Icelandic-English Dictionary*. With an introduction and life of Richard Cleasby by George Webbe Dasent. Oxford: Clarendon Press 1874.

Clunies Ross, Margaret: "Giants," in: Jens Peter Schjødt; John Lindow; Anders Andrén (eds.): *The Pre-Christian Religions of the North: Histories and Structures. Vol. III: Conceptual Frameworks: The Cosmos and Collective Supernatural Beings*. 4 vols., Turnhout: Brepols 2020, vol. 3, 1527–1557.

Collingwood, W. G.; Jón Stefánsson (trans.): *The Life and Death of Cormac the Skald. Being the Icelandic Kormáks-saga rendered into English*. (=Viking Club Translation Series 1), Ulverston: W.M. Holmes 1902.

Collingwood, W. G.; Jón Stefánsson: *A Pilgrimage to the Saga-Steads of Iceland*. Facsimile edition ed. by Matthias Egeler, [London]: Viking Society for Northern Research— University College London 2015 (originally published Ulverston: W. Holmes 1899; open access at http://www.vsnrweb-publications.org.uk/).

Cook, E. T.; Wedderburn, Alexander (eds.): *The Complete Works of John Ruskin. Library Edition, Volume III: Modern Painters, Volume I*. London: George Allen— New York: Longmans, Green, and Co 1903.

Cormack, Margaret: "Saints, Seals, and Demons: The Stories of Selkolla," in: Daniel Sävborg; Karen Bek-Pedersen (eds.): *Supernatural Encounters in Old Norse Literature and Tradition*. (=Borders, Boundaries, Landscapes 1), Turnhout: Brepols 2018, 75–103.

Cormack, Margaret: "Catholic Saints in Lutheran Legend. Post-Reformation Ecclesiastical Folklore in Iceland," in: *Scripta Islandica* 59 (2008): 47–71.

Cormack, Margaret: "Holy Wells and National Identity in Iceland," in: Margaret Cormack (ed.): *Saints and Their Cults in the Atlantic World*. Columbia: University of South Carolina Press 2007, 229–247.

Cormack, Margaret: *The Saints in Iceland. Their Veneration from the Conversion to 1400*. Preface by Peter Foote. (=Subsidia hagiographica 78), Bruxelles: Société des Bollandistes 1994.

Cormack, Margaret: "Saints and Geography," http://www.saintsgeog.net, last accessed 3 December 2020.

Corrigan, John: "Emotion," in: Michael Stausberg; Steven Engler (eds.): *The Oxford Handbook of the Study of Religion*. Oxford—New York: Oxford University Press 2016, 510–524.

Corrigan, John: "Spatiality and Religion," in: Barney Warf; Santa Arias (eds.): *The Spatial Turn. Interdisciplinary Perspectives*. London—New York: Routledge 2009, 157–172.

BIBLIOGRAPHY 311

Corrigan, John (ed.): *The Oxford Handbook of Religion and Emotion.* Oxford—New York: Oxford University Press 2008a.

Corrigan, John: "Introduction: The Study of Religion and Emotion," in: John Corrigan (ed.): *The Oxford Handbook of Religion and Emotion.* Oxford—New York: Oxford University Press 2008b, 3–12.

Cosgrove, Denis E.: "Introduction to *Social Formation and Symbolic Landscape*," in: Rachael Ziady DeLue; James Elkins (eds.): *Landscape Theory.* (=The Art Seminar 6), New York—London: Routledge 2008, 17–42.

Cosgrove, Denis E.: *Social Formation and Symbolic Landscape. With a New Introduction.* Madison: The University of Wisconsin Press 1998.

Cosgrove, Denis: "Prospect, Perspective and the Evolution of the Landscape Idea," in: *Transactions of the Institute of British Geographers* 10/1 (1985): 45–62, https://doi.org/10.2307/622249.

Cosgrove, Denis; Daniels, Stephen: "Spectacle and Text: Landscape Metaphors in Cultural Geography," in: James Duncan; David Ley (eds.): *Place/Culture/Representation.* London—New York: Routledge 1993, 57–77.

Cosgrove, Denis; Daniels, Stephen (eds.): *The Iconography of Landscape. Essays on the Symbolic Representation, Design and Use of Past Environments.* (=Cambridge Studies in Historical Geography 9), Cambridge—New York: Cambridge University Press 1988.

Cresswell, Tim: *Place. An Introduction.* Second edition, Chichester: Wiley Blackwell 2015.

Dagrún Ósk Jónsdóttir: "'It Was Ill Done, My Mother, to Deny Me Life': Rejecting the Role of Motherhood in Icelandic Folk Legends," in: *Western Folklore* 81 (Fall 2022): 321–355.

Dagrún Ósk Jónsdóttir: "'You Have a Man's Spirit in a Woman's Heart': Women Who Break Hegemonic Ideas about Femininity in Icelandic Legends," in: *Folklore* 132/3 (2021): 290–312.

Dagrún Ósk Jónsdóttir: "'Obey My Will or Suffer': Violence against Women in Icelandic Folk Legends," in: *Journal of Ethnology and Folkloristics* 14/2 (2020): 17–43, doi: 10.2478/jef-2020-0014.

Dagrún Ósk Jónsdóttir; Jón Jónsson: *Álagablettir á Ströndum.* Strandir: Sauðfjársetur á Ströndum og Rannsóknasetur HÍ á Ströndum—Þjóðfræðistofa 2021.

Dagrún Ósk Jónsdóttir; Jón Jónsson: "Álagablettir á Ströndum," in: *Strandapósturinn* 51 (2019): 84–92.

Dégh, Linda: *Legend and Belief. Dialectics of a Folklore Genre.* Bloomington—Indianapolis: Indiana University Press 2001.

Deleuze, Gilles; Guattari, Félix: *A Thousand Plateaus. Capitalism and Schizophrenia.* Translation and foreword by Brian Massumi. London: Athlone 1988 (reprint London: Bloomsbury 2013).

DeLue, Rachael Ziady; Elkins, James (eds.): *Landscape Theory.* (=The Art Seminar 6), New York—London: Routledge 2008.

Dietrich, Sophie: "Der nordische Naturraum und das Erhabene: Eine Fallstudie," in: *Ecozon@* 5/2 (2014): 6–22, https://doi.org/10.37536/ECOZONA.2014.5.2.610.

Diljá Rut Guðmundudóttir: *"Og þá gól útburður…": Rannsókn á íslenskum útburðasögnum.* Lokaverkefni til BA-gráðu í Þjóðfræði, Reykjavík: Háskóli Íslands, febrúar 2016, http://hdl.handle.net/1946/23556, last accessed 18 July 2020.

Doran, Robert: *The Theory of the Sublime from Longinus to Kant.* Cambridge: Cambridge University Press 2015.

312 BIBLIOGRAPHY

Lord Dufferin: *Letters from High Latitudes, Being Some Account of a Voyage in the Schooner Yacht "Foam," 85 o.m., to Iceland, Jan Mayen, and Spitzbergen, in 1856.* London: John Murray 1857.

Duncan, James; Duncan, Nancy: "(Re)Reading the Landscape," in: *Environment and Planning D: Society and Space* 6 (1988): 117–126.

Dünne, Jörg; Günzel, Stephan (eds. in collaboration with Hermann Doetsch and Roger Lüdeke): *Raumtheorie. Grundlagentexte aus Philosophie und Kulturwissenschaften.* Frankfurt a. M.: Suhrkamp 2006.

Durkheim, Emile: *The Elementary Forms of the Religious Life.* Translated from the French by Joseph Ward Swain. London: George Allen & Unwin 1915 (third impression 1954).

Eck, Diana L.: *India. A Sacred Geography.* New York: Three Rivers Press 2012.

eDIL: Electronic Dictionary of the Irish Language. Edited by Gregory Toner, Máire Ní Mhaonaigh, Sharon Arbuthnot, Marie-Luise Theuerkauf, and Dagmar Wodtko, http://www.dil.ie, last accessed 25 July 2020.

Egeler, Matthias: "Narrativ und pragmatische Nutzung des Raums: Zur Verknüpfung von Erzähltradition und Alltagswelt am Beispiel der Überlieferungen über den Gründungsheroen Steingrímur den Troll (*Landnámabók* S163=H132)," in: Jan van Nahl; Wilhelm Heizmann (eds.): *Germanisches Altertum und Europäisches Mittelalter. Gedenkband für Heinrich Beck.* (=Ergänzungsbände zum Reallexikon der Germanischen Altertumskunde 142), Berlin—Boston: de Gruyter, forthcoming a.

Egeler, Matthias: "The Grave Mound of a Saga Hero: A Case Study in Context and Continuity between *Grettis saga* and Modern Folklore," in: *Religionsvidenskabeligt Tidsskrift* 74 (2022): 705–725, https://tidsskrift.dk/rvt/article/view/132135, last accessed 16 September 2023.

Egeler, Matthias: "An Ethnography of an Imaginary Road: Fear, Death, and Storytelling in the Icelandic Westfjords," in: *Folklore* 132 (2021a): 115–139, https://doi.org/10.1080/0015587X.2020.1788806.

Egeler, Matthias: "Giants in the Landscape: Hennøy, Surtshellir, and the Semantic Spectrum of Place," in: Sabine Heidi Walther; Regina Jucknies; Judith Meurer-Bongardt; Jens Eike Schnall (eds. in collaboration with Brigitta Jaroschek and Sarah Onkels): *Res, Artes et Religio. Essays in Honour of Rudolf Simek.* Leeds: Kısmet Press 2021b, 121–139.

Egeler, Matthias: "Saga Writing, Folklore, and Labour: The Death of Svanr in *Njáls saga*," in: *Arkiv för nordisk filologi* 135 (2020a): 33–49.

Egeler, Matthias: "Pilgrims to Thule: Religion and the Supernatural in Travel Literature about Iceland," in: *Marburg Journal of Religion* 22/1 (2020b): 1–55, https://doi.org/10.17192/mjr.2020.22.8011, last accessed 26 May 2020.

Egeler, Matthias: "Ortsnamen als religionswissenschaftliche Quelle," in: *Zeitschrift für Religionswissenschaft* 27/1 (2019a): 146–173.

Egeler, Matthias (ed.): *Landscape and Myth in North-Western Europe.* (=Borders, Boundaries, and Landscapes 2), Turnhout: Brepols 2019b.

Egeler, Matthias: *Atlantic Outlooks on Being at Home: Gaelic Place-Lore and the Construction of a Sense of Place in Medieval Iceland.* (=Folklore Fellows' Communications 314), Helsinki: Suomalainen Tiedeakatemia (Academia Scientiarum Fennica) 2018a.

Egeler, Matthias: "The Narrative Uses of Toponyms in *Harðar saga*," in: NORDEUROPA*forum* 2018b, 80–101, https://doi.org/10.18452/19529.

BIBLIOGRAPHY 313

Egeler, Matthias: *Islands in the West. Classical Myth and the Medieval Norse and Irish Geographical Imagination.* (=Medieval Voyaging 4), Turnhout: Brepols 2017.

Egeler, Matthias: *Avalon, 66° Nord. Zu Frühgeschichte und Rezeption eines Mythos.* (= Ergänzungsbände zum Reallexikon der Germanischen Altertumskunde 95), Berlin—Boston: de Gruyter 2015a.

Egeler, Matthias (ed.): *W.G. Collingwood & Jón Stefánsson: A Pilgrimage to the Saga-Steads of Iceland.* Facsimile edition, [London]: Viking Society for Northern Research—University College London 2015b. (Originally published Ulverston: W. Holmes 1899; open access at http://www.vsnrweb-publications.org.uk/).

Egeler, Matthias: "A Retrospective Methodology for Using *Landnámabók* as a Source for the Religious History of Iceland? Some Questions," in: *RMN Newsletter* 10 (2015c): 78–92, https://www.helsinki.fi/sites/default/files/atoms/files/rmn_10_2015.pdf, last accessed 7 April 2020.

Egeler, Matthias; Ruhland, Susanne: *The Life of Saint Enda, Abbot of Aran. A Translation of Vita Endei with an Essay on Landscape and Labour in the Life.* (=Cork Studies in Celtic Literatures 8), Cork: Cork Studies in Celtic Literatures 2023.

Einar Matthíasson; Eiríkur Þorláksson; Erna Sörensen; Kristín G. Guðnadóttir (eds.): *Kjarval.* Reykjavík: Nesútgáfan 2005.

Einar Ólafur Sveinsson: *The Folk-Stories of Iceland.* Revised by Einar G. Pétursson, translated by Benedikt Benedikz, edited by Anthony Faulkes. (=Viking Society for Northern Research, Text Series 16), [London]: Viking Society for Northern Research—University College London 2003.

Einar Ól. Sveinsson: *Brennu-Njáls saga.* (=Íslenzk fornrit 12), Reykjavík: Hið íslenzka fornritafélag 1954.

Einar Ól. Sveinsson: *Verzeichnis isländischer Märchenvarianten mit einer einleitenden Untersuchung.* (=Folklore Fellows' Communications 83), Helsinki: Suomalainen Tiedeakatemia 1929.

Emil Als: "Gamli tíminn í Goðdal," in: *Morgunblaðið*, 241. tölublað, 7. september 2003, 20–21.

Engelke, Matthew: "Material Religion," in: Robert A. Orsi (ed.): *The Cambridge Companion to Religious Studies.* Cambridge: Cambridge University Press 2011, 209–229, doi:10.1017/CCOL9780521883917.012.

Eskeröd, Albert: *Årets äring: etnologiska studier i skördens och julens tro och sed.* (= Nordiska Museets Handlingar 26), Stockholm: Nordiska museet 1947.

Evans-Pritchard, E. E.: *Witchcraft, Oracles and Magic among the Azande.* With a foreword by C. G. Seligman. Oxford: Clarendon Press 1937.

Faulkes, Anthony: *Snorri Sturluson: Edda. Prologue and Gylfaginning.* Second edition, [London]: Viking Society for Northern Research—University College London 2005.

Faulkes, Anthony: *Snorri Sturluson: Edda.* Translated and edited by Anthony Faulkes. London: J. M. Dent—Vermont: Charles E. Tuttle 1995.

Faulstich, Paul: "Mapping the Mythological Landscape: An Aboriginal Way of Being-in-the-World," in: *Ethics, Place and Environment* 1 (1998): 197–221.

Feldt, Laura (ed.): *Wilderness in Mythology and Religion.* (=Religion and Society 55), Boston—Berlin: de Gruyter 2012.

Felton, Debbie (ed.): *Landscapes of Dread in Classical Antiquity: Negative Emotion in Natural and Constructed Spaces.* London—New York: Routledge 2018.

Finnur Kristjánsson: "Fjárhús Árna á Eyri," in: *Samvinnan* 2/78 (1 March 1978): 8–11.

314 BIBLIOGRAPHY

Foucault, Michel: *Die Heterotopien. Les hétérotopies. Der utopische Körper. Le corps utopique. Zwei Radiovorträge.* Zweisprachige Ausgabe, übersetzt von Michael Bischoff, mit einem Nachwort von Daniel Defert. 3. Auflage, Berlin: Suhrkamp 2017.

Foucault, Michel: "Von anderen Räumen (1967)," in: Jörg Dünne; Stephan Günzel (eds. in collaboration with Hermann Doetsch and Roger Lüdeke): *Raumtheorie. Grundlagentexte aus Philosophie und Kulturwissenschaften.* Frankfurt a. M.: Suhrkamp 2006, 317–329.

Frog: "Otherworlding: Othering Places and Spaces through Mythologization," in: *Signs and Society* 8/3 (2020): 454–471.

Frog: "Germanic Traditions of the Theft of the Thunder-Instrument (ATU 1148b): An Approach to *Þrymskviða* and Þórr's Adventure with Geirrøðr in Circum-Baltic Perspective," in: Eldar Heide; Karen Bek-Petersen (eds.): *New Focus on Retrospective Methods.* (=Folklore Fellows' Communications 307), Helsinki: Academia Scientiarum Fennica 2014, 120–162.

Frog; Ahola, Joonas (eds.): *Folklore and Old Norse Mythology.* (=Folklore Fellows' Communications 323), Helsinki: The Kalevala Society 2021.

Garrard, Greg: *Ecocriticism. (The New Critical Idiom),* second edition, London—New York: Routledge 2012.

Garrard, Greg: "Ecocriticism," in: *The Year's Work in Critical and Cultural Theory* 18/1 (2010): 1–35, https://doi.org/10.1093/ywcct/mbq005.

Geertz, Clifford: *The Interpretation of Cultures. Selected Essays.* New York: Basic Books 1973.

Geir T. Zoega: *A Concise Dictionary of Old Icelandic.* Oxford: Clarendon Press 1910.

Gísli Gunnarsson: "Fátækt á Íslandi fyrr á tímum," in: *Ný Saga. Tímarit Sögufélags* 4 (1990): 72–81.

Gísli Jónatansson: "Nokkur örnefni í Kirkjubólshreppi," in: *Strandapósturinn* 23 (1989): 121–126.

Gísli Jónatansson: "Gömul eyðibýli og sel í Tungusveit," in: *Strandapósturinn* 19 (1985): 123–129.

Gladigow, Burkhard: "Religionsgeschichte des Gegenstandes—Gegenstände der Religionsgeschichte," in: Hartmut Zinser (ed.): *Religionswissenschaft. Eine Einführung.* Berlin: Reimer 1988, 6–37.

Glauser, Jürg; Hermann, Pernille; Mitchell, Stephen A. (eds.): *Handbook of Pre-Modern Nordic Memory Studies. Interdisciplinary Approaches.* 2 vols., Berlin—Boston: de Gruyter 2018.

Guðrún Níelsdóttir: "Sagnir úr Goðdal," in: *Strandapósturinn* 10 (1976): 66–69.

Gunnell, Terry: "Dvergar (Dwarfs)," in: Jens Peter Schjødt; John Lindow; Anders Andrén (eds.): *The Pre-Christian Religions of the North: Histories and Structures. Vol. III: Conceptual Frameworks: The Cosmos and Collective Supernatural Beings.* 4 vols., Turnhout: Brepols 2020a, vol. 3, 1559–1570.

Gunnell, Terry: "Álfar (Elves)," in: Jens Peter Schjødt; John Lindow; Anders Andrén (eds.): *The Pre-Christian Religions of the North: Histories and Structures. Vol. III: Conceptual Frameworks: The Cosmos and Collective Supernatural Beings.* 4 vols., Turnhout: Brepols 2020b, vol. 3, 1571–1580.

Gunnell, Terry: "Spaces, Places, and Liminality: Marking Out and Meeting the Dead and the Supernatural in Old Nordic Landscapes," in: Matthias Egeler (ed.): *Landscape and Myth in North-Western Europe.* (=Borders, Boundaries, and Landscapes 2), Turnhout: Brepols 2019, 25–44.

BIBLIOGRAPHY 315

Gunnell, Terry: "The Power in the Place: Icelandic Álagablettir Legends in a Comparative Context," in: Ülo Valk; Daniel Sävborg (eds.): *Storied and Supernatural Places: Studies in Spatial and Social Dimensions of Folklore and Sagas.* (=Studia Fennica Folkloristica 23), Helsinki: Finnish Literature Society 2018a, 27–41.

Gunnell, Terry: "The Álfar, the Clerics and the Enlightenment: Conceptions of the Supernatural in the Age of Reason in Iceland," in: Michael Ostling (ed.): *Fairies, Demons, and Nature Spirits. "Small Gods" at the Margins of Christendom.* London: Palgrave Macmillan 2018b, 191–212.

Gunnell, Terry: "The Development and Role of the *Fjallkona* (Mountain Woman) in Icelandic National Day Celebrations and Other Contexts," in: Guzel Stolyarova; Irina Sedakova; Nina Vlaskina (eds.): *The Ritual Year 11: Traditions and Transformation. The Yearbook of the SIEF (Société Internationale d'Ethnologie et de Folklore) Working Group on the Ritual Year.* Kazan—Moscow: T8 2016, 22–40.

Gunnell, Terry: "Nordic Folk Legends, Folk Traditions and Grave Mounds. The Value of Folkloristics for the Study of Old Nordic Religions," in: Eldar Heide; Karen Bek-Pedersen (eds.): *New Focus on Retrospective Methods. Resuming Methodological Discussions. Case Studies from Northern Europe.* (=Folklore Fellows' Communications 307), Helsinki: Academia Scientiarum Fennica 2014, 17–41.

Gunnell, Terry (ed.): *Legends and Landscape. Plenary Papers from the 5th Celtic-Nordic-Baltic Folklore Symposium, Reykjavík 2005.* Reykjavík: University of Iceland Press 2008.

Gunnell, Terry: "Introduction," in: *Hildur, Queen of the Elves and Other Icelandic Legends.* Retold by J. M. Bedell, introduced and translated by Terry Gunnell. Northampton, MA: Interlink Books 2007, 1–26.

Gunnell, Terry: "Grýla, Grýlur, 'Grøleks' and Skeklers: Medieval Disguise Traditions in the North Atlantic?" In: *ARV. Nordic Yearbook of Folklore* 57 (2001): 33–54.

Günzel, Stephan: *Texte zur Theorie des Raums.* Ditzingen: Reclam 2013.

Hackett, Rosalind I. J.: "Sonic (re)turns," in: *The Immanent Frame,* published January 17, 2018, https://tif.ssrc.org/2018/01/17/sonic-returns/, last accessed 13 August 2020.

Hackett, Rosalind I. J.: "Sound," in: Steven Engler; Michael Stausberg (eds.): *The Oxford Handbook for the Study of Religion.* Oxford: Oxford University Press 2016, 316–328.

Hackett, Rosalind I. J.: "Sound, Music, and the Study of Religion," in: *Temenos* 48/1 (2012): 11–27.

Hahn, Johannes (ed. in collaboration with Christian Ronning): *Religiöse Landschaften.* (= Alter Orient und Altes Testament. Veröffentlichungen zur Kultur und Geschichte des Alten Orients und des Alten Testaments 301; Veröffentlichungen des Arbeitskreises zur Erforschung der Religions- und Kulturgeschichte des Antiken Vorderen Orients und des Sonderforschungsbereichs 493, Band 4), Münster: Ugarit-Verlag 2002.

Halbwachs, Maurice: *Stätten der Verkündigung im Heiligen Land. Eine Studie zum kollektiven Gedächtnis.* Herausgegeben und aus dem Französischen übersetzt von Stephan Egger. Konstanz: UVK Verlagsgesellschaft 2003.

Haraldur Ólafsson: "A True Environmental Parable: The Laxá-Mývatn Conflict in Iceland, 1965–1973: An Ecological and Anthropological Approach," in: *Environmental Review: ER* 5/2 (Autumn 1981): 2–38.

Hawes, Greta (ed.): *Myths on the Map. The Storied Landscapes of Ancient Greece.* Oxford—New York: Oxford University Press 2017.

Heidegger, Martin: "Building Dwelling Thinking," in: David Farrell Krell (ed.): *Martin Heidegger: Basic Writings from Being and Time (1927) to The Task of Thinking (1964).* Rev. and expanded ed., London: Routledge 1993, 343–363.

316 BIBLIOGRAPHY

Heisenberg, Werner: *Physics and Beyond. Encounters and Conversations.* (=World Perspectives 42), translated by Arnold J. Pomerans, New York: Harper and Row 1971 (reissue New York: Harper Torchbook 1972).

Helgi Guðmundsson: *Vestfirzkar sagnir. 1. bindi.* Reykjavík: Bókaverzlun Guðm. Gamalíelssonar 1933–1937.

Hermann Pálsson: "A Foundation Myth in *Landnámabók*," in: *Mediaeval Scandinavia* 12 (1988): 24–28.

Hermann Pálsson; Edwards, Paul: *The Book of Settlements. Landnámabók.* Translated by Hermann Pálsson and Paul Edwards. (=University of Manitoba Icelandic Studies 1), Winnipeg, Manitoba: University of Manitoba Press 1972 (reprint 2012).

Hermann, Adrian; Mohn, Jürgen (eds.): *Orte der europäischen Religionsgeschichte.* (= Diskurs Religion 6), Würzburg: Ergon Verlag 2015.

Hirsch, Eric D.; O'Hanlon, Michael (eds.): *The Anthropology of Landscape. Perspectives on Space and Place.* Oxford: Clarendon Press 1996.

Hirschkind, Charles: *The Ethical Soundscape. Cassette Sermons and Islamic Counterpublics.* New York: Columbia University Press 2006.

Hoelscher, S.: "Landscape Iconography," in: Rob Kitchin; Nigel J. Thrift (eds.): *International Encyclopedia of Human Geography.* Amsterdam—London—Oxford: Elsevier 2009, 132–139.

Hogan, Edmund; Ó Corráin, Donnchadh: *Onomasticon Goedelicum.* By Edmund Hogan (1910), digital edition revised and corrected by Donnchadh Ó Corráin (2017), https://www.dias.ie/celt/celt-publications-2/onomasticon-goedelicum/, last accessed 25 July 2020.

Holland, Eugene W.: *Deleuze and Guattari's A Thousand Plateaus.* London: Bloomsbury Academic 2013.

Honko, Lauri: "Four Forms of Adaptation of Tradition," in: Lauri Honko; Vilmos Voigt (eds.): *Adaptation, Change, and Decline in Oral Literature.* (=Studia Fennica 26), Helsinki: Finnish Literature Society 1981, 19–33.

hooks, bell: "Homeplace: A Site of Resistance," in: *bell hooks: Yearning. Race, Gender, and Cultural Politics.* Boston, MA: South End Press 1990, 41–49.

Howell, Frederick W. W.: *Icelandic Pictures Drawn with Pen and Pencil.* London: The Religious Tract Society 1893.

Hubbard, Phil; Kitchin, Rob (eds.): *Key Thinkers on Space and Place.* Second edition, Los Angeles—London—New Delhi—Singapore—Washington, DC: Sage 2011.

Hunt, Ailsa: "Pagan Animism: A Modern Myth for a Green Age," in: Ailsa Hunt; Hilary Marlow (eds.): *Ecology and Theology in the Ancient World: Cross-Disciplinary Perspectives.* London: Bloomsbury Academic 2019, 137–152. Bloomsbury Collections. Web. 12 Mar. 2021, http://dx.doi.org/10.5040/9781350004078.ch-011.

Icelandic Tourist Board, https://www.ferdamalastofa.is/en/research-and-statistics/numbers-of-foreign-visitors, last accessed 3 February 2021.

Ingi Guðmonsson: "Eyðibýli Kolbeinsvík," in: *Strandapósturinn* 15 (1981): 98–103.

Ingimundur Ingimundarson: "Þrjár systur: Fríða Ingimundardóttir, Klúku í Bjarnarfirði, fædd 22. nóv. 1908, dáin 1. júní 1983; Sína Karólína Ingimundardóttir, fædd 29. ágúst 1923, dáin 24. apríl 1977; Sína Vilhelmína Svanborg Ingimundardóttir, fædd 19. júlí 1913, dáin 12. desember 1948," in: *Íslendingaþættir Tímans,* 6. júlí 1983, 25. tbl., pp. 1–2.

Ingold, Tim: "Introduction," in: Monica Janowski; Tim Ingold (eds.): *Imagining Landscapes. Past, Present and Future.* Farnham—Burlington: Ashgate 2012, 1–18.

BIBLIOGRAPHY 317

Ingold, Tim: "Ways of Mind-Walking: Reading, Writing, Painting," in: *Visual Studies* 25/ 1 (2010): 15–23.

Ingold, Tim: *The Perception of the Environment. Essays in Livelihood, Dwelling and Skill.* London: Routledge 2000.

Ingold, Tim: "The Temporality of the Landscape," in: *World Archaeology* 25 (1993): 152–174.

ISLEX-orðabókin = ISLEX-orðabókin—Stofnun Árna Magnússonar í íslenskum fræðum, https://islex.arnastofnun.is/is/, last accessed 13 January 2021.

Jakob Benediktsson: *Íslendingabók. Landnámabók.* (=Íslenzk fornrit 1), Reykjavík: Hið íslenzka fornritafélag 1968.

Jakob Benediktsson: "*Landnámabók.* Some Remarks on its Value as a Historical Source," in: *Saga-Book* 17 (1966–69): 275–292.

Jamie, Kathleen: "A Lone Enraptured Male," in: *London Review of Books* 30/5 (6 March 2008), https://www.lrb.co.uk/the-paper/v30/n05/kathleen-jamie/a-lone-enraptured-male, last accessed 21 July 2021.

Janowski, Monica; Ingold, Tim (eds.): *Imagining Landscapes. Past, Present and Future.* Farnham—Burlington: Ashgate 2012.

Jóhann Sigurjónsson: *Eyvind of the Hills. The Hraun Farm.* Translated by Henninge Krohn Schanche. (=Scandinavian Classics 6—Modern Icelandic Plays), New York: The American-Scandinavian Foundation—London: Humphrey Milford—Oxford: Oxford University Press 1916.

Jóhann Sigurjónsson: *Fjalla-Eyvindur: Leikrit í fjórum þáttum.* Reykjavík: Heimskringla 1950.

Jóhannes Halldórsson (ed.): *Kjalnesinga saga.* (=Íslenzk fornrit 14), Reykjavík: Hið íslenzka fornritafélag 1959.

Jón Árnason (ed.): *Íslenzkar þjóðsögur og ævintýri.* Second edition by Árni Böðvarsson and Bjarni Vilhjálmsson, 6 vols., Reykjavík: Bókaútgáfan Þjóðsaga—Prentsmiðjan Hólar 1961.

Jón Jónsson (ed.): *Þorsteinn Guðbrandsson í Kaldrananesi: Dagbók 1918. Handritadeild Landsbókasafns Íslands—Háskólabókasafns (Lbs 3807–3809 8vo).* [Hólmavík]: Rannsóknasetur HÍ á Ströndum—Þjóðfræðistofa 2018a, https://www. hi.is/sites/default/files/mas/pdf/thorsteinn_gudbrandsson_dagbok_1918_-_vefur. pdf, last accessed 20 December 2020.

Jón Jónsson: "Dagbókarritarinn og Kaldrananes 1918," in: Jón Jónsson (ed.): *Þorsteinn Guðbrandsson í Kaldrananesi: Dagbók 1918. Handritadeild Landsbókasafns Íslands— Háskólabókasafns (Lbs 3807–3809 8vo).* [Hólmavík]: Rannsóknasetur HÍ á Ströndum— Þjóðfræðistofa 2018b, https://www.hi.is/sites/default/files/mas/pdf/thorsteinn_gu dbrandsson_dagbok_1918_-_vefur.pdf, last accessed 20 December 2020.

Jón Jónsson: *Á mörkum mennskunnar. Viðhorf til förufólks í sögnum og samfélagi.* (= Sýnisbók íslenskrar alþýðumenningar 23), Reykjavík: Háskólaútgáfan 2018c.

Jón Kr. Guðmundsson: *Sprek úr fjöru. Þjóðlífsþættir.* Kópavogur: Bókaútgáfan Hildur 1989.

Jón Kristjánsson; Björn Kristmundsson: "Búðarvogur," in: *Strandapósturinn* 11 (1977): 9–18.

[Jón Sigurðsson; Guðbrandur Vigfússon]: *Biskupa sögur.* 2 vols., Kaupmannahöfn: S. L. Möller 1858–1878.

Jón Thorarensen: *Rauðskinna hin nýrri. Þjóðsögur, sagnaþættir, þjóðhættir og annálar.* 3 vols., Reykjavík: Þjóðsaga 1971.

318 BIBLIOGRAPHY

Jón Þorkelsson: *Þjóðsögur og munnmæli. Nýtt safn*. Reykjavík: Sigfús Eymundsson 1899.

Jón Viðar Sigurðsson: "The Christianization of the North Atlantic," in: Jens Peter Schjødt; John Lindow; Anders Andrén (eds.): *The Pre-Christian Religions of the North: Histories and Structures. Vol. IV: The Christianization Process*. 4 vols., Turnhout: Brepols 2020, vol. 4, 1649–1693.

Jónas Jónasson: *Íslenzkir þjóðhættir*. Reykjavík: Rafnar 1934.

Jordan, Peter: *Material Culture and Sacred Landscape. The Anthropology of the Siberian Khanty*. Walnut Creek—Lanham—New York—Oxford: AltaMira Press 2003.

Josephson-Storm, Jason A.: *The Myth of Disenchantment. Magic, Modernity, and the Birth of the Human Sciences*. Chicago—London: University of Chicago Press 2017.

Kålund, P. E. Kristian: *Bidrag til en historisk-topografisk Beskrivelse af Island*. 2 vols., Kjøbenhavn: Gyldendalske Boghandel 1877–1882.

Käppel, Lutz; Pothou, Vassiliki (eds.): *Human Development in Sacred Landscapes. Between Ritual Tradition, Creativity and Emotionality*. Göttingen: V&R Unipress 2015.

Kári Pálsson: *Íslenskir blótsteinar. Bakgrunnur, samhengi og útbreiðsla*. BA ritgerð, Þjóðfræði, Reykjavík: Háskóli Íslands, Félagsvísindasvið, Febrúar 2019, http://hdl.han dle.net/1946/32132, last accessed 28 December 2020.

Karve, I.: "On the Road: A Maharashtrian Pilgrimage," in: *The Journal of Asian Studies* 22 (1962): 13–29.

Kehrer, Günter: "Religion, Definition der," in: Burkhard Gladigow; Karl-Heinz Kohl (eds. in collaboration with Hildegard Cancik-Lindemaier, Günter Kehrer, Hans G. Kippenberg, and Matthias Laubscher): *Handbuch religionswissenschaftlicher Grundbegriffe, Band IV: Kultbild—Rolle*. Stuttgart—Berlin—Köln: Verlag W. Kohlhammer 1998, 418–425.

Kennedy, John: "The Saga of Finnbogi the Mighty," in: Viðar Hreinsson (ed.): *The Complete Sagas of Icelanders. Including 49 Tales*. 5 vols., Reykjavík: Leifur Eiríksson Publishing 1997, vol. 3, 221–270.

Kieschnick, John: "Material Culture," in: John Corrigan (ed.): *The Oxford Handbook of Religion and Emotion*. Oxford—New York: Oxford University Press 2008, 223–238.

af Klintberg, Bengt: "Scandinavian Folklore Parallels to the Narrative about Selkolla in *Guðmundar saga biskups*," in: Daniel Sävborg; Karen Bek-Pedersen (eds.): *Supernatural Encounters in Old Norse Literature and Tradition*. (=Borders, Boundaries, Landscapes 1), Turnhout: Brepols 2018, 59–74.

Knott, Kim: *The Location of Religion. A Spatial Analysis*. London—Oakville: Equinox 2005.

Koerner, Joseph Leo: *Caspar David Friedrich and the Subject of Landscape*. Second, revised edition, London: Reaktion Books 2009.

Kong, Lily: "Mapping 'New' Geographies of Religion: Politics and Poetics in Modernity," in: *Progress in Human Geography* 25 (2001): 211–233.

Kong, Lily: "Geography and Religion: Trends and Prospects," in: *Progress in Human Geography* 14 (1990): 355–371.

Krebs, Angelika: "Why Landscape Beauty Matters," in: *Land* 3 (2014): 1251–1269, doi:10.3390/land3041251, http://www.mdpi.com/2073-445X/3/4/1251, last accessed 14 December 2020.

Kripal, Jeffrey J.: "Sexuality and the Erotic," in: John Corrigan (ed.): *The Oxford Handbook of Religion and Emotion*. Oxford—New York: Oxford University Press 2008, 162–180.

Kugele, Jens: "Kultort als sakraler Raum. Überlegungen zu Begriff, Konzept und Theorie," in: Matthias Egeler (ed.): *Germanische Kultorte. Vergleichende, historische und rezeptionsgeschichtliche Zugänge*. (=Münchner Nordistische Studien 24), München: Utz 2016, 11–48.

BIBLIOGRAPHY   319

Kühne, Olaf; Weber, Florian; Jenal, Corinna: *Neue Landschaftsgeographie. Ein Überblick*. Wiesbaden: Springer 2018.

Kuldkepp, Mart: "The People, the Bishop, and the Beast: Remediation and Reconciliation in Einarr Gilsson's *Selkolluvísur*," in: Daniel Sävborg; Karen Bek-Pedersen (eds.): *Supernatural Encounters in Old Norse Literature and Tradition*. (=Borders, Boundaries, Landscapes 1), Turnhout: Brepols 2018, 105–122.

Kwilecki, Susan: "Religion and Coping: A Contribution from Religious Studies," in: *Journal for the Scientific Study of Religion* 43 (2004): 477–489.

Ladino, Jennifer K.: *Memorials Matter: Emotion, Environment and Public Memory at American Historical Sites*. Reno—Las Vegas: University of Nevada Press 2019.

Landsyfirréttardómar og hæstaréttardómar í íslenzkum málum. V. bindi: 1895–1898. Reykjavík: Ísafoldarprentsmiðja 1901.

Lane, Belden C.: *Landscapes of the Sacred. Geography and Narrative in American Spirituality*. Expanded ed., Baltimore—London: Johns Hopkins University Press 2002.

Latham, Alan: "Edward W. Soja," in: Phil Hubbard; Rob Kitchin (eds.): *Key Thinkers on Space and Place*. Second edition, Los Angeles—London—New Delhi—Singapore—Washington, DC: Sage 2011, 380–386.

Lawing, Sean B.: "The Place of the Evil: Infant Abandonment in Old Norse Society," in: *Scandinavian Studies* 85 (2013): 133–150.

Lea, Mike; Lea, Kate (eds.): *W.G. Collingwood's Letters from Iceland. Travels in Iceland 1897 by W.G. Collingwood and Jón Stefánsson*. Cardiff: R.G. Collingwood Society 2013.

Lefebvre, Henri: *The Production of Space*. Translated by Donald Nicholson-Smith. Malden—Oxford—Victoria: Blackwell 1991.

LeVasseur, Todd; Peterson, Anna (eds.): *Religion and Ecological Crisis: The "Lynn White Thesis" at Fifty*. New York—London: Routledge 2017.

Lévi-Strauss, Claude: *The Savage Mind*. Chicago: The University of Chicago Press—London: Weidenfeld and Nicolson 1966.

Lilley, Keith: "Denis Cosgrove," in: Phil Hubbard; Rob Kitchin (eds.): *Key Thinkers on Space and Place*. Second edition, Los Angeles—London—New Delhi—Singapore—Washington, DC: Sage 2011, 120–126.

Lindsay, W. M. (ed.): *Isidori Hispalensis Episcopi Etymologiarvm sive Originvm libri XX. Tomvs II (Libri XI-XX)*. Oxonii: E typographeo Clarendoniano 1911.

Luhrmann, T. M.: *How God Becomes Real. Kindling the Presence of Invisible Others*. Princeton—Oxford: Princeton University Press 2020.

Macfarlane, Robert: "Off the Grid: Treasured Islands," in: Huw Lewis-Jones (ed.): *The Writer's Map. An Atlas of Imaginary Lands*. London: Thames & Hudson 2018, 94–101.

Macfarlane, Robert: *Mountains of the Mind. A History of a Fascination*. London: Granta Books 2008 (first edition 2003).

Macfarlane, Robert: *The Wild Places*. London: Granta Books 2007.

Magnús H. Magnússon: "Ný kirkja vígð í Árneshreppi á Ströndum," in: *Morgunblaðið*, Tuesday 10 September 1991, p. 59, https://timarit.is/page/1750253, last accessed 29 December 2020.

Magnús Rafnsson (ed.): *Rún. Lbs 4375 8vo*. Hólmavík: Strandagaldur ses—Museum of Icelandic Sorcery and Witchcraft 2018a.

Magnús Rafnsson (ed.): *Tvær galdraskræður. Lbs 2413 8vo; Leyniletursskræðan Lbs 764 8vo. Two Icelandic Books of Magic*. Hólmavík: Strandagaldur ses 2018b.

320 BIBLIOGRAPHY

Magnús Rafnsson: "Goðdalur—saga og fornleifar," http://www.galdrasyning.is/index. php?option=com_content&view=article&id=234&Itemid=100040&lang=en, last accessed 5 January 2021.

Malinowski, Bronislaw: *Coral Gardens and Their Magic. A Study of the Methods of Tilling the Soil and of Agricultural Rites in the Trobriand Islands*. 2 vols., London: George Allen & Unwin 1935.

Malinowski, Bronislaw: *Argonauts of the Western Pacific. An Account of Native Enterprise and Adventure in the Archipelagoes of Melanesian New Guinea*. (=Studies in Economics and Political Science 65), with a preface by Sir James George Frazer. London: George Routledge & Sons—New York: E. P. Dutton & Co. 1922.

Mariña, Jacqueline: "Friedrich Schleiermacher and Rudolf Otto," in: John Corrigan (ed.): *The Oxford Handbook of Religion and Emotion*. Oxford—New York: Oxford University Press 2008, 457–473.

Martineau, Jane (ed.): *Victorian Fairy Painting*. London: Royal Academy of Arts— Iowa: The University of Iowa Museum of Art—Toronto: The Art Gallery of Ontario— in association with: London—Merrell Holberton Publishers 1997.

Matthías Johannessen: "A Banquet in the Rocks," in: Einar Matthíasson; Eiríkur Þorláksson; Erna Sörensen; Kristín G. Guðnadóttir (eds.): *Kjarval*. Reykjavík: Nesútgáfan 2005, 545–547.

McDannell, Colleen: *Material Christianity. Religion and Popular Culture in America*. New Haven, CT—London: Yale University Press 1995.

McKittrick, Katherine: "bell hooks," in: Phil Hubbard; Rob Kitchin (eds.): *Key Thinkers on Space and Place*. Second edition, Los Angeles—London—New Delhi—Singapore— Washington, DC: Sage 2011, 242–248.

McManus, Denis: "Being-in-the-World (In-der-Welt-sein)," in: Mark A. Wrathall (ed.): *The Cambridge Heidegger Lexicon*. Cambridge—New York—Port Melbourne— New Delhi—Singapore: Cambridge University Press 2021, 103–110.

McTurk, Rory: Review of *Harðar saga*. Edited by Þórhallur Vilmundarson and Bjarni Vilhjálmsson. *Íslenzk fornrit*, XIII. *Hið íslenzka fornritafélag*. Reykjavík, 1991. In: *Saga-Book* 24 (1994–1997): 164–172.

Meining, D. W. (ed.): *The Interpretation of Ordinary Landscapes. Geographical Essays*. New York—Oxford: Oxford University Press 1979.

Merivale, Amyas; Millican, Peter: *Hume Texts Online*, https://davidhume.org/, last accessed 11 August 2020.

Merriman, Peter: "Marc Augé," in: Phil Hubbard; Rob Kitchin (eds.): *Key Thinkers on Space and Place*. Second edition, Los Angeles—London—New Delhi—Singapore— Washington, DC: Sage 2011, 26–33.

Meyer, Birgit: *Mediation and the Genesis of Presence. Towards a Material Approach to Religion*. Utrecht: Universiteit Utrecht 2012.

Meyer, Birgit; Houtman, Dick: "Introduction: Material Religion—How Things Matter," in: Birgit Meyer; Dick Houtman (eds.): *Things. Religion and the Question of Materiality*. New York: Fordham University Press 2012, 1–23.

Miller, W. Watts: "Hope," in: John Corrigan (ed.): *The Oxford Handbook of Religion and Emotion*. Oxford—New York: Oxford University Press 2008, 276–289.

Mitchell, Stephen: "Continuity: Folklore's Problem Child?" In: Daniel Sävborg; Karen Bek-Pedersen (eds.): *Folklore in Old Norse—Old Norse in Folklore*. (=Nordistica Tartuensia 20), Tartu: Tartu University Press 2014, 41–58.

BIBLIOGRAPHY 321

Mitchell, W. J. T. (ed.): *Landscape and Power*. Second edition, Chicago—London: University of Chicago Press 2002a.

Mitchell, W. J. T.: "Preface to the Second Edition of *Landscape and Power*: Space, Place, and Landscape," in: W. J. T. Mitchell (ed.): *Landscape and Power*. Second edition, Chicago—London: University of Chicago Press 2002b, vii–xii.

Mitchell, W. J. T.: "Introduction," in: W. J. T. Mitchell (ed.): *Landscape and Power*. Second edition, Chicago—London: University of Chicago Press 2002c, 1–4.

Mitchell, W. J. T.: "Imperial Landscape," in: W. J. T. Mitchell (ed.): *Landscape and Power*. Second edition, Chicago—London: University of Chicago Press 2002d, 5–34.

Moberg, Jessica: "Material Religion," in: James R. Lewis; Inga Tøllefsen (eds.): *The Oxford Handbook of New Religious Movements: Volume II*. Second edition, Oxford—New York: Oxford University Press 2016, 380–390.

Mohn, Jürgen: "Religionswissenschaft: Zur Geschichte, Problematik und Profilbildung einer komparativen Wissenschaftsdisziplin mit Blick auf die Universität Basel," in: *Bulletin VSH-AEU* 36/1 (April 2010): 18–28.

Mohn, Jürgen: "Heterotopien in der Religionsgeschichte. Anmerkungen zum ‚Heiligen Raum' nach Mircea Eliade," in: *Theologische Zeitschrift* 63 (2007): 331–357.

Moor, Robert: *On Trails. An Exploration*. New York—London—Toronto—Sydney—New Delhi: Simon & Schuster 2016 (paperback edition 2017).

Morris, William: *The Collected Works of William Morris, with Introductions by His Daughter May Morris. Volume XIV: The House of the Wolfings. The Story of the Glittering Plain*. London—New York—Bombay—Calcutta: Longmans, Green and Company 1912.

Morris, William: *The Collected Works of William Morris, with Introductions by His Daughter May Morris. Volume VIII: Journals of Travel in Iceland, 1871, 1873*. London—New York—Bombay—Calcutta: Longmans, Green and Company 1911.

Muir, John: *The Yosemite*. New York: The Century Co. 1912.

Mundal, Else: "Barneutbering," in: *Norskrift* 56 (1987): 1–74.

Murray, Kevin: "Genre Construction: The Creation of the *Dinnshenchas*," in: *Journal of Literary Onomastics* 6 (2017): 11–21, https://suny-bro.primo.exlibrisgroup.com/permalink/01SUNY_BRO/1k4d56r/alma998418424804805, last accessed 17 September 2023.

Naughton, Nora: "God and the Good People: Folk Belief in a Traditional Community," in: *Béaloideas* 71 (2003): 13–53.

Nora, Pierre: *Les lieux de mémoire*. 3 vols. in seven parts, [Paris]: Gallimard 1984–1992.

Ó Dónaill, Niall (ed.): *Foclóir Gaeilge-Béarla*. Baile Átha Cliath: Oifig an tSoláthair 1977.

OED = *Oxford English Dictionary Online*, Oxford University Press, June 2020, https://www-oed-com.emedien.ub.uni-muenchen.de/, last accessed 25 July 2020.

Ólafur Davíðsson: *Íslenzkar þjóðsögur*. Þorsteinn M. Jónsson bjó til prentunar. Bjarni Vilhjálmsson sá um útgáfuna. 4 bindi. 3. útgáfa. Reykjavík: Bókaútgáfan Þjóðsaga 1978–1980.

Olavius, Olaus: *Oeconomisk Reise igiennem de nordvestlige, nordlige, og nordostlige Kanter af Island. Tilligemed Ole Henchels Underretning om de Islandske Svovel-Miiner og Svovel-Raffinering, samt Vice-Markscheider Christian Zieners Beskrivelse over nogle Surterbrands-Fielde i Island*. 2 parts, Kiobenhavn: Gyldendals Forlag 1780.

Olavius, Olaus: *Oekonomische Reise durch Island in den Nordwestlichen, und Nord-Nordostlichen Gegenden. Auf Königl. Dänischen Befehl herausgegeben und durch*

322 BIBLIOGRAPHY

nöthige Kupfer erläutert. Aus dem Dänischen ins Deutsche übersetzt. Dresden— Leipzig: Breitkopfische Buchhandlung 1787.

Ólína Þorvarðardóttir: "Man and Nature in Icelandic Rural Narratives," in: Kalle Pihlainen; Erik Tirkkonen (eds.): *Rustica Nova. The New Countryside and Transformations in Operating Environment.* (=Publications of the Institute of History / University of Turku 17), Turku: University of Turku 2002, 157–164.

Olshausen, Eckart; Sauer, Vera (eds.): *Die Landschaft und die Religion. Stuttgarter Kolloquium zur Historischen Geographie des Altertums 9, 2005.* Stuttgart: Franz Steiner 2009.

Otto, Rudolf: *Das Heilige. Über das Irrationale in der Idee des Göttlichen und sein Verhältnis zum Rationalen.* Vierzehnte neu durchgesehene Auflage, Gotha: Leopold Klotz 1926 (first ed. 1917).

Paffen, Karlheinz: *Das Wesen der Landschaft.* (=Wege der Forschung 39), Darmstadt: Wissenschaftliche Buchgesellschaft 1973.

Paturel, Simone Eid: *Baalbek-Heliopolis, the Bekaa, and Berytus from 100 BCE to 400 CE. A Landscape Transformed.* (=Mnemosyne Supplements 426), Leiden— Boston: Brill 2019.

Pavord, Anna: *Landskipping. Painters, Ploughmen and Places.* London—Oxford— New York—New Delhi—Sydney: Bloomsbury 2016.

Pentikäinen, Juha: *The Nordic Dead-Child Tradition: Nordic Dead-Child Beings, a Study in Comparative Religion.* (=Folklore Fellows' Communications 202), Helsinki: Suomalainen tiedeakatemia (Academia Scientiarum Fennica) 1968.

Petzoldt, L.: "Ortssagen," in: Heinrich Beck; Dieter Geuenich; Heiko Steuer (eds.): *Reallexikon der Germanischen Altertumskunde. 22. Band. Östgötalag—Pfalz und Pfalzen.* Von Johannes Hoops. Zweite, völlig neu bearbeitete und stark erweiterte Auflage, Berlin—New York: Walter de Gruyter 2003, 305.

Pfeiffer, Ida: *Visit to Iceland and the Scandinavian North.* Translated from the German of Madame Ida Pfeiffer. Second edition, London: Ingram, Cooke, and Co. 1853.

Propp, V.: *Morphology of the Folktale.* First edition translated by Laurence Scott with an introduction by Svatava Pirkova-Jakobson. Second edition revised and edited with a preface by Louis A. Wagner. New introduction by Alan Dundes. (=American Folklore Society Bibliographical and Special Series 9 / Revised Edition / 1968 = Indiana University Research Center in Anthropology, Folklore, and Linguistics Publication 10 / Revised Edition / 1968), Austin: University of Texas Press 1968.

Purkiss, Diane: *Fairies and Fairy Stories. A History.* Stroud: Tempus 2007.

Ragnar Edvardsson: *Fornleifaskráning í Kaldrananeshreppi, Strandasýslu. Lokaskýrsla.* (= Fornleifastofnun Íslands FS185–99133), Reykjavík: Fornleifastofnun Íslands [2002], http://www.drangsnes.is/images/stories/adalskipulag/FS185–99133_Kaldrananesh reppur_Strandasyslu.pdf, last accessed 17 July 2019.

Ragnhildur Sigurðardóttir; Anthony J. Newton; Megan T. Hicks; Andrew J. Dugmore; Viðar Hreinsson; A. E. J. Ogilvie; Árni Daníel Júlíusson; Árni Einarsson; Steven Hartman; I. A. Simpson; Orri Vésteinsson; Thomas H. McGovern: "Trolls, Water, Time, and Community: Resource Management in the Mývatn District of Northeast Iceland," in: Ludomir R. Lozny; Thomas H. McGovern (eds.): *Global Perspectives on Long Term Community Resource Management.* (=Studies in Human Ecology and Adaptation 11), Cham: Springer Nature 2019, 77–101.

Rebanks, James: *The Shepherd's Life. A Tale of the Lake District.* n.p.: Penguin Books 2015.

Rinschede, Gisbert: *Religionsgeographie.* Braunschweig: Westermann 1999.

BIBLIOGRAPHY 323

Ristow, G.; Jászai, G.: "Golgotha," in: Engelbert Kirschbaum SJ (ed. in collaboration with Günter Bandmann, Wolfgang Braunfels, Johannes Kollwitz, Wilhelm Mrazek, Alfred A. Schmid, Hugo Schnell): *Lexikon der christlichen Ikonographie. Zweiter Band. Allgemeine Ikonographie. Fabelwesen—Kynokephalen.* Rom—Freiburg—Basel—Wien: Herder 1970, cols. 163–165.

Robinson, Tim: *Oileáin Árann. A Companion to the Map of the Aran Islands.* Roundstone: Folding Landscapes 1996a.

Robinson, Tim: *Setting Foot on the Shores of Connemara & other Writings.* Dublin: The Lilliput Press 1996b.

Rodaway, Raul: "Yi-Fu Tuan," in: Phil Hubbard; Rob Kitchin (eds.): *Key Thinkers on Space and Place.* Second edition, Los Angeles—London—New Delhi—Singapore—Washington, DC: Sage 2011, 426–431.

Rose, Gillian: *Feminism & Geography: The Limits of Geographical Knowledge.* Minneapolis: University of Minnesota Press 1993.

Rose-Redwood, Reuben; Alderman, Derek H. (guest editors): Themed section "New Directions in Political Toponymy," in: *ACME: An International E-Journal for Critical Geographies* 10/1 (2011): 1–41, https://acme-journal.org/index.php/acme/issue/view/67, last accessed 22 November 2020.

Rose-Redwood, Reuben; Alderman, Derek; Azaryahu, Maoz: "Geographies of Toponymic Inscription: New Directions in Critical Place-Name Studies," in: *Progress in Human Geography* 34/4 (2010): 453–470.

Rubin, Julius: "Melancholy," in: John Corrigan (ed.): *The Oxford Handbook of Religion and Emotion.* Oxford—New York: Oxford University Press 2008, 290–309.

Ruel, Malcolm: "Christians as Believers," in: *Belief, Ritual, and the Securing of Life.* Leiden: Brill 1997, 36–59.

Rüpke, Jörg: *Historische Religionswissenschaft. Eine Einführung.* (=Religionswissenschaft heute 5), Stuttgart: W. Kohlhammer 2007.

Samuels, David W.; Meintjes, Louise; Ochoa, Ana Maria; Porcello, Thomas: "Soundscapes: Toward a Sounded Anthropology," in: *Annual Review of Anthropology* 39 (2010): 329–345, https://doi.org/10.1146/annurev-anthro-022510-132230, last accessed 15 August 2020.

Sävborg, Daniel: "The Icelander and the Trolls—The Importance of Place," in: Ülo Valk; Daniel Sävborg (eds.): *Storied and Supernatural Places: Studies in Spatial and Social Dimensions of Folklore and Sagas.* (=Studia Fennica Folkloristica 23), Helsinki: Finnish Literature Society 2018, 194–205.

Sävborg, Daniel: "Are the Trolls Supernatural? Some Remarks on the Terminology for Strange Beings in Old Norse Literature," in: *Annali: Sezione Germanica (Nuova serie)* 26 (2016): 119–129.

Sävborg, Daniel: "Scandinavian Folk Legends and Icelandic Sagas," in: Eldar Heide; Karen Bek-Pedersen (eds.): *New Focus on Retrospective Methods. Resuming Methodological Discussions: Case Studies from Northern Europe.* (=Folklore Fellows' Communications 307), Helsinki: Academia Scientiarum Fennica 2014, 76–88.

Sävborg, Daniel: "Haugbrot, Haugbúar and Sagas," in: Svavar Sigmundsson; Anton Holt; Gísli Sigurðsson; Guðmundur Ólafsson; Orri Vésteinsson (eds.): *Viking Settlements and Viking Society. Papers from the Proceedings of the Sixteenth Viking Congress, Reykjavík and Reykholt, 16–23 August 2009.* Reykjavík: Hið íslenzka fornleifafélag and University of Iceland Press 2011, 437–447.

324 BIBLIOGRAPHY

Sävborg, Daniel; Bek-Pedersen, Karen (eds.): *Supernatural Encounters in Old Norse Literature and Tradition*. (=Borders, Boundaries, Landscapes 1), Turnhout: Brepols 2018a.

Sävborg, Daniel; Bek-Pedersen, Karen: "The Supernatural in Old Norse Literature and Research: An Introduction," in: Daniel Sävborg; Karen Bek-Pedersen (eds.): *Supernatural Encounters in Old Norse Literature and Tradition*. (=Borders, Boundaries, Landscapes 1), Turnhout: Brepols 2018b, 1–14.

Sävborg, Daniel; Bek-Pedersen, Karen (eds.): *Folklore in Old Norse—Old Norse in Folklore*. (=Nordistica Tartuensia 20), Tartu: Tartu University Press 2014a.

Sävborg, Daniel; Bek-Pedersen, Karen: "Folklore in Old Norse—Old Norse in Folklore. Introduction," in: Daniel Sävborg; Karen Bek-Pedersen (eds.): *Folklore in Old Norse—Old Norse in Folklore*. (=Nordistica Tartuensia 20), Tartu: Tartu University Press 2014b, 7–13.

Sävborg, Daniel; Valk, Ülo (eds.): *Storied and Supernatural Places: Studies in Spatial and Social Dimensions of Folklore and Sagas*. (=Studia Fennica Folkloristica 23), Helsinki: Finnish Literature Society 2018a.

Sävborg, Daniel; Valk, Ülo: "Place-Lore, Liminal Storyworld and Ontology of the Supernatural. An Introduction," in: Daniel Sävborg; Ülo Valk (eds.): *Storied and Supernatural Places: Studies in Spatial and Social Dimensions of Folklore and Sagas*. (= Studia Fennica Folkloristica 23), Helsinki: Finnish Literature Society 2018b, 7–24.

Schafer, R. Murray: *The Soundscape: Our Sonic Environment and the Tuning of the World*. Rochester, VT: Destiny Books [1994] (original edition 1977).

Schama, Simon: *Landscape and Memory*. New York: Vintage Books 1996 (original edition: London: HarperCollins 1995).

Schenk, W.: "Landschaft," in: Heinrich Beck; Dieter Geuenich; Heiko Steuer (eds.): *Reallexikon der Germanischen Altertumskunde. 17. Band: Kleinere Götter—Landschaftsarchäologie*. Von Johannes Hoops. 2., völlig neu bearbeitete und stark erweiterte Auflage. Berlin—New York: Walter de Gruyter 2001, 617–630.

Schiller, Friedrich: *Sämtliche Werke*. Auf Grund der Originaldrucke herausgegeben von Gerhard Fricke und Herbert G. Göpfert. 6 Bände, 6. Auflage, München: Hanser 1980.

Schjødt, Jens Peter; Lindow, John; Andrén, Anders (eds.): *The Pre-Christian Religions of the North: Histories and Structures*. 4 vols., Turnhout: Brepols 2020.

Schleiermacher, Friedrich: *Über die Religion. Reden an die Gebildeten unter ihren Verächtern*. Mit einem Nachwort von Carl Heinz Ratschow. Stuttgart: Reclam 1969 (original edition 1799).

Schneider, Norbert: *Geschichte der Landschaftsmalerei. Vom Spätmittelalter bis zur Romantik*. 3. Auflage, Darmstadt: WBG 2011.

Schulz, Dorothea E.: "Soundscape," in: David Morgan (ed.): *Key Words in Religion, Media and Culture*. New York—London: Routledge 2008, 172–186.

Schulz, Katja: *Riesen. Von Wissenshütern und Wildnisbewohnern in Edda und Saga*. (= Skandinavistische Arbeiten 20), Heidelberg: Universitätsverlag Winter 2004.

Sebo, Erin: "Does OE Puca Have an Irish Origin?" In: *Studia Neophilologica* 89 (2017): 167–175.

Shields, Rob: "Henri Lefebvre," in: Phil Hubbard; Rob Kitchin (eds.): *Key Thinkers on Space and Place*. Second edition, Los Angeles—London—New Delhi—Singapore—Washington, DC: Sage 2011, 279–285.

Sideris, Lisa H.: "Science as Sacred Myth? Ecospirituality in the Anthropocene Age," in: *Journal for the Study of Religion, Nature and Culture* 9 (2015): 136–153, doi: 10.1558/jsrnc.v9i2.27259.

BIBLIOGRAPHY 325

Sigfús Blöndal: *Islandsk-dansk ordbog*. Reykjavik: I kommission hos Þórarinn B. Þorláksson og hos H. Aschehoug, København og Kristiania 1920–1922.

Sigurður Bergsteinsson; Þór Hjaltalín: *Þiðriksvellir við Steingrímsfjörð. Fornleifarannsókn haustið 2000*. (=Rit Fornleifaverndar ríkisins 2012: 2), n.p.: Fornleifavernd ríkisins 2012, http://www.minjastofnun.is/media/skjol-i-grein/Thidriksvellir---fornleifaranns okn.pdf, last accessed 9 September 2020.

Silko, Leslie Marmon: "Landscape, History, and the Pueblo Imagination," in: Cheryll Glotfelty; Harold Fromm (eds.): *The Ecocriticism Reader. Landmarks in Literary Ecology*. Athens—London: The University of Georgia Press 1996, 264–275.

Simek, Rudolf: *Trolle. Ihre Geschichte von der nordischen Mythologie bis zum Internet*. Köln—Weimar—Wien: Böhlau 2018.

Simmel, Georg: "Philosophie der Landschaft," in: *Die Güldenkammer. Eine bremische Monatsschrift* 3/2 (1913): 635–644 (digitized without pagination at https://socio.ch/ sim/verschiedenes/1913/landschaft.htm, last accessed 6 January 2021).

Simmel, Georg: "Böcklins Landschaften," in: *Die Zukunft* 12 (1885, no. 47 of 10 August): 272–277 (digitized at https://socio.ch/sim/verschiedenes/1895/boecklin. htm, last accessed 6 January 2021).

Skúli Guðjónsson: "Þrjár þjóðsögur úr Bæjarhreppi," in: *Strandapósturinn* 8 (1974): 95–101.

Smith, Jonathan Z.: *Relating Religion. Essays in the Study of Religion*. Chicago—London: The University of Chicago Press 2004.

Smith, Jonathan Z.: *To Take Place. Toward Theory in Ritual*. Chicago—London: University of Chicago Press 1987.

Smith, Jonathan Z.: *Map Is Not Territory. Studies in the History of Religions*. (=Studies in Judaism and Late Antiquity 23), Leiden: E. J. Brill 1978.

Soja, Edward W.: *Thirdspace. Journeys to Los Angeles and Other Real-and-Imagined Places*. Malden, MA—Oxford—Carlton: Blackwell 1996.

Stacey, Timothy: "Imaginary Friends and Made-Up Stories: How to Explore (Non) Religious Imaginaries Without Asking Belief-Centred Questions," in: *Secularism and Nonreligion* 9 (2020), article 3, http://doi.org/10.5334/snr.125.

Stapleton, Timothy: "Dasein as Being-in-the-World," in: Bret W. Davis (ed.): *Martin Heidegger: Key Concepts*. Abingdon—New York: Routledge 2014, 44–56.

Statistics Iceland, https://hagstofa.is/, last accessed 23 November 2020.

Statistics Iceland Travel Survey 2007–08, https://statice.is/statistics/business-sectors/tour ism/travel-survey/, last accessed 3 February 2021.

Stefán Gíslason: "Að breyta bæjarnöfnum," in: *Bændablaðið*, þriðjudagur 27. maí 2008, bls. 8, https://timarit.is/page/5758351, last accessed 13 January 2021.

Stewart, Pamela J.; Strathern, Andrew: *Landscape, Memory and History. Anthropological Perspectives*. London—Sterling, VA: Pluto Press 2003.

Stoll, Mark R. *Inherit the Holy Mountain. Religion and the Rise of American Environmentalism*. New York: Oxford University Press 2015 (paperback ed. 2017).

Stubbe, Hannes: "Gefühle/Emotionalität," in: Christoph Auffarth; Jutta Bernard; Hubert Mohr (eds. in collaboration with Agnes Imhof and Silvia Kurre): *Metzler Lexikon Religion. Gegenwart—Alltag—Medien. Band 1: Abendmahl—Guru*. Stuttgart—Weimar: J. B. Metzler 1999, 449–455.

von Stuckrad, Kocku: *Die Seele im 20. Jahrhundert: Eine Kulturgeschichte*. Paderborn: Wilhelm Fink 2019.

326 BIBLIOGRAPHY

Sveinbjörn Rafnsson (ed.): *Frásögur um fornaldarleifar. 1817–1823*. (=Stofnun Árna Magnússonar á Íslandi—Rit 24), 2 vols., Reykjavík: Stofnun Árna Magnússonar 1983.

Sverrisson, S. E., 24. júní 1890: "No. 50—Landamerkjaskrá fyrir jörðinni Hvítuhlíð í Óspakseyrarhreppi í Strandasýslu," in: *Landamerkjabók Strandasýslu*, pp. 75–76, https://icdb.landsbokasafn.is/document/ICDB/Strandas%C3%BDsla;%20Landamerk jab%C3%B3k%201884–1892/, last accessed 9 February 2022.

Tally, Robert T. Jr.: *Spatiality*. London—New York: Routledge 2013.

Tangherlini, Timothy R.: "'It Happened Not Too Far from Here . . .': A Survey of Legend Theory and Characterization," in: *Western Folklore* 49 (1990): 371–390.

Taylor, Bron: "Dark Green Religion: A Decade Later," in: *Journal for the Study of Religion, Nature and Culture* 14 (2020): 496–510, http://doi.org/10.1558/jsrnc.34630.

Taylor, Bron: *Dark Green Religion. Nature Spirituality and the Planetary Future*. Berkeley—Los Angeles—London: University of California Press 2010.

Taylor, Bron R. (ed.): *The Encyclopedia of Religion and Nature*. 2 vols., London—New York: Thoemmes Continuum 2005a.

Taylor, Bron: "Introduction," in: Bron R. Taylor (ed.): *The Encyclopedia of Religion and Nature*. 2 vols., London—New York: Thoemmes Continuum 2005b, vol. 1, vii–xxi.

Thompson, Stith: *The Types of the Folktale. A Classification and Bibliography*. Antti Aarne's *Verzeichnis der Märchentypen* (FFC No. 3) translated and enlarged. Second Revision. (= Folklore Fellows' Communications 184), Helsinki: Suomalainen Tiedeakatemia 1961.

Thora S. Steffensen; Omar Palmason: "The Meeting of Old and New: Luminol Application to a Suspected Ritualistic Heathen Stone From Viking Times," in: *Proceedings of the American Academy of Forensic Sciences, AAFS Annual Meeting/New Orleans, Louisiana* 11 (February 2005), 287, https://aafs.org/common/Uploaded%20files/Resources/Proc eedings/2005_Proceedings.pdf, last accessed 28 December 2020.

Þórhallur Vilmundarson: "Formáli," in: Þórhallur Vilmundarson; Bjarni Vilhjálmsson (eds.): *Harðar saga. Bárðar saga. Þorskfirðinga saga. Flóamanna saga. Þórarins þáttr Nefjólfssonar. Þorsteins þáttr uxafóts. Egils þáttr Síðu-Hallssonar. Orms þáttr Stórólfssonar. Þorsteins þáttr tjaldstoeðings. Þorsteins þáttr forvitna. Bergbúa þáttr. Kumlbúa þáttr. Stjörnu-Odda draumr*. (=Íslenzk fornrit 13), Reykjavík: Hið íslenzka fornritafélag 1991, V–CCXXVIII.

Tilley, Christopher: *Interpreting Landscapes: Geologies, Topographies, Identities. Explorations in Landscape Phenomenology 3*. Walnut Creek, CA: Left Coast Press 2010.

Tilley, Christopher: *Body and Image. Explorations in Landscape Phenomenology 2*. Walnut Creek, CA: Left Coast Press 2008.

Tilley, Christopher; with the assistance of Wayne Bennett: *The Materiality of Stone. Explorations in Landscape Phenomenology 1*. Oxford—New York: Berg 2004.

Tilley, Christopher: *A Phenomenology of Landscape. Places, Paths and Monuments*. Oxford—Providence, RI: Berg 1994.

Tolia-Kelly, Divya P.: "Landscape and Memory," in: Peter Howard; Ian Thompson; Emma Waterton (eds.): *The Routledge Companion to Landscape Studies*. London—New York: Routledge 2013, 322–334.

Tolkien, J.R.R.: *On Fairy-Stories*. Expanded edition, with commentary and notes. Edited by Verlyn Flieger and Douglas A. Anderson. London: HarperCollins 2014.

Torri, Davide: *Landscape, Ritual and Identity among the Hyolmo of Nepal*. (=Vitality of Indigenous Religions, no number), London—New York: Routledge 2020.

BIBLIOGRAPHY 327

Townend, Matthew: *The Vikings and Victorian Lakeland. The Norse Medievalism of W.G. Collingwood and his Contemporaries.* (=Cumberland and Westmorland Antiquarian and Archaeological Society Extra Series 34), [Kendal]: Cumberland and Westmorland Antiquarian and Archaeological Society 2009.

Tuan, Yi-Fu: *Landscapes of Fear.* Minneapolis: University of Minnesota Press 2013 (original edition 1979).

Tuan, Yi-Fu: "A View of Geography," in: *Geographical Review* 81 (1991): 99–107.

Tuan, Yi-Fu: *Topophilia. A Study of Environmental Perception, Attitudes, and Values.* With a new preface by the author. New York: Columbia University Press 1990 (original edition Englewood Cliffs, NJ: Prentice-Hall 1974).

Tuan, Yi-Fu: *Space and Place. The Perspective of Experience.* London: Arnold 1977.

Tuan, Yi-Fu: "Geopiety: A Theme in Man's Attachment to Nature and to Place," in: David Lowenthal; Martyn J. Bowden (eds. with the assistance of Mary Alice Lamberty): *Geographies of the Mind. Essays in Historical Geosophy in Honor of John Kirtland Wright.* New York: Oxford University Press 1976, 11–39.

Turville-Petre, G.; Olszewska, E. S.: *The Life of Gudmund the Good, Bishop of Holar.* [London]: The Viking Society for Northern Research 1942.

Tweed, Thomas A.: *Crossing and Dwelling. A Theory of Religion.* Cambridge, MA—London: Harvard University Press 2006 (paperback edition 2008).

Tylor, Edward B.: *Primitive Culture: Researches into the Development of Mythology, Philosophy, Religion, Art, and Custom.* Vol. I, London: John Murray 1871.

Þorsteinn Erlingsson: *Þjóðsögur Þorsteins Erlingssonar.* Reykjavík: Ísafoldarprentsmiðjan 1954.

Þorsteinn M. Jónsson: *Gríma hin nýja.* 10 bindi. Reykjavík: Bókaútgáfan Þjóðsaga 1964–1965.

Uther, Hans-Jörg: *The Types of International Folktales. A Classification and Bibliography. Based on the System of Antti Aarne and Stith Thompson.* 3 vols. (=Folklore Fellows' Communications 284, 285, 286), Helsinki: Academia Scientiarum Fennica 2004.

V[altýr] St[efánsson]: "Fjóra sólarhringa í snjóflóði. Frásögn Jóhanns Kristmundssonar í Goðdal," in: *Lesbók Morgunblaðsins* 23. janúar 1949 (3. tölublað, 24. árgangur): 21–25.

Valk, Úlo: "Legends as Narratives of Alternative Beliefs," in: Zoja Karanović; Willem de Blécourt (eds.): *Belief Narrative Genres.* Novi Sad: International Society for Folk Narrative Research 2012, 23–29.

Vergunst, Jo; Whitehouse, Andrew; Ellison, Nicolas; Arnar Árnason: "Introduction: Landscapes beyond Land," in: Arnar Árnason; Nicolas Ellison; Jo Vergunst; Andrew Whitehouse (eds.): *Landscapes beyond Land. Routes, Aesthetics, Narratives.* (=EASA series 19), New York—Oxford: Berghahn 2012, 1–14.

Viðar Hreinsson: *Jón lærði ok náttúrur náttúrunnar.* Reykjavík: Lesstofan 2016.

Vogt, Jochen: "Benjamin, Walter," in: Heinz Ludwig Arnold (ed.): *Kindlers Literatur Lexikon (KLL).* Stuttgart: J.B. Metzler 2020, https://doi-org.emedien.ub.uni-muenc hen.de/10.1007/978-3-476-05728-0_5914-1.

Walsham, Alexandra: *The Reformation of the Landscape: Religion, Identity, and Memory in Early Modern Britain and Ireland.* Oxford: Oxford University Press 2011.

Warburg, Aby: *Werke in einem Band.* Auf der Grundlage der Manuskripte und Handexemplare herausgegeben und kommentiert von Martin Treml, Sigrid Weigel und Perdita Ladwig, unter Mitarbeit von Susanne Hetzer, Herbert Kopp-Oberstebrink und Christina Oberstebrink. Berlin: Suhrkamp 2018.

328 BIBLIOGRAPHY

Wattchow, Brian: "Landscape and a Sense of Place: A Creative Tension," in: Peter Howard; Ian Thompson; Emma Waterton (eds.): *The Routledge Companion to Landscape Studies*. London—New York: Routledge 2013, 87–96.

Weber, Max: "Die 'Objektivität' sozialwissenschaftlicher und sozialpolitischer Erkenntnis," in: Max Weber: *Gesammelte Aufsätze zur Wissenschaftslehre*. 6., erneut durchges. Aufl., hrsg. von Johannes Winckelmann, Tübingen: Mohr 1985, 146–214. (Erstdruck in: *Archiv für Sozialwissenschaft und Sozialpolitik* 19 (1904): 22–87.)

Weber, Max: "Science as a Vocation," in: *From Max Weber: Essays in Sociology*. Translated, edited, and with an introduction by H. H. Gerth and C. Wright Mills. New York: Oxford University Press 1946, 129–156.

Wellendorf, Jonas: "The Interplay of Pagan and Christian Traditions in Icelandic Settlement Myths," in: *Journal of English and Germanic Philology* 109 (2010): 1–21.

White, Lynn, Jr.: "The Historical Roots of Our Ecologic Crisis," in: *Science* 155/3767 (10 Mar 1967): 1203–1207.

Williams, Raymond: *The Country and the City*. London: Chatto & Windus 1973.

Willson, Margaret: *Seawomen of Iceland. Survival on the Edge*. Seattle: University of Washington Press 2019.

de Witte, Marleen: "Accra's Sounds and Sacred Spaces," in: *International Journal of Urban and Regional Research* 32 (2008): 690–709, https://doi.org/10.1111/j.1468-2427.2008.00805.x, last accessed 15 August 2020.

Worthing, Katherine Geneviève: "The Landscape of Clearance: Changing Rural Life in Nineteenth-Century Scottish Painting." Thesis submitted for the degree of Doctor of Philosophy in the Department of History of Art, University of Glasgow, March 2006, http://theses.gla.ac.uk/5498/, last accessed 11 April 2022.

Yeats, W. B.: *Fairy and Folk Tales of the Irish Peasantry*. Edited and selected by W. B. Yeats. London: Walter Scott—New York: Thomas Whittaker—Toronto: W. J. Gage 1888.

Yelle, Robert A.: *Sovereignty and the Sacred. Secularism and the Political Economy of Religion*. Chicago—London: The University of Chicago Press 2019.

Yelle, Robert A.: *The Language of Disenchantment. Protestant Literalism and Colonial Discourse in British India*. Oxford—New York: Oxford University Press 2013.

Yelle, Robert A.; Trein, Lorenz (eds.): *Narratives of Disenchantment and Secularization. Critiquing Max Weber's Idea of Modernity*. London—New York—Oxford—New Delhi—Sydney: Bloomsbury 2020.

Young, Jean: *Letters from Iceland, 1936*. [Birmingham]: The University of Birmingham, School of English 1992.

Young, Simon: *The Boggart. Folklore, History, Place-Names and Dialect*. Exeter: University of Exeter Press 2022.

Zinser, Hartmut: *Grundfragen der Religionswissenschaft*. Paderborn—München—Wien—Zürich: Schöningh 2010.

Index

For the benefit of digital users, indexed terms that span two pages (e.g., 52–53) may, on occasion, appear on only one of those pages.

For the purpose of alphabetization in this index, the Icelandic letter Æ/æ is treated like ae, Þ/þ like th, ð like d, ö like o. Following Icelandic convention, Icelanders are alphabetized according to their given (first) name.

Tables and figures are indicated by t and f following the page number

Adams, Ansel, 102–3
Ægishjálmur, 262–65, 264f
álagablettir, 1, 49–52, 57, 65–66, 69–70, 98, 106–7, 108, 110, 138, 148, 206–18, 230–34, 236–37, 241–45, 249–55, 268, 285–86, 291, 292–93, 299, 301–2, 302t
Alex, Rayson K., 240–41, 248–49
Álfaborg, 273–74
Álfakirkja. *See* Kirkjuhvammur
álfar. See elves
Álfhóll (Kleifar in Selströnd), 82–84, 185–86
Álfhóll (Melar), 207
Álftaskarð, 139–40, 141–42, 145–46, 147f
Andri Snær Magnason, 251–54
Aravað, 234–36
Árnes, 42–43, 80–81, 94–95, 113, 121, 262–65
art, 256–77. *See also* painting
Ásmundarnes, 149–50
Asparvík, 131–32, 135
Asplund Ingemark, Camilla, 28, 107, 192
Assmann, Aleida, 76, 80
Assmann, Jan, 76, 77–78, 83
Augé, Marc, 31, 80–81, 258–59

Bachelard, Gaston, 20–21, 30, 32, 85–86, 184–85, 194–95, 197–98, 202, 205, 218, 219, 236–37
Bakhtin, Mikhail, 181–82
Bakkagerði, 273–75
Basso, Keith Hamilton, 123–24, 135–36, 161, 164–65, 181–82, 284, 286, 287–88

bells (church bells), 43–44, 53–54, 55, 56–57, 57t, 58, 177–78, 179, 180–81, 182–85, 186, 187–88, 189t, 189, 224, 237–38, 288–89
Bender, Barbara, 84–85
Benjamin, Walter, 218–21, 237–38, 291–92
Bjarnarfjörður, 129–30, 149–50. *See also* Goðdalur; Kaldrananes; Kross; Svanshóll
Bohr, Niels, 23–25, 26, 227
Bólbali, 223–24, 225f, 230–34. *See also* Goðdalur
Bólbarð, 2, 223–24, 225f, 230–34. *See also* Goðdalur
Borgarfjörður eystri. *See* Bakkagerði
Bræðrabrekka, 145
Broddadalsá, 61
Broddanes, 61, 88, 236
Brúará, 98
Brunngil, 99, 229
Búðarvogur, 200–2, 201f
Búhóll, 207
Búrfellsvatn, 91
Burke, Edmund, 190–91, 289–91. *See also* sublime
Byrgiseyrar, 91–92
Byrgisvík, 201f, 207

chronotope, 181–83
city, 7–8, 15–17, 29, 178, 256–77, 278, 279–80, 293–302
Claude Glass, 16–17, 275, 278, 297, 301–2
collective memory. *See* Halbwachs, Maurice

330 INDEX

Collingwood, William Gershom, 267–71, 272, 276, 297–98, 299
constructivism, 18–19
Cormack, Margaret, 130–31, 134–35
Corrigan, John, 197–98, 202
Cosgrove, Denis, 16–20, 35, 104, 161, 163–64, 256–57, 265–67, 280, 294–95, 297
Cresswell, Tim, 15–16, 19, 33, 297
cultural memory, 76, 77–78, 80, 83. *See also* Assmann, Jan

Dalholtsmýri, 206, 207
dark green religion, concept of, 240–41, 244–45, 250, 292–93, 301–2
Deborah, S. Susan, 240–41, 248–49
Dégh, Linda, 11–13
Deleuze, Gilles, 31
DeLue, Rachael Ziady, 19–20, 137
disenchantment, 45, 107
dominant traditions. *See* Eskeröd, Albert
Doran, Robert, 269–71
Drangar (farm), 145, 201f, 207
Drangar (trolls), 113–17, 116f
Drangaskörð, 262–65
Drangsnes, 38–39, 43–44, 119, 120f, 183–84
draugur, 60, 169–76. *See also* ghosts
Lord Dufferin, 268–71
Durkheim, Emile, 46–48

Eck, Diana L., 4–5, 87–88, 102–3, 104, 122–23, 281, 285–86
eco-fear, 240–41, 248–50
Einar Hákonarson, 259–60
Einbúi. *See* Asparvík
Einfætingsgil, 111–12
Ekkjusteinn, 192–95, 203
elves, 51–57, 62–63, 64, 65–66, 78–81, 82–84, 85–86, 98, 101–2, 105–6, 139–42, 145–46, 148, 149–50, 160, 185–89, 192–94, 203, 204, 208–12, 224, 231, 233–34, 237–38, 242–43, 245–50, 252, 272–75, 276–77, 278, 285–86, 288–89, 298–99, 301–2, 302t
emotional topography, concept of, 28, 192
Erinnerungsräume. See Assmann, Aleida
escapism, 33, 176–77, 219–20, 291–92, 298–99

Eskeröd, Albert, 87–88, 102–3, 285–86
essentialism, 18–19
Evans-Pritchard, E. E., 50–51

fairies. *See* elves
Fell, 181–83, 193–94, 288–89
Felton, Debbie, 28
Feykishóladraugur. *See* Feykishólar
Feykishólar, 60, 135–36, 169–77
Finnboga saga ramma, 24–27, 131. *See also* Finnbogi the Strong
Finnbogastaðir, 43f, 43–44, 112–13, 114f, 115f, 121, 122, 131, 207
Finnbogi the Strong, 24–27, 43f, 43–44, 112–13, 114f, 131
Fjalla-Eyvindur, 157
Flateyjardalur, 24–25
Flókatunga, 43–44, 112–13, 115f
fornmannahaugur. See founders' burial mounds
Foucault, Michel, 30–31, 49–50, 75–76, 82–83
founders' burial mounds, 57–59, 92–102, 105–10, 179–85, 229, 233–34, 301–2
Friedrich, Caspar David, 272, 299–301
Frog, 46–47

Galdrasýning á Ströndum, 260–62
Gálgahóll, 82, 83, 185–86
Geertz, Clifford, 17–18, 46–47, 123
Geirmundarstaðir, 185–86
geopiety, 27–28, 191–92, 193–94
Gestsstaðir, 155–56, 158–59, 234
Gestur (in Miðdalur), 58, 234
ghosts, 59–61, 65–66, 87, 126–36, 138, 144–46, 158–59, 169–77, 236, 272–73, 276–77, 284, 286–87, 297–99, 301–2, 302t, See also *draugur*; *útburður*
Gilsfjörður, 113–17, 116f, 120f, 121–22
Gilsstaðir, 192–94, 203
Gíslakot, 169–71
Gjögur, 279–83, 286, 287–88
Gladigow, Burkhard, 151
Gljúfravað, 234–36
Goðafoss, 223–28, 233–34, 236–37
Goðdalur, 1, 4, 10n.20, 21, 49, 76, 186, 209–10, 218–38, 261–62, 291–93

INDEX 331

Goði (hill), 223–24, 228–30, 233–
34, 236–37
Góðilækur, 199, 200*f*
Grænaflöt, 207
Grímsey, 55, 116*f*, 117, 119, 119*f*, 120*f*,
156, 201*f*
Guattari, Félix, 31
Guðlaugur Jón Bjarnason, 262–67, 275–
76, 277, 293–95, 299
Guðmundur Arason. *See* Guðmundur
the Good
Guðmundur the Good, 40–42, 61–62,
65–66, 97, 151–54, 160, 162–63, 197–
202, 203, 204, 258, 285–86, 287, 289–
91, 301–2. *See also* Gvendarbrunnur;
Heilsubót
Gull-Bárður, 99
Gullbrá, 92n.59, 182–83
Gullfoss, 234
Gullhóll (Kleifar in Kaldbaksdalur), 207
Gullhóll (Þorpar), 98, 209–10, 211, 212*f*
Gullhóll (Tröllatunga), 100–1, 101*f*
Gvendarbrunnur, 42, 61–62, 65–66,
197–202

Hackett, Rosalind I. J., 178–79, 288–89
Halbwachs, Maurice, 76, 83–84, 85–86
Halldór Homer, 168–69
Hallgrímskirkja, 279–83, 287
Haugvatnshólmi, 233–34
Heiðarbæjarheiði, 155, 158–59, 161–62
Heidegger, Martin, 21–23, 32–33, 50n.157,
219–21, 236–37, 258–59
Heilsubót, 42, 198. *See also*
Gvendarbrunnur
Heisenberg, Werner, 23–25, 26, 27–28
Helgukot, 169–71
Hellar, 233–34
Hempusteinn, 78–82, 83, 85, 89
Hestur (Goðdalur), 186, 223–24, 225*f*,
226–27, 226*f*, 233–34, 236–37. *See
also* Goðdalur
Hetch Hetchy Valley, 252–53, 254–55
heterochronia, 30–31, 75–76, 82–83
heterotopia, 30–31, 49–50, 75–76, 82–83
hidden people. *See* elves
Hirschkind, Charles, 178
Hlaðhamar, 145

Hnyðjueyri, 88–91
Hof, 230
Hofstaðir, 43–44, 112–13, 115*f*, 183–84
Hólmavík, 7–8, 38–39, 43–45, 61–62, 68–
69, 71, 82, 165, 198–99, 213–15, 215*f*,
216, 245–46, 248–49, 252, 254–55,
257–67, 275–77, 293–94, 297
hooks, bell, 34, 219
Howell, Frederick W. W., 299–301
Hrófá, 132, 139–40
Hrófberg, 198, 201*f*
Hrútafjörður, 38, 44, 166, 167, 200–2
huldufólk. See elves
Huldufólksbrekka, 209–11, 215–
16, 244–45
humanistic geography. *See* Tuan, Yi-Fu
Hume, David, 205–6, 291
Hvalsá (farm), 159–60, 161–63
Hvalsárdalur. *See* Feykishólar
Hvalsárdrangur, 159, 160*f*
Hvammur, 182–83
Hvannadalshnúkur, 299–301
Hveramýri, 148, 207, 208
Hvít. *See* Hvítarhlíð
Hvítarhlíð, 57, 105–12, 122, 281
Hvítarleiði. *See* Hvítarhlíð
Hvítserkur, 56n.171, 183–84

iconography, analytical concept of, 17–18
indigenous reverential eco-fear, concept
of. *See* eco-fear
Ingemark, Dominic, 28, 192
Ingold, Tim, 19–20, 121, 137, 138, 141–42,
181–82, 281–82, 286–87

Jamie, Kathleen, 256–57, 299–301
Jóhannes Sveinsson Kjarval. *See* Kjarval
Jón Guðmundsson the Learned, 179–
80n.261, 193–94
Jón Stefánsson, 267–68, 299

Kaldbakur, 153–54, 201*f*, 207, 233–34
Kaldrananes, 34–35, 43–45, 62–63, 92–
102, 209–10
Kálfanes, 61–62, 198–202
Kálfanesskeið, 213–15, 215*f*
Kárahnjúkar Dam, 251–52
Karve, Iravati, 104

332 INDEX

Kastali, 155f, 157–59
Kattegat, 165–66, 176–77
Keralín, 133–35, 136, 139–40, 297–98
Kerasteinn, 133, 139–40
Kerlingarfoss, 90, 234
Kerlingartóft, 207
Kieschnick, John, 203–4
Kirkjuból. *See* Sesselja
Kirkjuhvammur, 211
Kjarval, 272–75, 276
Kleifar (Kaldbaksvík), 207, 233–34
Kleifar (Selströnd), 82–86, 127–28, 185–86
Kleppa, 43–44, 43f, 105, 112–13, 114f, 115f, 121, 122, 183–84, 207
Kleppustaðir, 43–44, 112–13, 115f
Klúka (Bjarnarfjörður), 149–50
Kolbeinsá, 200–2
Kolbeinsvík, 151–54, 160, 161–62, 206, 207, 258, 287
Kollafjörður, 88–89, 99, 105, 113–23, 179–85, 199, 211, 236, 258, 286
Kórklettar, 186
Kráka, 90–91
Krákufoss. *See* Kráka
Krákutún. *See* Kráka
Krebs, Angelika, 191–92
Kripal, Jeffrey J., 202–3
Kross (Kaldrananes), 92–102
Krossholt, 62, 97
Krossnes, 78–81, 84–85, 86, 148, 207, 208
Kvíjaklettabrekka, 208–9
Kwilecki, Susan, 217

Landseer, Edwin, 295–96
Laugufoss, 234
Laxá. *See* Mývatn
Lefebvre, Henri, 29–30, 163–64
Leikvöllur, 159–60, 161–62
lieu de mémoire. See Nora, Pierre
Ljótunn, 99
Ljótunnarstaðir, 99, 200–2, 201f
Ljúfa, 99
Ljúfuholt, 99
Ljúfustaðir, 99, 211
Lön, 233–34
Lorraine, Claude, 275, 301–2
Lynn White thesis, 239–55, 292–93

Macfarlane, Robert, 77, 138, 237–38
Malarhorn, 117

material culture, concept of, 203–4
Matthías Johannessen, 272
mediation, 8–9, 275–77, 297
medium, landscape as, 125–36, 237–38, 256, 265–67, 272, 276–77, 287–88, 294–95, 297
Melar, 207
Meyer, Birgit, 8–9, 13, 276, 287–88
Miðdalsgröf, 155–56, 158–59
Miðdalur, 58, 155–59, 160, 161–63, 234, 284–85
Mitchell, W. J. T., 35, 125, 163–65, 176–77, 204, 265–67, 276, 280, 287–88, 297
mnemonic pegs, place-names as, 84, 85
Mókollsdalur. *See* Mókollshaugur
Mókollshaugur, 58, 99, 179–85, 188, 233–34. *See also* founders' burial mounds
Morris, William, 268–71
Muir, John, 252–55, 271n.43
Munaðarnes, 211–12
musealization, 261
mysterium tremendum et fascinans, 189–91, 241
Mývatn, 194–95, 241–42, 245

Naustvík, 207
Neðri-Hamar, 186–87, 187f
Neðstibrunnur, 200–2
New Nature Writing, 256–57
New Year's Eve, 1, 192–93, 220–21
non-place, 31, 258–59
Nónsteinar. *See* Geirmundarstaðir
Nora, Pierre, 76, 80, 83
nostalgia, 33, 162–63
numinous, concept of the, 189–91

Óberjuflói, 145
Oddshólar. *See* Oddshóll
Oddshóll, 62–63, 166–69, 170f, 176–77
Ófeigsfjarðarflói, 262–65
Ólína Þorvarðardóttir, 241–42
Önundarhaugar, 99, 229, 233–34
otherworlding, 46–47
Otto, Rudolf, 151, 162–63, 189–92, 241, 287, 289–91
Óveiðisá, 91

painting, 14, 15, 16–17, 19, 84–85, 93f, 137, 190–91, 256–77, 281–82, 293–96, 297–98, 301–2

INDEX 333

Paradís, 61, 65–66, 66*f*, 301–2
Pausanias, 64n.184, 110, 284
Pavord, Anna, 275
Pentikäinen, Juha, 130–31, 134–35
pilgrimage, 41–42, 61–62, 104, 122–23, 199, 268–71
positivism, 18–19
Prestbakki, 44, 62–63, 166, 167
Propp, Vladimir, 48–49, 102–3
Púkabreið, 142–46, 147*f*, 148, 299–301
Púki (place), 145, 169–70
púki (devil), 142–43, 145, 148. *See also* Púkabreið

Rauf, 242–45
real-and-imagined, 30, 177–79
Rebanks, James, 149
resistance, 219. *See also* subversion
Reykjaneshyrna, 42–43, 43*f*
Reykja(r)fjörður, 91, 207
Robinson, Tim, 102
Rönkufoss, 234
Rönkuvað, 234–36
Rose, Gillian, 33, 219–20
Ruskin, John, 267, 271–72, 274–75, 276, 301–2

sacred music, 178–79
Satansflói, 145
Sauðabólshöfði, 212–13
Sävborg, Daniel, 10–12, 13, 28, 239, 292–93, 295
Schafer, R. Murray, 187–88
Schama, Simon, 77, 81–82, 83, 137, 148–49
Schleiermacher, Friedrich, 8–9, 189–90, 287
secularization, 45, 269–71. *See also* disenchantment
Selárdalur, 185, 192–93
Selkollusteinn, 129–30, 135
Sesselja, 128–29, 258, 282, 284
Sigríðartjörn, 234–36
Sigurður Jónsson. See *Sveitin mín*
Silko, Leslie Marmon, 19–20, 148–49, 254–55, 299–301
Simmel, Georg, 137n.165
Skerpingsstaðir, 43–44, 112–13, 115*f*
skessa, 111–12, 153–54, 156, 159. *See also* trolls

Skiphóll, 99, 229
Skjaldabjarnarvík, 38, 186, 201*f*, 236
Skottar, 236
Skyrkollusteinn, 207
slæðingur, 61, 143. *See also* ghosts
smooth and striated space. *See* Deleuze, Gilles
Snartartunga, 242–45, 268
Soja, Edward W., 30, 177–78
soundscape, 59–60, 75, 177–89, 288–89
Staður (Hrútafjörður), 167
Staður (Steingrímsfjörður), 43*f*, 43–44, 94–95, 112–13, 115*f*, 121, 129–30, 181–82, 183–84, 201*f*, 288–89
Steinadalsheiði, 113–17, 116*f*, 120*f*, 121–22
Steinadalur, 159, 199–202, 201*f*, 204
Steingrímsfjörður, 37, 57, 82, 97, 98, 99, 105, 117–18, 119, 121–22, 126, 127–30, 132, 133, 139, 155, 159, 181–82, 193, 209–10, 212–13, 233–34, 262–65
Steingrímshaugur, 58, 99, 100–1, 181–82. *See also* founders' burial mounds
Steingrímur the Troll, 37, 57, 99, 100–1, 181–82, 184–85
Stoll, Mark R., 239–40
Stóra-Ávík, 207
Stóra-Fjarðarhorn, 193–94
Stóra-Hvalsá, 145, 166–69, 170*f*
Stórhóll, 207
Stórusteinar. *See* Geirmundarstaðir
Strákadys, 65
Stúlkuhóll, 246–49, 252
sublime, concept of the, 148, 190–92, 256, 269–71, 272, 282, 289–91, 295–96, 299, 301–2, 302*t*
subversion, 34, 35, 163–77, 280, 287–88
supernatural, definition of, 10–11
Svanshóll, 10n.20, 62–64, 186, 208–10, 231–32
Svartagil, 234–36
Svartiflói, 131–32, 135, 143–46, 148
Sveitin mín, 194–97, 202–4, 289–91
symbolic forms, 17–18

taskscape, 74, 137, 281–82, 286–87, 299, 302*t*
Taylor, Bron, 240–41, 245, 292–93, 301–2
Þambárdalur, 268. *See also* Þambárvellir
Þambárvellir, 90, 111–12, 234

334 INDEX

theatre, metaphor of, 85–86, 135–36, 161–62
thick description, 17–18, 45
Þiðriksvallavatn, 91–92, 245–49
Þingeyrar, 183–84
thirdspace, 30, 177–78
Þjóðbrók, 183–84
Þjófalág, 155f, 156–57, 158–59
Þjórsá. *See* Tröllkonuhlaup
Þömb, 90, 111–12, 234
Þorbjarnarhóll, 234–36
Þórhallur Vilmundarson, 81
Þorpa-Gudda, 125, 126–29, 135–36, 298–99
Þorpar, 98, 126–28, 209–10, 211
Þröskuldagil, 236
Tilley, Christopher, 84, 137, 148–49, 165–66
Tóftardalur, 132, 139–40, 141–42, 145–46, 147f
topophilia, 20, 27–28, 191–92, 193–94, 197–98, 202–3
Torfholt (Byrgisvík), 207
Torfholt (Kaldbakur), 207
Tóttardalur. *See* Tóftardalur
tradition dominants. *See* Eskeröd, Albert
traditionsdominanter. *See* Eskeröd, Albert
Trékyllisheiði, 112–13, 115f
Trékyllisvík, 42–43, 80–81
Tröllatunga, 62–63, 97, 100, 101f, 201f
Tröllkonuhlaup, 251–53
trolls, 9–10, 37, 43–44, 43f, 51–57, 64, 65–66, 66f, 74, 90, 99, 100–1, 105, 108, 110–23, 138, 151–54, 155f, 156, 158–63, 181–85, 188–89, 234, 241–42, 251–54, 258, 265–67, 268, 272–73, 276–77, 278, 281, 286, 288–89, 298–99, 302t

Tuan, Yi-Fu, 23–24, 26, 27–28, 29, 32–33, 191–92, 193–94, 202–3, 205–6, 217, 218, 258–59
Tungudalur, 132, 133, 139–40
Tungugröf, 139–40
Tungukot, 234–36
Tweed, Thomas A., 8–9, 104, 150–52, 162–63, 191–92, 205–6, 287
Tylor, Edward Burnett, 8–9, 12–13

Útburðarbás, 131
Útburðarhraun, 131–32, 135, 272–73
útburður, 59–60, 129–35, 141–42, 178–79, 301–2. *See also* ghosts
Uxi, 116f, 117, 119, 119f, 120f, 122–23

Valk, Úlo, 11–13, 28, 239, 287–88, 292–93, 295
Veiðileysa, 90–91, 131–32, 135, 152, 272–73
Víðidalsá, 62–63, 131–32, 142, 143–45, 209–11, 244–45
Víðivellir, 129–31, 134, 135–36
Viljinn, 63–64, 71–72, 209–10
Vonarholt, 234

Warburg, Aby, 17–18
Weber, Max, 45, 46, 107, 205–6
Williams, Raymond, 15–16, 19, 297
witchcraft, 36–37, 50–51, 71, 168, 182–83, 184, 259–60, 265–67. *See also* Galdrasýning á Ströndum
de Witte, Marleen, 178

Ýluskarð, 132–35, 139–40, 141–42, 145–46, 147f, 178–79, 272–73, 297–98, 299
Yosemite National Park, 102–3, 252–53
Young, Jean, 146